D1557577

Debussy Letters

Debussy Letters

Selected and Edited by
François Lesure and Roger Nichols

Translated by
Roger Nichols

Harvard University Press
Cambridge, Massachusetts
1987

Originally published as *Claude Debussy: Lettres 1884–1918* by
HERMANN, éditeurs des sciences et des arts, Paris, 1980

This revised English edition with additional letters and translation
© Faber and Faber Ltd and the President and Fellows of Harvard College 1987

English translation and additional material
© Roger Nichols 1987

All rights reserved

The publishers are grateful to the Ministère de la Culture, Paris,
for help with the costs of translation

Printed in Great Britain

10 9 8 7 6 5 4 3 2 1

Library of Congress Cataloging-in-Publication Data

Debussy, Claude, 1862–1918.
  Debussy letters.

  Revised ed. of Lettres 1884–1918, with additional
letters and translation.
  Bibliography: p.
  Includes index.
  1. Debussy, Claude, 1862–1918—Correspondence.
2. Composers—France—Correspondence. I. Lesure, François.
II. Nichols, Roger.   III. Title.
ML410. D28A42 1987   780'.92'4   [B]   87–385
ISBN 0–674–19429–2

780.92
D289d

Contents

List of Illustrations   vii
Introduction by François Lesure   xi
Translator's Preface   xxiii
Chronology   xxv

THE LETTERS   1

1884–1887
Childhood
Musical studies
The Prix de Rome   1

1889–1893
Influences
Friendships
Early Works   23

1893–1896
The birth of *Pelléas*
Friendship with Pierre Louÿs
Prélude à l'après-midi d'un faune   50

1896–1901
Georges Hartmann
The *Nocturnes*
The break with Gaby
Marriage to Lilly   86

1901–1904
Pelléas et Mélisande   119

1904–1906
Divorce
La Mer
Marriage to Emma   145

1906–1909
Notoriety
Stage projects   170

1909–1910
The Russian Ballet
Images for orchestra   204

1910–1911
Journeys
Le Martyre de Saint-Sébastien   226

1912–1914
Jeux
The ballet world
More travels   254

1914–1918
The War
The Final Years   290

Bibliography of Debussy's letters   337
Index of works   339
General Index   343

Illustrations

1 Debussy in Rome in 1885.   7
2 Debussy on the steps of the Villa
  Medici.   9
3 Portrait of Madame Vasnier by
  Jacques-Emile Blanche, 1888.
  Photo: Bulloz.   19
4 Debussy at Luzancy in 1893.   25
5 Debussy with Raymond Bonheur
  and Ernest Chausson in 1893.   27
6 Debussy's friend Robert Godet.   29
7 Maurice Denis's cover for the first
  edition of *La Damoiselle élue*.   53
8 Gaby Dupont photographed by
  Pierre Louÿs.   55
9 Pierre Louÿs sitting at his
  harmonium.   62
10 A drawing of Debussy's fiancée,
   Thérèse Roger.   67
11 Debussy photographed by Pierre
   Louÿs in May 1894.   71
12 Debussy's editor and benefactor,
   Georges Hartmann.   79
13 Debussy and Zorah Ben Brahim,
   Louÿs's mistress, 1897.   91
14 Lilly, Debussy's first wife.   107
15 Debussy in Pierre Louÿs's
   apartment around 1900.   115

16 Albert Carré, director of the
    Opéra-comique. *Bibliothèque
    nationale.*   121
17 Maurice Maeterlinck and
    Paul Dukas.   125
18 André Messager, conductor of the
    première of *Pelléas et Mélisande.*   127
19 Photograph of Debussy taken on
    11 May 1902.   129
20 Louis Laloy, friend and
    biographer.   143
21 Debussy at Pourville in 1904 with
    Emma.   151
22 Camille Chevillard, conductor of
    the Lamoureux concerts.   157
23 Jacques Durand, Debussy's
    publisher from 1905.   159
24 Debussy at his work-table, around
    1905.   161
25 Debussy's daughter, Chouchou.   165
26 Maggie Teyte, the second
    Mélisande.   193
27 André Caplet and Debussy.   207
28 An 'official' photograph by Nadar.   213
29 Léon Bakst's drawing for 'the magic
    chamber' (*Le Martyre de Saint-
    Sébastien* Act II)   239
30 Léon Bakst's costume for the seven
    seraphim in *Le Martyre.*   241
31 Debussy and Chouchou at
    Houlgate, 1911.   245
32 Debussy and Stravinsky
    photographed by Satie.   257
33 Karsavina, Nijinsky and Schollar
    in *Jeux*, May 1913.   271
34 Portrait of Debussy by Ivan Thièle,
    1913. *Tretiakov Museum, Moscow.*   275
35 Emma and Claude Debussy
    around 1913.   281

36 André Hellé's design for the
   Durand edition of Debussy's *Boîte à
   joujoux*.   287
37 Debussy at Le Moulleau in 1916.   311

All rights to illustrations reserved by the publisher, except where another source is indicated.

Introduction
by François Lesure

This volume of letters allows us to see one of the greatest composers of our century at close quarters for the first time, conversing with friends and contemporaries and facing up to a variety of everyday occurrences, while through it all maintaining unsullied his vision of an artistic ideal.

Composers are in general not good letter writers. Among French composers Debussy, together with Berlioz and Chabrier, is an exception – a brilliant stylist, witty, deliberately caustic and prodigal with vivid turns of phrase. In writing to nearly seventy-five correspondents he covers a wide range of topics relating to art, literature and the aesthetic currents of his time, and the picture that emerges is as much of the composer as of the man. Because he is seen reacting to immediate events, his correspondence makes an indispensable complement to his writings as 'M. Croche'. All previous volumes of his letters have shown his relations with a single correspondent: here we can follow the pattern of his letter-writing day by day, throughout his adult life, and the result is all the more revealing because Debussy was in the habit of keeping his friendships in separate compartments.

There is a certain pathos in the dialectic which is revealed in these letters between the work, standing outside time in its determined urge towards self-renewal, and the man, trying without success to escape from society's conventional moral code. We must resist the temptation to paint his life entirely in shades of black – it was, after all, not without its successes – but even so there is no mistaking the intransigent solitude that marks the artist.

Although Debussy claimed (in letter 68, 14 July 1898) that he was as 'simple as a blade of grass', painting his portrait is not easy. An accumulation of the various opinions that have been expressed about him leads only to puzzlement at his complex nature: rude, taciturn with bouts of gaiety, shy, childish, sensitive, soft-hearted, insincere, moody and even, by some accounts, ill-natured. The most extreme opinion of all came from Paul Valéry, 'that monster of a Debussy . . .', but we should bear in mind that the poet was smarting under a sense of ingratitude at the time. All the descriptions ever given of Debussy are somehow incomplete and unsatisfactory, in that they apply to him only as a young man or rely on hearsay rather than personal observation. Debussy allowed only narrow facets of himself to be seen by the outside world, especially during the first thirty years of his life. Those, like Raymond Bonheur, Henri Lerolle and Pierre Louÿs, who knew him well at this time have left little in the way of intimate details, suggesting either that they regarded such material as secret or merely that Debussy kept that kind of thing to himself. It was only fifty years after his death that the world learned about the dramatic event which coloured his childhood: the conviction and imprisonment of his father in the aftermath of the Commune. One wonders whether even the various women in his life knew about it. When, later on in life, Debussy came to express his deepest thoughts in his letters, it was not to friends like Robert Godet or Paul-Jean Toulet but to his publisher Jacques Durand, who was in no sense a member of his intimate circle.

In conversation with Victor Segalen in October 1907 Debussy gave the following definition of his character: 'With me, everything is instinctive and unreasoning. I'm not totally master of myself. And there are times when I can do nothing, when I'm confronted by a wall and wonder whether I can jump over it or not.' He was aware that his behaviour sometimes appeared contradictory (a very typical word in his vocabulary) and on at least one occasion, in 1910, he tried to express this ambivalence in a curious passage in a letter to his publisher: 'this overpowering need to escape from myself into activities which seem inexplicable because the man who appears in them is not one anybody recognizes, although he represents perhaps the best side of me'.

If one compares some of his comments with others it is hard not to get a whiff of double-dealing or opportunism. This occurs from the earliest years. When he writes to M. Vasnier from Rome, thanking him for the 'room' he has 'been kind enough' to make for him in his family, one is left having to choose between cynicism and naïvety to designate this description of Debussy's relationship with the mistress of the house. Similarly the tone in which he refers to his friendship with Ernest

Chausson seems forced when we know the material support that went with it. At a crucial juncture, in March 1894, he went to the lengths of making a confession which it is hard to take seriously: 'It seems to me that up to this moment I've been walking in darkness and have had the misfortune to meet some truly unpleasant fellow travellers . . . If I've wandered into some evil spots, I've also contracted a distaste for them which will for ever keep me from harm.'

Debussy lived somewhat 'out of the world'. That, in fact, was his reply to the well-known questionnaire, sent out supposedly by Marcel Proust in 1889, asking where he would like to live. The theme of destiny was one he frequently returned to: 'my hard luck' (to Chausson in 1893), 'destiny treats me with an unpleasant irony' (to Louÿs in 1900), 'the typical trick of a destiny which is obstinately against me' (to Durand in 1911), etc. This thoughtful, melancholy side of him is practically imprinted on his face in almost all the photos of him that survive. Sociability was not one of his traits – he was ill at ease in formal gatherings – but he could be openness itself with people who took the trouble to seek him out and whose credentials were beyond dispute. He was called 'secretive'. Certainly he was not a ready talker and to his wife Emma he made an ironical reference to the 'somewhat restrained charms' of his conversation. He gave the impression of being haughty and indolent and only in the company of close friends did his true self emerge. Beneath a slightly rough exterior his tastes were refined in the extreme. In the words of Alfred Bruneau, 'he deliberately kept his distance'. Whether among friends or professional colleagues, he preferred not to seem to take himself seriously and he appreciated a certain lightness of touch in others, not spelling everything out in detail.

The place of women in his life cannot be overlooked. He was timid in approaching them and his forceful sensuality sometimes came out as brusqueness. His first wife claimed that he was a man of pleasure more than a man of passion and various female singers, such as Mary Garden, Maggie Teyte and Lucienne Bréval, have expressed the same view more forthrightly. Even so, many of the letters in this volume show that tenderness came naturally to him.

He valued friendship highly, as the early years of his life testify. But it seems as if he liked to enshroud his friends in a certain degree of mystery and keep each one apart from the others. René Peter, in his memoirs of the composer, records how amazed he was to discover the people Debussy had known and never mentioned to him. But there can be no doubting the sincerity of declarations like 'you, my dearest friend . . .', to Caplet; 'your friendship is as vital to me as bread', to Godet; 'there are things that I've talked about only to you', to Messager; and, to Segalen, 'you are one of the rare people to whom I talk about myself'. Among all his friendships, the one with Pierre Louÿs remains unique in its mischievous, conspiratorial tones and its almost unrelieved flippancy, through which one has to peer to make out the two men's firm affinities, as well as the areas of aesthetic discord. Debussy's style is generally clear, even if unorthodox. Only when tact or friendship force him to utter praise he does not feel, do his phrases become sibylline, as with Paul Dukas over *Ariane et Barbe-bleue,* or with Walter Rummel the day after he had given a recital. He was a conscientious correspondent, too. He replied even to people who wrote to him out of the blue, like the 16-year-old Francis Poulenc who asked a random question simply to obtain his autograph. The ones he could not stand were the gossips – Gabriel Mourey and Charles Morice were both convicted of this charge at different times. Finally, these letters bring home to us a side of Debussy which has so far been neglected: the support he gave to young musicians. He has been accused of indifference to new music, but Falla, Séverac, Lacerda, Varèse and others benefited from his help and encouragement. Debussy the 'happiness addict' (letter to Poniatowski, 1893) was also an 'affection addict' (letter to Pierre Louÿs, 1903).

His relationship with his parents was difficult for many years. He was the eldest of four children and his mother's favourite. She gave him some kind of sporadic education and, according to Paul Vidal, 'turned his stomach by always wanting him to be with her and to make sure he was working hard'. He felt bitter towards his father too, who wanted to make money out of his virtuosity and complained when he was only moderately successful in the Conservatoire piano classes. Achille-Claude (as he was then known) gave the impression of being stand-offish and selfish. Whenever he did make a little money from piano lessons he spent it on books or watercolours, much to his parents' fury. Nevertheless, he was over thirty before he left home and later on, when success had descended, he treated both his parents with an affection which we must regard as totally sincere.

Debussy was anxious to escape these restrictive surroundings and discover another way of life. The important influences on him came through his travels with Mme von Meck and through such different milieux as the Vasniers, the Librairie de l'art indépendant, Mallarmé's salon and the various cafés he frequented, like the Café Weber, the Café Pousset and Reynold's Bar. His friends were not so much musicians as writers and painters, and from them he learned to believe that academic rules and forms, if observed too rigidly, would bar the way to the renewal of music he was aiming for. So he rebelled against the constraints imposed on him and learned to fashion his own constraints, more in keeping with what he was. His fellow students at the Conservatoire or at the Villa Medici seemed to him to be wedded to traditions that were out of date and, what is more, to have a distasteful desire to 'succeed'. He found his freedom in the circles of the avant-garde, that is to say the Symbolists, and the number and calibre of the writers he knew is very striking, including Henri de Régnier, Camille Mauclair, Catulle Mendès, André Gide, Paul Valéry, Mallarmé and Pierre Louÿs. Equally impressive is a list of the authors he read: Bourget, Banville, Poe, Rossetti, Swinburne, Charles Cros, Jules Bois and Maurice Bouchor, not forgetting Baudelaire and Laforgue, both of whom provided many a quotation in his letters. Later on he was to add to these Nietzsche and Schopenhauer, Carlyle and Conrad, Gerhart Hauptmann, Dickens, Alexandre Dumas, Jules Renard and the songs of Paul Delmet. As for Wagner, Debussy's critical attitude totally amazed his non-musical friends. For them Wagner was the *ne plus ultra* of contemporary music and they could not see that this giant was blocking the way to progress and that, for all his genius, he had to be cast aside. Debussy's mission led him to turn away from the Meyerbeer-inspired products of the Opéra, the strict, classical forms of Saint-Saëns and the sonatas of d'Indy and his followers, in favour of music from Russia and the Far East. What was the point of spending his evenings in the concert hall, when the so-called contemporary programmes were restricted to music he knew by heart thanks to his long apprenticeship at the Conservatoire? In a letter to Paul Dukas he declared, 'I'm not thinking about music any more, or at least very little.' In the same vein he valued Robert Godet's ability to 'see beyond music' and advised his pupil Raoul Bardac to 'forget all about music from time to time'. No other composer has ever been so committed to finding ways of revitalizing music from outside the musical world.

The years between 1890 and 1900 were in some ways, for all their financial problems, the happiest of Debussy's life. A bohemian existence suited him, going to the circus, to the Chat Noir, pantomimes, occult meetings, browsing in Bailly's bookshop, listening or dreaming at Mallarmé's salon, meeting friends on the boulevards and ending the day at the Auberge du Clou or the Café Weber. Musicians hardly figured on the scene. The group centred on the Société nationale had little to offer him, and men like Vidal and Pierné were colleagues rather than friends. Among the musicians he had known at the Conservatoire he made an exception of Raymond Bonheur, but only because he was a poetry enthusiast. As for Chausson, who encouraged him to get married and tried to settle him into a middle-class way of life, he was more a patron than a real friend. The painters and writers were not so strictly bound by convention as the musicians were. We can see this in the case of Henri Lerolle, who went on seeing him after his brother-in-law Chausson had broken off relations. Debussy took his companion Gaby Dupont with him when he went to cafés but did not risk being seen with her in middle-class drawing rooms. His engagement to Thérèse Roger was a mistake for which he paid dearly and his recovery from this was helped by his ever closer friendship with Pierre Louÿs. Over the next twenty years Debussy was to forget the hardships of this time and remember only the taste of freedom and friendship which Gaby symbolized: 'I miss the C. Debussy who worked so happily on *Pelléas* because, between ourselves, I've never met him again' (1904); 'the period when I wrote my String Quartet was not exactly one of extravagant luxury but, even so, it was the best time of all' (February 1911).

His life with Lilly Texier was really no more than an episode. It has often been said that she never inspired him to write anything and that he never dedicated anything to her, but that is to be unfair to her. She was an attractive young woman; he married her at a time when he needed social stability and after three years he was tired of her. In any case, explaining Debussy's output in terms of his love-life is a doubtful procedure. But if tying the changes in style down to the influence of certain women and hunting for the sources of his inspiration is to miss the point, none the less it is not simply a weakness for anecdote that suggests we should look closely at his liaisons: very often these explain why certain friendships began or ended when they did.

His separation from Lilly, and her attempted suicide, were talking-points for the whole of Paris society. For the second time in his life Debussy saw several of his friends break off contact. But whereas in 1894 the drama was played to a tiny audience, now it was blown up to extraordinary proportions. The explanation was that, since the production of *Pelléas* two years earlier, Debussy had become a public figure and, as the leader of a school, his every action was closely watched – not to mention those people whom it amused, therefore, to find fault with him for whatever reason.

Out of all the friends he made as a young man only three stayed with him: Robert Godet, Paul Dukas and Erik Satie. Chausson broke with him after his brief engagement to Thérèse Roger and then died prematurely (it needed all Pierre Louÿs's persuasive powers to get Debussy to send a card, with Louÿs's own, to Chausson's funeral). He almost never saw Raymond Bonheur, even though he invited him to the *Pelléas* première. Gustave Doret, Ysaÿe, and Henri Lerolle abandoned him as a result of what they believed his behaviour to have been, and Messager did likewise. These defections hurt Debussy so deeply that he even thought Paul-Jean Toulet had joined his detractors (see letter 137, 5 May 1906).

He found some solace, at least temporarily, in his love for Emma Bardac and the birth of his daughter Chouchou. The move to the avenue du Bois de Boulogne marked a decisive step in his life. It was a well-appointed town house with a small garden, removed from the noise of the city (except for that of the suburban railway which passed nearby). The household included two servants and an English governess and was provided with a telephone, even if its irregular functioning caused complaints. To the outside world, his life was on a secure material footing – but this, in fact, Debussy was never to enjoy. For him, as for Baudelaire and Wagner, the need for money remained a constant obsession. He bullied his publisher for advances and had several times to resort to borrowing from professional moneylenders, who then plunged him into sudden crises. The foreign conducting tours he undertook between 1908 and 1914 were merely palliatives to help him ride the worst of the storms. He kept up the struggle, he admitted, in order to preserve 'a material comfort one has enjoyed for a long time and which one cannot believe has now become impossible to afford' (letter 245, 15 July 1913). It was an 'affair of honour' with respect to Emma, whom he had married only after they had lived together for three years.

The horizon darkened perceptibly between 1907 and 1909, the year in which the first signs of his illness appeared. As early as October 1907 Debussy wrote to Caplet: 'I am not content . . . Can it be that I am definitely not cut out for domestic life?' In 1910 a real crisis occurred, which we can follow as the months progress: 'I am at a dangerous turning-point in my history' (23 March); 'my life is as broken and miserable as ever' (30 March); 'I'm pretty wretched; there's more than a touch of the Usher family . . . The best family I've got!' Things were no better the following year: 'When the holiday's over, we then have to admit we don't know why we came. Is it really because we've lost the ability to enjoy things together?' (25 August 1911); 'sometimes I am so wretchedly lonely' (18 December). Many more such tragic confidences could be quoted, of yet another disappointment in love and a final protest as his 50th birthday approaches. To be sure, the teasing dedications, the deeply affectionate letters from abroad – all the external signs of love were to remain to the end. But Emma's health was not strong and she was capricious. She refused to let her husband travel to Boston where Caplet might, perhaps, have put on a *Pelléas* the composer would have approved of. He would have liked to go by himself but did not dare. His letter of 15 July 1913 to Durand on the subject of family discord, pathetic in tone, gives one or two details: 'My only energy is intellectual; in everyday life I stumble over the smallest pebble, which another man would send flying with a light-hearted kick!'

There we have the true picture of a creative artist. The crisis of 1910–11 turned into resignation. But things were not the same as they had been in 1904. Now there was Chouchou, as well as the fear of starting all over again at nearly 50, for a man who twice before had lost many of his friends for similar reasons. Fret as he might at the restrictions of bourgeois morality, Debussy could no longer break through them; and it was a little late to discover that he was 'not cut out for domestic life'. His future was fixed and he was to remain with his family despite the heartrending complaints that continued to escape him: 'I've been gnawing away at boredom in this house for too long' (29 July 1914). In his blackest moments he contemplated suicide. The rest of the time he was full of expressions of affection, especially on his travels abroad, which left both his wife and himself emotionally exhausted. All the fragility of Debussy's character and the ambivalence of his feelings come to the fore in these years of maturity.

He was happy to lose himself in his work. His chief projects were the operas on the two stories by Edgar Allan Poe, neither of which he finished. Ideas were suggested to him by others: writers such as Gabriel

Mourey, Victor Segalen and Louis Laloy for operas, Diaghilev for ballets, while Fauré invited him to sit on juries at the Conservatoire and journalists came wanting interviews. But there was no question of Debussy being isolated. He and Emma left his 'lair' to go to the theatre and friends came to visit, both old (those few who remained) and new: Paul-Jean Toulet, who unfortunately left Paris for Saint-Loubès in 1912, the Laloys, Stravinsky and the ever-faithful André Caplet. But for the most part these visitors were collaborators, performers and, with increasing frequency, doctors who, in the last months of 1915, diagnosed a cancer. From 1916 Debussy began to utter his bitterest complaint of all, that he could no longer satisfy 'that desire always to go still further, which for me used to be the stuff of life . . .'

Debussy's letters make up a kind of diary, filled with confidential remarks about the musicians of his time and about the earliest performances of his own works. The reader would search in vain through his articles in the *Revue blanche* or in *Gil Blas* to find the sort of uninhibited comments to which he gives vent in his letters: Berlioz 'a prodigious humbug', Bizet 'the Maupassant of music', Fauré 'the musical servant of a group of snobs and imbeciles', Gustave Charpentier the 'grubby Prix de Rome' with his 'chlorotic cantilenas', Richard Strauss 'the symphonic domestic', d'Indy 'the Schola contractor', Ravel the 'fakir-cum-enchanter'. Obviously we must make allowances in such remarks for Debussy's singular love of paradox. His caustic tongue was unsparing not just towards his rivals but towards those who had at some time disappointed his expectations. Among publishers, Heugel was a 'thoroughly nasty man', Messrs Durand were 'the barbarians of the place de la Madeleine', not to mention 'that ass Hamelle'. Among critics, Pierre Lalo was the 'evil Jesuit', Calvocoressi the 'lackey' and Jean-Aubry a 'poor little mosquito, easily brushed aside'.

His sharpest barbs were reserved for performers. When it came to the performance of his music Debussy was the most demanding composer of his time, and maybe of any previous time as well. Among singers, Maggie Teyte was 'a more than distant princess', Rose Féart 'indescribably ugly and lacking in poetry', while Bourbon had 'a pretty voice but enunciates like a house-painter'. Among conductors, Chevillard 'ought to have been a tamer of wild beasts', Sylvain Dupuis 'smacks more of an ox than of a maestro' and Lamoureux is 'a cubic conductor'. As for pianists, Debussy summed them all up in a letter to

Varèse: 'I can't tell you the extent to which my piano music has been deformed; so much so that I often have a job to recognize it.'

Few wholly escaped his deadly shafts, even if these are not all to be taken at face value. Debussy's intransigence was total only when it came to defending the one art which for him took the place of religion, and in this area at least he cannot be accused of double-dealing. At times he is blindingly frank: explaining to René Peter that the young man's draft of a play is foundering in a sea of facility, or refusing to entrust his prose to the editor of a periodical which disagrees with his own point of view; while d'Annunzio's poetic style is described to its author as 'over-fine'.

In defence of an authentic tradition, however, Debussy's tone became enthusiastic. He was as passionate in pleading with a Hungarian correspondent to respect the music of the gypsies as he was in urging Stravinsky to 'remain a great Russian artist'.

His judgements of contemporary composers are a little less sweeping, but none the less he allowed himself in his letters the freedom denied him in his articles. Realists and 'people's composers', like Gustave Charpentier and Alfred Bruneau, are manhandled without reserve. Enough has been said about his attitude to Wagner for it not to need repeating, but we learn new details of his relations with Dukas and Ravel – in the latter case fuel seems to have been heaped on the flames by the critics, Pierre Lalo especially. Stravinsky, right from the start, was hailed without reservations; these Debussy was to express only later as part of his campaign for French nationalism. His views on Richard Strauss, too, follow a complex course. *Ein Heldenleben*, in 1900, is 'all the same, a good, solid piece', but after that Strauss is lumped together with Schoenberg and, in the early part of the war, condemned in the cause of defending French music.

From all this it is clear that Debussy's pronouncements must never be taken at face value. Like many Symbolists, he liked to surround himself with mystery and ambiguity. Did he or did he not like Wagner and the Ballets Russes? His opinions seem contradictory only to those who choose to ignore the specific occasions that gave rise to them. If we take these into account his attitudes are unified and coherent in the extreme, based on his hatred of dogma and his fight against *a priori* forms, 'parasitic development passages' and empty padding, and on his commitment to making music both free and deeply serious.

When it came to his own music Debussy was quite open in describing his difficulties and satisfactions. He was naturally reticent about mentioning his personal 'chemistry' or a particular 'setting of a harmony in context' and it comes as something of a shock to find him writing that he has discovered 'a rather novel way of handling voices' or of mixing 'a low oboe with violin harmonics'. More typically, he turned to paradox, declaring, for instance, that 'you learn more about orchestration by listening to the sound of leaves blown by the wind than you do by poring over treatises'. He was quite straightforward in admitting that writing music is hard work and described his difficulties not only (as we might expect) to his various publishers, but to his friends as well. The *Nocturnes* and the orchestral *Images* were mulled over for months at a time; *The Fall of the House of Usher* and *The Devil in the Belfry* for years. Much more rarely did Debussy boast of success. Once at least, during the rehearsals of *Ibéria* in 1910, elation broke through: Debussy caught the immaterial nature of the orchestral sound linking 'Parfums de la nuit' and 'Le matin d'un jour de fête' in the phrase 'it sounds like improvisation'.

Some of these letters contain veritable professions of faith in the general field of musical aesthetics and could, with advantage, replace some of the catchphrases in which Debussy has often found himself imprisoned. 'Composers aren't daring enough' (to Lerolle in 1894); 'Music is a very young art in technique as well as in understanding' (to Durand in 1907); and a remark, pregnant with meaning, that he made to Charles Levadé in 1903: 'They categorize me, so I can't exercise the influence on music that I'd like to.'

Translator's Preface

To the 255 letters in François Lesure's collection (*Claude Debussy: Lettres 1884–1918*, Paris, 1980) I have added a further 56. The numbers of these are appended below; they are further designated in the text by the sign † against the number of each letter. Six of these are as yet unpublished in the original French (numbers 66, 76, 83, 118, 166, 251).

Although in making my translation I have tried to avoid slang, I have made no attempt to give it a period flavour; Debussy's ironical style is hard enough to render without that, and in any case his mind and manner of expression are often, like his music, surprisingly modern. I have retained the original French for his opening formulae. English has no equivalent for these, carefully judged as they always are to suit the addressee ('cher grand ami', for instance, in his letter to Ysaÿe, number 59). His closing formulae, on the other hand, seem to me by and large less meaningful and here English does provide a reasonably adequate range of possible renderings. There is however no convenient way of indicating in the letters themselves which correspondents Debussy addressed as 'vous' and which as 'tu'. A list of 'tutoyés' seems the best solution, namely: both his wives (though not in the express letter to Emma, number 116), Chouchou, Raymond Bonheur, Alfred Bruneau, Charles Levadé, Pierre Louÿs, René Peter, Gabriel Pierné and Eugène Ysaÿe.

I have added to M. Lesure's notes where I thought it helpful to the English-speaking reader. These additions are followed by the initials R.N. Notes to the 56 additional letters are also mine. Debussy's punctuation has, in a few places, been simplified. Passages omitted from the letters are indicated thus [. . .]. Debussy's misspellings of proper names have been preserved in the letters, but corrected in the notes.

I should like to express my sincere gratitude to François Lesure for his help in preparing this translation. I am also indebted for numerous favours to Margaret Cobb, David Grayson, Richard Langham Smith, Robert Orledge, Maître Henri Thieullent, the Pierpont Morgan Library, and to the Faculty Committee and staff of the Harry Ransom Humanities Research Center at the University of Texas at Austin.

Roger Nichols
September 1986

List of 56 letters additional to those in the original French edition

Letter number: 6, 7, 36, 37, 39, 66, 76, 83, 89, 92, 108, 109, 118, 125, 145, 156, 157, 161, 165, 166, 169, 170, 175, 178, 182, 186, 196, 200, 201, 208, 214, 216, 220, 224, 232, 240, 241, 249, 250, 251, 253, 265, 268, 270, 271, 272, 273, 276, 283, 285, 289, 291, 293, 295, 296, 306.

A note on the sources

Since this translation is by definition addressed to English-speaking readers, a detailed list of original sources seems of doubtful value. Scholars will naturally be familiar with François Lesure's original French edition of this book, the bibliography of which (as that in this translation) is conveniently listed for the most part by correspondent, and with the sources listed in the correspondence section of Claude Abravanel's *Claude Debussy: A Bibliography*, (Detroit Studies in Music Bibliography, No. 29), Detroit, 1974, Items 1578–1684. The location of those letters not found or mentioned in the above volumes, namely the six letters published here for the first time, is given below:

66, 83, 251	Harry Ransom Humanities Research Center at the University of Texas, Austin
76, 118	Pierpont Morgan Library, New York
166	Archive Durand, Paris

Chronology

1862   Born at Saint-Germain-en-Laye, just outside Paris, on 22 August.

1872   Enters the Conservatoire.

1881   First visit to Moscow. Meets Mme Vasnier.

1884   Wins Prix de Rome.

1885   Leaves for the Villa Medici, Rome. Hears Liszt play.

1887   Returns to Paris. Composes *Printemps*.

1888   First visit to Bayreuth. Completes *La Damoiselle élue*.

1889   Visits Bayreuth again. Universal Exhibition in Paris.

1892   Completes first set of *Fêtes galantes*. Meets Gaby Dupont.

1893   First performances of *La Damoiselle élue* and the String Quartet.

1894   First performance of *Prélude à l'après-midi d'un faune*.

1895   Completes first version of *Pelléas et Mélisande*.

1897   Gaby Dupont attempts suicide. *Chansons de Bilitis* completed.

1899   Marries Rosalie (Lilly) Texier.

1901   First complete performance of *Nocturnes*. First articles in the *Revue blanche*.

1902   First performance of *Pour le piano*. Première of *Pelléas et Mélisande* at the Opéra-comique.

1903   Made Chevalier of the Legion of Honour. Meets Emma Bardac.

1904   First performance of *Estampes*. Composes second set of *Fêtes galantes* and *L'Isle joyeuse*. Sets up house with Mme Bardac. His wife Lilly attempts suicide. Many of his friends desert him.

1905   First performances of *L'Isle joyeuse* and *La Mer*. Completes first set of *Images* for piano. Divorce from Lilly. Birth of daughter Claude-Emma (Chouchou) to him and Emma Bardac.

1907 Belgian and German premières of *Pelléas*.

1908 Marries Emma Bardac. Conducts in London. First performances of second set of *Images* and *Children's Corner*. American and Italian premières of *Pelléas*. Begins work on a setting of Poe's tale *The Fall of the House of Usher*.

1909 Visits London twice: to conduct, and to supervise English première of *Pelléas*. Begins first book of *Préludes*.

1910 First performances of *Ibéria* and *Rondes de printemps*. First book of *Préludes* published. Meets Stravinsky. Father dies. Conducts in Vienna and Budapest.

1911 First performance of *Le Martyre de Saint Sébastien*. Serious money problems. Conducts in Turin.

1912 Composes *Jeux*.

1913 Hundredth performance of *Pelléas* at the Opéra-comique. First performance of *Gigues*. Première of *Jeux*. Conducts in Moscow and St Petersburg.

1914 Conducts in Rome, The Hague and Amsterdam.

1915 Edits works of Chopin. Mother dies. At Pourville composes *En blanc et noir*, Cello Sonata, Sonata for flute, viola and harp, and piano *Etudes*. Undergoes operation.

1916 Edits violin sonatas of J. S. Bach. Final version of libretto of *The Fall of the House of Usher*.

1917 Composes Violin Sonata. Plays piano at first performance – his last concert in Paris.

1918 Dies in Paris on 25 March.

Childhood
Musical studies
The Prix de Rome

No sign of musical or artistic talent appears anywhere among Debussy's ancestors. Six generations back they were living in a small village on the Côte-d'Or. As for the lowly, temporary jobs held by his father, none of them can have had any great influence on him. As a young boy in Saint-Germain-en-Laye Achille-Claude received from his mother the barest minimum of education. Then he was sent off to join his aunt Clémentine in Cannes and thanks to her he had some piano lessons at the age of eight or nine. It was around this time that his father was made a captain in the forces of the Commune and then charged and sentenced to a year's imprisonment. In the prison camp at Satory Debussy *père* met Charles de Sivry whose mother, Antoinette Mauté de Fleurville, was a pianist and claimed to have been a pupil of Chopin. She realized the boy was musically gifted and from that moment the idea of his becoming a sailor was abandoned.

On 22 October 1872 Achille-Claude was admitted to the Paris Conservatoire. Student exercises were never much to his taste and his career there was not particularly distinguished. He won a first prize in solfège[1] but only a second prize for piano-playing and his father, who had hopes that he would become a virtuoso and make a lot of money, was extremely disappointed. He failed to excel in the harmony class either, being already reluctant simply to apply established procedures, but he did better in keyboard harmony and scorereading and began to compose songs. The first step in his career was the opportunity, in 1880, to serve in the musical establishment of Tchaikovsky's patroness Mme von Meck, thanks to whom he made his first journeys to Italy and Russia and discovered the pleasures of a moneyed existence. In the meantime he met Marie-Blanche Vasnier, a woman of thirty-two

[1]

married to a building contractor. She had a good voice and sang the songs he wrote for her, on poems by Théodore de Banville, Paul Bourget and Théophile Gautier. Their liaison soon caused gossip among Debussy's friends.

On 28 June 1884 he won the Prix de Rome with his cantata *L'Enfant prodigue*. This classic start to a musical career gave him little pleasure because it meant leaving Paris for the Villa Medici in Rome and being separated from Mme Vasnier for two years. But M. Vasnier's pleading together with the promptings of common sense – he had very little money – eventually persuaded him to go. Once there, he was unhappy with the atmosphere of the Villa, with his fellow students and, more often than not, with the works he was trying to write; so much so that he seems to have taken no pleasure whatever in his new surroundings.

[1]   Solfège is a system of basic musical instruction in which ear-training and sight-reading play a large part; in particular, pupils are asked to sing and name each note of a melody in relation to a fixed 'doh'. (R.N.)

1 TO GIUSEPPE PRIMOLI[1]

Mon cher ami   Late 1884

I'm writing to ask you a great favour. Perhaps you'll be surprised I've chosen you, when we've only known each other for such a short time. But my uncouth ways have not made me many friends and that's why I'm turning to you, as I know you're kind and sympathetic to my problems. My parents are not rich and I can't afford my Prix de Rome dinner. I've tried to sell some of my music but without success. Everything has been against me. I've run up one or two debts which I shall have to settle before I leave for Rome and I can't even buy any flowers for her *'who loves them so much'*.[2] So I'm asking you to lend me 500 francs.

It distresses me to make such demands on you when you've already contributed so much to my spiritual well-being.

Now it's my material life that needs your support. But, as I said, I ask this only because of the friendship I feel you have for me. And my parents are in such dire straits, I don't want to be a further burden to them.

With all best wishes
Claude Debussy

I'll repay you 100 francs at a time as soon as the instalments of my grant start coming through.[3]

[1] Count Primoli, 1851–1927, called 'Gégé', was the son of a Roman lawyer and Princess Charlotte Bonaparte: 'a young man of thirty with a miserable home life, who comes to the Villa Medici to find a little solace for his domestic troubles' (Paul Vidal to

Henriette Fuchs, 16 June 1884). That year he stayed from 10 June to 29 November in the apartment put at his disposal by his aunt, Princess Mathilde. He was connected with a number of writers, notably with Maupassant, and at his death left over two hundred paintings by Watteau.

[2] Marie-Blanche Vasnier, whom Debussy had met in 1881 in the singing class of Madame Moreau-Sainti, for which he acted as accompanist. He dedicated more than twenty songs to Madame Vasnier between 1881 and 1884.

[3] At that time the students at the Villa received 167.50 francs a month.

2 TO HENRIETTE FUCHS[1]

Chère Madame   Thursday 15 January 1885

I write, grave sinner that I am, to ask your pardon. You know I was competing for the city of Paris prize, and I've been working hard, but all for nothing as it happens because I couldn't finish in time. After this forced labour my brain has taken rather a knock and I've not been well.

But I should not like to leave without seeing you. May I ask you to suggest a day when I can receive your pardon and you can receive my farewell?

Yours affectionately
C. Ach. Debussy

[1] Henriette Fuchs was an amateur singer who ran a choral society called La Concordia. Debussy acted, erratically, as accompanist between 1883 and 1885, replacing his friend Paul Vidal who had left for Rome. We learn from this letter that Debussy intended to go in for the 'grand prix musical de la ville de Paris' so as to avoid leaving for the Villa Medici.

3 TO EUGÈNE VASNIER[1]

                                                                    Marseilles
Cher monsieur Vasnier   27 January 1885

I have very little to say to you, above all out of fear of troubling you with my troubles. I assure you I'm doing everything I can to keep my courage up, even to the extent of forgetting you. Now don't think of this as ingratitude. Anyway, don't worry, I shouldn't succeed.

I'll write to you at greater length when I get to Rome.

Yours sincerely
Ach. Debussy

[4]

Please pass on my best wishes to Madame Vasnier and embrace
Marguerite and Maurice for me.   Villa Medici

[1] Eugène-Henri Vasnier, a building contractor whose guest Debussy was both in Paris
and at Ville d'Avray.

4 TO EUGÈNE VASNIER

Rome

Cher monsieur Vasnier   early February 1885

Here I am in this abominable Villa and I can assure you my first
impression is not a good one. The weather is terrible – wind and rain.
You must admit there was hardly any point coming to Rome to find the
same weather we have in Paris, especially for someone who looks on all
things Roman with a jaundiced eye.

My fellow students came to collect me at Monte-Rotondo where we
had to spend the night in a dirty little room, all six of us. If you could only
see how they've changed! No more of the friendliness of Paris. They're
stiff and seem convinced of their own importance – the Prix de Rome has
taken them over.

The evening of my arrival at the Villa I played my cantata, which some
of the students liked but not, I may say, the musicians. Frankly I find the
artistic environment and the camaraderie my mentors go on about
considerably overrated. With one or two exceptions conversation is not
easy and I can't help thinking of those splendidly silly conversations *we*
used to have – they taught me such a lot and opened my mind in so many
ways, yes, I miss them. Everybody here is such an out-and-out egoist,
every man for himself. I've heard the three musicians, Marty, Pierné and
Vidal,[1] running each other down; Marty and Pierné running down Vidal,
Pierné and Vidal running down Marty, and so on.

And then back to my vast room, with a five mile walk between one
piece of furniture and the next. I've been so lonely I've cried.

I'd come to rely too much on your friendship and intelligence and on
the fact that you were interested in what I was doing and were willing to
discuss it. I'll never forget all you have done for me, or how welcome you
made me inside your family circle. I shall do everything I can to prove to
you that I am not ungrateful.

Once again, I must ask you not to forget me but to go on being my
friend. I have a feeling I shall need it.

[5]

I've tried to work and I can't; still, I do what I can. I don't need to remind you how much I love music and you can imagine how frustrated I am to be feeling like this. But I can't live this sort of life. The others may enjoy it, but I don't; and it's not pride that makes me hate it so much. It's simply that I can't get used to it – I haven't got the right sort of personality or the intellectual energy to make it work.

I repeat, I'm afraid I may come back to Paris sooner than you expect. Maybe that would be very silly, but what's the alternative? I'm afraid of going against your wishes and of trying your friendship too far, which is the last thing I would want. But certainly, if you can still find it in you to sympathize with my difficulties, you won't be able to accuse me of cowardice. I'm not very well, as always because the atmosphere in Rome doesn't agree with my system. I'd willingly work my head off its shoulders, but the only result is a fever that lays me out and leaves me helpless.

Very many thanks for your letter. I know your time is not your own but, if it's not asking too much, please write back a long letter to remind me of those wonderful conversations.

> Yours most sincerely and affectionately
> Ach. Debussy

Please give my best wishes to Madame Vasnier. Is Marguerite well? And is she still studying my songs? I'm very fond of Marguerite and I'd like to make a real musician of her. I think that would please you and for me it would be a source of pride – at least I would not have been completely useless.[2]

Embrace her for me, and also that young clown of a Maurice.

> Once again, my respect and affection
> Ach.

[1]   Georges Marty and Gabriel Pierné shared the Prix de Rome in 1882. Paul Vidal won it outright in 1883.

[2]   Debussy had been giving the Vasniers' daughter piano and harmony lessons. Later she described him as a teacher quite without patience and unwilling to come down to her level.

5 TO EUGÈNE VASNIER

Villa Medici

Cher Monsieur   4 June 1885

You must be thinking that something serious has happened to keep me

1 Debussy in Rome in 1885 during his first year at the Villa Medici.

so long from replying to your kind letter. That serious something is quite simply another very bad attack of fever. Over the last few days I've at last been feeling better and hope I'm rid of it.

It has, understandably, done nothing whatever to increase my sympathy for the Villa. On the contrary I've thought often of getting out of these wretched barracks, where life is so miserable and fever all too easy to come by. And yet there are people who have sung the praises of the Italian climate! I find this a little sinister, especially at present. Unfortunately my plans for escape were thwarted by your letter, tightly packed as it was with sensible advice – so tightly that I had no room to slip in the thinnest proviso. The contents are justified by the fact that I'm still here and about to start work. I hope that's good news for you. It would help me to discuss my work with you – it would cheer me up and remind me of 'our evenings of yesteryear'.

I've changed my mind about my first 'envoi'. *Zuleima*[1] is not the right sort of thing at all, so I shan't be going ahead with it as I intended. It's too old and too stuffy. Those great stupid lines bore me to death – the only thing great about them is their length – and my music would be in danger of sinking under the weight. Another thing, and more important, is that I don't think I'll ever be able to cast my music in a rigid mould. I hasten to add I'm not talking about musical form, merely from the literary point of view. I would always rather deal with something where the passage of events is to some extent subordinated to a thorough and extended portrayal of human feelings. That way, I think, music can become more personal, more true to life; you can explore and refine your means of expression.

I don't know if I've already mentioned to you Banville's *Diane au bois*?[2] I think I have. Well, that's what I'm starting on to be my first 'envoi'. Another reason for choosing *Diane* is that it's nothing at all like the usual poems set for 'envois', which are basically no more than improved cantatas. Heaven knows, one was enough! I may as well take advantage of the one good thing the Villa has to offer (as you said), complete freedom to work, in order to produce something original and not keep falling back into old habits. Of course, the Institut won't agree, as it naturally believes its own habits are the only ones that count. So much the worse for it! I'm too fond of my freedom and my own way of doing things. If my physical freedom is circumscribed, at least I can get my own back on the intellectual front. But seriously, the nub of the matter is that my sort of music is the only sort I can write.

2 Debussy with his Prix de Rome colleagues on the steps of the
Villa Medici.

What I still have to find out is whether I shall be strong enough to do it. Anyway, there are some people for whose satisfaction I'm prepared to do my utmost. The rest I'm not bothered about.

You, as I hope you know, are among those I like to please. If you do indeed know that, then write to me soon – a nice long letter to keep my spirits up – and spend a few moments lightening the burdens of my prison, because my spirits won't stay high indefinitely. That's more than I can manage and I think it's already an impressive feat for an idealistic character like myself to have kept them high for several months.

Ach.

[1] At the end of each year students at the Villa had to send back to Paris an 'envoi' as testimony to their progress, in the case of the musicians a substantial choral or orchestral work. Debussy's symphonic ode *Zuleima*, to a libretto put together by Georges Boyer from Heinrich Heine's *Almanzor*, has not survived. It drew from his examiners the response that 'M. Debussy seems to be tormented these days by the desire to produce music that is bizarre, incomprehensible and unperformable'. (R.N.)
[2] A 'comédie héroïque' published by Banville in 1864. Debussy had already done some work on it in Paris. The only parts that survive are an overture for piano duet and a duet between Diana and Eros (Act II, scenes 3 and 4), for soprano, tenor and piano accompaniment. See letter 8.

6† TO EUGÈNE VASNIER

Villa Medici
Cher Monsieur Vasnier   August 1885

It's my turn to ask your forgiveness for being so slow in answering. But, for a reluctant Roman like myself, the heat has been absolutely intolerable, so much so that when I sat down to play the piano it began to sweat like a living person. And then there's been the invasion by small, nocturnal insects, not only making sleep impossible but turning you into something resembling a colander as well.

Hébert[1] claimed we were making them up and that he'd never noticed them. 'It's a slander upon the Villa,' he said. But he's so mad about Italy anyway, he turns its most ridiculous aspects into miracles. The other evening he even went so far as to say that in Rome the drunks never lurch because *they drink the wine of heroes*! I must say, there's no denying the heroism with which they slash each other with knives, but I can't help wondering whether lurching wouldn't be better for them . . .

So I left Rome and went to Fiumicino on the coast. I only meant to stay a week or so, but it was such a lovely place I didn't get back here till the day before yesterday. Primoli was in Paris and let me have his villa, which is quite delightful, like the descriptions Bourget[2] gives of his favourite 'cottages', apart from the sky which (let's admit it) is a thousand times better than the one you find in England.

I was able to satisfy my savage instincts as thoroughly as possible; I didn't know anybody and didn't have to talk to anybody except to ask for food (which was quite a strain). I did some work (almost good, too) and went for walks as if I'd been doing it all my life. Perhaps my seaside has been almost as good as yours – no people or casinos, obviously, but then that's why I liked it [. . .]

[1] The painter Ernest Hébert, the director of the Villa Medici. He played the violin and Debussy used to accompany him. They had heated discussions about Wagner, who was not one of Hébert's favourites.
[2] Paul Bourget, 1852–1935, the novelist, poet and critic, who had travelled widely in England. Debussy knew him personally and made nine settings of his poems in the 1880s. Six of them are dedicated to Mme Vasnier.

7† TO EUGÈNE VASNIER

Villa Medici
16 September 1885

. . . I must ask you to forgive me for the uninteresting contents of this letter, but what can I find to say about a life where nothing goes on except boredom? I swear to you I've done everything to combat it, tried everything I know, but without success.

You may say I've no right to be bored, surrounded as I am by all that's beautiful and designed to stimulate the imagination. That's all very well, but one can't change one's nature . . .

You speak of the tranquillity the Villa has to offer. God knows, I could do with a bit less of it, no matter what the cost; it weighs me down and I can't live underneath it.

You may say again that that's not serious, but the worst thing is that my work is suffering badly. Every day I sink deeper into mediocrity and good ideas have abandoned me. You must admit, this state of affairs gives me the right to reflect on the future. You were kind enough to say I ought to be very happy at setting such high standards for myself. Well, this time it seems they haven't been high enough: it hasn't taken me long to see that my apparent happiness when things were going easily was in fact false and empty.

[11]

I really feel now that what I've been through so far this year is enough to prove that I'll never do any good here – *it's been a wasted experience and has merely set me back*. In all honesty I think it would be a disservice to ask me to remain here for a second year, it would only provide further obstacles and remove from me altogether the facility for working I once possessed. No one, I hope, can say I haven't tried. This wasted year is proof enough that I have.

So I intend to hand in my resignation at the end of the year. Knowing your affection for me, I ask you not to think this is a mistake. It is not on my own behalf any more that I'm speaking, but on that of my future [. . .]

8 TO EUGÈNE VASNIER

Villa Medici

Cher Monsieur   19 October 1885

Forgive my long delay in replying, but these last few days I've been down again with fever. I've only just got up, though I still feel very tired.

You say you don't understand a word of my letter. I'm sorry about this. Maybe I didn't explain myself properly. Or maybe you don't believe the fears I expressed about my work. I'll say no more about them, as that would probably bore you. In any case it's hard to put into simple words the despondency that weighs on me. May I just say that my complaints were not about the boredom of staying in the Villa, but about my future – that was all.

Don't think that my fellow students are influencing me. To begin with, I hardly see them, and what they think of my work is of absolutely no interest to me.

The reasons you give against my leaving the Villa are, as always, valid and I know your sympathy is what prompts them. So it must seem very odd to you that I don't respond in a reasonable manner. But I really wonder whether it wouldn't be better to put up with the fuss my return to Paris would cause, rather than submit to this feeling of helplessness that gets worse every day. But enough. Writing that letter did bring me, if nothing else, the consolation of knowing that you haven't forgotten me, and that I can still rely on your friendship.

And so to the news I owe you about the Bourget songs, and *Diane, Salammbô, Zuleima*. I've written one more song, and the rest are like

[12]

the Duke of Marlborough;[1] as for *Diane*, one scene is finished, though I'm not at all happy with it – it's far from being right. Apart from anything else, it could be that I've taken on something too ambitious. There's no precedent to go on and I find myself compelled to invent new forms. I could always turn to Wagner, but I don't need to tell you how ridiculous it would be even to try. The only thing of his I would want to copy is the running of one scene into another. Also I want to keep the tone lyrical without it being absorbed by the orchestra.

I'm keeping *Salammbô*[2] for when I get back to Paris. I've got one or two sketches which could be worked up.

Zuleima is dead and I'm not going to be the one who revives her. I don't want to hear any more about the subject, as it's not at all the sort of music I want to write. I'm after music that is supple and concentrated enough to adapt itself to the lyrical movements of the soul and the whims of reverie.[3]

Zuleima is too much like Verdi and Meyerbeer . . . Forgive me!

As you see, none of this is very important, and I'm not proud at having to admit to such feeble results – which is why I was reluctant to tell you about them.

> Forgive me
> With all best wishes
> A. Debussy

[1] Presumably a reference to the folk song 'Malbrough s'en va-t-en guerre' in which the English general, like Debussy's songs, comes to an untimely end. (R.N.)
[2] There is no trace of these sketches inspired by Flaubert's novel.
[3] This definition is amazingly close to the earlier one of Baudelaire: 'a prose that is poetic, musical, without rhythm and without rhyme, supple and concentrated enough to fit the lyrical movements of the soul and the undulations of reverie . . .' (letter to Arsène Houssaye introducing *Le Spleen de Paris*, ed. C. Pichois, Vol. I, 1975, pp. 275–6).

9 TO EUGÈNE VASNIER

Villa Medici
Cher Monsieur   24 November 1885

Feeling as guilty as I do, I won't embark on excuses but would ask you to forgive me and not to put my behaviour down to indifference.

Much of my slackness in not writing to you stems from the life I lead, which is turning me more and more into a savage. At times I'm so completely laid low that when the time comes to write I say to myself:

'What's the point?' There's nothing anyone can do to rescue me. I must just stay quietly in my corner and put up with a misery that most people find incomprehensible.

The fact of the matter is, I shall die without recanting on the subject of the Villa Medici and the benefits it lavishes on its artists. I shall remain deaf to the most persuasive sermons and equally (forgive me) to your kind remonstrances.

In many ways it's like being a junior officer on full pay, and such a life has nothing to teach me. In fact I'm glad to find I have the strength of character not to get involved, except where there's absolutely no avoiding it. As a result my fellow students have come to regard me with a certain animosity. They accuse me, unfairly, of trying to parade my individuality, or else they philosophize all over me in a style which, I dare say, they picked up in the bars on the boulevard Saint-Michel. I may say they get some tough, logical propositions in return.

I must tell you about my only outing this month. I went to hear two masses, one by Palestrina, the other by Orlando de Lassus, in a church called the Anima.[1] I don't know if you know it (it's hidden away in a maze of small, shabby streets). I liked it very much; it's very simple and pure in style, quite different from so many of the others, which are dominated by a riot of sculptures, paintings and mosaics – all rather too theatrical for my taste. The Christ in these churches looks like some forgotten skeleton, wondering sadly what it's doing there. The Anima is certainly the right place to hear that kind of music, the only church music I regard as legitimate. That of Gounod & Co. strikes me as the product of hysterical mysticism – it's like a sinister practical joke.

The two above-named gentlemen are true masters, especially Orlando, who is more decorative, more human than Palestrina. I'm truly amazed at the effects they can get simply from a vast knowledge of counterpoint. I expect you think of counterpoint as the most forbidding article in the whole of music.

But in their hands it becomes something wonderful, adding an extraordinary depth to the meaning of the words. And every now and then the melodic lines unroll and expand, reminding you of the illuminations in ancient missals. And those are the only occasions when my real musical self has given a slight stir.

I'm working hard. I must make up in quantity for not being able to rely on quality. *Diane* is giving me a lot of trouble. I can't manage to find a musical idea that gives me the look of her, as I imagine it. In fact

[14]

it's quite difficult, because the idea must be beautiful but cold – it mustn't give any hint of passion. Love comes to Diane only much later and then it's only really by accident; I'll have to get it across through the transformation of this idea, step by step as Diane loses her resistance to love, but the idea must keep the same contour throughout.

I was glad to learn that you were going to approach Baudry for Mme Vasnier's portrait. I think he's the only artist who could do her justice.[2]

As for the rumour about my death, I dare say it's been spread by someone complaining of the scarcity of my correspondence. I'm not well and I'm not ill. I'm just suffering from a malaise which I can't describe, but which comes from living away from where I belong.

Write to me soon, and tell me that you don't hold my attitude against me and that *you do not forget what you know*. My spirits are low at the moment and I don't know that I have the patience to hold out for a satisfactory solution.

> Yours affectionately
> Ach. Debussy

[1]   Santa Maria dell' Anima, near the Piazza Navone.
[2]   This portrait of Mme Vasnier was reproduced in the May 1926 number of the *Revue musicale*. Baudry won the Prix de Rome for painting in 1850 and this was one of his last works – as mentioned in the following letter, he died a few weeks afterwards.

10 TO EUGÈNE VASNIER

> Villa Medici
> 29 January 1886

[. . .] I must tell you how sorry I was to hear of Baudry's death. You know how much I admired him. For me he was a representative of 'great art' in the most modern sense of the term. It won't be easy to replace him, especially now that everyone with one or two exceptions is preoccupied by detail, thereby putting great art inexorably beyond their reach.

In your case the portrait of Mme Vasnier had brought you nearer to the artist and so his death is a double blow. May I therefore add my sincere regrets to your own.

You ask for news of my envoi. There lies much of the reason for my long delay in writing. I'm hard at it – one day I think I'm on the right track, the next I'm afraid I've made a mistake. Never before has a work filled me with such misgivings. It's so difficult to portray the countless emotions a character undergoes and still keep the form as simple as possible; and in *Diane* the scenes were constructed with no thought of their being set to music, so they could seem too long and it's the very devil to keep up the interest and ward off yawns of boredom.

But there's no point complaining about the text; I chose it, and I must take responsibility for the decision. I mention it only to show you how involved and frustrated I am.

I've hardly any news of Bourget. He sent me his last book with a brief note to say he was very busy, and that was all . . . No sign of George Eliot.[1]

My descriptive powers are not vivid enough to give you a real idea of Fiumiselino.[2] All I can tell you is that it's a charming spot where the Romans come for the sea-bathing. There's a little port with little boats, all very picturesque and delightful. I've put in some solid work on recovering my health, as you've already guessed.

I told you that Primoli had a lovely villa there. I've already paid one very pleasant visit there and in all likelihood I'll go again to finish *Diane* after the cold weather. There I can enjoy complete solitude, which is all I need at the moment.

The Villa Medici is currently very full as Hébert brought some guests back with him. A Monsieur Hochon has also arrived. They're all, it seems, very sophisticated people – I don't know if you're acquainted with them. I've met them once and they were full of kind wishes sent by Guiraud.[3] But all that's neither here nor there and does absolutely nothing to make me love the Villa more. Luckily I've found a way to get myself out of boring social occasions: I told Hébert I'd sold my evening dress and that my financial resources did not permit me to have another suit made. He thought I was mad, but who cares? I got what I wanted because he's too much of a decorum-worshipper to allow a mere lounge-suit to appear amid the splendour of décolleté gowns and tail-coats.

That's all my news for the time being. My only request is not to forget me.

Yours affectionately
A. Debussy

[1]   George Eliot, 1819–80, had considerable influence in France at this time. (But this reference is obscure – perhaps Debussy had ordered one of her books from the bookseller Baron? R.N.)

[16]

² A property belonging to Primoli at Fiumicino, on the coast near Rome.
³ Ernest Guiraud, 1837–1892, Debussy's composition teacher at the Conservatoire.

11 TO CLAUDIUS POPELIN[1]

Villa Medici

Cher Monsieur Popelin

24 June [1886]

You will have heard from Gustave the good news about my leave. There's no need to tell you how happy I am about it. But what I must say is that my previous two months in Paris[2] have not changed my views at all, and have only strengthened my feelings in some directions. They are too powerful to be ignored, as when I am away from what causes them I cease to live – it is surely 'ceasing to live' when you find you can no longer control your imagination. As I told you, my wishes and ideas function only *through her*,[3] and I'm not strong enough to break the habit. I'm rather nervous of telling you this, as it's a long way from following your advice to try and turn this love into a steady friendship. It's mad, I know, but the madness stops me thinking. And when I do think it only leads to further madness and, worse, to the realization that I have not done enough to further this love.

Forgive me, please. You know how much I value your friendship; it is to this friendship I turn in asking for forgiveness. I'm very fond of Gustave and miss him very much at the moment: without him I'd probably have left for good. I promise you, I've been through such periods of despair that I've needed him here to set me straight and revive my spirits. And may I say that the only consolation I can find in all these miseries is that they have done something to help me get to know both of you. I may not have the right to say how warmly I feel towards you, but never mind, I can't prevent myself.

As for M. and Mme Hébert, they can be sure that I'll do whatever I can to prove to them how grateful I am for their friendship.

I expect to leave on the 1st or 2nd July. It looks as though Gustave will be in Paris at that time. I hope I may look forward to seeing you as well?

Please tell Gustave that my father is quite better but that he's still worried,[4] as I am at not being able to do more for him. And please tell him too that I've given his butterflies their camphor.

Yours respectfully
A. Debussy
Very best wishes to Gustave.

[17]

[1] Claudius Popelin-Ducarre, a painter on enamel, celebrated mainly for his affair with Princess Mathilde. His son Gustave won the Prix de Rome for painting in 1882 and was one of Debussy's fellow students at the Villa.

[2] Debussy had already had two months' leave between February and April.

[3] Still Mme Vasnier.

[4] These worries probably came to a head with his dismissal on 12 April 1887 from the Compagnie Fives-Lille.

12 TO EMILE BARON[1]

Villa Medici
23 December 1886

Mon cher ami

Not having *two houses* to think about, I can't use that as an excuse for being so slow to reply; I offer instead a period of acute problems in my work – including moments of downright despondency. Ideas have been slipping away from me with an extraordinary determination. Imagine playing blind man's bluff with a group of sylphs and you'll have some idea of what I've been through.

At least my brain is not too exhausted to realize I've been thoroughly tiresome these last few days, which is not to say what an interesting person I am the rest of the time, far from it, but there are moments when I'm capable of the finer feelings; to set against others when I would sell my father and mother for an accidental. But enough of these unpleasant details.

We agree entirely about Becque.[2] In fact (and this isn't flattery) your judgement of things and people is really excellent; as soon as you come to realize that Wagner isn't a cheap buffoon, you'll be a perfect friend.

What do you think about the splendid flop of the Meyerbeer faction in the person of Salvayre?[3] Even though the most discerning part of the public is made up of grocers and chiropodists, I think they've had enough of cavatinas and all that rubbish, showing off the singers' technique and the heroes' pectoral muscles. The funny thing is, they're right behind innovations in literature and the new forms introduced by the Russian novelists (I'm quite surprised Tolstoy hasn't overtaken Flaubert yet), but when it comes to music, they want that to stay just as it was; a slightly dissonant chord is almost a signal for revolution. You must admit it takes a bit of understanding.

Have you read, or glanced at, Richepin's *Braves Gens*? It reminds me of Ohnet,[4] only well written. I much preferred his previous brutal style, and feel that this man in the orange suit is turning green.[5]

[18]

3 Portrait of Madame Vasnier by Jacques-Emile Blanche, 1888.
Photo: Bulloz.

Nothing new here except *L'abbesse de Jouarre*.[6] The only marked effect it's had has been on the French, shuddering as they see one of their most distinguished authors descend to third-rate histrionics.

If possible, I'd like my paper as soon as you can, as I shall soon be out of it; but I'm in no hurry for the stamp. Please would you send me Becque's *Michel Pauper*?[7] (You can cancel the *Revue indépendante*, I'm getting it from my brother.) Anything new I leave to your discretion.

Yours affectionately
A. Debussy

1   A friend of Debussy's who was a bookseller in the rue de Rome. He advised Debussy and kept him in touch with the current literary world.
2   Henry Becque was a playwright whose best-known works are *Les Corbeaux* and *La Parisienne*. He is regarded as a forerunner of the 'theatre of cruelty'.
3   *Egmont*, an opera by Gaston Salvayre, had been given at the Opéra-comique on 6 December. The only comment in the press was on a brief ballet sequence, which was pronounced 'delightful'.
4   The novelist Georges Ohnet wrote a long series of 'battles of life' – dully executed portraits of the contemporary middle classes.
5   Members of the French Institute wear green uniforms at their meetings. (R.N.)
6   One of Ernest Renan's 'philosophical dramas', which had just been published.
7   This five-act play had been put on in 1870 at the author's own expense.

13 TO EMILE BARON

                                                              Villa Medici
         Mon cher ami   9 February 1887

Now it's my turn to hope you won't accuse me of indifference for not replying to your letter earlier, especially as it contained news of your troubles. You have all my friendly sympathy and my prayers that you may soon be rid of them.

As for me, my excuse is my 'envoi'. It's getting me down seriously. Compared with mine, a convict's life is one of irresponsible ease and luxury. I've decided to write a work of a special colour, re-creating as many sensations as possible. I'm calling it *Printemps*,[1] not 'spring' from the descriptive point of view but from that of living things.

I wanted to express the slow, laborious birth of beings and things in nature, then the mounting florescence and finally a burst of joy at being reborn to a new life, as it were.

[20]

There's no detailed programme, of course, as I have nothing but contempt for music organized according to one of those leaflets they're so careful to provide you with as you come into the concert hall. I'm sure you see how powerful and evocative the music needs to be, and I'm not sure I shall be wholly successful in this.

You mentioned in your letter that you feel the need to transport yourself to a city of 'eternal spring'. Well, don't ever come to Rome! At the moment, for all its sunny reputation, it's more like Moscow: entirely covered with snow and cold enough to freeze you solid.

The inhabitants seem puzzled by the whole thing and are most reluctant to exchange their usual short jackets for heavy overcoats. But the ruins are a nice colour, clean-looking, and their cold, correct outlines have taken on a certain whimsy. It's a thousand times better than their ordinary pipe-clay colour under a boring blue sky. Yes, please send me *Francillon*[2] and also the *Revue indépendante* and J. Adalbert's *Paysages de femmes*, published by Vanier.

I hope you'll be quite recovered by the time you get this letter.

> Yours affectionately
> A. Debussy

My best wishes to Alexandre. Please send me also the *Nouvelle revue* for 15 February which contains a story by Bourget.[3]

[1]   This orchestral piece in two movements was finished that February and was played in piano duet form at one of the Director's parties. It served as Debussy's second 'envoi' and the Institut greeted it with reserve, warning the young composer against 'this vague impressionism which is one of the most dangerous enemies of truth in the world of art'. (This is the earliest recorded use of the term 'impressionism' in connection with Debussy. R.N.)
[2]   A play by Alexandre Dumas the younger, first performed on 17 February at the Théâtre français.
[3]   Debussy's information was inaccurate: this number of the *Nouvelle revue* contained some of Bourget's sonnets.

14   TO EUGÈNE VASNIER

Rome

Cher Monsieur Vasnier   Thursday [March, 1887]

I am going to need not only your friendship but your indulgence and your pardon!

I've tried everything, but I cannot stay here. I've followed the advice you've given me and I swear I've put the greatest possible goodwill into my efforts. The end result has only been the realization that I could never live and work here.

You'll say perhaps this is rather a sudden decision and that I haven't taken long enough to think about it but, I promise you, I've thought about it a great deal. I know what would happen to me if I stayed – total obliteration. Ever since I've been here I feel dead inside. I really want to work, and go on till I produce something solid and original. And another thing – you know how I always get serious doubts when I'm working; I need someone whose judgement I can rely on to reassure me. That's what I found so often in you – you gave me courage. Whenever you approved of something I'd written I used to feel stronger. There's no chance of that here. My fellow students make fun of my misery and I needn't look for encouragement from that quarter.

I know for a fact, if things don't turn out well many of my acquaintances will desert me. I'd rather work twice as hard in Paris. Everything may be laid on for me here but it's all so monotonous; it sends you to sleep, as I've said, or else saps your nervous energy, as in my case. I leave it to you to make the best of all this!

I leave on Saturday and get to Paris on Monday morning.[1] Please don't be too hard on me. Your friendship's the only thing I'll have left, so allow me to keep a little of it in my need.

    Yours sincerely
    A. Debussy

[1] According to the regulations, every student had to remain at the Villa for a minimum of two years. By 5 March Debussy had fulfilled this condition and so did not cut short his official stay there, contrary to what historians have long maintained.

Influences
Friendships
Early works

Debussy's stay in Rome was not, then, particularly profitable. When he came back to Paris in March 1887 his friendship with the Vasniers lasted only a few months, and new friendships took its place: with Robert Godet, Raymond Bonheur, soon to be followed by Chausson and Pierre Louÿs, as well as the artists and writers he met in cafés, in the bookshop belonging to Edmond Bailly (who published his *Damoiselle élue*) or in Mallarmé's salon. Chief among his new experiences were two visits to Bayreuth in 1888 and 1889, from which he returned apparently regarding Wagner as an enemy, even if he could never quite escape his influence; and the Paris Universal Exhibition in 1889 which led him to discover the scales and textures of Javanese music and the concentration of means employed in Annamite theatre. For all the material difficulties of this period, it furnished Debussy with a large collection of new ideas and allowed his aesthetic attitudes to achieve their final form.

The compositions of these years include the *Cinq Poèmes de Baudelaire*, a *Fantaisie* for piano and orchestra, not performed or published in Debussy's lifetime, and a major operatic project, *Rodrigue et Chimène*, on a rather earthbound libretto by Catulle Mendès. Despite Debussy's claims, he did finish it in piano score but then came to the conclusion that he had taken a wrong turning. With the String Quartet, however, the true voice of the mature Debussy is impossible to mistake.

He seems to have formed no lasting sentimental attachments during these first years of freedom from Rome. Then, in 1892, he met a pretty, green-eyed girl from Normandy, called Gaby Dupont, who was to be his partner in poverty until 1898.

15 TO ERNEST CHAUSSON[1]

Mon cher ami   Thursday 7 March 1889

I've intended several times to revise the orchestration of *Printemps*, but I've always been prevented by something, either musical or part of the daily grind; which is still the case at the moment. Also copying chorus parts and making a piano reduction all takes time and I'm afraid of being late.

I ought also to give you some particulars about *Printemps*. It's not really a choral work (the chorus part is *wordless* and more like an orchestral group). It's a *symphonic suite with chorus*. So the interest lies mostly with the orchestra and one of the difficulties of the chorus parts is the way they and the orchestra blend in together. The whole thing's a matter of ensemble and the mingling of the colours; both need a light touch.

I know it doesn't call for a large orchestra, but the writing's complex. Don't you think the salle Pleyel is too small for this kind of music? Of course, if you'd like to come and judge for yourself, I'm entirely at your disposal. I could show you *La Damoiselle élue*[2] at the same time. Perhaps her reticent charms would be more suitable?

Anyway, please reply straight away as I want to make every effort to preserve the goodwill of the Société nationale.

Yours
Achille Debussy

[1] Chausson, with d'Indy, Bréville and Camille Benoit, was one of the most active committee members of the Société nationale de musique. Debussy had been admitted as a

4 Debussy playing the piano in Chausson's house at Luzancy in 1893.

member on 8 January 1888, but neither *Printemps* nor *La Damoiselle élue* was performed at this time. The society was founded in 1871, with the motto 'Ars gallica', to help young French composers to have their works performed.

[2] Debussy's third envoi, which he wrote after returning from Italy. This 'poème lyrique' after Dante Gabriel Rossetti had received the following report from the Académie des Beaux-arts: 'The music . . . is not devoid of imagination or of charm, but it still shows tendencies, popular at the moment, towards relying on expressive and formal systems . . .' *La Damoiselle élue* was finally given at the Société nationale de musique on 8 April 1893.

16 TO ROBERT GODET[1]

25 December 1889

I'm very happy and would like, if I may, to put a little of what I feel into words (I'll be brief). Yes, our friendship does make me happy. I'm young and proud enough to have been sure it would develop, encouraged too by the secret thought that meeting troubles head-on like that did deserve an occasional sympathetic ear. This may be an old-fashioned way of looking at things, but luckily we aren't 'modern-minded'. I feel great friendship for you and I want to say so and proclaim the fact out loud. No need for any noisy razzmatazz, just that I enjoy doing so, that's all.

I should inform you that I've been hatching typhoid fever, which luckily turned into pneumonia. I'll spare you the unpleasant details. I'm still having to stay in bed and undergo a stately convalescence – the sort where a boiled egg becomes something of quite outstanding import-ance. I think it's the blood getting its revenge.

I'm sure I'll find Holland very much to my taste, both because of what you say about your life there and because it has been kind enough to allow my music to figure among its delights. Which is exactly what my music is for: to be absorbed by souls and things of goodwill. To have mastered yours so soon is already a brighter feather in my cap than the approval of the 'élite' public, under the baleful Wagnerian influence of Monsieur Lamoureux, with his pince-nez and his ceremonially pointing finger.

I've no idea why I go on so about this, though it's beautifully put. I'm not happy about the printers but I hope to send you the songs before 6 January.[2] In any case, will you please send me your most recent address?

My illness has seriously interrupted work on the *Fantaisie*.[3] The world seems to be surviving the disappointment. My envois won't be

5 Debussy boating on the Marne with Raymond Bonheur and
Ernest Chausson in 1893.

played this year, as the session is devoted to works by Vidal, the Festival Vidal, forsooth! But next year we'll have the Festival Debussy: a thoroughly delightful occasion. I hope you'll be there to help me through it.[4]

Before my illness I went to see *Tobie*,[5] but I don't think my views on it are wholly indispensable.

Mercier[6] held a little get-together to hear two cantos of Keats's *Endymion* in translation. It's very fine, once you get used to the atmosphere: some quite steamy scene-painting and a very nonchalant Diana instead of the heavy portrait others might have made of her.

I saw your friend Dardel[7] who seems to be a nice straightforward sort with a good laugh. Mercier as translator struck me as distinctly superior to the everyday Mercier. For one thing he drops that outer skin covered in riddles. Not that they're hard to solve, but there are too many of them for comfort, especially as he's a nice man underneath. We went to the café Vachette,[8] of course, and Monsieur Jean Moréas took Schopenhauer under his protection – I don't know why, as no special invitation was offered. Mercier attacked him and Dardel smiled throughout, which was really the only possible line to take.

Be charitable to this convalescent chatter, I just like to feel that you're there, otherwise I tend to get seriously depressed. The world looks ugly and boring, and then there are the exciting ideas which come to nothing! (Perhaps it's just as well.)

So goodbye, and I wish it wasn't for so long.

Yours
C. A. Debussy

No news of Brayer. Lamoureux must be casting a spell on him . . . at the very least.[9]

---

[1] Debussy had got to know this son of a Protestant minister from Neuchâtel about a year earlier, through Maurice Bouchor. He was four years younger than Debussy and they remained on friendly terms until Debussy's death.

[2] The *Cinq Poèmes de Baudelaire* were due to be published in February.

[3] The *Fantaisie* for piano and orchestra should have been Debussy's fourth envoi, but he never sent it to the Institut.

[4] This concert of his envois at the Institut did not take place.

[5] *Tobie*, a play by Bouchor, had received its first performance on 15 November at the marionette theatre in the passage Vivienne.

[6] Henry Mercier was a friend of Verlaine, Rimbaud, Charles Cros and Bouchor. His translation of Keats was never published or even finished.

[7] Otto de Dardel.

6 Debussy's friend Robert Godet.

⁸ The café Vachette was the regular haunt of the symbolist poet Jean Moréas.
⁹ Jules de Brayer was the organizer of the Concerts Lamoureux. He had lent Debussy a copy of Mussorgsky's *Boris Godunov* at a time when the work was unknown in France. (The reference to the spell is probably a further joke at the expense of Lamoureux's Wagnerian inclinations. R.N.)

17 TO VINCENT D'INDY[1]

Cher Monsieur d'Indy   20 April 1890

Night, the Bringer of Wise Counsel, bids me inform you of the following sad news.

But first I must express to you my profound gratitude for all your friendly efforts on my behalf.

It seems to me that playing just the first movement of the *Fantaisie* is not only dangerous but must inevitably give a false impression of the whole. On reflection, I would rather have a passable performance of all three movements than a fine performance of the first through your good offices.

It wasn't a rush of blood to the head or any kind of ill feeling that moved me to take such drastic action.[2] I hope anyway that you will agree with my point of view. Please believe me when I say how sorry I am to have been so apparently remiss in fulfilling my obligations towards you. You still have my gratitude, at least, and my sincere friendship.

Cl.A. Debussy

¹ The secretary and one of the founders of the Société nationale de musique. He was a consistent champion of music by young French composers, even when (and Debussy is very much a case in point) it was not to his personal taste.
² Debussy's *Fantaisie* had been put down for one of the concerts of the Société nationale. D'Indy was to conduct, but the programme turned out to be too long, so he decided to perform only the first movement. At the final rehearsal Debussy quietly removed the orchestral parts from the stands.

18 TO RAYMOND BONHEUR[1]

Cher ami   [5 October 1890]

I've been wanting to write to you for days, so please forgive a number of horribly banal problems that have come along to prevent me.

[30]

I'm reluctant to tell you that my nose has been luxuriating in the rare and delicate incense you've scattered over my songs,[2] in case I'm taken for an ultra-respectable idol. People would expect me to perform miracles and take up exhausting attitudes in times of crisis. Actually, I've absolutely no desire for my music to upset my contemporaries and keep them awake at night. All I want is the approval of people like you, who find literary programmes not sufficiently solid or engaging as a basis for music and prefer the sort which can be taken on its own terms. I don't see the point in putting a label at the head of one's list of priorities; that's descending to the level of a market stall-holder.

We should write music which contains the whole of our life, not just a little bit of it made attractive only by an elegant setting and by the idle conversation of those who don't compose* (music). Then literature and philosophy can be left with an absolutely free hand.

I look forward to your views one of these days.

Yours
Claude A. Debussy

* and particularly of those who do!

[1] A composer who had been one of Debussy's fellow students at the Conservatoire, Bonheur was a friend of Charles Cros, Albert Samain and Francis Jammes. Many of his works have remained unpublished.
[2] Undoubtedly the *Cinq Poèmes de Baudelaire*.

19 TO ROBERT GODET

Paris
Cher ami   Thursday [12 February 1891]

Obviously I'm sad you're so far away. Even so, I've not been master of myself of late and, as all I could have offered was a soul in blatant disarray, I felt silence was the best policy. I'd like to have had you there with me and told you my sufferings, great and small, face to face. It's not the same, having to rely on tear-jerking epithets – it all comes out dry and turgid. But Heaven knows, I've missed you! I hope this outburst from the heart will serve as an apology for my silence. In any case it wasn't really silence because I desperately needed to unburden myself, but there was no one to talk to!

In fact I'm still very confused. I wasn't expecting that business we talked about[1] to end so miserably and cheaply, with tales being told and unmentionable things said. I found a bizarre transposition taking place: precisely as her lips pronounced those unforgiving words, echoes of her once-loving voice resounded within me. This battle between the wrong notes (not accidental, alas!) and what I heard inside me was so overwhelming, I hardly understood what was going on. Since then understanding has forced itself upon me. I've left a large part of myself hanging on those thorns and it'll be a long time before I get back to my pursuit of art the great healer! (An ironic phrase, if you like, when art offers every kind of suffering there is – and we all know what happens to people who are healed by it.) I loved her so much, but with a sort of despairing passion because it was easy to see she was never going to commit herself utterly and she refused to be drawn when questioned about the strength of her feelings! Now I must try and find out whether she really possessed what I was looking for, or was I chasing a Void? In spite of everything, I'm still mourning the loss of the dream of a dream![2] Maybe it's not so bad, after all! Anything rather than those days when death seemed the only solution, and I was the one keeping vigil over the corpse!

Forgive me opening my wounds in this egotistical manner, I sound as though I'm pleading for sympathy over what is hardly a unique experience, but I'm just taking advantage of your kind heart. I'll say no more about it. All I need is to know you understand this arrogant weakness of mine, wanting to share my life with someone before making sure she feels the same way.

And then there are all the usual day-to-day worries, time wasted doing fatuous tasks, and Music running off in terror at all the uproar. The *Fantaisie* will see daylight shortly, when Lamoureux, who's impossible to get hold of, he's so busy cutting up *Tristan and Isolde* into bleeding chunks for the delectation of his intellectual audiences.[3] Oh! Those ridiculous mugs and their mysterious greetings: 'Are you going to *Tristan* on Sunday?' What right have they to go on like this? They should be utterly terrified, as though they'd agreed to witness some forbidden Rite.

If only this cubic conductor could give way to an angel, forcing the mob to bow their heads like a field of corn before an unseen wind!

Not that I'm forbidding them to listen – now that some of the pleasures of art are a commercial proposition we must all lend our

[32]

support – it's just that they should be made to show more respect and not sit round the table, sipping their evening coffee, and muttering: 'Good old Wagner! Good old Bach! . . . etc.' (though at least it's short). Judgements like these may appear harmless, but they always have unpleasant consequences.

What of you, meanwhile, in that alien city? (From Java to London![4] Truly Fate is extraordinary.) Brayer tells me he had a letter from you saying you were a great admirer of Turner and Rossetti, I'm delighted, and with good reason: I hope these two artists will keep you from seeing the rest! I was dreadfully worried by your letter, you sounded so discouraged. Only the extreme nature of my own misery kept me from replying instantly. And anyway there would have been no point adding my woes to yours. Still, I had a vision of you friendless and surrounded by people in ugly check suits. And that's not slick sentimentality, I promise you, but a real proof of my profound affection for you.

Now please tell me as soon as you can what you think of this idea: if I got some money together, do you think I could come and join you in London? I'd love to spend some time with you, it's what I need to heal the wounds and get back on my feet again, and you're one of the few people who doesn't see life from the crudely materialistic point of view. I'm tired of having the future reduced to a rigid schedule. Then again there are streets here where I can't walk without torment, hearing the melancholy echo of footsteps from happier times.

Try and give me some idea of what I should do.

If, as I very much hope, you approve of my plan, then I look forward to seeing you soon. But do as you think best! The last thing I want is to add to your problems.

Yours
Cl. A. Debussy

Reply to me at 27 rue de Berlin. Brayer will be writing to you in a few days and asks me to send you his best wishes.

---

[1] A love affair that took place between Debussy's attachments to Mme Vasnier and Gaby Dupont. We know nothing else about it.
[2] A phrase in imitation of Edgar Allan Poe.
[3] This must presumably refer to an intended performance of the *Fantaisie* under Lamoureux's direction. Debussy, possibly from indignation at Lamoureux's treatment of *Tristan and Isolde*, leaves out the verb in this clause. The *Fantaisie* was not

performed until 1919, the year after the composer's death, and was published in 1920.
(R.N.)
4 In the spring of 1890 Godet had been out to the Dutch East Indies and then became
London correspondent of *Le Temps*.

20 TO ROBERT GODET

Mon cher Ami   [30] January 1892

Even though I knew something of what you were going through, the distance between us has been causing me some anxious moments. So I was really delighted to get your letter and sorry to be kept so far from you by *le Temps*.[1] Unfortunately, a number of things have stopped me from writing earlier, but I don't think the above sentiments are any the less heartfelt for the delay!

My life is hardship and misery thanks to this opera.[2] Everything about it is wrong for me. I remember you used to like the colour of my pens – well, the poor things are sad and exhausted now. I long to see you and play you the two acts I've finished, because I'm afraid I may have won victories over my true self.

Between times, I've written a couple of songs[3] with the pens I have left! They're dedicated to you, not just to give you pleasure but as a proof of my friendship. I know such proof is impossible, but please forgive the attempt in the name of sincerity.

I've any number of things I want to say to you, but there's no point unless we're together. Then, maybe, we'd see an end to this awful feeling I sometimes have of being an exile with no future except to plod on dismally from day to day. To get to be a 'somebody', it seems, you have to use a bit of showmanship, and Music won't wait for the Hereafter.

Until we meet
Yours most sincerely
Cl. A. Debussy

1 '. . . la longueur du *Temps*', a pun referring to both physical and temporal separation.
(R.N.)
2 *Rodrigue et Chimène*, on a libretto by Catulle Mendès which Debussy had had since April 1890. He abandoned the opera soon after this letter and gave the manuscript to Gaby Dupont.
3 'Le son du cor s'afflige' and 'L'échelonnement des haies', two of the *Trois mélodies* on poems of Verlaine.

21 TO JULES BOIS[1]

Tuesday evening [February 1892]

I must remain firm, my dear Bois, and say that, whatever the cost to our friendship, I have not the necessary confidence in the enterprise to write the music I promised for *Les Noces de Satan!*[2] The orchestra seems to me not to exist except on a scrap of paper; as for knowing the names of the people involved and where they come from,[3] Monsieur Burger is the only one with this information, and although he's always in and out he can't do everything.

Forgive me and above all don't think there's any ill-will on my part. It's just that the whole thing deals too much in the Unknown! And could turn out to be a 'nasty experience'.

I would like to remain quite simply your friend, without drums or trumpets.

Claude A. Debussy

[1] A young 'metaphysical' writer, interested in the occult. Three years later he was put on the Vatican index for his book *Le satanisme et la magie*. Erik Satie wrote a Prelude for his play *La Porte héroïque du ciel* (1893).
[2] This esoteric, one-act verse drama by Jules Bois was to be performed at the Théâtre d'art on 31 March. The magazine *Le Saint Graal* announced in its number of 20 March that the piece would have 'music by Debussy'. The music was in fact written at the last moment by the Opéra archivist, Henry Quittard.
[3] The dramatis personae included, apart from Satan, Psyche, Adam and Eve, Mephistopheles, the courtesans etc.

22 TO LAURENT TAILHADE[1]

Monsieur   Sunday 18 June [1892]

I happened to read the number of *L'Initiation* for June '92 and, in the review of a book by Édouard Dubus, found my name mentioned.[2] I must confess I am amazed by this and still more by the fact that you mention me without probably knowing any of my music – I have published very little and caused too little discussion to attract even the lowliest of snouts.[3]

Your choice of names is unfortunate: they are known only to a few people, including, I believe, some of your friends.

The warm admiration I have for you compels me to think it is all a misunderstanding; I am unwilling to accuse you in your turn of

[35]

displaying a measure of ignorance, at least as regards myself.

>Yours sincerely
>A.D.

[1] A satirical poet and one of Mallarmé's Tuesday circle. His lively disposition led him into several duels.

[2] The review of Dubus's book *Quand les violons sont partis* began with the words: 'At this period of quackery, vapidity and desperate ignorance; at this period when the public snout is attracted by Péladanesque claptrap, the painting of Henry de Groux and the music of Achille de Bussy . . .' Debussy's reply, given above, was published in the next issue. [Joseph Péladan, 1858–1919, was a French writer and eccentric who assumed the title of *Sar* and grouped together a number of French painters under the title of 'Salon de la Rose-Croix'. In 1891 he wrote the text of *Le fils des étoiles* for which Satie composed incidental music. R.N.]

[3] In 1899 Tailhade was to publish a volume called *A travers les groins* (*Through the snouts*), which made something of a stir.

23 TO ANDRÉ PONIATOWSKI[1]

>Thursday/Friday 8/9 September 1892

First of all I must give you at least something in the way of a general reaction!

Astonishment, certainly, to find anyone in these selfish and uncaring times who is keen to grow flowers outside his own garden! This entitles you to a place among the high nobility of old who weren't content just to accept their station in life, but were determined to beautify it with the products of art; the last of whom was that unfortunate king of Bavaria[2] – no madman he, except in the eyes of the vulgar commonsensicals who surrounded him. I know flattery is easy enough, but, believe me, I'm not flattering you, just giving a candid description of the facts: your attitude is that of the best sort of dilettante! Try as you may to disguise your motives as eccentricity or the desire to do a good turn, I thank you from the bottom of my heart, a part of me which has suffered under the Barbarians of our time (so very much tougher than their predecessors, armed as they are with stupidity). I acknowledge too the rare tact with which you handle my fine envisionings. I say no more, not wanting to annoy you or make you think I'm more sentimental than I really am.

You ask me to be discreet. I shall find that easy enough knowing that things like this need close and tender care. Noising them abroad leads inevitably to fatuous comment, or else to tortuous explanations. I'm very sorry that for all-too-practical reasons I had to leave Paris, as this has given us not much time to play with. Your letters reached me on 2 September! Bailly[3] didn't know my address, and honestly admitted he didn't think they contained anything of interest – (truly, Fate can sometimes play cruel tricks!).

I'm very worried in case everything has fallen through. The only advantage in taking a few days to reply is that I've had time to reflect on your offer and to consider how far it goes beyond what I could have hoped for. I've also had a chance to combat that blinding enthusiasm which comes over those who catch even a glimpse of the Golden Fleece! As you very rightly say, my best work does perhaps stem from the dismal existence I've led up to now and it could even be that my less than princely life-style is more conducive to creativity than the carefree ease, the soporific silk that money and leisure fold around the brain. But the Debussy who spends his day at the work-table, whose sole delight is catching butterflies at the bottom of an inkwell, he's not the only one. There is another Debussy who is receptive to the idea of adventure and mixing a little action with his dreams. As long as he can get back to them afterwards and not have to watch them being mown down, as they so often are, by base reality. Besides, I should be grateful for this capacity I have to see everything in ideal terms; it's thanks to that I've been able to resist the influences of the so-called artistic environment in Paris, about which you're so unsparing. Unfortunately, you're absolutely right! I've been a part of it but only, as it were, from a position of insuperable pride. For all my own misery, I found those people even more wretched, and if you knew the conceit that comes out in those discussions – they're not just failures, they're envious crawlers to boot! To *make it* in Paris, however it's done and however you understand the word, means secretly relying on everything that's mediocre, shabby, wrong and shameful, which is precisely why I'm delighted to accept your proposals, if there is still time.

First, we must look realistically at the question of my commercial value on the American market. You mention Rubinstein, Tchaikovsky, etc., but they were musicians with a reputation and for them, if I may so put it, the outlook was favourable. In my case it's not so good, as I'm totally unknown and, what's more, my music is on the abstruse side: audiences must go out to meet it as it has no intention ever of *making advances* towards them, and with good reason. I have the advantage of your influence over there and, to judge from your letters, your considerable financial backing, but maybe it's as well to point out that

[37]

we can't count so certainly on the less practical, utilitarian ingredients of the enterprise.

I must also make it clear that I shall have to be supplied with *everything* for the journey. Tailors, shirtmakers, etc., are people out of a fairytale as far as I'm concerned, and have been so for years. I wouldn't want you to take on such a large responsibility if I felt I couldn't give you something in return. Of course I've absolutely made up my mind to accept your offer but it's my duty to mention my scruples even though I have a powerful desire to go on with never a backward look.

As for music, I should have at least:
1. Three *Scènes au Crépuscule*[4] almost finished – that's to say the orchestration is all worked out, it's just a matter of writing it down.
2. A complete Fantasy for orchestra and piano. For this, you might try and find out whether there's a pianist we could count on.
3. A little oratorio in a mystic, slightly pagan vein.[5] So there would be enough to make up a concert. I think it's better to start with a bang. I take some courage from the concert programme you sent me. The audience may not have understood any of it but at least they were prepared to sit and listen, which is rare when you think of the *select few* that usually go to contemporary music. You know what mine is like, indeed you're one of the minority who understand what it is about, including the speculative side to it which most people approach like aborigines examining a medieval manuscript. I don't imagine the Americans will get as close to it as that, it's not their style.

To conclude: I'm happy to accept and make the journey, but I would ask you to think carefully over the things I've said, even if they only come from my not being a man of action. As you might expect, I look forward eagerly to hearing from you.

Write to me at 42, rue de Londres: I can be sure then that your letters will reach me *direct*.

My best wishes from across the world, and I hope to see you soon.

Claude Debussy[6]

[1]   Prince Poniatowski, 1864–1955, was at various times an industrialist, a banker and a planter. He was also a writer who moved in various literary and artistic circles, and was a friend of Mallarmé and Degas. Late in life he wrote his memoirs (*D'un siècle à l'autre*, 1948). Wanting to be of some practical help to Debussy, he planned a concert for him in the USA with his friends the American conductors Anton Seidl and Walter Damrosch.
[2]   King Ludwig II, Wagner's patron. (R.N.)
[3]   See letter 25 to Poniatowski of February 1893.

⁴ The original title of the *Nocturnes*. It was taken from a group of poems by his friend Henri de Régnier, published in *Poèmes anciens et romanesques*.
⁵ Probably *La Damoiselle élue*.
⁶ From now on Debussy signed himself Claude, instead of Claude-Achille or Achille. In the remaining letters in this volume the full signature 'Claude Debussy' has been abbreviated to 'C.D.' He had left his parents' home and moved into a furnished apartment.

24 TO ANDRÉ PONIATOWSKI

Wednesday 5 October 1892

Your message has reached me, for which many thanks. I'm astonished you haven't received my letter; it was *posted on 9 September* so it ought to have reached you in the normal course of events. Could it be that the cholera and the subsequent quarantine of shipping is responsible for this further chapter in my run of bad luck? You can imagine the extent of the hopes aroused in me by your letters, both from the material point of view, and for the chance to give some body to my dreams – so far they've led a very private, sheltered existence. As it is, I can't begin to describe the state my nerves are in. If you had in fact received my letter, then there was no possible reason for us to lose so much time and see jeopardized the splendid plans you had laid on my behalf.

Whatever happens, I shall always be grateful to you for keeping me in mind, an act of imagination in an otherwise utilitarian world, and for helping me escape from the black hole which my life has tended to become. I shall have the courage now to keep going in spite of everything, the failures that crush even the strongest and the enemies ranged against me. It's strange, but even though my name is almost unknown there are innumerable people who detest me. They spread stories about me in establishment circles, the sort of stories likely to give my music a bad smell for evermore. So you can understand easily enough how much I look forward to being rid of them, once and for all, and to satisfying my great ambition – to run my own show in my own way and root out the imbecility in musical understanding that these last few years have fostered in the gentle listeners of our time.

I end this letter as I did the first one: I'm entirely at your disposal and look forward eagerly to hearing from you.

Yours affectionately
C.D.

[39]

Mon cher ami   Thursday February 1893 [sic]

Even though a letter I wrote to you several months ago has obviously not reached you, you're still right to reproach me for my excessive silence. This may seem all the more strange when writing to you is one of my real pleasures in life, and thinking about you a great comfort amid the multitude of dismal preoccupations. I'll try and explain briefly why I haven't written: first, there have been several unpleasant incidents in my family circle, in which I was necessarily involved. Then my mother decided I was not providing what a son ought to, no fame was accruing, and so began a needling campaign. Some of the weapons were emotional, but some were simply unkind. It's clear that those castles in the air built on the anticipation of my fame have fallen horribly to earth! Add to that the daily grind, the struggle to keep going through it all, and you have a rough picture of what my life's been like.

So if I had written to you in 'this state of mind' to use the language of Bourget's followers, you wouldn't have been cheered by the result. Being worried doesn't, I think, give one the right to wrong other people. Besides which, however real one's sufferings are they look rather quaint and dramatic on paper. Anyway the best thing is not to take all these hardships too seriously. They support what I might call the Cult of Desire. And when all's said and done, Desire is what counts. You have this crazy but inescapable longing, a need almost, for some work of art (a Velázquez, a Satsuma vase[1] or a new kind of tie), and the moment of actual possession is one of joy, of love really. A week later, nothing. The object is there and you spend five or six days without looking at it. The only time the passion returns is when you've been away for several months. It's like the sun, which is so wonderful when you feel it again on an April morning and then all through the summer we're tired of it. You could write down a formula for desire: 'everything comes from it and returns to it'. By a rather elegant piece of trickery, the desire to be happy works pretty much on the same lines. One is never happy except by comparison or by giving oneself a certain limit to aim at, whether it's so many millions in cash or so many children, to provide some relaxation from the onward drive to glory. I don't know whether, like me, you're a 'happiness addict';[2] that's to say, whether your wish to be happy in a particular way, using your own resources and with the highest of motives, condemns you to be written off for the most part as

[40]

either a blackguard or a poor idiot. How wise you are to spend your time coping with railways and figures! You're spared the melancholy spectacle afforded to those who love art by the people who are its so-called modern representatives. We've just had a *Werther* by Massenet,[3] displaying an extraordinary talent for satisfying all that is poetically empty and lyrically cheap in the dilettante mind! Everything in it contributes to providing mediocrity and it's all part, too, of this appalling habit of taking something which is perfectly good in itself and then committing treason against its spirit with light, easy sentimentalities: *Faust* eviscerated by Gounod, or *Hamlet* more honoured in the breach than the observance by Monsieur Ambroise Thomas. Those who put their energies into forging banknotes are prosecuted, but nothing happens to these other forgers whose aim, equally, is to be rich. I should have every sympathy with an author who printed a notice on his works saying, 'It is forbidden to park your music anywhere on this book.'

There's also a new star on the musical horizon called Gustave Charpentier, destined, it seems to me, to achieve glory, riches and complete freedom from aesthetic considerations. He's taking over from Berlioz who was, in my opinion, an inveterate practical joker who came to believe in his own jokes. Charpentier hasn't even got Berlioz's moderately aristocratic nature. He's a man of the people: to the extent, it seems, of writing an opera to be called *Marie* and set in Montmartre. The work which has just endeared him to the populace is called *La Vie du Poète*.[4] The faded romanticism of the title tells us something about it but what you cannot possibly imagine is the work's total absence of taste — what you might call 'the triumph of the Brasserie'.[5] It smells of tobacco and there are whiskers all over it. Just to give you one brief example, the final movement of the symphony represents the Moulin Rouge where the poet (surprise, surprise!) has reached his ultimate degradation, complete with a prostitute who utters orgasmic moans.

Poor music, when I see people like that dragging you in the mud!

And of course all the little snobs, terrified of being taken for lifeless cretins, cry, 'What a masterpiece!' It's suffocating! But music, don't you know, is a dream from which the veils have been lifted. It's not even the expression of a feeling, it's the feeling itself. And they want to use it to tell lurid anecdotes, when the newspapers do that perfectly well! It's not easy to put up with this sort of thing. It's like being arm in arm with a beautiful woman whom you love and seeing her other arm being taken

[41]

by a lout! It amounts very nearly to a personal insult. I may not be more talented than such people but at least I can say that I adore music, which I must admit is something unusual when I see the terrible way music's treated and everyone taking it as a matter of course.

These last few days I've found some consolation in a very satisfying musical experience. It was at Saint-Gervais, a church where an intelligent priest[6] has taken the initiative in reviving the wonderful sacred music of earlier times. They sang a Palestrina mass for unaccompanied voices. It was extremely beautiful. Even though technically it's very strict, the effect is of utter whiteness, and emotion is not represented (as has come to be the norm since) by dramatic cries but by melodic arabesques. The shaping of the music is what strikes you, and the arabesques crossing with each other to produce something which has never been repeated: harmony formed out of melodies! (When you're next in Paris I promise I'll get you to come and hear it – better than my prose, which can't possibly do justice to miracles like this!) I also heard a mass by Vittoria, a Spanish primitive. It's full of rough, ascetic mysticism and all with the same simple means as the Palestrina.

When you hear music like this you ask yourself why such a magnificent way of writing turned off on to paths where nothing lay in store for it but misfortune. Because it's the very essence of the music that's been transformed, and for it to have ended up at the Paris Opéra is cause for the wildest astonishment!

Needless to say, there were very few musicians there. Perhaps they had the good taste to know they'd be out of place; and certainly they could only have felt disgust at the gossip and commercialization which is the stuff of their existence. There were rather more literary men and poets, the people who have been most successful in guarding the sovereignty of their art. As for the remainder, there were some of the well-to-do, very unhappy at having to get up so early, as well as society hostesses looking rather put out.

Anyway, it gives one courage to go on living in one's dream! And the energy to go on searching for the Inexpressible which is the ideal of all art.

I've revised the *Scènes du Crépuscule* quite extensively. I've also finished a string quartet, and a set of *Proses lyriques* to my own words which Bailly[7] is going to publish. Now there's someone worth getting to know! He's a wise little man, endowed with truly artistic ideas, and his determination sometimes puts mine in the shade.

[42]

Much as I should like to give you further proof of my friendship, I mustn't take up more of your valuable time. I'll content myself with sending you best wishes for your success and the assurance of my friendly sympathy.

If I need an excuse for writing at such length, please find it in my wish to be forgiven for my silence and in the pleasure I get from sharing my thoughts with you.

Yours
C.D.

I think I owe you a debt of gratitude for your generosity, which gave me at least some peace of mind.[8]

1   A particularly fine variety of Japanese earthenware, decorated with gold, made in the province of Satsuma since the fifteenth century. Debussy was a keen collector of Japanese prints and *objets d'art*.

2   A phrase ('maniaque du bonheur') taken from Jules Laforgue's poem, 'Solo de lune'.

3   *Werther* had its première at the Opéra-comique on 16 January.

4   *La Vie du Poète*, symphony-drama in 3 acts and 4 scenes for soloists, choir and orchestra (1892). Charpentier himself wrote the text. Gounod was enthusiastic about the work, but some conservative listeners were shocked. *Marie* was the original title of *Louise*, which was not produced until 1900.

5   A 'brasserie' is a bistro specializing in beer. (R.N.)

6   The Abbé De Bussy (sic), the vicar of Saint-Gervais, had just joined Charles Bordes in founding an association to encourage the spread of Renaissance music.

7   Edmond Bailly was not only a bookseller and publisher but also an expert on magic and the occult. He inhabited a tiny bookshop in the Chaussée d'Antin with his wife and his cat Aziza and sold copies of symbolist literature only to customers he liked. He preferred to spend the time talking to his friends, including Pierre Louÿs and Henri de Régnier. He published Debussy's *Cinq Poèmes de Baudelaire*, although his name does not appear on the edition. The String Quartet and the *Proses lyriques* were bought by Durand and Fromont respectively.

8   In his book *D'un siècle à l'autre* (p. 310), Poniatowski explains that he felt 'morally obliged' to see that Debussy had 'if not wealth, at least the opportunity to work in peace for a year or two'.

26   TO ODILON REDON[1]

Cher Monsieur Redon   Thursday 20 April [1893]

I cannot possibly tell you how happy I am that *La Damoiselle élue* should have procured for me such a memento of you.

It is, and will remain, as precious to me as your artistic sympathy.

Yours most sincerely
C.D.

[43]

[1]   The painter had many opportunities to meet Debussy, not only in Bailly's shop but also at the houses of Chausson, Jacques-Emile Blanche and Jean de Tinan. On this occasion he had expressed to Debussy his admiration for *La Damoiselle élue* (performed on 8 April 1893) by offering him one of his engravings. The following July Debussy responded by sending Redon a score of *La Damoiselle* with the dedication: 'A l'artiste rare . . .'.

27   TO ERNEST CHAUSSON

Cher ami   Sunday [7 May 1893]

You must allow me to reproach myself for not replying earlier to your letter, which made me very happy. I wouldn't want to offend you by saying I was astonished, but anyway it confirmed things which, coming from you, I'm more than delighted to believe!

When I think back to our last conversation, among the dustsheets, I feel sad at being separated from you, and the assurance of your friendship is all I need to wipe away the slightly disconcerting memory of your departure, just when everything was going so well.

It's good to share confidences on all sorts of topics, because even among friends you often find their true thoughts being withdrawn from you. It's upsetting – rather like people who have a beautiful garden and then surround it with those railings shaped like spearheads. Long live those who open their gates wide! You may say there are gardens where the flowers are not for picking, but we could go on along those lines for a long time. I'd rather just say that I'm very fond of you and that your support is certainly one of the things in my life I care most about! I feel more than I can say on this subject.

The halting intellects that hover round the Opéra (as Monsieur Bauer[1] would say) had the pleasure yesterday of hearing Catulle Mendès explaining *Das Rheingold*. A huge success – though why is beyond me. The general impression seemed to be that 'Wagner should light a large candle to Mendès' for having recalled so many erring souls to the true religion! (It's enough to make one choke!) Be it noted that his lecture was dedicated to playing down the role of the composer to glorify the poet. A roundabout way, in fact, of saying that if he, Mendès, hadn't actually written any music it was because music was something one could quite well do without. I tell you, if fire from heaven, which perhaps doesn't manifest itself often enough, had descended during this cosy little gathering it would have set the seal on a unique occasion.

[44]

I offer my profoundest apologies to Wagner for getting mixed up in all that.[2] But the time will shortly come when this gentleman gets a merry revenge on Paris, and the two of us will be thè sufferers because he'll become one of those fortresses the public likes to use to block all new artistic ideas. And as, in all honesty, we can't pretend his music's bad we shall have no option but to keep quiet. I've come to the conclusion that as far as music goes I should like to be my own grandson! Or else just think what excellent monks we'd have made, walking together in a slightly over-lush cloister garden, discussing how to perform Palestrina's latest mass!

My heart has been through one last, desperate crisis but now things are calm again. Please thank Mme Chausson for me. I'm sure the little flask she gave me has helped in this.

I expect you're still working extremely hard.[3] Allow me to offer my sympathy and to say I fully expect fine things to come out of it. I bring this overlong letter to a close with the thought that I'll see you on Wednesday. So I needn't worry my head writing things which are better said.

> Yours ever
> C.D.

[1] See letter 97, note 1, p. 124.
[2] Apart from being a poet, novelist, playwright and influential critic, Mendès had been one of the earliest and most outspoken of Wagner's defenders in Paris. In 1869 he went with Judith Gautier and Villiers de l'Isle-Adam to see Wagner at Triebschen. The Paris première of Die Walküre was set for 12 May and to help the audience understand it he gave an afternoon lecture on Das Rheingold, from the point of view of its being a prologue to the Ring. The lecture was illustrated with numerous music examples sung by six singers with two pianists playing a reduction of the orchestral score: Raoul Pugno and Debussy.
[3] At this time Chausson was nearing the end of his nine years' work on Le roi Arthus, an opera on his own libretto, first performed in Brussels in 1903, after his death. (R.N.)

28 TO ERNEST CHAUSSON

Cher ami   Monday afternoon 22 May 1893

I feel rather guilty at not writing to you this week. I haven't any excuses other than various banal tasks and ill humour, and anyway I was expecting to see you on Saturday. But, alas, there was a knock on my door in the afternoon and it was Bachelet (!) in his role as Mme Sulzbach's envoy, asking me to come and play her the Cinq Poèmes de

Baudelaire. I'd have liked to have your advice about whether to accept, but I did![1]

I'm extremely bored without you here. I feel like a tiny footpath, abandoned by everyone for the main road. I find myself suffering frequently from the illusion that I'm on my way to see you and it's sad to think your door won't in fact be opening for quite some time and cheering my homeward footsteps. Don't be too hard on this sensitivity and, above all, don't think I'm putting it on. After all there's no harm in grafting a little sadness on to the things we love and which give us such pleasure.

I'm rid of *Das Rheingold*, which is a bit of a bore where the gold is concerned but Rhinewise I'm delighted. The last session was grotesque and boring.[2] Catulle Mendès's language about *Die Walküre* was such that mothers who, in all innocence, had brought their daughters were obliged to walk out on the passionate outbursts of this unseemly priest. From now on, anyway, May, the month of renewal, will become the month of *Die Walküre*: some simple souls see this work as being the renewal of music and the death of the old, outdated formulae. I don't agree, but never mind.

The amusing thing about all this was an article by Dujardin, followed by a reply from Wilder's son-in-law, avenging the memory of the said Wilder with a quotation from a translation of *Das Rheingold* by Dujardin – altogether it gives off a pretty rotten smell (the article is in the *Revue wagnérienne*).[3]

I leave you and look forward to our meeting on Wednesday. I'll wait for you *here* as we agreed.

Yours
C.D.

---

[1] Alfred Bachelet was an acquaintance of Debussy's at the Conservatoire; he won the Prix de Rome in 1890. Mme Sulzbach was a benefactress of the Société nationale de musique and the dedicatee of Chausson's song *Ballade* (1896).

[2] After the success of Mendès's first lecture two further afternoon sessions were arranged for 11 and 18 May.

[3] Edouard Dujardin was the founder of the *Revue wagnérienne* which appeared between 1885 and 1888. Victor Wilder was a writer on music who translated Wagner into French verse in the style of an opera libretto. The Wagner family removed the translation rights from him and gave them to Alfred Ernst.

Cher ami   Sunday afternoon [2 July 1893]

I really must settle down and write to you – not that I don't want to, but I'm hopelessly depressed and it seems not quite the moment to burden you with my feelings! Please don't accuse me of a lack of courage, when you've been so busy getting me back on to an even keel and giving my life some purpose!

Now that you're no longer with me my heart bleeds for times past and I can't seem to get a grip on things. I try and work like a navvy but can't manage to overcome this black melancholy which makes me dissatisfied with everything I write. I dare say it's only a bad patch I just have to get through, but what makes it worse is that it means fighting against myself, and that's a battle I don't always win.

I've finished the third *Prose lyrique*,[1] for better or worse. I hope you'll allow me to come and go through it with you. As for the last movement of the Quartet, I can't get it into the shape I want, and that's the third time of trying. It's a hard slog!

I'd be really happy to know that with you it's all going well. Bear in mind I care about your work as much as about mine and I'd be truly delighted. And may I, in passing, utter a gentle reproach at not having heard from you, which makes me uneasy!

The manuscript of the *Moralités légendaires*[2] belongs to Dujardin, who claims to set great store by it, at least until he has to pay his gambling debts. Vanier undoubtedly has the manuscripts of the *Complaintes* and of *Notre-Dame de la Lune*, and with him I'm sure there'd be no problem. If you'd like me to get in touch with this sinister bibliophile,[3] I'm at your disposal.

I'm still looking for an apartment and Dupin[4] and I can be found climbing innumerable staircases. On one of them, strange to relate, I even met one of my creditors and the next day had a letter threatening me with all sorts of unpleasant proceedings.

Please write soon, to lessen a little the distance between us.

Yours
C.D.

[1] 'De fleurs', which was dedicated to Mme Chausson.
[2] Debussy's acquaintance with Laforgue's writings, especially the *Moralités* and the *Complaintes*, left its mark on him, as we can see from numerous passages in his letters and in the words of his *Proses lyriques*.

[47]

³ Léon Vanier, who published works by symbolist and 'decadent' writers up until 1903, including Mallarmé, Régnier, Laforgue, Viélé-Griffin, Tailhade, etc.
⁴ The financier Etienne Dupin was one of Debussy's most loyal friends. He was the dedicatee of the *Cinq Poèmes de Baudelaire* and it was thanks to him that Debussy went to Bayreuth in 1888. He was assassinated in Mexico in 1899.

30 TO ERNEST CHAUSSON

Cher ami   Saturday 26 August 1893

Claude Achille has had to postpone the pleasure of writing to you these last few days thanks to a nasty fever which has kept me in bed in a miserable, dazed condition and made my fingers dance about the bedcover like so many hares.

It started one gloomy evening after we'd said goodbye to you. Bonheur and I wandered around and everything we could think of to say was painfully boring. When I got home I felt thoroughly depressed and our departure took on the proportions of an irreparable accident! I could see a succession of long days, like an avenue of dead trees, and myself as an orphan, deprived of your friendship. I realize it's a common enough situation, but I took it badly and couldn't shake it off. You there, me here, and nothing I could do about it. However I figured it in my mind, it always added up to the same thing! So when your letter came it found me constructing projects which by the light of the fever seemed sensible enough. I hate to cause you distress with tales of my misfortune, when you're one of the few people who deserve to be happy and when you're so tactful and considerate about pointing out the aspects of things that most people are keen to hide. My gratitude to you is greater than I can say and I'm profoundly happy to be your friend because in you artistic qualities are completed by human ones and, when you're kind enough to show me your music, you can't imagine the great sympathy I feel for you, seeing you at work with emotions which to me are foreign but whose expression by you fills me with joy. If I've sometimes spoken a touch brusquely on the subject please put it down to impatience. After all, if your garden has a tree in it that promises flowers in abundance, it's surely natural to want to see them bloom?

As for your sermons, I shall always treasure them. You're like an elder brother in whom one has total confidence and from whom even grumbles are taken in good part. Forgive me if, so far, I haven't managed to satisfy you, but rest assured that reproaches from you

[48]

would cause me such heartache that I'm bound to do everything in my power not to deserve them.

Like you I'm convinced that one must keep on trying, but when this effort is tainted with the difficulties of making ends meet it all becomes distressing sometimes, especially when you see what little interest it inspires in the rest of the world which is happy to exchange effort for 'facility'. If, in our sufferings for art, we want to keep its ideals and illusions free from stain then it's a dreadful struggle because people claim they don't want to be bothered with questions that don't really affect them – and few of them get even that far!

In modern civilizations, the artist will always be someone whose usefulness becomes clear only after his death, and even then it serves as the pretext for mindless pride, often enough, and inevitably for vulgar speculation. Far better for him never to mix with his contemporaries, and anyway why bother to involve them in any kind of public manifestation of his talents, when so few of them can appreciate the satisfaction he feels! It's enough to be 'discovered' much later on, given that certain recent triumphs will have to shoulder terrible responsibilities in the years to come.

You have my warmest good wishes and please remember me to Mme Chausson, Etiennette, Marianne and Jean Sebastien Michel.

> Yours
> C.D.

When I called in at the Boulevard de Courcelles I heard excellent news of M. Chausson.[1]

---

[1] Chausson was on holiday at Royan.

The birth of *Pelléas*
Friendship with Pierre Louÿs
Prélude à l'après-midi d'un faune

A new chapter in Debussy's life opened when he started to compose *Pelléas et Mélisande*. After obtaining Maeterlinck's permission in August 1893 he set himself feverishly to the task, in the knowledge that he had at last found a text that conformed with his artistic ideals.

On the material and emotional fronts his life was still unstable. He had left the parental home for good and lived first in lodgings, then in a very modest apartment in the rue Gustave-Doré, still accompanied by Gaby. He spent much of his time among the Symbolists, either in Bailly's bookshop or among the friends of Mallarmé. His artistic development was swift at this period but he went through an unhappy episode when his engagement to a singer called Thérèse Roger was swiftly broken off, alienating him from friends like Ernest Chausson who were firmly attached to middle-class values. But his friendship with Pierre Louÿs grew closer and was a considerable support in his bachelor existence. Even if the first performance of *Prélude à l'après-midi d'un faune* on 22 December 1894 did not register in the minds of musicians as an important occasion, it at least brought him some attention. In this work, as Pierre Boulez has written, 'the art of music began to beat with a new pulse'.

31 TO ERNEST CHAUSSON

Cher ami   Sunday [3 September 1893]

Try as I may, I can't regard the sadness of my existence with caustic detachment. Sometimes my days are dull, dark and soundless like those of a hero from Edgar Allan Poe;[1] and my soul is as romantic as a Chopin Ballade! Too many memories come crowding into my solitude and I can't get rid of them. One must simply live and wait! It remains to be seen whether I've picked a lucky number or not for the Happiness bus. If not, I'd be quite happy to stand! (Forgive this reach-me-down philosophy!)

The bell has tolled now to mark my 31st year, and I'm still not confident that my musical attitudes are right; and there are things I can't yet do (write masterpieces, for example, or, among other things, be completely serious – I'm too prone to dream my life away and to see realities only at the very moment they become insuperable). Maybe I'm more to be pitied than blamed, but in any case in writing this I count on your pardon, and your patience.

I had a visit from Henry de Régnier[2] who, as I hardly need say, is full of goodwill towards you. I took the trouble to polish up my manners and played him *L'Après-midi d'un faune* which he claimed was as hot as a furnace. He also liked 'the way it vibrates'! (Make of that what you will.) But when he turns to poetry he becomes extremely interesting and is obviously a man of delicate sensibilities.

He was talking to me about certain words in the French language, saying that their gold had been tarnished from knocking about too much in the rude world, and I thought to myself it was much the same

[51]

with certain chords whose sound has been cheapened by use in mass-produced music; not a grippingly original thought, I know, unless I go on to say that these chords have lost their symbolic values at the same time.

Music really ought to have been a hermetical science, enshrined in texts so hard and laborious to decipher as to discourage the herd of people who treat it as casually as they do a handkerchief! I'd go further and, instead of spreading music among the populace, I propose the foundation of a 'Society of Musical Esotericism' and you may be sure M. Helmann[3] won't be a member and nor will M. de Bonnières![4]

While I've been writing this the girl in the flat above has been sawing away on the piano at something in D major. An appalling din and all too living proof that what I've said makes sense.

As for you, are you working hard, are you content, and are you no longer surrounded by dear little children making a noise like half a million thunderstorms? Have you really made up your mind to kill poor Guinevere?[5] The last of the music you showed me raised my highest expectations! I wait with confidence. As for me, I'm working furiously but – whether it's my misanthropic existence, I don't know – anyway I'm not happy with what I'm doing. It would be rather nice to have you here; I'm nervous of working in a void and my music is tending to sound like that of a young savage, without my being able to resist it, what's more.

Your poor Claude-Achille waits like another Sister Anne for the pleasure of your return.

> Yours, with affection
> C.D.

Stop Press

I've just finished the last of the *Proses lyriques*. I have dedicated it to Henry Lerolle, partly because I wanted to, partly so as not to stray outside the circle of friends.[6]

I've had a letter from Vincent d'Indy, very friendly, with praises that would bring a blush to the lilies that sleep between the fingers of the *Damoiselle élue*.[7]

From the acid remarks of M. de Bonnières (courtesy H. de Régnier): 'Poor Vincent (d'Indy), when he's in evening dress he does rather look like a village locksmith.'

C.A. Debussy is finishing a scene of *Pelléas et Mélisande*, called 'A well in the park' (Act IV, scene 4)[8] on which he would be glad to have the opinion of E. Chausson. There should perhaps be a way of organizing rail

7 Maurice Denis's cover for the first edition of *La Damoiselle élue*.

excursions between Paris and Royan to celebrate the occasion. No need for me to stress its considerable importance.

A letter too from G. Street[9] saying he only came back from the country yesterday and promising to support my application to Mme Desrousseaux . . .

[1]   Replying to a questionnaire in 1889, Debussy put down Poe and Flaubert as his favourite prose writers. According to André Suarès he was working 'on a symphony . . . based on Poe's tales and particularly on *The Fall of the House of Usher*'. (Debussy's words 'mes journées sont fuligineuses, sombres et muettes' are taken directly from Baudelaire's translation of *Usher*, 'journée fuligineuse, sombre et muette'. R.N.)

[2]   The symbolist poet must have got to know Debussy in Bailly's bookshop and had acted as intermediary between Debussy and Maeterlinck in obtaining permission to set *Pelléas* to music.

[3]   Helmann was at Bayreuth at the same time as Debussy in 1889.

[4]   Robert de Bonnières was a reporter and novelist who put on concerts in his apartment in the avenue de Villiers. Works by d'Indy, Fauré and Chausson figured largely.

[5]   The heroine of Chausson's opera *Le roi Arthus*.

[6]   See letter 45. Debussy had written 'De soir', the last of the *Proses lyriques*, in July. The dedicatees of the other three songs of the cycle were Vital Hocquet (a plumber with, according to Debussy, 'painter's eyes'), Raymond Bonheur and Mme Chausson. (R.N.)

[7]   This work had just been published by Bailly with a cover designed by Maurice Denis. (See p. 53)

[8]   The early sketches for *Pelléas* have been reproduced in facsimile (Minkoff, Geneva, 1977).

[9]   Georges Street was a composer of piano pieces, operettas, etc.

32 TO ERNEST CHAUSSON

Cher ami   Monday 2 October 1893

The only excuse I have for not writing to you for so long is that I've been working very hard! Anyway you've been kind enough to assume that this must have been the reason. Idleness comes into it too, when I'm faced with writing things I'd much rather say to you! Yes, time drags and, let me say, my sadness at not seeing you grows as the days go by. Ignore this repetition of the same complaints; I'd just like you to know that among the irksome things in my grey life your absence takes first place.

I was premature in crying 'success!' over *Pelléas et Mélisande*. After a sleepless night (the bringer of truth) I had to admit it wouldn't do at all. It was like the duet by M. So-and-so, or nobody in particular, and worst of all the ghost of old Klingsor, alias R. Wagner, kept appearing in the corner of a bar, so I've torn the whole thing up. I've started again and am trying to find a recipe for producing more characteristic phrases. I've

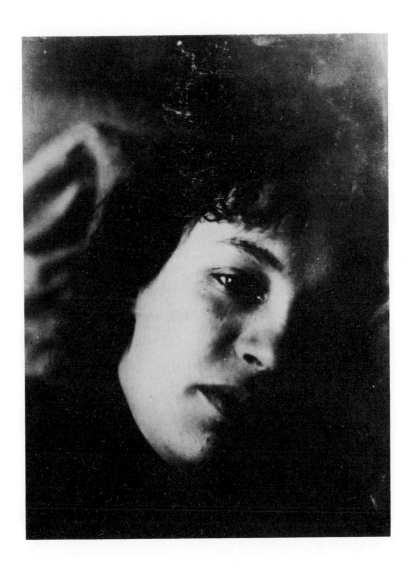

8 Gaby Dupont photographed by Pierre Louÿs.

been forcing myself to be Pelléas as well as Mélisande and I've gone looking for music behind all the veils she wraps round herself, even in the presence of her most devoted admirers! As a result I've discovered something which you may perhaps find valuable – I'm not bothered about the rest of them. I found myself using, quite spontaneously too, a means of expression which I think is quite unusual, namely silence (don't laugh). It is perhaps the only way to give the emotion of a phrase its full value and, even if Wagner has used it, it seems to me it's only in an absolutely dramatic fashion, rather as in other doubtful dramas like those of Bouchardy, d'Ennery and others![1]

If only the times were less depressing and it was possible to get people interested in something other than the latest shape of bicycle! I don't know why I say this, as I've no intention of setting up as a spiritual dictator over my contemporaries, but even so it would be nice to found a school of Neomusicians where care would be taken to keep music's wonderful symbols intact and to bring back respect for an art which so many outsiders have dragged in the mud. There the mob would learn at least a few lessons about filtering its enthusiasm and about distinguishing between a Franck and a Massenet, who would be relegated with all his crew to the rank of talentless mountebanks. For them and their tawdry products one or two booths at a fair would be enough – mind you, we owe this state of things to that inscription on our public monuments: Liberty, Equality, Fraternity, words fit for cab-drivers at best!

Thanks to the machinations of Etienne Dupin I went to see *La Dame de Monsoreau*.[2] I think you and Mme Chausson would enjoy it. It has sword-thrusts as fast as demisemiquavers, dramatic thrusts likewise, Henry III's sons as pretty as butchers' boys and about as elegant, an operatic tenor called 'Bucci' flashing his eyes at the gallery like a toreador, but also an excellent Chicot. It was an absolutely splendid evening, marred only by the fact that the box we were in when we went to see *Le Bossu* was now full of the most ridiculous-looking people.[3]

I saw Messager,[4] who in some inexplicable surge of friendship invited me to dinner! His talk of music was fairly bizarre: 'A few more years of work,' he says, 'and then I'm retiring to the country and exchanging my evening clothes for a permanent flannel waistcoat'; which, you may think, is rather like someone who's understandably tired after a lifetime of selling socks now starting to dream of growing pumpkins. He spoke enthusiastically about a *Manon* by Puccini[5] and also about some rhapsodies by Svendsen.[6]

[56]

They're singing a Vittoria mass at Saint-Gervais next Sunday. I intend to be there and I'll tell you all about it.

I don't see anything interesting on the book front, unless a volume by Bloy holds any attractions for you.[7]

I'm trying to think of a title for your Concerto[8] but haven't come up with anything so far. I imagine, like me, you're thinking of something very simple? Talking of which, you're having the parts engraved straight away, aren't you? Bailly wasn't sure about it. I'd also like to have the manuscript if you still want me to look over the final proof. It's a splendid work and, what's more, something of a turning-point too!

I hope you'll be able to work consistently on *Le roi Arthus* until we see each other again. I feel you ought to finish it as soon as you can; there are other works anxiously awaiting your attention.

> Yours affectionately
> C.D.

[1] Joseph Bouchardy, 1810–1870, and Adolphe Dennery, 1811–1890, writers of cheap melodramas.
[2] The play by Dumas and Maquet had been revived with great success on 14 September 1893 at the Porte Saint-Martin.
[3] *Le Bossu* by Bourgeois and Féval had been given in the same theatre on 3 February 1893.
[4] André Messager, 1853–1929, was at this time more a composer than a conductor.
[5] *Manon Lescaut* had received its première in Turin on 1 February 1893.
[6] Johan Svendsen, the best-known Norwegian composer after Grieg, was quite popular in France.
[7] Undoubtedly *Sueur de sang (1870–71)* which had just been published with three original drawings by Henry de Groux (Paris, E. Dentu).
[8] The Concerto for piano, violin and string quartet op. 21 by Chausson was published by Bailly in 1894.

33 TO ERNEST CHAUSSON

Cher ami   Monday [23 October 1893]

Your letters are soon going to be like those books by Francis Poictevin[1] in which the most unexpected changes of scene follow each other in dizzy succession. As for me, sitting here in my corner, my thoughts turn to a place on the boulevard de Courcelles[2] which has pleasant memories for me. So I'm sorry to see you enjoying your long exile, especially when my hopes of seeing you again are answered by such baleful question marks! It's a real pity I'm not a magician like Merlin. You can imagine me materializing one day amid the apple-blossom and treating you to a

[57]

pretty little speech, while the delightful and slightly chromatic music of the breezes blends with your Merlinesque harmonies. Something along the lines of: 'Ernest Chausson, 'tis time, my friendship finds you wanting. Leave this *King Arthur*, the cause of such torment, whose savage insistence that you tell his story is blinding you to life. Find peace in the friendship of Claude! Claude needs you!

I'm sure you couldn't resist imperative harmonies like those!

One thing I'd like to see you free yourself from is your preoccupation with the inner parts of the texture. By which I mean that too often we're concerned with the frame before we've got the picture; it was our friend Richard Wagner, I think, who got us into this fix. Sometimes the frame is so ornate, we don't realize the poverty of the central idea. And here I forbear to mention the occasions when magnificent inner parts adorn ideas like sixpenny dolls! It would be more profitable, I feel, to go about things the other way round, that's to say, find the perfect expression for an idea and add only as much decoration as is absolutely necessary. Certainly some composers we know are like priests hanging incomparable jewels on idols made of deal! Look at the attenuation of symbol at the centre of some of Mallarmé's last sonnets, in which none the less the workmanship is of the finest; and look at Bach, where everything conspires wonderfully to highlight the central idea and where the delicacy of the inner parts never absorbs the principal line. You're well aware of all these points, of course, and I mention them only by way of conversation.

So far I've had no news of the Société nationale but what you tell me fills me with alarm. What sort of future is there for me on board this vessel? It looks reminiscent of the one that carried the Honourable

[58]

Arthur Gordon Pym.[3] No doubt there'll be a lot of performances of the Russians, out of patriotism. It's a pity they couldn't take advantage of Admiral Avellan's[4] presence to invite him to a concert. Tiersot, the bard,[5] would have pronounced some words of welcome, I'm sure. But enough of this pleasantry. There are murky days ahead!

The Royan–Jehin combination[6] sounds excellent, but only completely excellent if you're going to be back there. Then luck really would be on my side!

So, tiresome though it may be for me, I wish you a happy stay at Arcachon among the pine trees. I stayed in a villa there once called the villa Marguerite;[7] I hope that'll make you think frequently of your good friend Claude.

C.D.

I enclose my sketch for the cover of the Concerto. Now I need you to send me the information for the title page.

I've sold 'your quartet'[8] to the Barbarians of the Place de la Madeleine for 250 francs! They were cynical enough to admit that what they were paying me didn't cover all the labour this 'work' entailed. At any rate it will always be a pleasure for me to see your name attached to it. It represents for me the beginning of a friendship which, in time, is due to become the best and most profound of my life.

I should have written to you on Saturday but I had a visit from Lerolle. I was delighted to see him, of course, and no doubt he has written telling you extraordinary things about *Pelléas*. He's so sympathetic towards me that probably you shouldn't believe more than half of them. Just for a moment he revived memories of that happy time we both, I imagine, look back on with nostalgia.

Bailly can't get hold of Madame Rouquairol over the payment for the *Damoiselle*. Would you be kind enough to give me her new address?

---

[1] Poictevin, 1854–1904, was a writer whose novels were published between 1882 and 1894. Larousse refers to his 'enigmatic and paradoxical ideas' and to his 'form reaching out beyond the conventional to the bizarre'. Debussy's allusion is to another of Chausson's holidays, this time at Arcachon.

[2] Chausson's house on the boulevard de Courcelles was decorated by Henri Lerolle and contained paintings by Degas and Manet, as well as by Carrière and Puvis de Chavannes.

[3] The main character in Poe's *Narrative of Arthur Gordon Pym of Nantucket*.

[4] The admiral in charge of the Russian fleet in the Mediterranean who had been given an enthusiastic public welcome in Paris.

[5] Julien Tiersot, 1857–1936, a librarian at the Conservatoire who was also a musician and a specialist in folklore.

[6] Jehin was the conductor of the orchestra at the Royan casino. Chausson had been working to get him to offer Debussy a job.

[7] Debussy stayed in Arcachon in the summer of 1880 with Mme von Meck.

[8] Debussy's Quartet was to have its first performance on the following 29 December. It was published by Durand in 1894 with a dedication to the Ysaÿe Quartet. Chausson seems not to have liked the work. We do not know whether this was Debussy's reason for changing the dedication or whether it was because of their quarrel after the breaking off of Debussy's engagement to Thérèse Roger.

34 TO ERNEST CHAUSSON

Cher ami   Thursday evening [early December 1893]

I must ask your forgiveness for the long silence which, out of your great goodness of heart, you're on your way to granting already. A lot's been going on, some of it annoying, some pleasant – I'll stick to the latter as the other is nothing very new.

As a result of making friends with Pierre Louÿs,[1] whom I think you know, I made a brief journey to Brussels. The only interesting thing about the place as far as I'm concerned is that Ysaÿe[2] lives there, so my first visit was to him. You won't be surprised when I tell you he greeted my appearance literally with shouts of joy, clasped me to his enormous chest and addressed me as familiarly as if I were his baby brother. Then I had to tell him the news about everyone, especially you, although I could only tell him what I knew from letters. After that music and more music. In the course of one memorable evening I played one after the other the Cinq Poèmes, La Damoiselle élue and Pelléas et Mélisande. I was as hoarse as if I'd been out on the street selling newspapers. Pelléas had the honour of melting some of the listeners' hearts (they were English girls, I believe) and as for Ysaÿe, he was delirious. Really I can't bring myself to repeat what he said! He liked 'your' quartet too and has given it to his colleagues to look at.

I saw Maeterlinck and spent the day with him at Ghent.[3] To begin with he behaved like a girl being introduced to her future husband but then he thawed out and was charming. When he talked about the theatre he was absolutely fascinating. For Pelléas he's allowing me to make whatever cuts I like and went as far as to suggest some important ones – extremely useful ones even! He claims he doesn't understand anything about music and wanders through a Beethoven symphony like a blind man through a museum. But in fact he's all right and talks in the

[60]

most entrancing and simple way about his extraordinary discoveries. At one point I thanked him for entrusting *Pelléas* to my care and he did his best to demonstrate that he was the one who ought to be grateful because I was being kind enough to set his words to music! As my opinion is diametrically the opposite, I had to use all my diplomacy — not that nature has endowed me liberally in that direction.

So you see, my journey was more profitable than Urien's![4]

C.D.

[1] Pierre Louÿs told his brother, in a letter of 25 November, that he and Debussy had been constant companions for the previous two months. They had thought about living together in a large apartment at Neuilly. See the following letter.

[2] See letter 46.

[3] The visit took place in November. Louÿs' description of the scene, some years later, is rather different: 'I had to do all the talking for him because he was too shy to speak; and as Maeterlinck was shyer still and simply didn't reply, I also had to give Maeterlinck's answers. It was a scene I'll never forget . . .' (letter to his brother, 20 April 1914).

[4] *Le Voyage d'Urien*, one of Gide's earliest works, had just been published by Bailly with illustrations by Maurice Denis.

35 TO PIERRE LOUŸS[1]

Cher ami [late 1893]

In the name of a friendship which, even if not of long standing, is still dear to me, I ask you to forgive my display of bad temper this afternoon. Please believe I've suffered considerable remorse.

It's not the sort of thing, I think, to leave a cloud on our horizon.

If you wish, I shall learn Victor Hugo's longest play off by heart and recite it, on my knees and barefoot, in the place de la Concorde!

I place my truly contrite heart in your hands and trust in your goodwill.

Yours ever
Claude

I'll await Parsifal's sword in the course of the afternoon.

[1] Louÿs, 1870–1925, was a brilliant writer and a friend of Gide and Valéry. He had met Debussy at Mallarmé's salon and was to become Debussy's closest friend, acting on frequent occasions as his prop and stay. Wagner was the subject of passionate discussions between them.

Cher ami   Monday afternoon 8 January 1894

I've just been to see Jehin and it's not exactly thrilling. In fact it's just a dreary accompanist's job in all its horror! And not a chance of having fun with the orchestra. It pays 350 francs, which is not much of a return for what one would have to put up with, *and it takes up every day as well as every evening.*

It would need you living at Royan for me to turn a blind eye to all this mediocrity. In any case Jehin had already made his arrangements and would only take me if these fell through. I'll wait for your reply before replying! It looks as though my hopes may not come to anything.

My spirits at the moment are leaden, and melancholy bats wheel in the bell-tower of my dreams! All my hopes now are centred on *Pelléas et Mélisande* and God alone knows whether this hope is any more than just a puff of smoke!

With my warmest good wishes and New Year greetings to everybody, not forgetting King Arthur.

Yours
C.D.

Cher ami   Tuesday [early 1894?]

It's the fault of Mélisande! Please forgive both of us.

I've spent days trying to capture that 'nothing' that Mélisande is made of and haven't always had the courage to give you all the details. Anyway, you're familiar with the kind of struggles that are involved, but I don't know whether, like me, you've ever gone to bed with a vague desire to burst into tears, rather as though you'd been prevented during the day from seeing somebody you were very fond of.

At the moment it's Arkel who's tormenting me. He comes from beyond the grave and has that objective, prophetic gentleness of those who are soon to die – all of which has to be expressed with doh, ray, me, fah, soh, lah, te, doh!!! What a profession!

I'll write at greater length tomorrow. For now, just my greetings and best wishes.

C.D.

[62]

9 Pierre Louÿs sitting at his harmonium.

38 TO PAUL DUKAS[1]

Cher ami   11 January 1894

You're the one who's difficult. And that's why I won't play you *Pelléas*. I'll explain. The various performances I've given of it so far have been necessarily fragmentary and the impression they've produced has been confused, not to say contradictory. So I'd rather wait till I've got one or two acts finished and can give you, at least, a more or less complete idea.[2] I hope you'll be touched by such renunciation and will realize it's aimed only at giving you more satisfaction in the long run; I hardly need tell you the value I place on your criticisms as well as on your encouragement.

Yours ever
C.D.

[1] Debussy had got to know Dukas in Guiraud's class at the Conservatoire. The two composers remained on friendly terms until Debussy's death.
[2] According to the sketches of *Pelléas* that have survived, Debussy had by this time finished Act IV, scene 4 and part of Act I.

39† TO ERNEST CHAUSSON

Cher ami   Monday 5 February 1894

No doubt you're fed up with that wretched Claude Achille, but really he's nothing but the helpless victim of a multiplicity of occupations! Indeed, I no longer recognize myself! I'm to be found in the salons executing smiles, or else conducting choruses at the house of the Countess Zamoiska! Oh yes, and while I'm immersing myself in the beauty of these choruses I tell myself it's a just punishment for this dreary music to be flayed by fearless society ladies. Then there's Mme de Saint-Marceaux[1] who's discovered that I'm a first-rate talent! It's enough to make you die laughing. But really, you'd have to be a hopelessly weak character to be taken in by all this rubbish. It's so fatuous! Like G. Fontaine,[2] for example, asking me who wrote the words of 'Harmonie du soir'! But at least I have Lerolle with whom I can come clean. You'll understand if I tell you I like him a lot; and then he shows such a lively sympathy for *Pelléas* that I can't help but be grateful to him.

I started the Wagner sessions last Saturday; it all went very well, nobody fidgeted, not even Mme Rouquairol (she didn't even talk). As for me, I was absolutely flattened. No question, but Wagner's a very exhausting fellow.

I should say that all this activity is no replacement for you. I miss you and am suffering from the long exile from your friendship! I should also say that I was really upset for several days by what you said about my quartet, as I felt that after all it only increased your partiality for *certain things* which I would rather it encouraged you to forget. Anyway I'll write another one which will be for you, in all seriousness for you, and I'll try and bring some nobility to my forms. I'd like to have enough influence with you to be able to grumble at you and tell you you're heading in the wrong direction! You put such strong pressure on your ideas that they no longer dare present themselves to you, they're so afraid of not being dressed in a way you'd approve of. You don't let yourself go enough and in particular you don't seem to allow enough play to that mysterious force which guides us towards the true expression of a feeling, whereas dedicated, single-minded searching only weakens it. I'm convinced you have within you all the expression you could want, so it worries me to see you exhausting yourself in needless conflict. One has to tell oneself that when it comes to art we are nothing, merely the instrument of some destiny, and we have to allow it to fulfil itself! Maybe I've no right to talk to you like this, so forgive me and realize it's just that I want so much to see you become what you should be; something on the very highest level, because that is where you belong, more than any of us. Accept what you will out of all this, I've really no intention of offering you advice! I'd simply like to give you the courage to believe in yourself.

Will you be in Brussels till 1 March to hear the Debussy Festival?[3] (If there are people who don't like that kind of music, they're going to have a terribly boring time.)

I'm delighted you're pleased with the edition of your Concerto. It looks as though Bailly has been something of a first mover in this excellent enterprise!

There are tussles at the Société nationale; at some of the concerts you'd think it was the Institut the day of the Prix de Rome competitions. I play the piano for them, with that disdain for principles you know so well.

Do you still intend to make a reduction of your quartet for piano duet? I'm only afraid this would get in the way of other, more interesting work. But in all this do what seems to you best.

Hoping to see you soon
Yours affectionately
C.D.

[1] Mme de Saint-Marceaux ran one of the most prestigious musical salons in Paris, to which Fauré and later Ravel were frequent visitors.
[2] The Fontaine family were related to Chausson.
[3] This 'festival' was a concert organized by Octave Maus, the leader of the group known as the *Libre esthétique*. It was given on 1 March, surrounded by an exhibition of paintings by Renoir, Gauguin, Redon, Sisley, Pissarro, Signac, and Maurice Denis, among others. It included *La Damoiselle élue* as well as the Quartet and the *Proses lyriques*.

40 TO PIERRE DE BRÉVILLE[1]

Cher ami   [February 1894]

Before leaving for Brussels I wanted to tell you myself that I am engaged to Mademoiselle Thérèse Roger.[2]

Please see in this hasty note a proof of my friendly sympathy – I wish I could have done more to show it before now.

Yours
C.D.

[1] A composer and a pupil of César Franck who went to Bayreuth with Debussy in 1888. He was one of the most active members on the committee of the Société nationale de musique.
[2] A salon singer, whose mother was a music teacher. She had been one of the soloists in *La Damoiselle élue* and on 17 February 1894 gave the first performance of two of the *Proses lyriques* at the Société nationale accompanied by the composer. Their engagement, which came as a surprise to Debussy's closest friends, was soon to be broken off.

41 TO ERNEST CHAUSSON

Cher ami   Thursday evening [8 March 1894]

I too have been meaning to write for days and days, but I'm in such a turmoil, with life seeming to take on a whole spectrum of new colours, that it all takes a bit of getting used to. I'm filled with a mixture of great joy and not a little misery. It seems to me that up to this moment I've been walking in darkness and have had the misfortune to meet some

[66]

10 A drawing of Debussy's fiancée, Thérèse Roger, by
André-Charles Coppier.

truly unpleasant fellow travellers. Now that a sunny road is open before me I'm afraid at not having deserved such happiness, and at the same time I'm fiercely determined to defend it with all the power at my disposal! Your advice about marriage has touched me deeply, I assure you, and it seems to me (novice that I am in the business) absolutely right. Certainly happiness is always to be found in ourselves rather than in people who might appear to be the motivating force behind it, so when we want someone else to be glad about our happiness it's always a matter of suggestion. But I really feel I've offered my life once and for all and that from now on it'll be lived for just one person!

If I've wandered into some evil spots, I've also contracted a distaste for them which will for ever keep me from harm. I'm still young enough to be able to say I'm bringing an absolutely new heart to this new life and I have feelings within me which for good reasons have never been expressed; luckily I've kept them intact, always in the hope that one day I would have the pleasure of seeing them bloom.

The Brussels concert[1] was a marvellous occasion for me, chiefly because I owe a large part of its success to Th . . .[2] who sang like a fairy! This arrangement was completely fortuitous and it turned out to be an unforgettably romantic intermezzo; it was so nice to be able to whisper sweet nothings to one another in the midst of so many strangers!

Ysaÿe played like an angel! The Quartet moved people in a way it didn't in Paris, the orchestra was admirable and the large audience, which came simply to enjoy itself, was disarmingly keen to understand.

The *Proses lyriques* were less of a success (not that it matters), and especially the one dedicated to Madame Chausson! Which only goes to show *it's really intended for people of quality!*

I also had a good going-over from Kufferath[3] in the *Guide musical*. I don't really see what more I could ask for!

You don't tell me anything about your music. You know how keen I am to see you finally satisfied and (forgive the egoism) how much I'd like to be able once again to show you what I'm doing. But it's a friendly sort of egoism because I feel that without music we're not really close to each other.

And now I've a difficult request to make of you. I'll be brief about it: I need your help once again! I'd like to pay off all my debts in the near future and, while not wanting to put pressure on you, I give you full powers of judgement in the matter. When we get back to Paris, I'd like to come to some agreement as to how I can pay you back! There'll be some debts I shall never be completely free of! But as they only concern my profound affection for you I'm content for them to remain that way.

In the hope that from now I shall be worthy of your continuing friendship.

Yours
C.D.

Please thank Madame Chausson for the charming letter she wrote to Mademoiselle Roger.

[1] This was the 'Debussy Festival' referred to in letter 39.
[2] Thérèse Roger.
[3] Maurice Kufferath's review of the *Proses lyriques* contained the lines: 'At times it was pure cacophony. If it was not done for a bet, one is left with the sad conclusion that it was the result of defective hearing, just as the output of certain painters suggests defective vision.'

42 TO ERNEST CHAUSSON

Cher ami   Friday 16 March 1894

The only distress I felt at your letter was to think that you believed such things of me! My fault was only a certain waywardness in material matters and for that I've been most severely punished. What's more, your influence on me has been seriously for the good and it would indeed be unprincipled of me to stop being 'serious' at the very moment when I need this quality more than ever![1]

I've not hidden any of my debts from Mme Roger and I fully intend to tell her that a certain friend is being kind enough to become my sole creditor! In any case there's nothing else I could do. I need a life that's transparent, without any mysterious depths. It's a transformation I'm undergoing and almost as much an intellectual as moral one. So it's vital you lend me another *fifteen hundred francs*! First I must pay some debts and then I absolutely have to buy a dress for my mother![2] Forgive the detail but it's so that you can see I really do need the money! I need hardly add that I'm *determined to remove this burden from our friendship as soon as possible*!

Forgive me for mentioning these tiresome matters! And please believe that, as your friend, I'm far from happy at getting you to play

[69]

the role of Providence in my life so often. Could I, lastly, ask you to let me have an answer as soon as possible?

Yours ever
C.D.

¹   Some of Chausson's friends had told him that Debussy had not broken off relations with Gaby Dupont. It was a difficult time for the composer, during which Pierre Louÿs declared that he had stood up for Debussy 'against a couple of dozen people'.
²   According to a letter written by Lerolle to Chausson on 25 February, the wedding was fixed for 16 April and an apartment had been rented for the happy couple in the rue Vaneau.

43 TO PIERRE LOUŸS

Cher ami   Friday [20 July 1894]

I'd never doubted for a moment that the 'inversion' of Bayreuth was Biskra, but Heaven knows the second's the chord I prefer[1]. When it comes to it Bayreuth's a bad influence, a universe rather too tightly hemmed in by the chord of the seventh. Biskra's bound to be better at producing new aggregations.

In this affair
What's Wagner's share?
And who's . . . Biskra?
It's Cosima.

I envy you dressing up in bright clothes. How English you must look surrounded by all that baked earth!

Here it's positively arctic, everyone's putting their furs on for a bit of warmth and the trees are putting their leaves back in their album; there must be a chemical process we can use to take the place of summer. The only winners are those endowed with sangfroid.

I'm living with Pelléas and Mélisande for company, and very accomplished young people they are, as always; I've decided to do the vault scene, but in a manner which you'll be good enough to find interesting when you see it. I'm having dinner with Robert[2] who's a good substitute for gypsies during the meal. Just in case it makes you feel happy, I must say I miss you – nobody else plays me Bach with those delightfully imaginative touches with which you alone know how to adorn such antiquities.

Yours as ever
C.D.

[70]

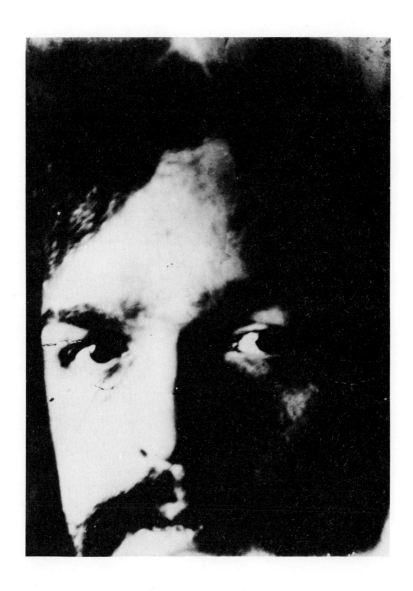

11 Debussy photographed by Pierre Louÿs in May 1894.

[1]   Louÿs had left Paris for Bayreuth. Then, under the impact of Gide's evocative descriptions, he changed his mind and went to Biskra in Algeria.
[2]   Paul Robert was a painter and a friend of both Debussy and Louÿs. He painted a portrait of Debussy.

44 TO PIERRE LOUŸS

20 August 1894

[. . .] I've been so involved with semiquavers lately I haven't had the energy to tell relevant anecdotes pertaining to the said semiquavers; I've been working like a carthorse, finishing the vault scene, the scene when they have emerged out of the vault, the scene with the sheep.[1] [. . .]

The music by Bizet you included in your letter looks like one of his better things. He was the Maupassant of music; like Maupassant, he enjoys a brothel kind of celebrity. After all, we've all in our time been invited by a woman to step into the room just over there 'on the ramparts of Seville'. Anyway it's rather nice to go to Spain after dinner for a mere 7.50 francs! . . . No one's ever really pointed out how few chords there are in any given century! Impossible to count how often since Gluck people have died to the chord of the sixth and now, from Manon to Isolde, they do it to the diminished seventh! And as for that idiotic thing called a perfect triad, it's only a habit, like going to a café! [. . .]

C.D.

[1]   Act III scene 2, Act III scene 3, and Act IV scene 3 respectively.

45 TO HENRI LEROLLE[1]

Mon cher Lerolle   28 August 1894

I think of you too often to apologize for not replying sooner to your letter. It was welcome nourishment for my spiritual journey on which I've rather been feeling the lack of your friendly support, and I must tell you most earnestly how very encouraging I find it — don't take this as being empty sentimentality (although sentimentality isn't what M. Casimir Périer thinks it is).[2] I think of you as an elder brother whom one is fond of even when he grumbles, because you know he does it out of the kindness of his heart − an idiosyncratic view of things, maybe, and if you don't always find it acceptable please don't say so too forcefully, it would really upset me! Pelléas and Mélisande started off by sulking and refused to come down off their tapestry, so I had to start playing round with some different ideas; then they got rather jealous and came and leant over me, and Mélisande addressed me − you know that frail and gentle voice of hers: 'Leave these silly little thoughts, good only for the great musical public, and let your dreams dwell upon my hair. You know there can be no love like ours.'

I've finished the vault scene. It's full of impalpable terror and mysterious enough to make the most well-balanced listener giddy. The climb up from the vaults is done too, full of sunshine but a sunshine reflecting our mother the sea. I hope it'll make an attractive scene; anyway, you'll see for yourself − the last thing I want to do is influence you. I've also finished the scene with the sheep. Here I've tried to get across something at least of the compassion of a child who sees a sheep mainly as a sort of toy he can't touch and also as the object of a pity no longer felt by those who are only anxious for a comfortable life. At the moment I'm on the scene between the father and the son. It's terrifying, the music's got to be profound and absolutely accurate! There's a 'petit père' that gives me nightmares.[3]

I had the idea, for the death of Mélisande, of putting some of the orchestra actually on stage so that her death would be, from the sound point of view, a kind of richly coloured one. What do you think? I've started some pieces for violin and orchestra which'll be called *Nocturnes*.[4] I'm going to split up the orchestral groups so as to try and achieve nuances with the groups by themselves. Composers aren't daring enough. They're afraid of that sacred idol called 'common sense', which is the most dreadful thing I know − after all, it's no more than a religion founded to excuse the ubiquity of imbeciles! Ultimately we must just cultivate the garden of our instincts and officiously trample on the flower-beds[5] all symmetrically laid out with ideas in white ties.

My life here is as simple as a blade of grass and I have no pleasures apart from working (quite enough for you, you poor wretch!).

I had dinner with André Gide[6] some time ago. He's like an old spinster, timid, gracious and polite in the English manner, but he's charming and very swift at coming up with subtle and ingenious ideas. He has a horror of Wagner − a sure sign of a refined intelligence. Perhaps he's too preoccupied with striking an attitude, but that's very much a contemporary disease. Pierre Louÿs is back from Algeria, with a burnous which is every bit as curious as any of his descriptions.

Paris looks like a watering-place for rich invalids. You see people going round looking amazed and women with a slightly Viennese elegance and piercing blue eyes! And then there's the fact that I go for regular walks in the Bois de Boulogne, now it's free of the criminal element, and that Lucien Fontaine[7] continues to sing like a sentimental bull.

Yours ever
C.D.

My best wishes to Mme Lerolle and the rest of your family. (I like the design on your seal.)

[1] Lerolle was a painter, some fifteen years older than Debussy, who specialized in decorative panels. He was also an amateur violinist and was close to Duparc, Bordes, d'Indy, Bonheur and especially Chausson, his brother-in-law.
[2] Casimir Périer, who had been elected President of the Republic on 27 June, was well known for his grandiose ideas and his crises of conscience. He was to resign suddenly the following year.
[3] In Act III scene 4 the child Yniold has to sing this phrase no fewer than 28 times (30 times in the original uncut version). It was one of the passages seized on by hecklers at the early performances. (R.N.)
[4] The new form of the *Scènes au Crépuscule* mentioned in a letter to Poniatowski (see letter 23).
[5] 'Marcher sur les plates-bandes' means 'to interfere in somebody else's business'. (R.N.)
[6] Writing to Louÿs on 27 July 1894, Debussy speaks of a dinner with Gide and Valéry.
[7] Lucien Fontaine was a businessman who had asked Debussy to conduct the small amateur choral group he had founded. It was for this group that Debussy wrote the first version of the *Chansons de Charles d'Orléans*.

46 TO EUGÈNE YSAŸE[1]

Mon cher grand ami   22 September 1894

I've been so slow writing to you, I'm afraid this letter may find you on the 'great boats that go upon the waters', on your way to bring good music to the rectangular Americans. Please forgive me, but I've been drawing endless semiquavers on papers whose 32 staves appear with relentless regularity. I'm exhausted to the point of not daring to write even to my best friends, and you can certainly consider yourself one of those.

I'm working on three nocturnes for solo violin and orchestra. In the first one the orchestra is strings only, in the second flutes, four horns, three trumpets and two harps and in the third one both groups come together. It's an experiment, in fact, in finding the different combinations possible inside a single colour, as a painter might make a study in grey, for example.

I hope you'll think it interesting – my main interest is that you should like it. I'm not abandoning *Pelléas* in the meantime and the further I get the more I'm beset by the darkest misgivings . . . One has to pursue one's musical dream and it needs the merest nothing to dissipate it; then there's the self-control one has to exercise in suppressing anything irrelevant or long-winded. The result is I'm feeling like a stone that's been run over by carriage wheels.

I wish you every success – you have the right to expect it.

> Yours ever
> C.D.

[1] The Belgian violinist had founded the Ysaÿe Quartet in 1892. They gave the first performance of Debussy's Quartet on 29 December 1893 at a concert of the Société nationale de musique in the Salle Pleyel.

47 TO STÉPHANE MALLARMÉ

> Cher maître   21 December 1894[1]

I need not say how happy I should be if you were kind enough to honour with your presence the arabesque which, by an excess of pride perhaps, I believe to have been dictated by the flute of your faun.

> Yours respectfully
> C.D.

[1] The first performance of the *Prélude à l'après-midi d'un faune* took place next day. Debussy had been attending the poet's Tuesday salon for at least two years. Though he did not go regularly, he did meet a number of artists and writers with whom he remained in contact: Ferdinand Hérold, Pierre Louÿs, P. Quillard, Charles Morice, André Gide, Paul Valéry, Camille Mauclair, James Whistler, etc. (Mallarmé did attend the performance on 22 December. See also letter 191. R.N.)

22 January 1895

But my dear good fellow! Remember the music of Java[1] which contained every nuance, even the ones we no longer have names for. There tonic and dominant had become empty shadows of use only to stupid children.

So no more dumping the superannuated thrills of your 'mi la ray doh' on us. I sincerely hope the charms of Paqua and Lola are fresher than that.[2] [. . .]

In the early morning the executioner plies his trade and a voice sobs:

> See what a fine young man goes there,
> Fine and loving!
> Fine and loving!
> See what a fine young man goes there
> His heart belongs to Lola fair.[3]

Everyone's clutching *Bilitis*, even Jean Lorrain, which must be quite a surprise for her. He compares her to pictures by Puvis de Chavannes – certainly they're not as beautiful as the ones in the book she learnt to read from.[4] [. . .]

Pelléas and Mélisande are my only friends at the moment. Indeed we're getting to know each other too well perhaps and every time we talk to each other we know perfectly well how it's going to end. And then, finishing a work of art is rather like the death of someone you love, isn't it? . . .

A chord of the ninth . . .

The accidentals are blue . . .

I take pleasure in imagining your artistic figures 'near the ramparts of Seville, drinking manzanilla'. You're going to be real experts on the castanet by the time you get back, a welcome addition to your meagre social talents.

I look forward to hearing whether so many centuries of civilization have tamed the celebrated 'Spanish arrogance', but whatever you do bring me back a guitar so that whenever I strike it it gives off a kind of subtle, sonorous dust, the relic of its savage melancholy of old.

There my communication ends, with my regrets that I can continue it only in thought. Let my friendship fill the gaps.

C.D.

[76]

All my best wishes to Hérold. He likes the 'minor' mode, I fancy, which is very right and proper in Spain.[5]

[1] A reference to the gamelan performances at the Universal Exhibition in 1889 which revealed to Debussy the music of the Far East, as they did to several artists.

[2] Indeed they were. Louÿs's previous letter mentions that he has taken up with Paqua who was fifteen. Hérold's girl, Lola, was sixteen. (R.N.)

[3] The refrain of *L'Amant d'Amanda*, a popular song of the time.

[4] Paul Duval, known as Jean Lorrain, was a sophisticated man-about-town whose vitriolic column 'Pêle-mêle' appeared once a week in the *Journal*. He was a poet, storyteller, journalist and novelist. His review of the *Chansons de Bilitis* had just appeared in *L'Echo de Paris*. After the first performances of *Pelléas* he wrote an article called *Les Pelléastres* which annoyed Debussy considerably.

[5] Louÿs had gone to Seville with A. Ferdinand Hérold, a poet and playwright. He was one of the regular visitors to Mallarmé's salon and the grandson of Louis Hérold, the composer of *Zampa*.

49 TO PIERRE LOUŸS

Cher ami   Friday [23] February 1895

I hope the beauty of the countryside, passionately reflected in the eyes of your various charming companions, is absorbing all your interest so you're not pining for any letters from me; in which case I won't bother myself hunting for vague excuses!

I'm working on things which will be understood only by our grandchildren in the 20th century; only they will see that 'clothes don't make a musician'. They'll rip the veils away from idols and discover that underneath there was only a miserable skeleton (murmurs of agreement from the celestial parliament, on the left).

I greet with joy your entry into the world of music; Messrs Durand[1] ask me to implore you to let them have the first refusal on your works.

Unfortunately I had to miss *Chilpéric*[2] but this evening I'm going to hear some music by E. de Polignac[3] which I hope will be a satisfactory replacement.

Beethoven's fourteenth quartet is without question one long practical joke, in spite of what these young metaphysicians say in *L'Art et la vie*.[4] People should stop lumbering us with old furniture which hasn't even retained its period smell.

Yours as ever
Claude

[77]

[1] The publishers on the place de la Madeleine who had brought out his Quartet and who, ten years later, were to become the exclusive publishers of his works.
[2] An 'opérette-bouffe' with words by Paul Ferrier and music by Hervé, which was given in a new version at the Variétés on 1 February 1895.
[3] The Prince Edmond de Polignac 'was a gracious prince, a great wit and a formidable musician', wrote Marcel Proust. 'Few people knew his compositions, but that was because he was so demanding about how his music should be played. He was terrified of concert halls' (*Chroniques*, 1927, p. 39). The concert given this Friday evening included, as well as Polignac's *Robin m'aime*, works by Chausson, Hüe, Erb, Planchet, Rimsky-Korsakov, Max d'Olonne, Fauré, Kunc and Guiraud. The conductor was Gustave Doret.
[4] A 'revue jeune' which appeared from 1892 to 1897. Debussy refers to an article by Maurice Pujo in the number for 1 January, discussing some of the Beethoven quartets played in the Salle d'Harcourt by the Crickboom Quartet.

50 TO PIERRE LOUŸS

Pierre, mon ami   11 May 1895

Hartmann[1] spent the whole of this morning involved with 'Schotts' of Mainz – he looks after their Paris interests, without forgetting yours! So we must try again later.

Now: *Cendrelune*[2] (2nd Act). The enchanted girls (nice to know them, no doubt)[3] have a slightly 1822 feel to them and it also seems to me they should meet Cendrelune somehow, perhaps in the course of some initial test of her moral fibre. The formal renunciation which the Green Lady desires would then really be the final test. The Green Lady's escape needs to make more impact. It could be done by Marie-Jeanne being restored to life, and Cendrelune* falling into her arms and saying the magic words that break the spell. Then, from the distance to begin with, we could hear the girls' voices replying (as sad as breadcrumbs behind a flowering shrub!) I'll be with you on Monday about 6 and we can discuss all this.

Yours
C.D.

*   Because Cendrelune is really too little to be playing at Parsifals.

[1] Georges Hartmann was Schott's agent in France; see letters 62 and 63.
[2] This project, for a 'musical tale in two acts and three scenes' was discussed at length by Debussy and Louÿs between 1895 and 1898. It originated from a commission by Carvalho for the Opéra-comique. Louÿs replied to Debussy the next day: 'Write *Cendrelune* yourself. You're perfectly capable of it. With all the changes this little libretto's gone through I can't recognize it any more . . .'
[3] Debussy's pun on 'enchantées' is untranslatable. (R.N.)

12 Debussy's editor and benefactor, Georges Hartmann.

Cher ami   Friday evening [9 August 1895]

I thought the second act of *Pelléas* would be child's play and it's the very devil! . . .

Anything resembling conversation doesn't really work in music and the man who discovers the secret of the 'musical interview' ought to be generously rewarded.

I hope I'll be able to get to see you next Tuesday at the usual time and that it'll be one of those days when we can be as nice and simple as a blade of grass.

Yours
C.D.

52 TO HENRI LEROLLE

Saturday 17 August 1895

Good Heavens, yes! Mon cher Lerolle, there was nothing for it, I had to finish *Pelléas* while you were a long way away![1] It's not been without its problems, either; especially the scene between Golaud and Mélisande! That's the point where things begin to move towards the catastrophe, and where Mélisande begins to tell Golaud lies and to realize her own motives, assisted in this by the said Golaud, a solid fellow for all that; it also shows you shouldn't be completely frank, even with young girls. I think you'll like the scene in front of the cave. I tried to capture all the mystery of the night and the silence in which a blade of grass roused from its slumber makes an alarming noise. And then there's the sea nearby, telling its sorrows to the moon and Pelléas and Mélisande a little scared of talking, surrounded by so much mystery.

I won't say any more, in case it turns out like those descriptions of a foreign country: you build a whole edifice of dreams on them and then reality wipes them out with a merciless sponge. Now my anxiety begins in earnest; how will the world behave towards these two poor creatures? – I hate crowds, universal suffrage and nationalistic phrases! – Take Hartmann, for example; he's a fair representative of average intelligence. Well, the death of Mélisande, as it stands at the moment, has as much effect on him as on a small bench! For him, it doesn't work! But then whenever a woman dies in the French theatre it has to be like the *Lady of the Camellias*; though you're allowed to replace the

[80]

camellias with some other flowers and the Lady by an Eastern princess! People can't get used to the idea that one might take one's leave discreetly like somebody who has had enough of planet Earth and is on his way to where the flowers of tranquillity bloom!

All in all anything which consists of trying to familiarize one's contemporaries with the sublime is a fool's game, except for oneself.

What you say about nature is absolutely true. Really to get to grips with nature you must be, don't you think, either an old oak-tree which has seen all its colours, and which doesn't need to shelter from the rain under a ridiculous instrument called an umbrella since it is its own umbrella, or else a shepherd whose conversation, entirely reserved for his sheep, is every bit as interesting as that of a member of the Jockey-Club! I hope too that you'll now let the mountains have some peace and will return to the trees on the avenue Wagram and to the piano in the rue Gustave Doré which misses its best friend.

> Yours ever
> C.D.

Please give my respects to Mme Lerolle and greetings to all your family as well as Ernest-Arthus Chausson.

[1] The sketch draft of parts of *Pelléas* which Debussy gave to Lerolle is dated June–July 1895.

53 TO HENRI LEROLLE

Mon cher Lerolle   Monday 23 September 1895

I was intending to answer your kind letter straight away, but that terrible Hartmann has forced me to work night and day on the *Fantaisie*[1] for piano and orchestra which Pugno is going to play at Colonne's concerts this winter, if the latter is not too appalled by my music. I'm due to see him on Tuesday.

I'm as sorry as you are that our two journeys should unfortunately have coincided, and if Monsieur Lerolle had told me in advance I could perhaps have done something about it! None the less I'm sorry, even though I was entertained at Mercin[2] like the Prince of Wales or any other prince you care to mention!

As for your jealousy about those who've heard the end of *Pelléas*, I tell you for your comfort than Bonheur and Dupin are so far the only ones thus honoured – take the word 'honoured' in any sense you choose. Like you, I think Bonheur's Chaldaean inscription is just right and in keeping with the feelings he's expressed; I look forward confidently to your agreement! Try and make this as soon as you can, as I feel it's six years since I last saw you!

To tell the truth I haven't done very much – extracting all that music from a single brain has left me exhausted. I intend now to finish the three *Nocturnes*. I've also been working on the libretto of *La Grande Bretèche*[3] which I'm going to go on with as I think I could make something quite disturbing out of it, which could easily become a marketable commodity abroad.

I'm going to Bonheur's on Thursday and no doubt we shall find all sorts of unpleasant things to say about you. I can't imagine why you insist on staying in a place with such an inharmonious name[4] and neglecting your friends.

> Yours ever
> C.D.

---

[1]   Debussy had already referred to this work in the letter of 13 February 1891 to Robert Godet, see letter 19. The *Fantaisie* was not performed in the composer's lifetime.
[2]   Mercin was Lucien Fontaine's country house near Soissons.
[3]   It seems this project, based on Balzac's novel, never came to anything.
[4]   Labergement Sainte-Marie (Doubs).

54 TO ALFRED BRUNEAU

Mon cher ami   Thursday [17 October 1895]

Many thanks for your kind article[1] about the *Prélude à l'après-midi d'un faune* and also for the example you provide of artistic solidarity! It's something pretty rare among composers! Especially with the 'successes', who immediately turn into dogs guarding a hard-won bone! All praise then to those like you who admit the existence of another art than their own; they're really the ones who matter.

> My thanks again and all best wishes
> C.D.

---

[1]   In his article in *Le Figaro* on 14 October Bruneau had remarked on Debussy's 'rare and original' temperament and on 'the truly exquisite moments' in the music, but added: 'Frankness obliges me to admit that I prefer something more clearcut, more robust and masculine.' What Debussy thought of Bruneau's music can be seen in letter 61.

55 TO PIERRE LOUŸS

Mon cher Pierre   Thursday 17 October 1895

At first I was cross with you in spite of the excellent reasons you had to offer. But all in friendship, I promise you, and in disappointment that you were the only person missing that day out of *three thousand six hundred people* whose only value, as far as I was concerned, was in their quantity![1]

But then I know all too well the contradictory actions life forces us into, and I'm not even cross with the *Mercure* as it's going to be responsible for something very fine.

So all's well and we're still friends.

See you on Sunday
C.D.

[1]   Pierre Louÿs was in the thick of publishing *Aphrodite* and so could not attend the *Prélude à l'après-midi d'un faune* on 13 October, its first performance at the Colonne concerts.

56 TO PIERRE LOUŸS

Mon cher Pierre   17 January 1896

I've had a suggestion from M. Houston Chamberlain[1] for a ballet on *Daphnis and Chloë* and even though this man's given his name to a percolator[2] I find his ideas murky! So tell him to come with you tomorrow, I really need more details. He hasn't even told me anything about the forces required: will it be for xylophone, banjo or Russian bassoon? He's still at the Wagner stage too (can you imagine?) and believes in the recipes propounded by that old poisoner!

Yours invulnerably
Claude

[1]   Houston Stewart Chamberlain was an Englishman brought up in France who settled in Germany. Here he made friends with Edouard Dujardin and devoted himself to the propagation of Wagner's music. Wagner's daughter Eva became his wife. It was Louÿs who had initiated the idea of this ballet project with Debussy.
[2]   Or nearly: the percolator was in fact called Chamberland.

Mon cher ami   Friday 10 April 1896

I must certainly add my voice to the European chorus of enthusiasm which has rightly greeted the unforgettable Chrysis.[1] But this enthusiasm seems to me to have gone astray over the licentious parts of the book. Facile and downright stupid comments were only to be expected when you consider the limitations people put on a work of art: it only counts as such if you use the attitudes and characters which have acquired the designation 'artistic' over the centuries.

Speaking personally, I find the book extraordinarily supple. The way you describe actions, too, is unique; you manage to make it all seem utterly human and perfectly harmonized at the same time (you know what I mean). And as for the beginnings and endings of the chapters, where you describe or arrest the arabesques of feeling and colour, they're magical.

Sometimes I feel the developments of your themes take on a value entirely of their own – the superb structure of the story is still there, but one is sad to lose sight of it with the rather abrupt incursion of over-rich material.

You will, I hope, take this observation in friendship, as it's given, and see in it my wishes for your increasing strength as a writer. Anyway it doesn't affect anything I've said or, indeed, my happiness at being a friend of such a man and artist – as I've long known you to be.

Yours
C.D.

[1] *Aphrodite* first appeared in instalments in the *Mercure de France* and was then published as a book in April 1896. The Galilaean courtesan Chrysis is the heroine.

58 TO HENRI GAUTHIER-VILLARS[1]

Thursday 10 October 1896

The *Prélude à l'après-midi d'un faune*, cher Monsieur, is it perhaps the dream left over at the bottom of the faun's flute? To be more precise, it is the general impression of the poem. If the music were to follow it more closely it would run out of breath, like a dray-horse competing for the Grand Prix with a thoroughbred. It also demonstrates a disdain for the 'constructional knowhow' which is a burden upon our finest intellects. Then again, it has no respect for tonality! Rather it's in a mode which is intended to contain all the nuances — I can give you a perfectly logical demonstration of this.

All the same it follows the ascending shape of the poem as well as the scenery so marvellously described in the text, together with the humanity brought to it by thirty-two violinists who have got up too early! As for the ending, it's a prolongation of the last line:

Couple farewell, I go to see what you became.

I realize that in replying to your solicitously urgent letter I am depriving myself of what you might have said on your own account and I am most anxious not to circumscribe your freedom in this respect.

Yours sincerely
C.D.

P.S. I spell my name 'Debussy', not 'de Bussy': one of my quirks.

[1] Gauthier-Villars wrote under the pseudonym Willy or 'the usherette at the Cirque d'été', first in *L'Echo de Paris*, then in *Comoedia*. He was renowned for his caustic reviews, larded with puns. His wife Colette was one of his 'collaborators' in publishing his books, together with three of Debussy's friends: Curnonsky, Jean de Tinan and Paul-Jean Toulet. He began as a music critic with the help of Alfred Ernst, one of Debussy's predecessors on the *Revue blanche*.

Georges Hartmann
The *Nocturnes*
The break with Gaby
Marriage to Lilly

From 1895 onward Debussy received support from an intelligent and understanding publisher, Georges Hartmann. *Pelléas* was now largely completed and Debussy was performing extracts at private gatherings, but he could obtain nothing more than vague promises of it being performed at the Opéra-comique. He composed an orchestral triptych, the *Nocturnes*, which he had great trouble finishing, but the various projects discussed with Pierre Louÿs came to nothing. In 1899 he finally broke with Gaby Dupont and in his desire for stability married Lilly Texier, a pretty, uncomplicated mannequin of twenty-five. Pierre Louÿs had himself got married some months before and now the two friends saw less and less of each other. With Hartmann's death in 1900, Debussy's material situation once again became insecure.

59 TO EUGÈNE YSAŸE

Cher grand ami   13 October 1896

I'm extremely touched by your kind letter and by the friendly anxiety it shows about Pelléas and Mélisande – poor little creatures, it's so hard to bring them out into the real world because, with someone like you as their godfather, the world is unwilling to let itself be convinced.

I must now set out modestly the reasons why I disagree with you on the question of performing extracts from *Pelléas*. Firstly, if this work has any merit, it lies above all in the connection between the movement on stage and the movement in the music. It's obviously the case therefore that this quality would disappear in concert performance and no one could be blamed for being totally impervious to the peculiar eloquence of the silences with which the work is studded. What's more, the simplicity of the means employed only makes its point in the opera house; in the concert hall I'd immediately have Wagner's transatlantic abundance hurled back at me, and be left looking like some poor devil who simply couldn't afford his . . . contrabass tubas! In my opinion Pelléas and Mélisande must appear *as they are*. People will have to take them or leave them and, if there has to be a fight, it will be worthwhile . . . Here's what I suggest instead: it's likely that by December I'll have finished something I've written on a poem by D. G. Rossetti: *La Saulaie*. Note that it's very important and written according to my latest experiments in musical chemistry.[1] You could add to that *Trois Nocturnes* for violin and orchestra, written for Eugène Ysaÿe, a man I like and admire. Furthermore these *Nocturnes* can be played only by him: if Apollo himself were to ask for them I should have to refuse. What do you say to that?

[87]

As for the *Marche écossaise*,[2] I must tell you I've redone the orchestration fairly thoroughly. Perhaps you'll be kind enough to tell me the precise occasion you want it for. I feel Demest[3] would do to sing *La Saulaie*, though it's a bit low, being written rather for a high baritone. Tell me what you think.

I've also started on the orchestration of two of the *Proses lyriques*[4] and in these the young singer you speak of would be splendid.

Once again my heartfelt thanks for your support. I don't think I need emphasize how much it means to me.

> With my best wishes to your charming family
> Yours affectionately
> C. D.

[1]   *La Saulaie*, a poem by Dante Gabriel Rossetti in a translation by Pierre Louÿs. Debussy was still working on it in 1900 (see letter 79) but, like most of his collaborative projects with Louÿs, it was never finished.
[2]   Originally this was a piece for piano duet, *Marche des anciens comtes de Ross*.
[3]   Désiré Demest, a Belgian tenor, 1864–1932.
[4]   Almost certainly 'De grève' and 'De soir'. But two years later he had given up the idea: 'it seems to me it's a complete waste of time to inflate them with any sort of orchestral uproar' (letter to Pierre de Bréville, 24 March 1898).

60   TO PIERRE LOUŸS

Mon cher Pierre   Tuesday evening 9 [February] 1897

You must be cursing me or else you've dismissed me for ever from your thoughts . . . No, I'm sure you haven't. I'm sure too that you've never been out of mine. I've been thinking about you a lot and even talking to you. Frankly it's not my fault if you keep having these strange compulsions to travel beyond Asnières[1] . . . I've been mixed up in a tiresome business, a sort of collaboration between Bourget and Xavier de Montépin[2] (not, after all, beyond the bounds of possibility). Gaby, she of the piercing eye, found a letter in my pocket which left no doubt as to the advanced state of a love affair, and containing enough picturesque material to inflame even the most stolid heart. Whereupon . . . Scenes . . . Tears . . . A real revolver and *Le Petit journal* there to record it all . . . It would have been nice to have you here, my dear Pierre, to help me recognize myself in all this third-rate literature. It's all senseless, pointless, and it changes absolutely nothing; you can't wipe out a mouth's kisses or a body's caresses by passing an india-rubber over them. It'd be a handy invention, an india-rubber for removing adultery.

However, poor Gaby has just lost her father and this intervention by death has sorted out the whole stupid business for the moment.

Even so I've been completely knocked sideways and, once again, mortified at feeling you so far away, so irredeemably far that I couldn't summon up the strength even for the simple task of writing to you. I felt it wouldn't go as it should – the words friends speak face to face can't be put on paper. Maybe you'll think it's all my fault. But there it is, at times I'm as sentimental as some milliner who could have been Chopin's mistress; I need to know that my heart is still capable of reacting, instead of peacefully pursuing researches into my personal chemistry, which entails a responsibility only to what's on paper.

Let's say no more on the subject, and rest assured I'm still your devoted friend.

I expect you know all there is to be known about the Mallarmé banquet.[3] I was monumentally bored. Mallarmé seemed to feel the same way and, in a voice like a melancholy Mr Punch, delivered a cross and frosty little speech. F.V.G.[4] carried on like a policeman and little La Jeunesse[5] like a disease; I made the acquaintance of M. José-Maria de Hérédia, which left me unmoved – one more person to greet in the street.[6]

Dukas's symphony, played by the orchestra, was a disappointment! . .[7] It turned into something tiny, like a mixture of Beethoven and Charpentier; I just don't understand it at all . . .

Talking of music, have you been working at *Cendrelune*? . . . Not that I deserve it . . . Still, it's a real favour to give me something to get on with, even if only to make a change from all these disturbances and sprinkle a little water on the sickly plant which my life resembles at the moment.

Forain (as you know) has asked me to compose some music for the mime-play written by his wife.[8] Have you read it? It's not bad at all, even though it's not finished. I found myself deeply implicated and I don't know how to get out of it, or how to tell him politely that it's no more than the beginnings of a nice idea.

Reply soon and forgive me sooner still . . .
Yours
C.D.

Not a word of all this when you write. Try and come back soon.

[89]

[1] Asnières is a suburb to the north-west of Paris. Louÿs was in Algeria.

[2] Xavier de Montépin, 1823–1902, author of pamphlets and successful plays *La Porteuse de pain*, *La Voleuse d'amour*, etc.

[3] A banquet was arranged for Mallarmé, on 2 February at Père Lathuile's restaurant, by a small group of his friends to celebrate the publication of *Divagations*. The banquet led to much soul-searching and annoyance and Gide and Valéry were among the most notable absentees.

[4] Francis Viélé-Griffin, a hardline symbolist poet who formulated his poetic system in his review, the *Entretiens politiques et littéraires*. It was in this same review that he had published the first two poems of Debussy's *Proses lyriques* (issue of December 1892).

[5] Ernest La Jeunesse, a critic who had just brought out a rather disrespectful publication *Les Nuits, les ennuis et les âmes de nos plus notoires contemporains*.

[6] One hopes Louÿs had forgotten this remark two years later, when he came to marry de Hérédia's daughter, Louise. (R.N.)

[7] Dukas's Symphony in C had been given its first performance at the Opéra on 3 January.

[8] Jean-Louis Forain, painter, designer and lively caricaturist. His wife's mime-play was called *Le Chevalier d'or*.

61 TO PIERRE LOUÿS

Mon cher Pierre   Tuesday 9 March 1897

I've already been much too slow answering your two lovely letters, for which eternal guilt shall be my lot . . .

First may I say how happy I am to know you're in better health; it made me sad and worried to think of you being ill when you were alone and so far away. I bitterly regretted, too, being only a poor little harpsichordist who's temporarily forbidden to make long journeys; otherwise, my dear chap, you would have seen me stepping off the boat like some modern Isolde and I'd have made you realize that friendship is the only permanent ointment which never disappoints the hopes invested in it. I hope, anyway, that by the time these lines reach you you'll be completely recovered and able to pursue your musical studies.

I'm no more up on the score of *Messidor*[1] than you are because life is short and better spent in a café or looking at pictures. How can you see such ugly people as Zola and Bruneau producing anything that's more than mediocre? Have you seen also the deplorable use they make in their two articles of patriotism, a jolly good excuse for saying 'It may be bad, but at least it's French!'[2] Good Lord, there's only one musician who's really French and that's Paul Delmet,[3] he's the only one who's caught the melancholy of the suburbs and the sentimentality which laughs and weeps on the sandy turf of the fortifications. Massenet remains this master's best pupil, but the others, with their social preoccupations and

13 Debussy and Zorah Ben Brahim, Louÿs's mistress, in Louÿs's
apartment in 1897.

their claims to encapsulate life in chords of the seventh, are no more than miserable hacks and if, in fact, they do have a view of life it's only through their laundress's latest bill.

I hope these few lines reach you as soon as possible, bringing with them all my friendly greetings; I'll send the rest tomorrow.

    Yours
    Claude

Gaby thanks you and sends you her nicest smile.

[1] This work, with words by Emile Zola and music by Alfred Bruneau, had received its first performance at the Opéra on 19 February.
[2] *Le Figaro* had printed on 20 February an article by each of them, concluding on a patriotic note.
[3] The singer and song-writer of the night-club *Le Chat noir*. In 1908, a newspaper item claimed that Debussy had collaborated with him.

62 TO GEORGES HARTMANN[1]

    Cher Monsieur Hartmann   Sunday 19 September 1897

Thank you for your kindness in replying so promptly. M. Heugel[2] is not worthy to be called a colleague of yours any longer and, quite apart from all the damage he's done to music, he strikes me as a thoroughly nasty man.

I'd prefer you to let me have the whole of the sum I'm asking for, I've got so many bills! ... and people are shouting insults under my window; even so I wouldn't want to put you in an awkward position and take the bread out of Margot's mouth. So please hand over as much as you can to one of my employees who'll call on you tomorrow morning.

Once again, my heartfelt thanks.

    Yours
    C.D.

See you on Saturday.

[1] A music publisher who had been active since 1870 and had supported several young composers, including Massenet. He then sold his business to Heugel (see footnote 2) in 1891. He was the dedicatee of the *Nocturnes*, and *Pelléas* was dedicated to his memory. For several years he gave Debussy a monthly subsidy of 500 francs.
[2] Henri-Georges Heugel, who directed the music publishing house *Au Ménestrel* from 1883 to 1916.

Cher Monsieur Hartmann   Friday evening 31 December 1897

I can find no way of escaping extreme sadness as this year comes to a dreary end, a year in which I did practically nothing of what I wanted to do; and, in making up my mind to send you my very best wishes, I think of all the happiness I have forfeited by not being able to live up to my expectations.

I wanted to bring you the *Trois Nocturnes* (dedicated to you) in which I've tried to give orchestral music a little life and freedom. Unfortunately I haven't finished them and am rather discouraged. I'm only afraid you may, as a result, think there's some ill-will on my part, which would pain me deeply.

I want you to know, once and for all, the true affection I have for you and the great trust I put in your friendship; please believe that in my worst moments it is a great comfort to be able to rely on it.

As soon as I can show you what I've done, I'll write to you. Until then, I remain

Yours sincerely
C.D.

Mon cher ami   Wednesday 19 January 1898

You must please allow me not to have any official opinion about the future of the Opéra-comique[1] . . . even though no one knows exactly why, it'll probably continue. As for the experimental opera house, that strikes me as a sinister joke; one doesn't experiment with music. Nobody loves music enough in France, neither those who make it nor those who listen to it, for an opera house to be able to support itself, and inevitably it'll be a question of various schemes in which music takes on the unlooked-for role of procuress.

The morality behind all this lies in the transformation which has come over Art in general. No longer is it something lofty and disinterested, but just a way of making money within the reach of those who are wedded to the respectable professions – in defence of my contemporaries I should say it's been going on a long time, and there's no reason to suppose it won't continue for a very long time as well.

This letter is meant as a private one to you – *not* for *Le Figaro*, please – as well as an opportunity for me to send you my best wishes.

C.D.

[1] On the death of Carvalho, the director of the Opéra-comique, the journalist Jules Huret sent a questionnaire to various composers on the path they thought the theatre should follow. He published the answers in his book *Loges et coulisses* (Revue blanche, 1901), but without Debussy's. Huret had acquired some notoriety in 1891 when he conducted a literary survey in *L'Echo de Paris* which provoked a considerable uproar.

65 TO PIERRE LOUŸS

Cher Pierre   Sunday 27 March 1898

Please forgive me before I start making excuses, as I haven't got any that are wholly convincing. Let's agree, once and for all, that you can rely on the constancy of my affection and that one or two adjectives more or less aren't going to undermine it.

I've been very miserable since your departure, in the most thorough-going way imaginable, and I've shed tears copiously – a simple gesture which unites the whole of humanity and the only thing left to me in my wretched condition. I can't explain further and as a friend you'll understand the rest.

Naturally I haven't worked much, with music quite rightly getting its own back for being neglected. Even so the *Chansons de Bilitis* are finished and I hope the third one will find the same favour in your eyes as the other two.

The three *Nocturnes* have been infected by my private life, first full of hope, then full of despair and then full of nothing! I've never been able to work at anything when my life's going through a crisis; which is, I think, why memory is a superior faculty, because you can pick from it the emotions you need. But those who write masterpieces in floods of tears are barefaced liars.

It would be very kind of you to do some work on *Cendrelune* as I need something to lavish my affection on and to hang on to. Otherwise I shall go mad and resort to suicide, which would be even more stupid. I promise you I'm not just bombarding you with fine words and there are times when I'm afraid of losing what was almost good in my character.

I haven't seen *Cyrano de Bergerac*[1] and I'm afraid it may be an act of wool-pulling.

[94]

You've probably received a letter from young René Peter who's the happiest man in the world now he's got your preface.[2]

Forgive this short letter but I'd only go on bemoaning my lot, which would be extremely boring for you and would do nothing to change the sequence of events which have so cruelly gone against me.

Most of all, I wish you were here with me, because you're the only friend I can trust.

Yours
C.D.

P.S. I gather the proofs of Peter's preface have been sent off to you: would you send them back as soon as possible and say what title you would prefer: Preface by P.L.; Introduction by P.L.; or any other version of your choice.

[1] Since 28 December the previous year Edmond Rostand's play had been having a great success at the Porte Saint-Martin.
[2] René Peter, the son of a well-known doctor and ten years younger than Debussy, had been a friend of his for some years. He was also close to Marcel Proust who wrote of his 'unwearying kindness'. Debussy had acted as middleman in getting Pierre Louÿs to write a preface for Peter's free-verse drama in one act, *Tragédie de la mort* (see note on the following letter).

66† TO RENÉ PETER

Mon cher René   6 May 1898

No doubt you've had hard things to say about me for not replying to your charming note . . . The thing is, I've had a fever with all the usual accompanying inconveniences; otherwise it was a common or garden fever without a trace of individual genius about it.

Sit down and let's talk: I've every intention of taking the Ballade of the Child whose head is wreathed in flowers and covering it with music, but so far I've had no luck rummaging through collections of popular songs. I think I'll abandon my researches and try and find something which owes nothing to anybody.[1]

So try to come and see me on Friday, either before or after lunch.

A toi
Dir
Yours

Tibi

Claude

My metal gullet speaks all languages.

[1] Debussy eventually (in April 1899) set the 'Chanson de la Mère' from Act I of Peter's play *Tragédie de la mort*, which was never staged. The manuscript, now in the Library of Congress, carries the title 'Berceuse ... sur une vieille chanson poitevine' and the dedication reads: 'Dear René, forgive this temporary assumption of a Poitiers accent, to assure you once again of my firm friendship.' The text of the song, written for unaccompanied solo voice, is printed according to Peter's own version (before Debussy gave it an 'accent poitevin' by suppressing mute *e*'s) in Margaret G. Cobb, *The Poetic Debussy*, Northeastern University Press, 1982, pp. 281–2.

67 TO ALICE PETER[1]

Ma chère amie   Tuesday evening [May–June 1898]

I meant to write to you at greater length, but so far the only length has been in the gap between my first letter and this one. Don't blame me, or anyone; just life, which is so short on joy and long on anxiety. In any case my silence has been supported by yours, so don't let's dwell on this break for which we've both been responsible.

'Play is resumed.'

I could relate to you my various troubles, still tiresomely similar to the ones you're familiar with; but fear not, I guard them as discreetly as an elephant. Naturally I've done nothing about *F.E.A.*![2] The early enthusiasm has been transformed into a kind of obstinacy and the opportunity to look at things coolly has led me to reflect, perhaps too much so. I feel that to get anywhere with this project one would have to be less confident and be better acquainted with the souls of all the characters. One never invents anything, unfortunately, and a knowledge of the human heart is the result of innumerable experiences. The task is made harder by the play's characters themselves who appear in so many different lights, it's impossible to keep a steady opinion of them for longer than an evening! ... (which leads me to say that philosophers certainly have a 'crust'!)

So one has to generalize throughout; for one thing, if you portray people in bulk you have a better chance of getting some of them right – in this respect I suggest *Les Tisserands*[3] is a much more accomplished masterpiece than is generally felt. To tell you the truth, I don't feel I have the muscle to clean out the Augean stables, which is rather what it would come to.

[96]

René mustn't let himself be upset by all this or prevented from aiming at some more immediate source of glory;[4] I'm just an old romantic who doesn't feel the need to make a splash at all costs! That's why I'm not writing to him but using you as a gentle and devoted buffer.

Don't forget me entirely and try and let me have some news of you . . .

Forgive this disorganized letter – it's really bound together by my very best wishes to yourself and to René.

> Yours
> C.D.

[1] René Peter's sister-in-law, who was by now more or less separated from her husband. She was the dedicatee of 'La Chevelure', the second of the *Chansons de Bilitis*. René Peter described her as a 'woman of the world . . . in the mature, practical sense of the word'; she saw that Debussy was 'ready to play the role of devoted servant and was happy to prolong the attachment as long as it suited him'.

[2] *Les Frères en Art*, a play which Debussy was planning to write in collaboration with René Peter. Its theme was the rivalry between artists who were intending to found an esoteric society (*F.E.A.*) in order to promote their works but prevent commercial exploitation. Extracts from what remains of Debussy's contribution were published by Edward Lockspeiser in *Revue de musicologie* 1970, pp. 165–76. See letter 32 to Chausson in which Debussy is already adumbrating the idea of such a society.

[3] A play by Gerhart Hauptmann, performed at the Théâtre Antoine on 29 May 1893 and published the same year. It deals with the problem of the proletariat in its struggles with capitalism.

[4] See letter 72.

68 TO GEORGES HARTMANN

Wednesday 14 July 1898
Cher Monsieur Hartmann   [in fact Thursday]

Your discomfort has brought you one advantage at least, that you are spared any possibility of taking the slightest part in the national festivities . . . It gets more and more banal and the flags flying from the windows of various establishment-minded households were not stirred by any breeze of patriotism. What's worse, people have to be hired these days to sing the *Marseillaise* as the mob don't know it any more! Charpentier's the only one devoted to it, crowning the Muses with orchestral accompaniment and the approbation of the Municipal Council. I hope such strenuous efforts will lead him to become a Member of Parliament. It's time we had a musician there, if only to put some rhythm into the shrieks and groans those gentlemen produce.

I need hardly say how delighted I was to receive your letter and how grateful I am for your patience and sympathy in listening to my problems. Nothing, alas, has changed and 'something is rotten in the state of Denmark' in the words of that elegant neurasthenic Hamlet. In addition my life is decorated with complications of a sentimental nature, turning it into the most awkward and involved thing I know. I'd need a lot of money to leap over let alone destroy the barriers erected by law to separate those who strive for their own kind of happiness; and as it takes all my time not to die of hunger I have to sit back impotently and watch all my fine, beautiful dreams being smashed to pieces. It may seem ridiculous but I assure you it's enough to make the strongest person seriously depressed, whereas I'm really as simple as a blade of grass and it's only from Music I ask the impossible (or do I?)

I suppose your tribute to the Waters of Carlsbad will bring about an improvement in your overall situation but, Heavens above, you must be bored, and that lively, civilized and comfortable apartment of yours must be missing you.

I've completed the *Nocturnes*, as I told you, but the orchestration isn't finished yet. It shouldn't take long. As for the *Chansons de Bilitis*, we talked about the cover and using the brown Japanese paper with the title in vermilion-red lettering. For the title on the inside page I'd like the same layout as for *L'Après-midi d'un faune*, but I imagine we'll have to wait for your return to discuss this?

Do you think it would be possible, when we see Carré[1] and Messager again, to draft some sort of contract so they can't keep us on a string indefinitely? I think next winter would be the right moment. *Pelléas* has been widely talked of and we shouldn't lose or lessen the impact the opera is likely to have in the matter of impressing novelty on contemporary sensibilities. But you manage these 'explosives' with a surer touch than I do and, as usual, I'm happy to leave everything in your capable hands. It's just that we shouldn't allow too much 'fluff' to accumulate in the ears of the dear music-lovers.

Saturday 23 July 1898

I've had to put off finishing this letter because of a very painful attack of neuralgia which has been disrupting my superb intelligence for the last week. Don't worry, it hasn't left any permanent scars. What I need, I think, is lots of sea air and peace and quiet, and a respite from seeing the head of my concierge, that homegrown Medusa. During this last bout

[98]

of illness I've had the most amazing nightmares: I was at a rehearsal of *Pelléas* when suddenly Golaud turned into a bailiff and began to adapt the notes of his role to the musical formulae favoured by such characters.

I'm afraid this letter may not reach Carlsbad until after you've left, which would be fine for you as it would mean you'd finished with this wretched treatment. Don't be too cross with me for being so slow in writing and, as proof, let me have news of your health as soon as you can.

Yours
C.D.

---

[1] Albert Carré, the director of the Opéra-comique, who waited a further three years before finally agreeing to put on *Pelléas*.

69 TO GEORGES HARTMANN

Cher Monsieur Hartmann   Tuesday 9 August 1898

Once again I've been fighting my way through a mass of difficulties and still don't know whether I'm done with them.

Your letter disturbed me considerably by attaching importance to something which seems to me of purely anecdotal interest.[1] Nearly three years ago Mauclair,[2] acting on Maeterlinck's behalf, contacted me about this business; naturally I replied that I would have nothing to do with writing incidental music for *Pelléas*; having understood and worked on this play to turn it into an opera I was not going to be involved in something which would have looked like a repudiation. Now certainly Maeterlinck could have let me know the project was going ahead anyway. But he's a Belgian! which is to say, a trifle vulgar and badly brought up, that's for sure – as I know from other instances, too complicated to go into here.

In fact I believe Fauré was commissioned to write the music by that English actress[3] without being aware of the history of the project, and that subsequently he hasn't had the good manners to keep me informed.[4]

But anyway I can't see his music lasting beyond this present production. If I may be so immodest, I don't see the two scores could possibly be confused – for one thing, mine's much longer. And then

Fauré is the musical servant of a group of snobs and imbeciles who will have nothing whatever to do with the other *Pelléas*. Once again, the most annoying thing is that you found it so impressive; as for me, I assure you nothing could matter to me less.

As I said earlier on, I'm bored and ill and dream of a little peace, failing which I shall definitely go out of my mind.

> Yours
> C.D.

¹ In 1898 the Prince of Wales Theatre in London put on several performances of Maeterlinck's *Pelléas* with incidental music by Fauré, written in one and a half months.
² Camille Mauclair, a poet, novelist and art critic, had with Lugné-Poë founded la Maison de l'Oeuvre at the Théâtre des Bouffes-Parisiens, to make symbolist plays more widely known.
³ The English actress was Mrs Patrick Campbell, who took the part of Mélisande in the London performances. Mary Garden relates going to town to see her in the role, some years later, with Debussy: in Act III 'Debussy almost screamed when Mrs Patrick Campbell unloosed an avalanche of jet-black hair! . . . We left the theatre at once . . .' *Mary Garden's Story* London, 1952, p. 77. (R.N.)
⁴ None the less, Debussy held the musical rights in the play and, as Edward Lockspeiser has pointed out, Fauré would have had to ask his permission for the incidental music to be performed. (R.N.)

70 TO GEORGES HARTMANN

Cher Monsieur Hartmann Friday 16 September 1898

I was really very pleased to get your letter; you may take it as a compliment that for a moment I forgot this bored, depressed individual I'm carrying around with me.

As you've been unable to ward off misfortune, even living as you are with a beautiful garden and the sea nearby, how would you find the limited décor offered by a charming little apartment on the fifth floor of the rue Gustave-Doré? . . .

Not that I'm claiming to hold a record for dissatisfaction, but being a townsman is a hard life, especially when the weather insists infuriatingly on being fine and tempts melancholic souls to think about nice spots in the country.

You're going to hear, and own, the three *Nocturnes*, which together have given me more trouble than the five acts of *Pelléas*. I hope it'll be open-air music that will vibrate in the breeze of Freedom's mighty wing. (Goodness, what fine writing! . . .)

I'm dying to make the acquaintance of the cigarette-holder. Knowing you, and I can't think of any reason why you should have changed, it must be 'really cool'.

And so back to cultivating my garden of melancholy and lining up bars by the kilometre. To think one could go on drawing them till one's dying day.

Yours as ever
C.D.

71 TO PIERRE LOUŸS

Mon cher Pierre   Sunday 16 October 1898

Since you are so kindly determined not to get in touch, I employ the means you have so generously granted me . . .

Fragerolle,[1] Paul Delmet and, more relevantly, Reynaldo Hahn have been basking in glory as a result of various exhibitions at which their respective methods of displaying genius have been much praised. The public acquired there a permanent taste for bad music which, none the less, will serve admirably for good (music).

Literature profited as well and the names of Baudelaire, Verlaine, etc., became less rebarbative. As elsewhere, we live on misunderstandings – that only made for one more after all, and a less bothersome example than the one dividing France and England.[2]

So M. Achille Segard is going to give a talk on the *Chansons de Bilitis*[3] which contain, couched in marvellous language, all that is passionate, tender and cruel about being in love, so that the most refined voluptuaries are obliged to recognize the childishness of their activities compared to the fearsome and seductive Bilitis.

Tell me now, what would my three little songs add to the straightforward reading of your text? Nothing at all, my dear fellow; in fact I'd say the result would be a clumsy dispersal of the audience's feelings.

Really, what's the point of making Bilitis sing either in the major or in the minor, considering hers is the most persuasive voice in the world? You'll say 'Then why have you set it to music?' But that, my dear Pierre, is another question . . . It's for a different occasion; but believe me when I say that if Bilitis is there, let her speak without accompaniment.

[101]

I won't bother to mention all the other material difficulties like, for example, finding a young person who, to please our pale, aesthetic selves, would devote herself utterly to studying these three songs and would be content with our expressions of deep gratitude. Then there is yours truly who has the tiresome habit of scattering wrong notes from both hands whenever he has to play in front of more than two people. I've been frank and hope you'll understand. I'm not shirking but trying to act in your interests . . .

Affectionately
C.D.

[1] Georges Fragerolle had been a pupil of Ernest Guiraud and then turned to writing operettas, notably for the theatre of the Chat Noir.
[2] The Fashoda affair, in which French and British military expeditions confronted each other on the Upper Nile.
[3] Louÿs had asked Debussy to accompany a singer in his *Chansons de Bilitis* for a talk given by Achille Segard. [The songs were eventually given their first performance on 17 March 1900 by Blanche Marot, accompanied by the composer. R.N.]

72 TO RENÉ PETER[1]

Mon cher René   Monday evening 24 October 1898

Saying to someone 'You've made a mistake' has never been easy for the one who had to say it, nor pleasant for the recipient of such a terse declaration; and anyway I'm not sure what gives one the right to say someone's wrong, no matter who they are . . . Where, as in this case, it has to be said from one friend to another, well, you can imagine I thought long and hard before writing to you. My first reason for disapproving of your play[2] is that it belongs to the kind of dramatic writing I most detest. Even if one accepts the play for what it is, the characters are lacking in colour and the whole thing is sketchy and unimaginative. There are some nice moments but the structure doesn't seem to me dramatic enough; in any case I think it's going to be many a year before this kind of play yields a masterpiece! . . . I must emphasize that the everyday details of life aren't a fit subject for this kind of treatment, they're too unpleasant and too lofty at the same time. If one tries to capture their mystery or their banality in some kind of dramatic transposition one is always going to fail. Mind you, I could be wrong. Given the extraordinary success some plays have had, there is reason for you to hope. But before you get involved in this sort of business I suggest you have a word with someone who's better informed than I am and in whose judgement you can have confidence.

As I see it, any success it brought you would be misplaced and a backward step. You can and must do better than this. It's only middle-of-the-roaders who are discouraged by setbacks; the others derive new strength from them and go on to find their own true alchemy. Those are the people you should be determined to find a place among.

Yours affectionately
C.D.

[1] Peter wrote several light comedies, one of which is here criticized by Debussy. Peter had asked him to give advice about writing plays and together they planned a dramatic satire, *F.E.A.*, see letter 67.
[2] Peter relates that after *F.E.A.* had been abandoned Debussy continued to give him advice about a comedy called *Le Roman de Rosette*. This could be the play referred to here.

73 TO GEORGES HARTMANN

Cher Monsieur Hartmann   Sunday 1 January 1899

Much as I should have liked to deliver my New Year wishes to you in person, I'm anchored to my bedroom by bronchitis . . . Life has been quite full lately: I've changed apartments[1] and then Mlle Dupont,[2] *my secretary*, has resigned her position. Altogether it's been extremely disturbing, and even if one's a composer one is none the less a man. You have every reason to complain, as you won't be receiving a visit either from me or from the three *Nocturnes*; I only hope your kind heart will retain some sympathy for me.

Yours ever
C.D.

[1] Debussy had just moved to 52 rue Cardinet.
[2] This is the first news of Gaby's final departure, after a liaison lasting some five years.

74 TO PIERRE LOUŸS

Mon cher Pierre   Tuesday 16 May 1899

There can be no doubt you've written some of the most wonderful books to be found in this *fin de siècle*, but nothing nearly as surprising as the wonderful one whose opening chapter you sent me this morning, in which you ask Mademoiselle Louise Hérédia for her gracious collaboration.[1]

You will allow me to be delighted at the news and I hope I don't need to insist on the warmth of my best wishes in this respect?

I've not had the pleasure of being introduced to the organist who dispenses harmonies to the parishioners of Saint-Philippe, but I shall apply myself to writing the couple of hundred bars you ask for.[2] They may not be amazingly beautiful but at least they'll be full of brotherly affection and necessarily of some additional feeling, as it'll be the first time I've ventured into this emotional area. I'm afraid it may be the last too as I've been close to Music for so long, I don't think there's room for marriage! . . .

With deepest affection, my dear Pierre, and please offer my sincerest best wishes to the young lady who is shortly to become Madame Louise Louÿs.[3]

Yours
C.D.

[1] Louÿs had announced his engagement to the poet's daughter the day before.
[2] Debussy wrote a March, but it has not survived.
[3] The final s of Louÿs was sounded – hence in his letter to Debussy he refers to his bride succumbing to her father's poetical influence in exchanging her maiden name for one that is 'more balanced and symmetrical.' (R.N.)

75 TO GEORGES HARTMANN

Cher Monsieur Hartmann   Monday evening 3 July 1899

This last week I've been in the hands of a most determined fever. My view of life became fantastic in the extreme, veering between a desire to throw myself out of the window and wanting to become a Swiss citizen! . . . In fact I've been extremely ill, which explains why I've been so slow to thank you for keeping your promise. I was delighted to get your letter, even if the rain had washed some of the joy out of it.

I can't imagine why the superintendent of the celestial waters is determined to dispense them to you every time you set foot in Carlsbad. As far as I know you are not an untoward admirer of water, unless it appears in the form of baths. If it's any consolation, it's raining in Paris too, to the despair of the couturiers . . .

Being ill, I couldn't get to Pierre Louÿs's wedding. Apparently it was very Parisian and very aesthetical. P.L. wore a frock coat with a velvet collar, grey trousers and a mauve tie . . . As a work of art, nearer to M. Le Bargy,[1] I'd say, than to Lucian of Samothrace . . .[2]

Have you seen the list of works M. Albert Carré is intending to put on next season? There's *Louise*, something by Pierné, *Le Juif polonais*,[3] etc. I'm sure I shall be enormously interested to hear them! But what is to become of poor little *Pelléas et Mélisande*? M. Carré must be a hardhearted man not to adopt two such charming children straight away. I'm really beginning to worry about their future and soon I'll no longer be able to feed them . . . You too are their father to some extent; couldn't something be done, do you think? I'm not very good at making requests unless I'm sure in advance they won't be refused – a rather difficult and contradictory position.

You ask what I'm doing! . . . I can only tell you what I'm going to do . . . I'm going to finish *La Saulaie*, then three more Nocturnes and the *Nuits blanches*.[4] When I'm not feverish there's a young lady I love with all my heart (a blonde, naturally) with the most beautiful hair in the world and eyes which lend themselves to the most extravagant comparisons . . . In short, she's good enough to marry! . . .

Finally, I hope you're feeling less depressed. If my letter helps towards that, it's a bonus on top of the pleasure it gives me to write it, and to assure you once again of my devotion and affection.

C.D.

[1] An actor of the Comédie française, well known for his elegance.
[2] The Greek orator and philosopher. Pierre Louÿs had published a translation of his *Scenes from Courtesans' Life* in 1894.
[3] The operas by Charpentier and Camille Erlanger were indeed performed at the Opéra-comique in 1900, and Pierné's *La fille de Tabarin* in 1901.
[4] Five songs were planned to Debussy's own words, making a second volume of *Proses lyriques*. Nothing survives except the first nine bars of one of them.

76† TO LILLY TEXIER[1]

Ma Lilly adorée   Monday evening 3 July 1899

It's strangely absurd to have you so far away, sleeping like a spoilt child as you do, and me not able to get a glimpse of that exquisitely pretty scene! . . . I'm here . . . trying to kill time . . . (he's an amazingly healthy old man) as the minutes pass heavily and unvaryingly . . . there's no laughter here with Lilly gone . . .

However much I urge myself to be patient, there are things in me which cry out for you like children lost in a forest . . . Too well my mouth remembers yours, your caresses have left an indelible mark, as hot as fire, as gentle as a flower . . . I yearn for the blush of your red lips . . . And when your eyes are no longer before me I'm rather like a blind man or a poor little boat that has lost its sails — two images of an equal and irreparable sadness —

You've made me love you more than a man is allowed to, perhaps. The need to destroy myself for your greater joy becomes so violent, at times it resembles a death wish . . . And I can also love you with the winning tenderness of a child. Indeed there are no ways of loving you that my love doesn't know or can't discover.

For me, hours spent without you spell boredom multiplied a hundred times! . . . It's the imperious impatience of a love which is hungry and which will smash windows to steal its bread, it's the need to live for someone else, and it's the most beautiful thing in the world. I promise you, it had to happen like this. Let's worry only about ourselves; let's make our love strong enough to bear every responsibility cheerfully and let's never demean it with those constricting little rules fit only for nonentities. Your love is Wisdom in its most beautiful form.

I love you
Claude

[1] Rosalie Texier, known as Lilo or Lilly, was twenty-five and a mannequin with the Callot sisters. Debussy was to marry her on 19 October. There is no information on her illness, referred to here.

77 TO RENÉ PETER

Vieux loup!   Thursday 10 August 1899

When you come on Saturday try to be extremely rich, because if I don't pay my rent, people (or something resembling them) will hang themselves in fury on my doorbell!

In any case it's not a question of 50,000 francs and, in passing, forgive me for playing once again the role of 'master-sponger'. I hope it'll be the last time.

Your friend
Hamlet

[106]

14 Lilly, Debussy's first wife.

78 TO DR ABEL DESJARDINS[1]

Cher ami   4 September 1899

Following your kind offer, this is to ask whether you would come here to see my little Lilly next Wednesday, at whatever time suits you best. Apart from being adorable she's a very brave person and if her condition is serious don't hesitate to tell her so; only please don't run her down in front of me.

Yours sincerely
C.D.

[1] Debussy had met Dr Desjardins at Chausson's house. His family was related to the Fontaines.

79 TO GEORGES HARTMANN

Cher Monsieur Hartmann   Sunday 24 September 1899

I don't wish to offend you, but I *have* written: once to Carlsbad and once to Bayreuth. So in fact you haven't been without news of the 'terrible' man, as you put it so forcibly! . . .

If I haven't handed the *Nocturnes* over to the engraver, it's because of my fearful meticulousness (which I'm the first to suffer from). Then I put them aside for a time and did some work on *La Saulaie*, another nightmare: and all in the search for 'simplicity', after which people will continue to complain about my byzantine complications. But you may tell Colonne he can count on me. Talking of which, do you think it's really a good idea to play *L'Après-midi d'un faune* before the *Nocturnes*? . . . I feel it's turning into an obsession, a faun for life! etc. . . . I'd prefer Colonne to reserve a space after the *Nocturnes* for *La Saulaie* of which I have high hopes, if the imp of the Perverse[1] is good enough not to haunt my brain.

It's been a fairly miserable summer with charming compensations and I should tell you that I'm going to marry the aforementioned compensations . . . It'll take place very soon without pomp or ceremony or bad music; there's really no need to disturb the universe for such a private matter! . . .[2]

Please let me know when you're back in Paris. I would love to see you

[108]

again and I've also got some things to tell you which won't fit into this letter.

Yours affectionately, despite my 'terrible' side

C.D.

[1] The title of a story by Edgar Allan Poe.
[2] The civil marriage between Debussy and Lilly took place on 19 October. The witnesses were Pierre Louÿs, Erik Satie and Lucien Fontaine. That morning Debussy had had to give a piano lesson to Mlle de Romilly (see letter 102) so that he could pay for the wedding breakfast.

80 TO ROBERT GODET

Cher ami   5 January 1900

Your mixture of tact and unexpectedness is quite your own . . . So I wasn't surprised by your letter and was confirmed in my view of you as a very dear friend, known only to me.

I tell you the anecdotal side of my life without more ado; two events are pre-eminent; first, moving flats; second, my marriage . . . yes, really, and you may remain seated! Mademoiselle Lilly Texier has exchanged her inharmonious name for that of Lilly Debussy, much more euphonious as I'm sure everybody will agree . . .[1] She is unbelievably fair, pretty as someone out of a story-book, and in addition not in the least 'modern style'.[2] Her tastes in music are not formed according to the latest pronouncements of 'Willy' H.G.V.,[3] only by her own likes and dislikes. Her favourite song is a round about a grenadier with rosy cheeks who wears his hat over one ear like an old trooper . . . It's indescribable and not exactly challenging.

I've started working again, something my brain has got out of the habit of doing in its moribund, depressed state and, I'm sorry to say, without any commission in the offing.

I'm working on La Saulaie, a poem by D. G. Rossetti – I'm sure I must have mentioned it to you? It's very fine, very 'alive', and one can even put a bit of one's own life into it, together with a few hairs . . .

I've finished the Trois Nocturnes, which you've heard bits of. I'm sorry you won't be there at the first performance, which takes place in a few weeks' time . . . Your presence would have given some point to a boring, senseless occasion! Life is full of bizarre consequences!

I had a visit from a young friend of yours, M. Jules Christen, who is

[109]

amazingly ugly; but very polite, even if a trifle early. He gives the impression of not knowing quite how to play his ugliness. Naturally I did what I could for him but I haven't heard any more; I hope he'll forgive me for not being either eminent or influential.

Those are the most urgent things I have to say to you, together with my eager desire to see you soon and at length . . .

Please give my best wishes to Mme Godet, and to you my fondest thoughts as always.

C.D.

I look forward very much to meeting your friend Rist.[4]

1   This reads like a parody of Pierre Louÿs, see letter 74 footnote 3.
2   In English in the original. (R.N.)
3   On Henri Gauthier-Villars, known as Willy, see letter 58 footnote 1.
4   The doctor Edouard Rist.

81 TO PIERRE LOUŸS

Cher Pierre   Tuesday 6 February 1900

I was at the rehearsal of 'the Charpentier family'! . . . which makes it very much easier to understand the forcefulness of your letter.[1] It was a necessity, I think, for this work to be written, performed and applauded. It fills to perfection the need for vulgar beauty and imbecile art proclaimed by the many . . .

Note how this man Charpentier takes the 'cries of Paris' (charming, natural, picturesque) and like a filthy Prix de Rome winner turns them into chlorotic cantilenas with harmonies which, to be polite, I'll call parasitic. Saints above, it's a thousand times more conventional than *Les Huguenots*[2] and even uses the same means, without appearing to! And they call that 'Life'! Heavens, I'd rather drop dead on the spot. It's the sentimentality of a gentleman returning home around four in the morning and being moved to tears by the sight of the roadsweepers and the rag-and-bone men – and he thinks he can record the souls of the poor!!! It's so stupid you have to be sorry for him.

Naturally Monsieur Mendès finds traces of Wagner in it and Monsieur Bruneau an opportunity to magnify Zola. Total: a really French work. There's something wrong with the arithmetic, that's for sure. It's more a question of stupidity than evil intentions; only people don't like beauty because it's a nuisance and doesn't accommodate itself to their nasty little souls. Many more works like *Louise* and there'll be no hope of pulling them out of the mud.

I assure you I'd be delighted if *Pelléas* was played in Japan. It'd be the same sort of people who'd welcome it, in the name of elegance and eclecticism. Frankly, I'm ashamed of the whole thing.

Thanks for you nice letter and see you soon, I trust!

Yours
C.D.

[1]   The première of Charpentier's *Louise* took place at the Opéra-comique on 2 February. Louÿs was there and in his letter to Debussy, written that same evening, complained that because he was in a box as somebody else's guest he had been unable to whistle. (R.N.)
[2]   An opera by Meyerbeer.

82 TO GEORGES HARTMANN

Cher Monsieur Hartmann   Sunday 4 March 1900

Lilly Debussy and Claude Debussy thank you for your timely good wishes . . .

You need a strong stomach to swallow Richard Strauss's *Ein Heldenleben*,[1] even so it's a good solid piece. Clearly his view of the beerhouse is loftier than Charpentier's and his hero is better acquainted with Nietzsche than with *la Goulue*.[2] And it all passed off without any kind of fuss . . . This man has something of the wild animal tamer about him.

Thank you again and best wishes from 'us both'.

Yours
C.D.

P.S. You've no idea how pleased I was to see the pretty jacket you've put on the *Three Nocturnes*. I have a specially receptive spot for things like that which is not often reached.
P.S.P.S. If it would make you happy to pay me a visit at 4 o'clock on Thursday, please consider my house your own.

[1]   On the afternoon of this letter Richard Strauss had conducted his symphonic poem at the Concerts Lamoureux.
[2]   The pseudonym of the dancer Louise Weber, 1870–1929. She was the star of many Parisian shows and Toulouse-Lautrec drew her portrait.

Cher Monsieur Hartmann   Tuesday evening March 1900

Having only one performance doesn't upset me unduly, it could even be a way of leaving the audience of the Concerts Colonne intrigued and wanting more! What bothers me is how little rehearsal time there is! This man (Colonne) doesn't know the first note of the *Nocturnes*. What is he going to do?[1] And then there are the Sirens? They sing things in which enthusiasm is absolutely no substitute for accuracy? These question marks are loaded with menace and I should like to know what you think. These *Nocturnes* in every sense belong to you and are dedicated to you! There mustn't be any miscalculation.

Yours affectionately
CD

[1] In the event the performance never took place, but see letter 89.

84 TO PIERRE LOUŸS

Mon cher Pierre   Wednesday 25 April 1900

I write this lying down, not because it's more convenient but because of heart trouble, a charming illness which I hope won't develop more than is convenient.

I couldn't of course be with Hartmann either during his last hours or at his funeral service. I feel a real sorrow at his death – he was a lucky find for me and he played his part with a smile and a good grace you don't often come across among philanthropists of art.[1]

I've no idea what'll happen to *Pelléas*, but it seems he's left his affairs in good order. General Bourjat is his executor.[2]

As for the miserable, frustrated state your life's in, I don't understand it. Damn it, you mustn't forget you're Pierre Louÿs, so be kind enough not to be awkward with me. At the risk of saying something stupid (much better than thinking it), *Le Roi Pausole*[3] shows a change of rhythm in your writing – I don't know whether the second is better than the first (I'm not one for competitions and classifications) but I'm sure it's a very good idea to do an about-turn from time to time; we all have a tyrant inside us and we have to find ways of knocking him on the head. For the moment it would be better if you would set your mind to being a bit calmer and stop thinking you have to act as a lighthouse for those walking late at night along the Boulevard Malesherbes. And what about one attractive Madame Pierre Louÿs who must be dying of worry?

I dare say all this is rather rambling, but I can assure you if I wasn't so tired there'd be a lot more of it.

Yours as ever
Claude.

[1] Debussy's publisher had died on 22 April.
[2] He was Hartmann's nephew and heir and insisted on Debussy paying back advances that had been agreed. Fromont bought up his stock of manuscripts and printed scores in 1902.
[3] Louÿs's novel, *Les aventures du Roi Pausole*, was being serialized in *le Journal* until 7 May. (R.N.)

85 TO PIERRE LOUŸS

Mon cher Pierre   14 May 1900

Since nothing can conquer your determination not to be there when I come and see you (you push perversity to the lengths of going to Le Havre!) here are a few indignant words.

I'd like to have said something about *Le Roi Pausole*, which I think is a *tour de force* from many points of view, but that doesn't fit in with my indignation . . . I must tell you that Hartmann left his affairs in total and complete chaos and that your poor friend Claude is at present without a publisher; and there's the further complication of a botched-up contract no one, not even God himself, would want to renew. Fate is certainly having a merry time with me! . . . I find the only publisher who can adjust himself to my delicate little soul and he has to go and die!!! I'm not a bad man but I'd like to give the whole of Nature a good pummelling . . . not to mention the people Hartmann restrained somewhat from declaring themselves my enemies. It's not exactly amusing and it's important Lilly doesn't have to bear too much of it; so I conjure up smiles which feel like tears and remain none the less,

Your
Claude

Mademoiselle   Friday 24 August 1900

I didn't want to come and see you after the concert because I was afraid I wouldn't be able to find the right words to say how grateful and how moved I was. I don't think anyone else could have sung *La Damoiselle élue* with so much feeling, sensitivity and sincerity. At times you were able to escape so totally from the material environment, it became other-worldly, and the way you delivered the words 'Tout ceci sera quand il viendra' remains one of the most profound musical experiences of my life, something I'm sure I shall never forget.

So please accept my deepest gratitude. And I'm sure a certain someone else must have been pleased too – no need to name him . . .

Lilly Debussy asks me to convey to you her admiration and, as soon as she can walk,[2] the two of us will come and thank you personally.

Hoping you will forgive me for not being able to express all I feel,

Yours sincerely
C.D.

[1]   Mlle Marot had just sung in *La Damoiselle élue* at one of the official concerts of the Universal Exhibition at the Trocadéro. She had also given the first performance of the *Chansons de Bilitis* on 17 March.
[2]   Lilly had suffered a miscarriage and had been in a clinic from 14 to 23 August.

87 TO PIERRE LOUŸS

Mon cher Pierre   Saturday 25 August 1900

Forgive me for being so slow in replying to your nice letter. I'm afraid various unpleasant occurrences will serve as excuses. Lilly has been in Dubois's clinic and was operated on several days ago, but that's not all; it seems her body in general is in a poor state and (between ourselves) she has tubercular patches at the top of both lungs. We are having to take immediate steps to deal with these, namely sending her to the Pyrenees for three or four months! You can imagine what a torment it's all been, quite apart from my financial situation, desperate as usual! I don't know any more how to cope with so many contradictory events.

I hope your stay in the gloom of Bourboule does you good – you really must follow the cure meticulously, but I won't take advantage of my seniority[1] to play the schoolmaster!

[114]

15 Debussy in Pierre Louÿs's apartment around 1900 photographed
   by Louÿs.

You have too many things still to say to allow yourself to be thwarted by some stupid illness.

My best wishes to Madame Pierre Louÿs.

Yours as ever
C.D.

¹ Debussy was the elder of the two by eight years. (R.N.)

88 TO PIERRE LALO¹

Monsieur   Monday 27 August 1900

Many years ago now I was forcibly removed from the Opéra for being too energetic in demonstrating my admiration for that charming masterpiece *Namouna*.²

Your father discovered wonderful harmonies, still considered as being dangerously explosive by some people, and there was also the magic his artistry exercised over some of us − an artistry that shone brightly, so different from the usual dishonesty you find in composers (if 'dishonesty' seems to you a trifle strong, let's say 'talent'.) Why are they remembered and he forgotten? That's magic too, but the nasty sort. So I thank you for your kind words about *La Damoiselle élue*; you will readily understand why I was so touched by them.

Yours sincerely
C.D.

¹ Pierre Lalo was the son of the composer Edouard Lalo and, as music critic of *Le Temps*, was one of the most influential voices in Parisian musical life. He supported Debussy until *Pelléas* but then changed his position, see letter 133.
² A ballet by Edouard Lalo, given at the Opéra rather unsuccessfully on 6 March 1882.

89† TO PIERRE LOUŸS

Mon cher Pierre   [6 December 1900]

No news from *Le Journal*, which at the moment suits me very well. The *Nocturnes* are due to be performed on Sunday by Chevillard.¹ Of course I'm at sixes and sevens and I'm also getting up early, which never does me any good. Seeing the sunrise is as much fun for me as having a hangover! Anyway, I hope you'll be there on Sunday; I think you'll like the *Nocturnes* more than most people. They're playing Liszt's *Faust Symphony* in the same programme – food and drink for a whole generation of composers, and a lesson in orchestration too. Chevillard is as charming as a cageful of bears and has really and truly taken over from his father-in-law.[2]

Yours
Claude

[1] Camille Chevillard was the conductor of the Concerts Lamoureux. 'Nuages' and 'Fêtes' were first performed on 9 December 1900, 'Sirènes' not until 27 October 1901 because it was not possible for Chevillard to have a female chorus.
[2] Chevillard took over the Concerts Lamoureux from the founder, Charles Lamoureux, after marrying his daughter.

90 TO PAUL DUKAS

Monday evening
Cher ami   [11 February 1901]

Thank you for your kindness in sending me your symphony; and your article on the *Nocturnes*[1] fills me with pride.

Your pen is normally more expansive but, may I say, there emanates from its underlying silence a persuasive force born of what amounts to a practically unique act of empathy. But then to have intelligence at the service of complete understanding is a luxury you're used to. None the less one has to mention these things from time to time, as they tend unfortunately to be out of place in casual conversation. In fact the music of 'Fêtes' was based, as always, on distant memories of a festival in the Bois de Boulogne; the 'ghostly procession' was, on that occasion, made up of cuirassiers! ... You won't hold it against me if in the meantime the trumpets have been muted and Liane de Pougy[2] is no longer present. The fanfares can be left in barracks and Liane de Pougy to the mercies of the immortal composer of *Louise*. Talking of which, have you noticed that since this opera was put on old clothes sellers are no longer giving their traditional cry; they're probably afraid Charpentier will make them pay royalties.

Anyway it's high time these poor, defenceless popular tunes were left in peace – they've never done anything to deserve the symphonic treatment!

To you, possessed of a brain of steel and a cold, blue, unbending will

[117]

(guarantees of your influence on the twentieth century, both now and later), to you I confess that I am no longer thinking in musical terms, or at least not much, even though I believe with all my heart that Music remains for all time the finest means of expression we have. It's just that I find the actual pieces – whether they're old or modern, which is in any case merely a matter of dates – so totally poverty-stricken, manifesting an inability to see beyond the work-table. They smell of the lamp, not of the sun. And then, overshadowing everything, there's the desire to amaze one's colleagues with arresting harmonies, quite unnecessary for the most part. In short, these days especially, music is devoid of emotional impact. I feel that, without descending to the level of the gossip column or the novel, it should be possible to solve the problem somehow. There's no need either for music to make people *think*! (The thinking most people do on this topic, even the best educated of them, is beneath serious consideration more often than not.) It would be enough if music could make people *listen*, despite themselves and despite their petty, mundane troubles, and never mind if they're incapable of expressing anything resembling an opinion. It would be enough if they could no longer recognize their own grey, dull faces, if they felt that for a moment they had been dreaming of an imaginary country, that's to say one that can't be found on the map.

Please add to the above all the things I've forgotten or can't express.

Yours ever
C.D.

When do we see you?

[1] In his column in the *Revue hebdomadaire* (February 1901), Dukas gave his opinion of the first performance of the *Nocturnes*. After admitting that as a composer Debussy was 'unclassifiable', he declared his preference for 'Nuages' and wondered whether, in 'Fêtes', the music had preceded the programme or vice versa. He ended up by complaining that the absence of a female chorus had prevented the performance of 'Sirènes'.
[2] Anna-Marie Chassaigne, known as Liane de Pougy, was a courtesan famous in Paris society for her beauty. See also letter 108 footnote 3.

Pelléas et Mélisande

On 3 May 1901 Debussy finally received Albert Carré's promise that *Pelléas* would be produced the following season. He hurriedly set to work revising the orchestration and, despite the last-minute problems caused by Maeterlinck over the casting, one of the masterpieces of French opera was given its première on 30 April 1902 with André Messager conducting. Although the critics were divided, *Pelléas* was supported from the start by a handful of friends and young musicians and became a real success, bringing Debussy sudden recognition. He defended his ideas on music in the columns of the *Revue blanche* (under the title 'M. Croche'), and later in *Gil Blas*. He was just 40 years old.

91 TO PIERRE LOUŸS

5 May 1901

As you are still . . . good old Pierre! I wouldn't like you to hear from a third party that: *I have a written guarantee from M. A. Carré* that he will put on *Pelléas et Mélisande* next season. All of which is surely no reason for you not deigning to tell me of your return?

Yours
C.D.

92† TO RAOUL BARDAC[1]

[Bichain][2]
Cher ami   Saturday 31 August 1901

As you see, I'm in no doubt about the form of address we should use in our letters. So in future please do the same.

My delay in replying certainly doesn't stem from any sort of indifference to the delicate feelings expressed in your letter; it's just that here in Bichain – and I'm sorry to think we shan't be seeing you – the minutes go past without one realizing.

I get the feeling, above all psychologically, of being at the opposite end of the earth from Paris. The nasty little fever that besets us all more or less can't wreak its havoc here – it dies of its own accord, and without a doubt the interplay between trees and riverbanks is a less impoverished counterpoint than ours; what's more, one finds good reasons not to be disagreeable . . . But if the setting's beautiful, one has

[120]

16 Albert Carré, director of the Opéra-comique.
Bibliothéque nationale.

to admit the people are less so; no need to tell you that 'the sower's proud gesture'[3] has been totally forgotten and when the Angelus gently enjoins the fields to sleep you never see anyone taking up solemn, lithographic attitudes[4] ... What you tell me about *Hérodiade*[5] is certainly all to your credit ... Time spent carefully creating the atmosphere in which a work of art must move is never wasted. As I see it, one must never be in a hurry to write things down. One must allow the complex play of ideas free rein: how it works is a mystery and we too often interfere with it by being impatient – which comes from being materialistic, even cowardly, though we don't like to admit it.

Thank you for the Quartet . . .[6] How to repay such a debt I don't know, unless simply by saying you can count on me, but then I don't imagine I shall ever be 'influential'. I've been too thorough in cultivating my indifference to my fellow human beings, which is probably the only way one can choose between them.

I'll be back in Paris around 10 September. I'm afraid there'll be more people pestering me than usual – which is to say, if you come and see me one evening it'll make me forget how tired I am.

> Affectionately
> C.D.

[1]　See letter 134, note 1, p. 167.
[2]　Bichain par Villeneuve-la-Guyard, a village in the Yonne district. His father-in-law had retired to it and Debussy spent several summers there between 1901 and 1904.
[3]　A line of Victor Hugo.
[4]　An allusion to Millet's pictures *L'Angélus* and *Les Glaneuses*.
[5]　The opera by Massenet.
[6]　Bardac had made an arrangement of Debussy's Quartet.

93　TO PAUL-JEAN TOULET[1]

> Cher ami　　　　　　　　　　　　　　　　　　7 November 1901

The lady who admitted to you, in a place this white paper would rather not mention, that she preferred Fontenailles[2] to Debussy was a very sensitive person, refusing to allow any discordant combinations to invade her feelings; if you see her again, present my compliments. The kindly attitude you, out of friendship, show towards my music could have had an opportunity of manifesting itself some Sundays ago at the Lamoureux concerts. They played my *Nocturnes* and some of the audience took this as an excuse for some vigorous whistling, especially

in the third one. This partiality for the other two annoys me slightly . . .
even so I think you would have enjoyed their voluptuous rhythms (No
whistling! . . .). I wrote to Monsieur Alioth and offer you my gratitude
for this brief outburst of provincial enthusiasm.

The best news of all, I trust, is that you'll be back in Paris soon.

> Yours as ever
> C.D.

[1] Toulet was a shy, imaginative, desperate poet in the mould of Laforgue. His
masterpiece, the volume of *Contrerimes*, was not published until after his death. Debussy
had known him since 1899 and was to be a more intimate friend of his after *Pelléas*.
According to René Peter, Debussy called Toulet 'that delicate grasshopper with faded
colours'.
[2] Count Hercule de Fontenailles, a composer of light ditties. In 1905 both he and
Debussy contributed to a volume of settings of poems by Paul Gravollet.

94 TO RENÉ PETER

> Cher ami   27 January 1902

The Maeterlinck business is settled and Carré agrees with me that his
attitude is little short of pathological.[1] But there are still nursing homes
in France.

> Yours
> C.D.

[1] Maeterlinck had been insisting that his mistress, Georgette Leblanc, take the role of
Mélisande. The rehearsals of *Pelléas* began on 11 January. On 14 April Maeterlinck was
to state to *Le Figaro* that the work was now 'alien' to him and that he hoped it would be
an 'immediate and resounding disaster'.

95 TO ALBERT CARRÉ

> Cher ami   Tuesday [March 1902]

Please forgive me for not replying at once to your charming and . . .
helpful letter. Living as I do like a machine with steam up, civility
disappears but friendship remains (at 58 rue Cardinet). Jusseaume[1],
after kicking up a lot of dust, has decided to come round to my way of
thinking, so things shouldn't be too bad! I'm going to Ronsin's[2] today
to see the rest of the models; let's hope God will support me in this new

trial of strength. Until tomorrow, with my warmest good wishes,

Yours
C.D.

[1] A designer at the Opéra-comique from 1898 to 1924. The critics thought of him as a creator of poetic landscapes, but he belonged to the traditional realist school.
[2] Eugène Ronsin was well known for his collaboration with a number of designers.

96 TO PAUL-JEAN TOULET

Cher ami   2 April 1902

Claude Debussy proposes and M. Messager disposes ... About 10 o'clock yesterday evening the aforementioned gentleman arrives to ask me for a linking section of 75 bars in the second act of *Pelléas* ... naturally he had to have them straight away so that was the end of the pleasant evening I was looking forward to.

Please forgive this disruption, none of my doing, and let's make it good as soon as we can.

Yours
C.D.

[1] Orchestral rehearsals of *Pelléas* had started on 8 March. By 2 April most of the sets had been tried out on the stage.

97 TO HENRY BAUER[1]

Mon cher maître   8 May 1902

Thank you for your splendid article on *Pelléas*. You will never know what a great solace it has been for me among so much detestable stupidity, as well as a valuable reward for twelve years of work.[2] I am proud to have been the recipient of such generous opinions from such a distinguished source.

My thanks again, together with my warm admiration
C.D.

[1] A reporter and critic, Bauer fought for the transformation of the theatre and was known in France especially for his support of Ibsen's dramas. Of *Pelléas* he wrote in *Le Figaro*: 'Today or tomorrow, Debussy's score will make its mark ...'
[2] Debussy exaggerates by three.

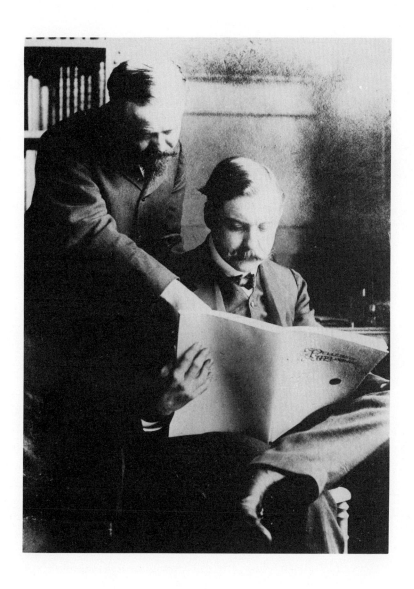

17 Maurice Maeterlinck having his attention drawn by Paul Dukas to
details of Debussy's score of *Pelléas et Mélisande*.

Mon cher ami   Friday 9 May 1902

Since you left[1] I've been about as gloomy as a path where feet no longer tread . . . I miss you all the time. Not exactly sensible, given our present topographical situations . . . But I won't bore you with my complaints. Let's talk a bit about *Pelléas* instead . . .

On Thursday we had to have a tidying-up session for Busser[2] – between ourselves, the directors of the Opéra-comique might have allowed him one complete rehearsal. He was nervous and didn't seem to know which end of the score to take hold of. Périer's voice seemed to be coming out of his umbrella! While Mademoiselle Garden[3] absolutely refused to look at the aforementioned Busser on the grounds that she was accustomed to looking at someone infinitely more to her liking – an opinion hard to contradict. All in all the impression was vague and foggy. Who knows what will happen next?

On Friday a splendid audience, including Monsieur Jean de Reszke.[4] They waited respectfully for Busser to arrive, looking like a man heading for a cold bath and not relishing the prospect . . . (The orchestra was splendid, carrying him along and prompting him to observe nuances . . .) He paid no attention whatever to the singers and threw chords at their feet without the least concern for harmonic propriety. Anyway it all sorted itself out more or less and after Act IV three curtains calls rewarded all these excellent people for their efforts.

In short: a good evening in which the only thing lacking was you . . . and a wholly irremediable omission it was! To explain: you knew how to bring the music of *Pelléas* to life with a tender delicacy I dare not hope to find elsewhere, sure as I am that in all music the interior rhythm depends on the interpreter's evocation of it, as a word depends on the lips that pronounce it . . . So your interpretation of *Pelléas* was deepened by the personal feelings you brought to it and from which stemmed that marvellous effect of 'everything in its place'. You know as well as I do, that's something you can't improve on. I'm only reawakening my regrets, I know, but too bad! You should know once and for all how I feel.

Yours most sincerely
C.D.

P.S. I'll write again on Sunday. Madame Debussy sends her best wishes.

[126]

18 André Messager, the conductor of the première of
Pelléas et Mélisande.

She had the honour of a visit from Mademoiselle Madeleine Messager and I think the two of them will be seeing more of each other in future.

¹ As well as being the composer of *Les deux pigeons* and *Véronique*, from 1898 Messager had been musical director of the Opéra-comique and the conductor to whom new works were entrusted. He was at the same time artistic director at Covent Garden, to which he was recalled after the première of *Pelléas*.
² Henri Busser, who had been a pupil of Guiraud and had won the Prix de Rome in 1893, was the chorus-master at the Opéra-comique. This was his first appearance on the conductor's podium.
³ The creators of the two name parts: Jean Périer and the 25-year-old Scottish singer Mary Garden.
⁴ A tenor of Polish origin, de Reszke had made his début in 1874 and went on to enjoy a brilliant career in London and New York, and then at the Paris Opéra. 1902 was the year he stopped singing in opera and turned to teaching.

99 TO ROBERT GODET

13 June 1902

It is I, Claude Debussy . . . though that's nothing to be proud of.

You will never know the remorse I feel at having treated you in such an indescribable manner. The great love I bear you only makes things worse for me! To tell you the truth, I'm suffering fatigue to the point of neurasthenia, a de luxe illness I never believed in till now. But I can only think that the labour and nervous strain of these last months have finally got the better of me, if I can't bear to write to Godet . . . I'm taking advantage of a moment when I'm feeling less etiolated than usual to beg you not to be offended and to rest assured that nothing is rotten in the state of Denmark.

As for your article,[1] I can't really thank you for it, it would sound like an insult . . . and anyway your sensitivity and understanding and your indefectible love of Beauty have been known to me too long for me to be surprised that you have simply behaved in character . . . Even so, in this case there is also a personal happiness at hearing words which only you could say, with the promise of a truth wholly and lastingly understood. That is as rare as the work itself.

To return to narrative, I may say the General[2] is making my life extremely uncomfortable and I foresee a string of legal documents stretching away into the future! It's a game I'm not well prepared for and to which I bring nothing, you might say, but innate incompetence.

I haven't been able to do anything about Dr Rudolf Louis,[3] for the

[128]

19 Photograph of Debussy taken on 11 September 1905.

reasons stated above: it's probably too late now and all my fault, which is no consolation!

I really can't wait for the *Pelléas* performances to finish! It's time they did, I may say: it's beginning to sound like a repertory opera! The singers are improvising, the orchestra's getting heavy (quite a *tour de force* of the fantastic and the unbelievable) and before long they'd be doing better to turn to *La Dame Blanche*.[4]

I'll write to you again in a few days when I'm in less of a hurry. For the moment I'd like you to get this as soon as possible.

Madame Debussy was very touched by your wife's letter and sends her affectionate greetings. Please remember me to Madame Godet.

>   Your true friend as ever
>   C.D.

[1] Godet's article on *Pelléas* had just appeared in *La·musique en Suisse*.
[2] General Bourgeat, the executor of the will of Debussy's late publisher Hartmann, was trying to get the composer to repay all the advances he had received.
[3] A German critic and author of various harmony textbooks.
[4] Boieldieu's opera had remained in the repertory almost continuously since its première in 1825.

100 TO ANDRÉ MESSAGER

>   Très cher ami   Wednesday 9 July 1902

My heart is not made of bronze . . . And your letter reminds me so much of happy times that I find it quite impossible to resist what you suggest. So I'll be taking the 9 o'clock train on Saturday evening and the chances are that on Sunday I'll at last be seeing your friendly face once again.[1]

The success of 'our Garden' doesn't surprise me;[2] you'd have to be wearing ear-stoppers to resist the charm of her voice, surely? Personally, I can't imagine a gentler or more insinuating timbre. It's tyrannical in its hold on one – impossible to forget.

My dear Messager, there's so much I have to tell you, I haven't the patience to put it all on paper . . . When I think that I'll be seeing you on Sunday, my heart beats madly in the depths of my throat[3] (if Maeterlinck will allow me to express myself after his manner).

But enough empty literature. My wife joins me in sending fondest best wishes.

>   Yours
>   C.D.

[130]

Please will you embrace Mélisande on behalf of both of us and thank her for the charming letter I received this morning?

1   Debussy joined Messager in London on 11 July for a few days.
2   Mary Garden was singing at Covent Garden. (R.N.)
3   A quotation from Act IV, scene 4 of *Pelléas*. (R.N.)

101   TO LILLY DEBUSSY-TEXIER

Très chère petite femme   London 16 July 1902

Your letter cheered me up immensely. In spite of everything I feel lonely and no longer to hear your commanding voice call 'Mî-Mî' makes me as melancholy as a guitar. I was very touched by your lack of courage. It's all very well to be the brave little woman, but there are times when the brave little woman needs to have her weaknesses. It adds an extra charm to her attractions. All of which is very nice, but not worth your left little toe. Would you believe, it's impossible to find a reasonable cup of tea? I wish I were back in the rue Cardinet with my little wife, who includes tea-making among her other gifts! You don't find women like that in England. They're fit to be the wives of horse-guards, with complexions the colour of uncooked ham and the allure of a young animal. They're ferociously perfumed and give themselves airs enough to make a street-walker gasp. All in all you probably have to travel sometimes if only to prove you'd have done better to stay at home. But I question whether I needed to undergo the tortures of absence to satisfy myself I couldn't do without you. Logical, but an operation on my morale I could happily have forfeited.

Messager and Mary Garden send their best wishes. I will stop now, as it's making me sad. I love my Lilo very much.

Your Claude

102   TO MME GÉRARD DE ROMILLY[1]

Chère Madame   [around 1902]

I have only got back to Paris today and, as letters weren't being forwarded, yours didn't reach me until now.

About the music . . . I really don't know what to say! It's difficult to talk about something incomplete in which you feel the underlying thought hasn't been expressed, deliberately or otherwise!

As it stands, it's a curious mixture and reminds me of certain American drinks made up of vegetables, champagne, fruit, etc. You can't tell whether they're excellent or revolting, but you drink them out of astonishment.

Not a watertight comparison, as I'm sure you'll appreciate . . . As for harmonizing this music or orchestrating it, that's a problem which can be solved only by the person who wrote it. You can't wrap music up like sweets! A musical ideal contains its own harmony (or so I believe); otherwise, the harmony is merely clumsy and parasitical. All the same there's something here and I look forward to hearing from you if you're interested. I'm glad it gave me the opportunity of hearing your news and Madame Debussy sends you her best wishes. We hope in any case to see you in Paris soon and I trust you won't forget your old teacher and his affection for you.

C.D.

Please remember me to your husband.

[1] Born Worms de Romilly, she married a General Gérard in 1902. From 1898 to 1908 she was one of Debussy's rare singing and piano pupils (cf. *Cahiers Debussy* nouvelle série no. 2, Paris, 1978), and he dedicated the 'Prélude' from *Pour le piano* to her. The music mentioned here consisted of songs an army officer had collected from the Bambara tribe in the Niger basin!

103 TO PAUL-JEAN TOULET

Cher ami   21 October 1902

The only reason I've been so slow in replying is the number of rehearsals we've had to have for the revival of *Pelléas* . . . They've taken up most of my time and knocked me out for the duration of what was left. And although I readily forgive you for not coming to see me before you left, I confess to being mildly hurt; especially as Kurne[1] tells me you won't be coming back to Paris before you set out. Let's say no more about it . . . it isn't every day one leaves for Tonkin and it'll make it all the more gratifying when we do see you again. And now, to the matter of the good Monsieur William.[2]

The second outline you sent suits me in all possible ways. Don't you think we need to make the first scene more interesting by using an off-stage choir to underline the various stages of Orlando's wrestling match? They could make comments like: 'He's done for! No, he's not! Bravo, sir! O feet of strength!'[3] But no, bad jokes aside, I think from the musical point of view it could lead to something new. For the various songs, too, I'd like to use a choir. The Duke's rich enough to pay for the Chanteurs de Saint-Gervais and their conductor to travel to the forest of Arden. We'll have to make an effective set-piece out of the wedding and end up with rejoicing. Take any chance you can find to replace the exact word with its lyrical counterpart. Which is not to say I don't like the style of the two scenes you've written: far from it; it's just in response to your fear of being too rhythmical . . . Don't worry, the music will take care of all that.

I have an idea to suggest, for what it's worth: could we not use scene 1 of Shakespeare's play, between Oliver and Charles the Wrestler, as an introduction?

Anyway, send me as much as you can before you leave, as I'm sure we're on to something splendid.

Yours
C.D.

[1]   Maurice Sailland, known as Curnonsky, was one of the group of friends who met at the Café Weber in the rue Royale.
[2]   The two of them had decided to collaborate on an adaptation of Shakespeare's *As You Like It*. The project was interrupted by Toulet's journey to Tonkin and only revived much later.
[3]   'Il n'a pas les foies gras!' (R.N.)

104 TO PAUL-JEAN TOULET

Cher ami   25 October 1902

As your arguments are better than mine, I give in without more ado. Yours is just another way of furthering my own desire to make clear the subtleties, the complexities indeed, in the plot of *As You Like It*, so I'm perfectly happy.

You don't say anything about my thoughts over the wedding ceremony, which I feel could provide a graceful ending . . . I think it could be the basis for a build-up on stage with actors in fine clothes making their entrances in a precise and rhythmical way and preparing for the arrival of Orlando's Rosalind. All that mixed with singing, but in the ancient manner, that's to say as an integral part of the action. Don't be afraid to develop the character of Touchstone; he's a man of such individual fantasy (as I'm sure you must agree?).

I'm terrified at the thought of you going so soon. You've made me so anxious to get my hands on all the details of this little human fairy story.

Don't forget me in the yellow air of Tonkin.

> Yours ever
> C.D.

105 TO PIERRE LOUŸS

> Cher Pierre   19 June 1903

You don't understand because it's so long since you saw me. Otherwise you'd realize how simple the situation is.

The things I've been upset by include a letter I wrote last year, asking if I could see you before I left for the country, which you answered in a tone of the vaguest intention . . . As far as I can see, nothing's changed since then? I haven't been able to avoid finding out, as one is bound to in such matters, that even if your door was firmly closed to me, it was open and welcoming to others. Don't worry, I won't mention them by name.

The fact that we're both newly married cannot and has no reason to change anything in our relationship. You've been too close a friend for anyone, even a *woman*, to think of affecting that. I can indeed assure you that she's as firmly your friend as I am.

So those are the cracks in the edifice . . . I'm well aware of the ridiculous sentimentality in all this. Let's just say I'm an 'affection freak' and leave it at that.

Either reply to this or come and visit us, and you'll see that you're as welcome as you ever were. And you'll find the little winged figure of Isis, too, to whom I've offered many a prayer on your behalf.

> Your friend as always
> C.D.

Très cher ami   29 June 1903

Orchestrating in a temperature of 30 degrees centigrade is taking enjoyment a little far! I can only do it, what's more, in the confines of my study. For reasons of convenience and concentration I lock my door and . . . the cool breath of the flutes does nothing to reduce the heat. That's also why I haven't yet thanked you for the fourth act of *Pelléas*. One has to be truly kind to burden oneself with a job like that.[1] God is my witness that my gratitude to you will cease only when I am dead.

Just imagine, my dear Messager, I've been listening to the Prix de Rome competition. You have no idea what goes on in that place . . . and how it breeds distaste for music. The gentlemen of the jury now find themselves in the business of handing out prizes to cantatas which don't even follow the hallowed tradition any longer but are termed 'dramatic'. And one has to sit and listen to it . . . It's enough to give you apoplexy! The distinguished candidate who got the prize this year strikes me as being Leoncavallo's best pupil.[2] Ye gods, what music! And all the artistic sensitivity of a pork butcher.

That evening I went to hear *La Guirlande*, an opera-ballet in one act by Rameau.[3] I'm sorry you weren't there! You more than anyone would have been able to appreciate this work's lifegiving delicacy.

I leave next week for Bichain. If you ever happen to be in the area . . . I needn't impress on you how happy we should both be to see you.

C.D.

I'll write to Mélisande soon. In the meantime would you embrace her for us both?

[1] Messager had been correcting the proofs of the orchestral score of *Pelléas* which was to be published by Fromont the following year.
[2] The winner of the Grand Prix de Rome in 1903 was Raoul Laparra, a pupil of Fauré, with the cantata *Alyssa*. Ravel suffered his third failure.
[3] Rameau's work was given on 22 June 1903 in the garden of the Schola Cantorum. It was on his way out from attending this performance that Debussy proclaimed: 'Long live Rameau! Down with Gluck!' See also his final article for *Gil Blas*, published on 28 June.

Bichain par Villeneuve-la-Guyard
[July 1903]

Forgive me . . . for some days I've been: the-man-who's-working-on-a-Fantasy-for-E♭-alto-saxophone[1] (try saying that three times without taking a breath . . .).

Considering this fantasy was commissioned, paid for and spent more than a year ago, you could say I'm behindhand – For one thing the idea didn't interest me greatly, and for another I wouldn't otherwise have been able to write you such a fine letter. The saxophone is a reedy animal with whose habits I'm largely unfamiliar. Is it suited to the romantic sweetness of the clarinets or the rather vulgar irony of the sarrusophone (or the contra-bassoon)? In the end I've got it murmuring melancholy phrases against rolls on the side-drum. Surely the saxophone, like the Grand Duchess, likes military men?[2] The whole thing's called 'Rapsodie arabe' . . . (long live the army, even so). The country's not boring at all, you see? The answer lies in not believing that the sun which sets on the hillsides of Bichain is any different from the one which goes to rest on the pale terraces of Biskra.

Say what you like, a volume of Villon is more use than a walking stick! And I'm all the more delighted to have it because it comes from your library; not that this makes its vocabulary any less uncouth, but from Claude Debussy's point of view it increases its value.

I've been to Sens. There's a lovely cathedral and some extremely irritating military men. We took the opportunity of having a good meal and drinking a Pommard which would make Kurnonsky's hair stand on end. That's pretty well the only outing we've had . . . To make up for this I've also written a piano piece which bears the title 'Une soirée dans Grenade'.[3] And I tell you, if this isn't exactly the music they play in Granada, so much the worse for Granada. No more need be said!

When you have a minute to spare, don't forget that you couldn't do better than devote it to me . . . You're the only person from whom I can bear to hear news about Paris. Indeed I even miss the place when I remember you're still there.

Yours as ever
C.D.

Please remember me to the delightful Madame Pierre Louÿs.

[136]

¹ The *Rapsodie* for saxophone and orchestra had been commissioned by Mrs Elise Hall, the president of the Boston Orchestral Club. Debussy gave it several titles ('fantaisie', 'rapsodie mauresque', 'rapsodie arabe') but left it unorchestrated at his death. This task was performed by Roger-Ducasse and the work was performed in May 1919.
² A reference to the rondo 'Ah! que j'aime les militaires!' in Offenbach's *La Grande-duchesse de Gerolstéin*.
³ The second of the *Estampes* for piano.

108† TO JACQUES DURAND¹

Bichain

Cher ami   Friday [August 1903]

I was just getting ready to send you the proofs . . .² You'll see, on page 8 of 'Jardins sous la pluie', there's a bar missing; my fault, in fact, as it's not in the manuscript. Even so, it's necessary from the point of view of number; the divine number, as Plato and Mlle Liane de Pougy would say, though each for a different reason, admittedly.³

I'm back in front of my manuscript paper and now my excursions go no further than round my worktable. Not everybody can be a sporting man!

You'll have to return to your piano practice if you don't want to make those nightmare *Estampes* more melancholy still by your somewhat wanton inexactitude!

I'm working at 'La Mer' . . . If God is kind to me, I'll be a good way through by the time I return.

Please give Mme Durand my best wishes.

Yours
C.D.

¹ The publisher who was to bring out almost all Debussy's music from now on. See letter 119 footnote 1.
² The *Estampes* were published the following October.
³ 'Liane de Pougy [. . .] was a well-known Parisian *demi-mondaine*. *Le divin nombre* as applied to her suggests a pun on the expression connoting 'the divine few' or 'the élite' (synonymously *le nombre des élus*), which would be consistent with her *demi-mondaine* reputation.' (R. Howat *Debussy in proportion* Cambridge University Press, 1983, p. 7 footnote 8). Obviously, there is also a grosser interpretation which cannot be altogether discounted.

Bichain
Cher ami   Thursday [August 1903]

The no. 8 is perfect ...[1] only, I think now the colour we originally chose for the lettering will be rather heavy. I offer the following combination as an ideal answer:

(*or pâle*)

    Estampes

        (*blue*)   (*blue*)

(*pale gold*) Pagodes – La Soirée dans Grenade

             (*blue*)

        Jardins sous la pluie

                (*pale gold*)

the blue to be that of the address at the top of this letter, the gold pale yellow.

To print it in gold won't be difficult or too expensive, as Ollendorf has published a number of books with that colour of cover. I'm boundlessly grateful to you for humouring my cover mania; as with all maniacs, it's a sure way to touch my heart.

    Yours ever
    C.D.

(Being as superstitious as an old crow, I won't say I'm working.)

[1] A reference to the typeface.

---

110 TO PAUL-JEAN TOULET

Bichain
Cher ami   Friday 28 August 1903

If friendship did not forbid the provoking of painful discussions, I'd have told you long ago how sad I was about your involvement with opium ... an imagination as finely balanced as yours is just the sort to suffer from it most. And now life has issued a warning, rather abruptly (as it always does), to say that this sinister drug is not for you; so it would be presumptuous of me to press the matter further. I'm delighted you're renewing your acquaintance with the characters of *As You Like It*, convinced as I am you'll be able to make something splendid out of them. I, in the meantime, have been working on *Le Diable dans le*

Beffroi;[1] forgive me, there's no ill-will at the bottom of this, it's just that, from the musical point of view, I need to bring certain ideas to fruition, and if I put them off they'll become a nuisance. In any case it won't make me forget the double debt I owe: to you as my friend, and to Shakespeare. And especially to the incomparable Rosalind. I must ask you not to fall in love with her, otherwise I might easily become jealous of your attentions.

Life in the country is singularly uneventful and I have no news. I did go to Sens. There's a lovely cathedral and soldiers in the mould of General André.[2] We took the opportunity of having an excellent meal and of drinking a Pommard which Kurnonsky would have talked about for the rest of his life.

> Yours
> C.D.

[1] There will be frequent references from here on to the two tales by Edgar Allan Poe which Debussy worked on right to the end of his life: *The Fall of the House of Usher* and *The Devil in the Belfry*. Several sketches which survive of this second project do in fact bear the date 'August 1903'.
[2] General André, the War Minister in Waldeck-Rousseau's cabinet, was making attempts to improve soldiers' living conditions.

111 TO OCTAVE MAUS[1]

Bichain

Mon cher ami   [September 1903]

I'm lingering amid autumn landscapes and forgetting all about musical protocol, including competitions, which are among its principal ornaments.

The question you put in your letter seems to me insoluble . . . As long as there are men, there'll be competitions, and whether they're open to the public or held *in camera* is six of one and half a dozen of the other, as they say.

What's more, it's devoutly to be wished that this ardour for finding ways of bringing art before the public should be cooled, otherwise there'll soon be more fake artists than real art – and I'm not even certain this moment hasn't already arrived.

Perhaps putting a stop to all publicity and prizes would be enough to set things, and people, straight and remind them of a forgotten truth . . . 'art is entirely its own reward'.

> Yours most sincerely
> C.D.

¹ After an incident at the violin competition at the Brussels Conservatoire, Octave Maus (see letter 39 footnote 6) sent out a questionnaire on the usefulness or otherwise of such occasions. The results were published in his review *L'art moderne*.

112 TO CHARLES LEVADÉ¹

Bichain

Cher ami   Friday 4 September 1903

I've no desire to write a 'history of orchestration through the ages' for you as I haven't brought the necessary documents to the country with me; and anyway the idea doesn't appeal. To be honest, you learn orchestration far better by listening to the sound of leaves rustling in the wind than by consulting handbooks in which the instruments look like anatomical specimens and which, in any case, contain very incomplete information about the innumerable ways of blending the said instruments with each other.

Your question about standard orchestral forces is a tricky one. Who can decide for you that they are exactly what you need? All the same, here they are: 3 flutes, 2 oboes, 1 cor anglais, 2 clarinets, 3 bassoons, 4 horns, 3 trumpets, 3 trombones, 1 tuba, 2 harps . . .

But take my advice, and don't burden yourself in advance with a system or a formula . . . By bar 10 you won't know what to do with it [. . .] Don't ever worry that you haven't got enough instruments! And remember above all that the brass are to be handled with extreme delicacy and are not instruments of bloodshed! Only in the ultimate extremity should a trombone blare . . . Take Wagner, who's the victim of his own system: in spite of a quartet of tubas and all the trumpets in the catalogue, the result is none the richer for them . . . And even with the examples of Berlioz, Charpentier, Ganne² and Puccini before you, don't be misled into thinking the triangle is an expressive instrument!

Don't be too envious of me, as no one will ever know how different my music really is from what people think.

If it weren't for a pinch of disdain in my make-up I might suffer, seeing how I'm categorized, so that I can't exercise the influence on music that I'd like to. But anyway it's not important [. . .]

Please believe how much I value your affection for me, in all its charming 'forwardness'; and don't hesitate to make whatever use you please of my unshakeable affection for you.

C.D.

[140]

Give my kindest regards to Mme Ch. Levadé, accompanying yourself
on the piano the while.

[1] Levadé won the Prix de Rome in 1899 and probably got to know Debussy in the days
when he was a regular customer at the Chat Noir and the Auberge du Clou. Levadé was a
friend of Erik Satie and the third *Gymnopédie* is dedicated to him.
[2] Louis Ganne, 1862–1923, was a composer of operettas. (R.N.)

113 TO ANDRÉ MESSAGER

Bichain

Cher ami   Saturday 12 September 1903

I'm by no means the 'little pig' you think . . . It's just that Fromont[1] is
by far the most determined busybody I know. When he does deign to
stir himself, you can be sure it'll be over something he'd have done
better to leave alone. Gulon[2] has had Act V for some time now – I'm
correcting the second proofs at the moment and they'll go off to him
this evening.

Talking of *Pelléas*, I'll get a clear proof of the final, corrected version
run off for you and, as Pothier[3] is so fond of you, perhaps you'd be kind
enough to ask him to make the corrections in the parts . . . Naturally I'll
stand the cost of all this.

A Quintet doesn't appear anywhere on my schedule. I'm working on
three symphonic sketches entitled: 1. 'mer belle aux îles Sanguinaires'; [4]
2. 'jeu de vagues'; 3. 'le vent fait danser la mer'; the whole to be called
La Mer.

You're unaware, maybe, that I was intended for the noble career of a
sailor and have only deviated from that path thanks to the quirks of
fate. Even so, I've retained a sincere devotion to the sea.

To which you'll reply that the Atlantic doesn't exactly wash the
foothills of Burgundy. . . ! And that the result could be one of those
hack landscapes done in the studio! But I have innumerable memories,
and those, in my view, are worth more than a reality which, charming
as it may be, tends to weigh too heavily on the imagination.

We mustn't be in too much of a hurry to cry 'Finis!' to *Le Diable* . . .
the scenario is more or less complete,[5] and I've more or less decided the
musical colouring I want to use. After that come the many sleepless
nights and a large quantity of hope.

Those people who are kind enough to expect me never to abandon
the style of *Pelléas* are well and truly sticking their finger in their eye.

[141]

Obviously they don't know that, if that were to happen, I'd turn instantly to growing pineapples in my bedroom, believing as I do that to repeat yourself is the most tiresome thing of all. Quite likely, the same people will find it scandalous that I should have abandoned Mélisande's shadows for the Devil's ironical pirouette, and will seize yet another opportunity to accuse me of being bizarre.

Don't forget your promise – we both hold you to it implacably.

> Yours most affectionately
> C.D.

My wife is quite well and sends you one of her prettiest smiles.

[1] Eugène Fromont was the publisher of *Pelléas*.
[2] A music engraver.
[3] A copyist.
[4] This title for the first movement was taken from a short story by Camille Mauclair which appeared in the *Echo de Paris illustré* in 1893. Debussy eventually changed it to 'De l'aube à midi sur la mer'.
[5] Only the scenario of *Le Diable dans le beffroi* was ever sketched out. None the less Debussy signed a contract with Durand on 14 October 1903, to cover the staging at the Opéra-comique of this 'musical tale in two acts and three scenes' based on the story by Edgar Allan Poe.

114 TO MESSRS ENOCH AND COMPANY[1]

Thursday 26 November 1903

I agree to complete the two remaining acts of *Briséis*[2] on the following conditions:
1. That my collaboration is approved by Monsieur Catulle Mendès and Chabrier's heirs.
2. That we agree in advance on the financial conditions attendant on my preparation of the score.

> I remain
> Yours faithfully
> C.D.

[1] A music publishing house directed by Wilhelm Enoch and linked with the firm of Costallat.
[2] An opera in three acts by Chabrier to a libretto by Catulle Mendès and Ephraim Mikhaël, based on Goethe's *The Bride of Corinth*. At his death in 1894 Chabrier left just the first act complete and orchestrated. Before he died he asked Vincent d'Indy to undertake the completion of the last two acts and this request was repeated by Chabrier's

20 Louis Laloy, friend and biographer.

heirs. But d'Indy refused to involve himself in something 'not even half sketched out'. The first act was given with some success at the Concerts Lamoureux in 1897, then at the Opéra in 1899. Debussy's agreement to take on the project must have been prompted largely by financial considerations.

115 TO LOUIS LALOY[1]

Mon cher ami   Sunday 3 April 1904

I've seen Mlle Marot[2] (a plumper Bilitis, but still musical); she'll sing the second *Prose lyrique* 'De grêve . . .' That should please you. I don't imagine Viñes[3] will refuse to accompany her. Would you like me to ask him? Although it seems to me you have ways of being useful to him which he can hardly be unaware of.

Have you read an article by Landormy in the *Revue bleue* in which he describes a conversation with C. Debussy? It's extraordinary that this so-called musician should have such defective hearing . . .[4]

When do I see you?

Yours ever
C.D.

P.S. Have you seen Hayot?[5]

[1] Debussy got to know Laloy shortly after *Pelléas* and remained close to him. Laloy was a critic and musicologist, specializing in Far Eastern music. He published the first French biography of the composer in 1909.
[2] See letter 86.
[3] The Spanish pianist who was to become Debussy's accredited interpreter and who had already given the first performances of the suite *Pour le piano*, on 11 January 1902, and of the *Estampes*, on 9 January 1904.
[4] Paul Landormy's inquiry into 'The Present State of French Music' appeared in the edition of 2 April. It is worth noting that this suspect article contains some of the remarks most often quoted as being Debussy's: 'the musical genius of France consists of a kind of fantasy within sensitivity' and 'music should humbly concern itself with giving pleasure'.
[5] A violinist and the founder of a well-known quartet.

Divorce
La Mer
Marriage to Emma

Lilly's kindness and naïve simplicity could not disguise her lack of culture or her bourgeois ideal of marriage. Debussy was already drifting away from her emotionally when he met Emma Bardac. She was lively and intelligent and she sang his songs. Debussy became more and more attracted by her until, in July 1904, he went off with her to Jersey and then to Dieppe, not returning to Paris until the end of September. Lilly tried to commit suicide and the news, which appeared in the press, led to many of his friends deserting him. The lovers rented a private house at 80 avenue du Bois de Boulogne. Here they were to remain and here their daughter Chouchou was born on 30 October 1905. New friends replaced old ones and Louis Laloy and Paul-Jean Toulet became very close to him. Meanwhile Debussy gave the publisher Jacques Durand the exclusive right to handle his work, in the hope of stabilizing his financial position. The critics were lukewarm in their appreciation of *La Mer* but Debussy's reputation now began to spread more widely and 'debussysme' became a talking-point.

116 TO EMMA BARDAC[1]

[express letter] Thursday [9 June 1904]

'The rain falls heavily upon the town.'[2] Would you be kind enough to grant me a few moments this afternoon? I would very much like to talk to you alone for once without counterpoint or development.

If you would like to come here that would make me extremely happy, but you must do what you want and I will be content with whatever meeting place you choose.

This is not a crazy whim but written with true feeling, and some anxiety.

> Yours ever
> C.D.

[1]   Emma, née Moyse, was seventeen when she married the banker Sigismund Bardac. She had one son by him (Raoul, a pupil of Debussy's) and one daughter (Hélène, known as Dolly). She was the inspiration behind Fauré's song cycle *La Bonne Chanson* (1894) and Debussy had just dedicated to her his *Trois Chansons de France*. In 1904 she was 42, the same age as Debussy.
[2]   A reference to Verlaine's poem, beginning 'Il pleure dans mon coeur/Comme il pleut sur la ville', set by Debussy as the second of his *Ariettes oubliées*, published first in 1888 and then in a revised edition in 1903. (R.N.)

117 TO PIERRE LOUŸS

Cher Pierre   Sunday 12 June 1904

I didn't reply immediately to your two letters because the first upset me and the second made me laugh too much . . . Anyway, I'm absolutely and entirely in agreement with you about our relationship; it's absurd,

[146]

fantastic and, what's more, incomprehensible. We're not even dead, which would at least be an excuse. Still, I wish all the time we could see each other again and our inability to organize it only makes me wish it more. I wouldn't ever ask you to climb the five storeys to my apartment – they knock too much breath out of me every day for me to do that. But in future, when you think it might be nice to see me, give me a day and a time and I'll be there, merry as a spring morning (though not as fresh, bearing in mind the white hairs I've acquired recently).[1]

We missed seeing your wife last week – particularly silly as my wife was visiting a friend in the same building. Please convey to Madame Pierre Louÿs our regrets.

> Yours as ever
> Claude

[1] As far as we know, this is one of the last letter's Debussy wrote to Louÿs. Even if they saw each other on occasion, their friendship was now at an end.

118† TO LILLY

Petite Lily-Lilo   Saturday 16 July 1904

I received your telegram over lunch . . . It made an extra dish, so to speak, and the nicest of all. Even so you must have got dreadfully hot and, though I'm pleased to know you arrived safely, I can't help wondering what sort of state the pretty parts of your poor little body must have been in? I'll say no more – this takes us out of bachelor territory.

I had dinner out, came home at 10 and worked until 3 in the morning. It went not too badly . . . at 6.30 I was woken up by what I was sure must be people digging holes in the wall, so vigorously it sounded as though they were going to break through into the bedroom. There are better kinds of alarm clock, but they come more expensive.

You mustn't think I got any pleasure out of putting you so deliberately on the train. It was hard for me! Only, for reasons I'll explain to you later, it had to be done . . . Also, I've got to find something new, otherwise my reputation will suffer; for some time I've been worried because I'm revolving in the same old circle of ideas. Now I think I've found a new path, which is why I daren't abandon it, whatever the cost. It's also a question of livelihood . . . even if I haven't always been nice to you, at least I must be supportive! In any case you couldn't bear a standard of living lower than ours is at present, so a choice had to be made between two evils . . . God grant that I've chosen the lesser of them. Life has its dangerous turning-points and in my case they're complicated by the fact that I'm both an artist (what a business!) and your husband. Try to understand me and not be resentful . . . and above all try not to miss any opportunity for laughing, as you like to so much.

> Yours passionately, tenderly
> Claude

My love to the Texiers.

119 TO JACQUES DURAND[1]

Grand-Hôtel Jersey

Cher ami   [July 1904][2]

Forgive me for being so dilatory and causing so much emotional disturbance as to provoke a telegram . . . The countryside here is marvellous, I'm at peace, which is better still, and I'm completely free to work, which hasn't been the case for a long time . . . So, if anyone has plans to appoint me Constable of St Helier – for such are the authorities called in these parts – then I'm quite ready for it.

The sea has behaved beautifully towards me and shown me all her guises. I'm still absolutely stunned (as that little silly of a Manon puts it).[3]

You'll receive by the same post the proofs of *Masques* and of *Fêtes galantes*. For the latter, please remember to print the following dedication: 'In gratitude to the month of June 1904' followed by the letters 'A.l.p.M.'[4] It's a little mysterious, but one has to make some contribution to legend!

I'll probably be back next week.

In any case, write to me *poste restante* at Dieppe from next Monday onwards.

> Yours sincerely
> C.D.

Go on telling *everybody* you don't know my address, including my dear family.

¹ Some months later Debussy was to give Durand exclusive publishing rights over his works in return for an annual income of 12,000 francs.

² Debussy had left Lilly and gone to Jersey with Emma Bardac.

³ 'Je suis encore toute étourdie' is Manon's opening aria in Massenet's opera.

⁴ 'A la petite mienne', an intimate form of address to Emma, reminiscent of a poem by Jules Laforgue, O geraniums diaphanes: 'O ma petite mienne, ô ma quotidienne . . .'

120 TO ANDRÉ MESSAGER

[Dieppe]

Très cher ami   Monday 19 September 1904

You're absolutely right to vilify me, but you have to reckon with the fact that for a time I thought you'd abandoned me and indeed it was only through Madame Messager that I learned of your friendly desire to see me when you came to Paris.

My life these last months has been bizarre in the extreme, far more than one might have wished. I'd rather spare you the details, which I find tiresome; better discussed face to face and over some of that excellent whisky of yore.

I've been working . . . not as I'd have liked . . . The result of too much worry, or perhaps of aiming too high? Never mind! I fell to earth frequently with enough bruises to keep me out of action for a good long time.

There are many reasons for this which I'll tell you one day . . . if I have the courage, because they are more than usually sad ones.

I suppose it's natural, after a certain age, to start feeling nostalgia for days gone by: I feel nostalgia for the Claude Debussy who worked so enthusiastically on Pelléas – between ourselves, I've not found him since, which is one reason for my misery, among many others.

I expect I'll see you in Paris in October, if you're back from the country by then . . . I need your friendship and support.

Yours affectionately
C.D.

121 TO ANDRÉ ANTOINE[1]

Dieppe

Cher Monsieur Antoine   20 September 1904

I am as upset as you are by the long delay and, above all, at the surprising announcement that the première of *Lear* is to take place so soon. Still, I'm, sure you agree we must make the best of it. In spite of your understandable desire to have the first night on 1 October, could you not, in view of the unfortunate state of things, trip the production up slightly and delay its progress? This would give time for the music to be organized — not that it has claims to enhance Shakespeare's reputation, but even so it's got to be there, surely? It would be a matter of eight days altogether. I hope you won't take it amiss if I say that such a delay would in no sense affect your customary punctiliousness any more than your habit of keeping your word. Otherwise I must in all honesty admit I do not see how I can have the music ready for 1 October. Bear in mind that, the writing of the music apart, the players will have to rehearse at least twice before they reach the orchestra pit!

Talking of which, can you promise me *thirty players*? Will the pit be large enough? It's the least I can get away with. Otherwise it'll be a wretched, ridiculous little noise like flies rubbing their back legs together!

No need to say how impatient I am to have your reply and how sorry I shall be if I have to turn down a project I'm so keen on; not to mention the pleasure of working with you.

Yours sincerely
C.D.

[1] René Peter acted as intermediary between Debussy and the director of the Théâtre libre. Two extracts from Debussy's incidental music survive, a 'Fanfare' and 'Le sommeil de Lear', but they were not used in Antoine's production, for which Edmond Missa finally provided the music.

122 TO JACQUES DURAND

Mon cher ami   [January 1905]

Forgive me for being so slow in replying to your two letters. But apart from working without respite I'm being hounded by the press campaign Madame Debussy has been kind enough to launch against me.[1] It seems I'm not allowed to get divorced like anybody else . . .

21 Debussy at Pourville in 1904 with Emma.

My position is quite simple: I want to be left in peace and not be a party to material complications which contain no possibility of a clear solution.

I'll be back towards the end of the month and will make a point of coming to see you as soon as I can.

> Yours ever
> C.D.

1   On 3 January *Le Figaro* published an inaccurate report that Lilly had tried to commit suicide a second time.

123 TO LOUIS LALOY

> Mon cher ami   Friday 14 April 1905

First of all, may I say I have regarded you as a friend throughout! And now your friendship has become still dearer to me thanks to your simple – but precious – gesture in writing to me as you have, with a sympathy and understanding which you obviously feel too strongly not to express. I've had to look on as desertions take place all round me . . . ! Enough to make me feel I've been stripped of anything one could call human. Even so I've been wanting for a long time to write to you (telepathy is no children's game, that's for sure) telling myself that you could not be like the others and putting my trust in the memory of past conversations in which we went somewhat beyond exchanging mere words!

I won't give you an account here of what I've been through: unpleasant, tragic and at times with an ironical similarity to light romantic fiction ... All in all it's been enough to depress me thoroughly. Was there some debt to life I had to repay? I don't know . . . but often I had to smile in case people suspected I might be about to burst into tears.

So you need be in no doubt how glad I am to find you still a friend; I'll also try and rediscover the Claude Debussy you used to know . . . if he's a little bowed down with care, I hope you'll forgive him and think rather of his friendship for you, which remains unshakeable.

> C.D.

Would you like to come and see me at 3 o'clock next Monday, at *10*

[152]

avenue Alphand? I'm sorry to be so particular, but I'm often out and I wouldn't want to miss you.

The avenue Alphand runs between sinister flanks of dressed stone into the rue Duret (avenue de la Grande Armée).

124 TO GABRIEL FAURÉ

Mon cher ami   Wednesday 28 June 1905

Forgive me for not writing earlier to offer you my congratulations . . .[1] But if they're going to put 'the right man for the job' in charge of the Conservatoire, who knows what will happen? And how much dust of old traditions there is to shake off!

Anyway you're there, which is splendid, and the artistic world should rejoice (even those members who are hypocritical or jealous).

Yours most sincerely
C.D.

P.S. Would you be kind enough to tell me where one can get hold of the photograph of you which appears on the cover of *Musica*?[2]

[1] Fauré had been appointed Director of the Conservatoire on 15 June.
[2] A photograph of Fauré at the organ of the Madeleine was featured on the cover of the issue dated July 1905.

125† TO JACQUES DURAND

                                          Grand Hotel Eastbourne
Mon cher ami   Wednesday 26 July 1905

Here I am and more or less settled in. It's a charming, peaceful spot. The sea unfurls itself with an utterly British correctness. In the foreground is a well-groomed lawn on which little chips off important, imperialist blocks are rushing around.

What a place for working in . . . ! No noise, no pianos, or only delightful mechanical ones, no musicians talking about painting and no painters talking about music . . .

In fact, a splendid place for cultivating egoism. What's more, so far I've only seen one pauper, and he looked comfortable . . . It can't be true, they must hide them away during the season.

I hope to be able to send you some music next week.

Yours ever
C.D.

126 TO JACQUES DURAND

Eastbourne
Mon cher ami   Tuesday 7 August 1905

So, after a year, the nightmare is finally over. . . !¹

I accept your congratulations in the matter. I feel now that I've done my duty as a gentleman, but I dare say reasons will be found for judging me severely and God knows what clowns will constitute themselves judges for the occasion! But I'm determined to live as I want to without bothering about the cheap literature my case will give rise to . . . the facts are really childishly simple.

The proofs of *La Mer* will reach you shortly.² I know what you mean by the 'shock' of this arrangement . . . It's not impossible to play but it's certainly not something you can expect anyone to sight-read.

All the same, I assure you it was hard to do . . . even if less hard because I knew the music.

In *La Mer*, I don't know who made the curious correction in 'Jeux de vagues' (p. 30, rehearsal number 33, 1st bar in the bass of the *seconda* part), but a # has been added to the E which I recommend to your attention.

As for the *Images* for solo piano, I expect to be sending you all three next week.

Don't you think it would be more 'aesthetic' – as the Belgians say³ – to publish the three pieces as a set? In an elegant and convenient format, like the Italian Peters one, for example, but better laid out! . . . I must admit I'm not so keen on the 'piece from' any more. It has an unfortunate, provisional look to it and lies about in odd corners like an orphan . . . I leave this to the wisdom of your editorial consideration.

Forgive this rather late reply. I'd been through a good buffeting and I spent the first few days of my stay here in more or less animal relaxation.

I hope you're in good health and your father too. Please give him my kindest regards.

Yours sincerely
C.D.

[154]

[1]   Debussy's divorce came through on 2 August.
[2]   Debussy had made a version for piano duet. This and the full score were both published by Durand later in the year. (R.N.)
[3]   Probably a reference to the *Libre esthétique*, see letter 39 footnote 3. (R.N.)

127 TO JACQUES DURAND

Eastbourne

Mon cher ami   Friday 19 August 1905

I've received your letter and enclosure and I hereby return to you the receipt for 500 francs, duly signed and monogrammed – and understood.

I'm touched by your impatience over the *Images*. What happened was this: the first piece, 'Reflets dans l'eau', doesn't satisfy me at all so I decided to write another based on different ideas and in accordance with the most recent discoveries of harmonic chemistry ... My apologies for this slight delay – which in any case won't last beyond the end of the week. I'm starting to see things clearly again in my imagination and my thinking machine is gradually getting back into gear.

I'm beginning to forget the man I am and to turn back into the man I ought to be, if the Gods permit!

All this metaphysics, mixed up with mechanics, is probably beside the point and not very easy to grasp, but then metaphysics is the art of making totally fatuous remarks in an obscure language. Chevillard[1] is bound to dismember *La Mer* unmercifully. It looks as though Giordano[2] takes himself for the Pope.

Yours as ever
C.D.

[1]   Camille Chevillard had been the conductor of the Lamoureux concerts since 1897. He had already given the first performance of the *Nocturnes* and was to do the same for *La Mer* on 15 October. As will be seen from later letters, Debussy was not one of his admirers. (See especially letters 132 and 150; though also letter 222).
[2]   Umberto Giordano was one of the leading lights of the Italian *verismo* school.

Grand Hotel, Eastbourne
Cher ami   Monday 28 August 1905

I left Paris without seeing you, which would have been unpardonable had my departure not resembled an escape . . . An escape from all these stupid, depressing goings-on, an escape from a self who was not permitted to think except by legal decree!

I've been here a month now. It's a little English seaside town, as ridiculous as these sorts of places always are . . . too many draughts and too much music, both of which I try and avoid but I don't really know where to go!

You've probably seen in the papers that Mme Debussy has gone back to being Mlle Lilly Texier. She should have stayed that way from the start and I'm sure that under her old name she will find success and fortune. I'm using the occasion to try and find myself a bit . . . I've written quite a lot of music, which hasn't happened for a long time.

I no longer get the *Mercure musical* . . . Perhaps this excellent magazine holds me responsible for the silence of M. Croche, the poor, disillusioned man![1]

Wait for my new address before you reply.

Yours ever
C.D.

If you're in touch with Déodat de Séverac,[2] tell him I'm not so stupid as to be ungrateful for what he sent me. The music he writes smells good and one can breathe to one's heart's content. Unfortunately I've lost his address; how can I thank him?

---

[1] Debussy wrote to Laloy on 2 May asking him, without much enthusiasm, if he would reserve a corner of the magazine for him, under the heading 'Interviews with M. Croche'. Debussy never in fact contributed to the magazine.

[2] Séverac lived in the Languedoc area of southern France. He was one of the first pupils of the Schola Cantorum which had just organized a concert entirely of his works, with Blanche Selva and Ricardo Viñes among the performers. Two years earlier, coming out of a Société nationale concert where one of his songs had been performed, Séverac saw coming towards him a man he had never met, who said to him, 'I like your music very much'. It was Debussy. (L. Laloy *La musique retrouvée*, p. 134.)

22 Camille Chevillard, conductor of the Lamoureux concerts.

Bellevue (Seine-et-Oise)

Mon cher ami   11 September 1905

On my way back from England I spent two days in Paris, like a perfect stranger, taking just enough time to annoy Choisnel[1] with some new corrections for *La Mer* . . . I'd be grateful if you'd oversee this matter personally: I'm not sure dear Gaston's eyesight is quite perfect!

I'm settled in here, I don't know exactly how long for. It's just the place for a brief holiday and, as it happens, at the moment it's almost deserted. Several neurasthenic Americans, and two or three Russians the Japanese have forgotten about.[2]

I hope to finish the three *Images* for two pianos very soon . . .

Colonne has written to me twice about *King Lear* – I'm working on that too.

Madame E. Hall, the 'saxophone-lady', is politely asking me for her fantasy; I'd like to oblige her, because she's been as patient as a Red Indian and deserves some reward.[3]

Have you played the *Images* . . . ? Without false vanity, I think these three pieces work well and will take their place in piano literature . . . (as Chevillard would say), to the left of Schumann or to the right of Chopin . . . as you like it.[4]

(I don't want to dedicate them to anyone.)

My congratulations on the admirable cows at Bel-Ebat,[5] and what a lovely house in the background. It must be altogether more attractive than dealing with musicians!

Let me know your news soon.

Yours
C.D.

P.S. Do you like the shiny outlines they've given the waves on the cover of *La Mer*?
P.S.P.S. Is that the definitive form of the edition?

---

[1]   Gaston Choisnel, a cousin and assistant of Jacques Durand.
[2]   Japan had just emerged victorious from her war with Russia. (R.N.)
[3]   See letter 107.
[4]   This phrase is in English in the original. (R.N.)
[5]   Durand's country house at Avon, near Fontainebleau. (Had he perhaps sent Debussy a postcard of it? R.N.)

23 Jacques Durand, Debussy's publisher from 1905.

TO LOUIS LALOY   Pavillon de Bellevue, Bellevue

Mon cher ami   13 September 1905

I've just spent several days in London – rather dreary, except for the music of the grenadiers who went past every morning with their lively 'bag-pipes' and raucous little fifes. Their marches sound to me like a drunken cross between Scottish popular songs and the Kake-Walck. Then two days in Paris like a stranger and now I'm settled in here, I don't know how long for.

It's a spot that doesn't seem to attract the crowds so it's peaceful, with only a few Americans shattered at not being able to find the usual brand of whisky and two or three Russians the Japanese have forgotten about.

While I was in Paris I saw an issue of the *Mercure musical* which contained an essay on *Pelléas*. In all humility, I found it remarkable;[1] I don't see how understanding of a work could go further. Reading it was a real pleasure and comfort; the *Pelléas* lovers were beginning to make me wonder a little what my intentions had been, their comments were all so reductive and fatuously prosaic. All the same, rest assured I shall not forget the friendship of the man who wrote these words, and whom I already regard with an affection no letter can do justice to.

The same issue of the *Mercure* contains some charming idiocies from the hand of Armande de Polignac.[2] Her ideas on the orchestra are touching and her views on music in general disarmingly individual. Let's hope she changes all that when the winter fashions come in!

As for the Byzantine cabinet-maker![3] I don't know what second-class sounds have done to him, but they've got to him somehow . . . !

The truth is that apart from you the people on the *Mercure musical* are a sinister bunch: and, worst of all, they're lamentably ill-informed. I really don't see M. Croche fitting in among this mass of brazen specialists. I feel very much like informing you of his demise, as follows: 'M. Croche, anti-dilettante, rightly disheartened by the musical *mores* of the age, has passed away peacefully amid general indifference. No flowers or wreaths by request, and above all no music.'

Don't be cross with me . . . I want you to do well and I'm afraid you may be too delicate and well brought up to cope with magazine folk.

Write to me as soon as you can. I'm anxious to know what you're doing . . . as a brother might be.

Yours
C.D.

[160]

24 Debussy at his work-table, around 1905.

What is Jean d'Udine?[4]

Is he a man or a Chinese hat?

[1] Laloy's article was *Le drame musical moderne: C. Debussy* (issue of 1 August 1905, pp. 233–50).

[2] The Countess A. de Chabannes-La-Palice, née Polignac, had been a pupil of Eugène Gigout. The *Annuaire des artistes* described her as 'a society lady of high birth ... extremely gifted ... her face is a marvel of charm and distinction'. Her article *Pensées d'ailleurs* appeared in the issue for 1 July 1905.

[3] Jean Marnold, co-editor of the *Mercure* and a prominent critic.

[4] A critic and propagandist of Dalcrozian ideas, whose real name was Albert Cozanet.

131 TO NICOLAS CORONIO[1]

Mon cher Coronio   [1905]

Your letter is a little late, as you are frank enough to admit. But if your attitude so far has not been markedly different from that so strangely adopted by my friends, at least you have the courage to take the bull by the horns.

I should be glad for you to explain why you are anxious about my reputation and, especially, how you reconcile it with another anxiety – a more pleasant one, I must admit.

Would you like to come tomorrow at 3 o'clock or Saturday around 5? I'd prefer tomorrow as I'm not sure I'll be free on Saturday.

Yours[2]

C.D.

[1] One of Debussy's few pupils, who had taken his time resuming contact after the composer's divorce.

[2] In English in the original. (R.N.)

132 TO JACQUES DURAND

Cher ami   Tuesday 10 October 1905

I've just spent five hours with Chevillard in two days, including a 3-hour rehearsal this morning ...[1]

That's a lot of Chevillard for a bachelor ... As you can imagine, I'm absolutely shattered. That man ought to have been a wild beast tamer. You have to admire the way he makes people work, but otherwise what a Caliban!!!

What's more, the parts have been badly proof-read . . . We spent a lot of time chasing mistakes and missing ties . . . There's still 'Jeux de vagues' to work our way through, the other two movements are more or less correct with only the final touches to be applied. This is the moment I'm afraid of with Chevillard; there's really so little artistry about him.

So there we are . . . I look for a little sympathy from you for putting up with so much ill-humour and ugly grimaces.

Yours
C.D.

1 The first performance of *La Mer* was to take place on 15 October.

133 TO PIERRE LALO

Mon cher ami   Wednesday 25 October 1905

There's no problem in your not liking *La Mer*[1] and I've no intention of complaining about it. I shall perhaps suffer regret that you haven't understood me and astonishment at finding you (though one such occasion doesn't establish a habit) in agreement with your fellow music critics. We may leave *La Mer* for a moment, but I can't follow you when you take it as a pretext for claiming all of a sudden that my other works lack logic and are held together only by a tenacious sensibility and a dedicated search for the 'picturesque' . . . a slogan which people use to designate things which have nothing to do with the true meaning of the word. But really! If my idea of music isn't the same as yours, I am none the less an artist and nothing but an artist . . . In fact the perpetual joy I find in writing music is certainly my principal defect, one which has often been the subject of bitter reproaches!

You say – keeping your unkindest cut for the last – 'that you do not see or smell the sea throughout these three sketches'! That's a large claim and I don't know who is going to evaluate it for us . . . I love the sea and I've listened to it with the passionate respect it deserves. If I've been inaccurate in taking down what it dictated to me, that is no concern of yours or mine. You must admit, not all ears hear in the same way. The heart of the matter is that you love and defend traditions which, for me, no longer exist or, at least, exist only as representative of an epoch in which they were not all as fine and valuable as people make

[163]

out; the dust of the past is not always respectable. If in the future we are no longer to understand one another, I shall still not forget all that *Pelléas* owes to you for your warm and unstinting support . . . Indeed, it's the main reason for my writing this letter.[2]

> Yours sincerely
> C.D.

[1] In his review of *La Mer*, published in *le Temps* on 16 October, the day after the first performance, Lalo's most trenchant paragraph ran: 'It seems to me Debussy has willed himself to feel rather than really feeling deeply and naturally. For the first time, listening to a descriptive work by Debussy, I have the impression of standing, not in front of nature, but in front of a reproduction of nature; a wonderfully refined, ingenious and carefully composed reproduction, but a reproduction none the less . . . I do not hear, I do not see, I do not smell the sea.'
[2] For Debussy's earlier relationship with Lalo, see letter 88.

134 TO RAOUL BARDAC[1]

> Saturday 24 February 1906
> Mon cher Rara   and even Sunday 25

You will forgive the date of this letter and . . . my idleness!

Now let's resurrect our memories of winter – as Monsieur Mallarmé's faun would say, in the revised version by Willy.[2] And what a winter! It's raining, the trees look like inconsolable widowers, the flowers are indoors, the poultry is out of doors and, for a change, overweening humans are trying to make good these deficiencies with orchestral descriptions. With the result that we heard *Schéhérazade* again. It doesn't improve with age and is more bazaar than oriental. I also have to admit that Chevillard doesn't in the least resemble the princess Boudour . . . He waves his arms like a news vendor and from behind looks like a bicycle salesman – all of which doesn't exactly make him a thing of beauty.

We also heard d'Indy's *Un jour d'été à la montagne*.[3] This is the d'Indy from the other side of the Cevennes. As I possess no precise information on the atmosphere of the above-mentioned locale, there's not much I can tell you about it. There seemed to be an inordinate amount of work for the bassoon and I was surprised to hear a piano – I thought you only found pianos on Swiss mountains?

You didn't have any luck placing your work with the Société nationale . . . Well, you mustn't be more upset by this than the occasion

[164]

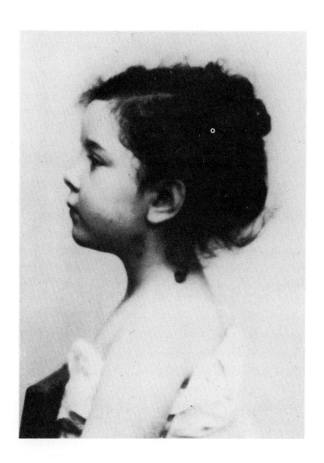

25 Debussy's daughter, Chouchou.

warrants. To begin with, you didn't have much in the way of support, and then you're not a member of any of those groups to whom permission is granted to dip their toes into music.

I'm not over sorry that Colonne is not going to play any of your music this year . . . This gives you time to prepare your entry. Take advantage of the opportunity and don't risk putting forward works which, if not bad exactly, could turn out to be nondescript. You have facility – and talent, there's no doubt about that – but you can never be too cautious about accepting the way forward your ideas suggest to you. Sometimes the result with you is music that's a little sloppy, hasty too, giving the disconcerting impression that you wanted to get to the end come what may. You know how little love I have for developmental padding. It's seen long service at the hands of the masters and it's time we started to replace it by a more rigorous selection of ideas; the line needs to take more account of the value of those ideas on the orchestral and ornamental front and, above all, the ideas must breathe. So often they're overwhelmed by the richness or the banality of the frame.[4]

Have patience, then! It's a major, even a domestic, virtue which solves many a problem.

But I don't want to dampen your day with a downpour of aesthetic and moral advice. It's not much use, anyway – aesthetics change with the centuries and I'm rather afraid morals do too.

Your daily schedule sounds splendid, with just enough time devoted to doing nothing. You're right to organize it like that – it's important to let your brain marinate under a hot sun. Spend time looking at flowers and snapshots – while your grey matter is still capable of responding.

Collect impressions. Don't be in a hurry to write them down. Because that's something music can do better than painting: it can centralize variations of colour and light within a single picture – a truth generally ignored, obvious as it is . . . You must even forget about music entirely from time to time. It was an idiot who proclaimed you had to write a lot to learn how to write . . . Anyway, it's not polite to make daily demands on the people you claim are your best friends.[5]

Your mother has a remarkable bout of 'flu . . . you know how she reacts against all kinds of medicine, which doesn't make life any easier.

Baby Claude[6] is going to have a change of nurse yet again. The last one, according to her own account, has been deceived by her husband! So she's off to investigate the disaster personally – doubtful psychology and deplorable housekeeping.

[166]

I won't say anything about what I'm writing . . . there's not much of it, and what there is I don't like at all. For want of a better excuse I blame it on the weather.

> Hoping to see you soon
> Yours ever
> C.D.

[1] Raoul was the son of Emma and Sigismund Bardac. He had been having a few lessons from Debussy since 1901, at least.

[2] 'O nymphes, regonflons des souvenirs divers' (Debussy's pun (divers/d'hiver) is very much in the Willy mould. R.N.).

[3] The two concerts Debussy refers to took place on the same day, 18 February 1906, but in two different halls: Rimsky-Korsakov's *Schéhérazade* at the Concerts Lamoureux (with the *Nocturnes*), *Jour d'été à la montagne* at the Concerts Colonne (with the *Prélude à l'après-midi d'un faune*).

[4] See also letter 33 to Chausson. (R.N.)

[5] Debussy is here personifying music. (R.N.)

[6] Debussy's daughter by Emma Bardac, soon to acquire the name Chouchou ('darling'). She was born on 30 October 1905.

135 TO LOUIS LALOY

Mon cher ami   Saturday 10 March 1906

I've been a bit worried these last few days about baby Claude's health – one has so little idea of what's going on inside such a tiny frame, it's easy to lose one's sang-froid. But now I hope the alarms are over and I offer my apologies for being so slow in replying.

Mme de Grefhule[1] was quite right to replace Debussy by Laloy – Laloy is in any case a much more sociable character than Debussy.

It's very kind of you to be so insistent on the subject of M. Croche . . . but he's no longer very well in touch with the musical *mores* of his age. What's the point, in any case, of spelling out his opinions to people who don't listen! Music is currently split up into lots of little republics in which everyone is determined to shout louder than the man next door. The result is such horrible music, one begins to fear a taste for the 'other sort of music' may not long survive; and it's no consolation to see a sort of pretentious mediocrity gaining ground. It's not only irritating but positively harmful.

You know, better than I do, the standard of writings about music. Today, if you don't know what to do or, especially, what to say, you improvise some art criticism!

As for the artists themselves, they've taken to profound dreaming about aesthetic problems – the strange thing is, they generally talk more rubbish than the other lot . . . altogether not very stimulating!

Don't you agree, we ought to adopt a more guarded attitude? We need to preserve a little of the 'mystery', which is eventually going to be rendered 'pervious' by all this gossip and tittle-tattle, with the artists joining in like so many aged actresses.

Certainly there are things that need saying. But who to? Who for? For people who oscillate between Beethoven and Maurice Ravel! It's lucky really that no one of our generation is a genius: in my view that would be the hardest and most ridiculous position of all to be in.

When are you coming to play bridge?

Yours
C.D.

Mme Debussy sends you her best wishes.

¹ Elisabeth de Caraman Chimay, Countess Greffulhe, was the model for Proust's duchess de Guermantes and the president of the Société des grandes auditions musicales de France.

136 TO JACQUES DURAND

Mon cher ami   Tuesday 20 March 1906

You are very kind, Colonne is very obliging . . . and no doubt you'll think I'm being tiresome when I say that 'Cortège' and 'Danse'¹ are perhaps too slim, both in interest and in duration, to fit comfortably into a season that has already included, one after the other, La Mer, the Nocturnes and the Images.²

Keen though I might be to hear a programme entirely of my works in chronological order, I'm still nervous of being accused of rummaging around in my bottom drawer just to keep my name on the posters . . . if I was dead, that would be an excellent excuse – though I'd prefer to put that off for a bit.

You know I like to oblige you when I can. So I hope you'll forgive me for not being completely in agreement with you; it doesn't happen often.

Yours sincerely
C.D.

[168]

[1]   Earlier in the year Debussy had revised the orchestration of the 'Cortège' and the 'Air de danse' from his Prix de Rome cantata, *L'Enfant prodigue*. They were first heard in public in a partially staged performance in the Salle Gaveau on 12 December 1907. (R.N.)
[2]   Ricardo Viñes gave the first performance of the first set of *Images* for piano at the Société nationale de musique on 3 March 1906. (R.N.)

137 TO PAUL-JEAN TOULET

Paris

Mon cher ami   Saturday 5 May 1906

I saw you today at Durand Ruel's and I'm astonished you didn't come and shake hands, as we always used to. If you'd been alone I'd have asked you why. I can't believe that with your attitude to life you approve of the behaviour of some of my so-called friends![1]

Forgive me for requesting an answer to this note. At least it gives me the chance to sign myself

Your sincere friend
C.D.

[1]   Toulet, replying three days later, expressed his indignation that Debussy could ever have thought he was one of his fair-weather friends. Their close relationship was resumed forthwith.

Notoriety
Stage projects

In addition to his work, and going to concerts, Debussy began in 1908 to appear as an orchestral conductor. *Pelléas* began to be given outside France, notably in Brussels and London, and Debussy went to supervise rehearsals personally. Among his projects, two in particular engaged his attention: *Le Diable dans le beffroi* and *La Chute de la maison Usher*, on the tales by Edgar Allan Poe, for which Debussy wrote his own libretti. Two other projects, stemming from his desire for self-renewal, never progressed beyond the initial stages: a version of *Tristan* with Gabriel Mourey, and *Siddhartha* with Victor Segalen. He was in demand for interviews, he was appointed a member of the Conseil supérieur du Conservatoire, and Louis Laloy published the first biography of him to appear in France.

Mon cher ami   Saturday 7 July 1906

I confess candidly I was waiting for a letter from you. So your reproaches come as a surprise because they seem to be accusing me, in the nicest possible way, of not keeping in touch ... A misunderstanding, simply; your letter, full of reassurance, is now to hand and here's mine full of remorse, if that's what you want.

I'm now one tooth the less, which hasn't altered my physique in any way, and I'm getting back to work with that mixture of enthusiasm and exhaustion which is my speciality, at the moment anyway.

If an ironical fate doesn't come and jumble up my manuscripts, I should have *Ibéria* finished next week[1] and the two other pieces by the end of the month.

After that I must get back to the Belfry and to the devil, who may well end up by resenting all this attention.

Talking of *Le Diable*, I think I've found quite a novel way of writing for voices; it has the further merit of being simple. But I don't have much confidence in it, so let it be a secret between the two of us ... I'm terrified of waking up one grey morning and finding it's idiotic.

In short, I'm making the fullest possible use of my existence, and if Music doesn't bestow any smiles on me, it's just that she's a hard mistress.

I hope to find you in good form when I see you on Monday.

Yours ever
C.D.

[171]

¹ In fact Debussy needed another two and a half years to finish this second movement of the orchestral *Images*: the score is dated 25 December 1908.

139 TO LOUIS LALOY

Mon cher ami   Monday 10 September 1906

According to Jules Simon – unless it was Simon, the friend of Christ – one should 'never ask a friend on his travels to write to you, because in so doing you reattach the thread with his daily life that he was intent on breaking'.¹ An admirably egotistical formula I apply rather often, supporting as it does my nonchalance as a correspondent!

So you're staying in an old house² which you've known since childhood. That's so much better than spending one's time in a café, or even at a concert without going to a café.

And when I tell you that no sooner was I back in Paris than I bumped into Colonne; that the most unpleasant plans are afoot, with contracts attached, for putting on *Pelléas* in Brussels, Vienna . . . etc. – why not Singapore or Peking! . . . At least one would have the thrill of travelling – well then, I hope your quiet stay far from these European manifestations gives you the strength to sympathize with me.

I'm delighted about your enthusiasm for Rameau. He deserves it for all the qualities in his music which ought to have protected us against Gluck's deceitful grandiloquence, Wagner's bombastic metaphysics and the old Belgian angel's false mysticism; all of which we have clumsily adapted to a manner of understanding the exact opposite of what that music demands, while we continue, like vain children, to ignore the perfect taste and strict elegance which make up the consummate beauty of Rameau's music. And, unfortunately, where there are signs that we're turning to him again, it's only out of idle curiosity. It's almost impossible for us to realize what we've lost in paying him so little attention, proud as we are of knowledge which was never intended for us and which might even be described as the negation of music . . . I feel a serious revolution is the only thing to get us out of this cosmopolitan stew.

I also discovered Lacerda³ was at Günten . . . How did that come about? Who's he staying with? The postal workers of that country don't function on the lines of M. Dupin in the story of the stolen letter . . . So I haven't had the nerve to write to him. If you see him, say I often think about him and his 'lower classes'. Try and come back soon. Mme Debussy remembers you and sends you her best wishes. As usual, my burden of years is now heavier by one – just turned 44!

Yours ever
C.D.

[1] Jules Simon, 1814–1896, was a philosopher and politician and the author of works on the condition of the working class. His statue stood under the office windows of Debussy's publisher, Jacques Durand.
[2] Laloy had just been appointed an assistant professor at the Sorbonne and was at his country home, preparing courses on Rameau.
[3] Francisco de Lacerda, 1869–1934, was a Portuguese composer whom Debussy had befriended. See also letter 168.

140 TO HECTOR DUFRANNE[1]

Mon cher Dufranne   26 October 1906

I hope you'll forgive my irritability during the *Pelléas* rehearsals,[2] which leads me to express myself more vigorously than I really mean to . . . You and Vieuille[3] are almost the only two who have maintained your understanding of my artistic aims in *Pelléas*; that's why I ask you to go on defending this work, which others don't seem to love as much as you do. In Act V, it seems to me the stage movements are a bit casual, perhaps? And please exaggerate, even, Golaud's poignant misery . . . to get over clearly all that he regrets not having said and done . . . and all the happiness which is lost to him for ever [. . .]

C.D.

[1] The Belgian bass-baritone made his debut at La Monnaie in Brussels in 1896 and at the Opéra-comique in 1900. He sang Golaud at the première of *Pelléas*.
[2] The revival of *Pelléas* was to take place at the Opéra-comique on 23 December.
[3] Félix Vieuille sang Arkel at the première of *Pelléas*. (R.N.)

141 TO LOUIS LALOY

Mon cher ami
                                    Tuesday 25 December 1906

At last some good news from you . . . first of all your marriage[1] (if you don't mind my saying so, of rather more interest than the *Mercure musical*). I'd certainly have come and brought you my friendly support, but that *Pelléas* you're so fond of has played a dastardly trick and is obliging its composer to leave for Brussels on Thursday morning . . . It's doubly annoying as I'm heading for a time of anxiety and pointless discussions, leaving behind me regret at having missed you . . . I speak for myself, naturally.

For the same reasons I can't possibly let you have anything on any topic whatever for the new-look *Mercure musical*.[2] But for the future I have in mind a collection of notes, opinions, etc. . . . . They've been left me by poor M. Croche, who grew tired of life — that most sensitive of men thought I couldn't in all decency go on with 'conversations' in which the Void bandied words with a vague Nothing-at-All! — he's left it up to me: to publish the papers or burn them. We can discuss what the best policy would be.[3]

So now I send you my best possible wishes; I won't be specific in case I forget anything or am indiscreet — every man's happiness is a private matter, to be jealously guarded. Mme Debussy joins me in all this.

I'll get in touch as soon as I'm back in Paris and, before we get down to bridge, perhaps we might make the acquaintance of Mme Laloy?

Yours ever
C.D.

[1]   With S. Babaïan.
[2]   The editors of this review were Laloy and Jean Marnold. It continued to name Debussy as one of its 'principal collaborators' even though he had never written anything for it.
[3]   This collection of articles was delayed by the war. It was finally published in 1919 under the title *M. Croche antidilettante*.

142 TO JACQUES DURAND

Brussels
Cher ami   7 January 1907

I've just come out of a rehearsal and sent you a telegram with the date of the première. How will it go? I've no idea, but the general feeling is it'll go very well!!!

There's actually a bell that ought to give a G and which, out of a spirit of Belgian contradiction, gives a C! . . . It sounds rather as if it's dinner-time in the castle and it makes Mélisande's deathbed scene less affecting.[1] So far I've seen only half a tower . . . a pale wooden well . . . and dungeons so realistic no one can get into them! Yniold is so young he still knows absolutely nothing about music, and it's the *dress rehearsal* tomorrow . . .[2] May the good Lord preserve my friends the artists of Belgium. The easiest thing would be to play the part of a reputable dead composer, with whom one can take what liberties one pleases. The orchestra and singers, I should say, may well be wishing this state of affairs on me quite seriously as it seems I'm the most demanding composer they've ever come across . . . and what's more I have the presumption to want my music performed properly.

So you're going to see something that falls short of perfection. Forgive me in advance, I've done everything I can to make it otherwise – certainly to the point of being unpleasant. May God and the King of the Belgians forgive me if I don't regard all the inhabitants of Brussels as men of genius or as possessors of infallible taste.

I intend to leave on Wednesday morning.[3] First of all, I've had enough and my little girl isn't very well; and secondly I could only offer you an imperfect performance.

Please give my best wishes to your father.

Yours
C.D.

[1]   The bell is first heard over an E minor chord . . . (R.N.)
[2]   Mary Garden sang Mélisande. One critic commented that the scenery was 'in the Renaissance style and rather more poetic' than at the Opéra-comique.
[3]   In fact Debussy did not stay for the première on Wednesday evening, 9 January.

143 TO SYLVAIN DUPUIS[1]

Mon cher ami   Tuesday 8 January 1907

Thank you from the bottom of my heart for the devotion and artistic loyalty you have brought in such large measure to the preparation of *Pelléas* . . . I shall certainly never forget what a pleasure it has been to work with you.

As I leave tomorrow morning, may I ask you to convey my respects to the gentlemen of the orchestra and to assure them of my gratitude for their patience and goodwill. They are both artists and good fellows, which is rare!

Once again my thanks, which go beyond what I can say in a letter.

Yours
C.D.

I enclose the score of *Salome* you were kind enough to lend me.

[1] Dupuis, 1856–1931, was a Belgian composer who was the principal conductor at La Monnaie in Brussels from 1900 to 1911.

144 TO MANUEL DE FALLA[1]

Monsieur   Sunday 13 January 1907

I received your letter only yesterday on my return from Brussels and hope you will forgive this late reply . . . What you ask is rather hard to give a definite answer to! It's not possible to write down the exact form of a rhythm, any more than it is to explain the different effects of a single phrase!

The best thing, I think, is to be guided by how you feel . . . The colour of the two dances[2] seems to me to be clearly defined. There's something to be got out of the passage between the 'gravity' of the first one and the 'grace' of the second; for a musician such as yourself that will not be difficult, and I am quite happy to leave the performance to your good taste.

Yours most sincerely
C.D.

[1] Debussy did not get to know the young Spanish composer until a few months later, when he came to live in Paris.
[2] Debussy wrote his two *Danses* for harp and orchestra in 1904. (Falla played a piano version of them in Madrid a few weeks after this letter, at the Teatro de la Comedia. R.N.)

145† TO LOUIS LALOY

Mon cher ami   Wednesday 23 January 1907

I've been back from Brussels for some time, but in such a bad state I didn't feel I could get in touch with you straight away. If the directors of La Monnaie were to be believed, everything was absolutely in order and all I had to do was congratulate everyone including the doorkeeper's father . . . Alas, things proved to be very much otherwise.

I had to spend a fortnight re-educating an orchestra whose Flemishness is about as flexible as a 100 kg. weight . . . the woodwind thick and noisy, the brass, on the other hand, stuffed with cotton wool . . . Added to which they have a disconcerting gift for mangling the simplest rhythm . . . In short, a constant and utterly exhausting struggle to arrive at something tolerable. We left on the morning of the première and, ironically enough, it was a triumph – according to the Belgians and my friend and publisher Jacques Durand.

When are you coming? Maybe the time hasn't been wasted for everybody, but it's too long since we saw each other.

I do hope Mme Laloy will come too; it would be a great pleasure to meet her.

Yours ever
C.D.

146 TO JACQUES DURAND

Cher ami   25 February 1907

Thank you for the *Histoires naturelles* . . . it's an extremely curious score! It's artificial and chimerical, rather like the house of a wizard! But 'le Cygne'[1] is very pretty music, even so.

Yours ever
C.D.

[1]   The third of Ravel's five *Histoires naturelles*, on prose-poems by Jules Renard. The first performance on 12 January had provoked something of a scandal.

147 TO LOUIS LALOY

Cher ami   Friday 8 March 1907

Nervous people are unbearable, so you must forgive me . . . ! We're very sorry your wife's been ill and hope she'll come with you on Tuesday evening; you're coming to dinner, aren't you?

As for Ravel, I recognize the marks of your usual ingenuity . . . Even if I don't feel he's quite found 'his way', he'll be able to thank you for pointing one out to him . . .[1]

But, between ourselves, do you really believe in 'humorous' music? For a start, it doesn't exist on its own; there always has to be a pretext, either words or a situation . . . Two chords with their feet in the air, or in any other curious position, will never be intrinsically humorous and could only become so in an empirical manner.

[177]

I agree with you Ravel is extraordinarily gifted, but what annoys me is the attitude he adopts of being a 'conjuror', or rather a Fakir casting spells and making flowers burst out of chairs ... The trouble is, a conjuring trick always has to have a build-up and after you've seen it once you're no longer astonished.

For the moment I'm happy if people find it entertaining. Given the way people torment and annoy music, she might be glad to hear the excuse that her only function is to bring a smile to the lips!

We look forward to seeing you both on Tuesday evening.
Yours
C.D.

[1] In an article in the review *S.I.M.*, the bulletin of the Société internationale de musique, of 15 March 1907, Laloy wrote: 'There are no grounds for thinking, as some do, that a welter of passion and romantic enthusiasm necessarily spells sincerity ... this gentle irony, far from diminishing emotion, on the contrary sharpens it and makes it more poignant.' (R.N.)

148 TO PAUL DUKAS

Cher ami   Wednesday 8 May 1907

Enthusiasm aside, my clearest impression is of a certain implacability in the beauty of *Ariane et Barbe-bleue*[1] which effaces everything that surrounds it ... What chance have the poor replicas of precious stones against the torrent of sound which floods the orchestra?

What chance has the efficiently electric sun? Or the flowers? But above all there's the seductive breath of freedom whose perfume fills the final act, making the five little human dolls yet more ineffectual and Bluebeard, their noble companion, yet more wretched! And throughout, at every turning, the music dominates the words.

My wife sends you her thanks for a wonderful day and I my sincere admiration.

Yours
C.D.

[1] The dress rehearsal of Dukas's opera had taken place the day before at the Opéra-comique.

Mon cher ami   Thursday 23 May 1907

I'm not 'Oedipus of the Café des Mille Colonnes' and I humbly confess I don't see how my opinions can help you?

Over the Russian concerts?[2] They're admirable — some slight nepotism in the programmes and, if they're to be called 'historical', some surprising gaps. But it was a really excellent idea to put on the first Act of *Boris*.[3]

Last Friday was the first time I'd heard *Salome*.[4] I don't see how anyone can be other than enthusiastic about this work — an absolute masterpiece . . . almost as rare a phenomenon as the appearance of a comet.

Yours as ever
C.D.

[1]   An impresario and the moving spirit behind the Théâtre des Champs-Elysées, opened in 1913.
[2]   Astruc and Diaghilev organized five Russian historical concerts at the Opéra between 16 and 30 May, in which Chaliapin was an outstanding success. (The music was mostly by the 'Five', but Josef Hofmann also played piano concertos by Scriabin and Liapunov, and Rachmaninov played his own Second Piano Concerto. R.N.).
[3]   The second concert, on 19 May, contained in fact two extracts from Act I (the scene of Pimen's cell and Varlam's drunken song), followed by the whole of Act II. (R.N.)
[4]   Richard Strauss conducted his opera at the Châtelet on 17 May. Rimsky-Korsakov was also present and called out to the singers to shut up. Debussy had looked at the score of *Salome* earlier in the year (see letter 143). (R.N.)

150 TO JACQUES DURAND

Cher ami   Wednesday 17 July 1907

I intended to try and see you today but I'm afraid it may be too late . . . and think I'd better write instead. First, the gossip. M. H. J. Wood[1] is definitely going to perform *L'Enfant prodigue* and for this I feel it would be best if I re-orchestrated it straight away . . . if you have to get a copy made of the score at the Conservatoire, it'll still have to be corrected — I'm pretty sure the 'original' orchestration smells of 'exams', 'the conservatoire' and tedium . . . What do you think?

I've got a firm date to conduct *L'Après-midi d'un faune* and *La Mer* in London on 1 February next year . . . and in April two concerts, one in Rome, the other in Milan. For one of these I think I might be able to offer myself the first performance of the *Images* . . .[2] again: what say you to this small revolution?

I've seen Colonne recently, not that it was particularly exciting. As for Chevillard, I refuse to let myself be assassinated by him ever again.[3]

Don't be too hard on me for being late: I'm working like a factory – and making progress despite the trauma and exhaustion of various leaps forward!

When are you coming to Paris? Next week? I must say hello to you and let you hear some music! With all my sympathies to your father,

Yours ever
C.D.

[1]   Henry Wood, the founder and conductor of the Promenade Concerts.
[2]   The *Images* were not to be performed for nearly another three years.
[3]   See letter 222 for a slightly different point of view.

151 TO VICTOR SEGALEN[1]

Mon cher ami   Friday 26 July 1907

I'm terribly late with this letter, but you know the bizarre state you get into when you're determined to find something and then, in spite of everything, it arrives at a moment maliciously selected by Lady Luck to thwart your most determined intentions . . .

The business about *Tristan* is simple. I read Bédier's *Roman de Tristan*[2] when it first came out and was so struck by it I immediately had the idea of turning it into an opera. I felt it was necessary to give Tristan back his legendary characteristics, so badly deformed by Wagner and by the suspect, metaphysical approach which, there more than anywhere, resists explanation . . . Then I forgot the idea until recently when Mourey,[3] whom I hadn't seen for years, turned up and spoke to me of his Tristan projects. My enthusiasm awoke – it had never really been asleep, I admit – and I accepted!

That's my crime, with my regrets at not telling you about it. You can simply write to Laloy – though why he hasn't published your essay by now I don't know![4] His present address is: Ker-Lann, Saint-Quay-Portrieux, Côtes du Nord.

As for Maeterlinck, you may be aware I'm on the worst possible terms with him. So do what you think best.

I'm leaving here at the end of the month, banished from my home by

[180]

a ridiculous boiler. It's very annoying, with all the things I have to do, and anyway I have a natural repugnance towards living in a hotel.

If I'm not going to see you before I get back at the end of September, would you be long-suffering enough to send me any new passages of *Siddhartha* . . . what you tell me of it whets my appetite enormously.

I don't need to underline my profound sympathy with your work and my wishes for its double success.

> Yours
> C.D.

From 2 August my address will be: Grand Hôtel, Pourville, Seine-Inf.

[1]   Segalen was a doctor in the Marines and a dramatic poet. He had introduced himself to Debussy in April 1906 and suggested to him a Buddhist drama, *Siddhartha*.
[2]   It appeared in 1900.
[3]   None of Mourey's collaborative ventures with Debussy came to anything. The composer found his prose 'not very lyrical'.
[4]   An essay on Maori music. It appeared in Laloy's *Mercure musical* (issue of 15 October 1907) under the pseudonym Max-Anély and dedicated to Debussy.

152 TO JACQUES DURAND

Grand-Hôtel Pourville near Dieppe
Cher ami   Tuesday 5 August 1907

Forgive me for having to leave the very day of our appointment! . . . The blame lies with the imperious boilermen.

In any case I did mean to write to you straight away but I fell victim to intolerable stomach pains, and the sea air only made them worse.

Today, for the first time, I'm beginning to feel more at ease and have stopped walking around looking lost, like someone who's forgotten his room number.

Naturally I like the suburban railway,[1] because one has to learn to cope with everything; even so, I confess it was a joy to see the Channel again . . . It's not as big as the Atlantic, obviously, but it has delicacy and some nicely distinguished harmonies! It's also deliciously hypocritical and lies to you with womanly smiles. If its finery is less dazzling than the Atlantic's it has a greater curiosity value. Don't worry, I'll say no more on the subject!

I hope that here I shall at last manage to finish the *Images*, once and for all. There were quite a few passages I wasn't happy about . . . it

[181]

was well written, but with that skill born of habit that's so hard to conquer and so tiresome.

I think I can see now what needs to be done, with no more of this mandarin kind of work, which I'm not made for at all.

I must tell you there are some most surprising things in the early orchestration of *L'Enfant prodigue* . . . I've found a cor anglais which quite blatantly plays fifths . . . and even thirds . . . it's really a pity such a cor anglais remains to be invented. My recollections of the performance which was given at the Institut are a bit hazy, but it must have had its interesting moments.[2]

Let's not deceive ourselves though! It's got to be revised and I'm working on it between times. I'll send it to you as soon as it's finished.

Where did some of the newspapers get the information about 'L'Histoire de Tristan'[3] – including *Le Temps*, such a serious and accurately informed paper? I saw Mourey[4] before I left, as enthusiastic as ever. Frankly, the whole project is so attractive, I'm almost frightened of getting the libretto.

Forgive me for still not slaking your thirst! It's all to your advantage, at least I hope so. You'll get a tastier wine for it being longer in the bottle.

> My respects to your father
> Yours as ever
> C.D.

[1]   The railway in question ran not far from his house in the avenue du Bois de Boulogne.
[2]   *L'Enfant prodigue* was given at the Institut (with piano duet accompaniment) on 27 June 1884. The singers were Rose Caron, Ernest van Dyck and Taskin.
[3]   The papers had announced that the work was to be performed at the Opéra-comique the following year.
[4]   See letter 171.

153   TO VICTOR SEGALEN

Pourville

26 August 1907

Mon cher ami

Thank you first of all for sending *Siddhartha*; now I can get a more or less complete impression of it . . .

It's an amazing imaginative conception! The only thing is, as it stands I don't know of any music that could plumb this abyss! Its only use would be to underline certain gestures or contribute to particular scenic effects. In other words, as an illustration much more than a perfect union with the text and with the terrifying immobility of the principal character. Please note, I'm not saying it's impossible; just that . . . it scares me stiff. If I asked you to scale down your conception to more normal proportions, I'd feel I was trampling rudely over part of your life's work – and that would bring no joy to anybody.

I hope though I may still express a sincere desire to have something of yours as a basis, without the danger of doing you a disservice?

You'll understand, I'm sure, that my objections are directed only at my own physical deficiencies. I have a secret, childish hope that everything will sort itself out as it does in fairy stories. And in many cases there was a more elegant denouement than followed from the brusque attentions of important, reasonable people.

Dans un monde sonore[1] is splendid stuff, in absolutely uncharted territory . . . One only hopes people will have the grace to understand what you're trying to say . . . I rather doubt it . . . they never admit that most of them are deaf and blind.

Don't you think something splendid might come out of the Orpheus myth? Gluck's version represents only the anecdotal, sentimental side and leaves out everything that portrays Orpheus as the first and most sublime of misunderstood geniuses. These ideas came to me while I was reading *Dans un monde sonore* where your use of Orpheus shows you're fully acquainted with the myth.

As for M. Riemann,[2] don't you think he's like someone reducing a beautiful sunset to a mechanical model?

I haven't asked you to come here because, apart from the sea, it's an odious place where the people are slightly more ridiculous than elsewhere. My strongest desire is to escape as soon as possible.

I'll let you know when I'm back in Paris and ask you to come round, if that's all right with you.

Yours
C.D.

[1] Segalen's novel had just been serialized in the *Mercure de France*.
[2] Hugo Riemann, the German musicologist. Debussy would have known of his theories of harmony through Jean Marnold's analyses of them in the *Mercure musical*.

Pourville
Cher ami   Tuesday 3 September 1907

As you see, beneath M. Sonzogno's[1] outward appearance of a recently discovered mummy there lurks the soul of a subtle dilettante . . . Have you considered what the word 'éclat' might refer to in respect of *Pelléas*? Might he be intending to introduce some *vocalises*?

But I'm pleased and congratulate you on such a successful outcome.[2] Your inquiry as to when I expect to be back in Paris revives my most insistent desire . . . But, as you know, boilermen consider themselves artists and according to the latest news from Paris it'll be ten days or a fortnight before the house is habitable.

It's very cold here and I've more or less recovered . . .

The *Images* will be ready as soon as I can finish *Rondes* to my satisfaction and as it needs to be. The music of this piece is peculiar in the sense that it's immaterial and one can't, therefore, handle it as though it were a robust symphony, walking on all four feet (sometimes three, but walking anyway).

Generally speaking, I feel more and more that music, by its very essence, is not something that can flow inside a rigorous, traditional form. It consists of colours and of rhythmicized time . . .

The rest of it's just a nonsense invented by unfeeling imbeciles on the backs of the Masters who in most cases were writing no more than the music of their period!

Bach was the only one who saw ahead to the truth.

In any case, music is a very young art, as much in technical matters as in 'knowledge'.

All the same, I think I can expect to be back in Paris around the 15th . . . If you'd like to send me the English version of *Pelléas*, I'm entirely at your disposal.

My respects to your father
Yours as ever
C.D.

---

[1] The Milanese publisher Edoardo Sonzogno.
[2] *Pelléas* was to be given its Italian première at La Scala on 2 April 1908.

[184]

155 TO GABRIEL PIERNÉ[1]

Cher ami   22 October 1907 7.30 p.m.

Thank you for your telegram which I found waiting for me on my return. You know I enjoy a performance of anything if it's conducted by you. Even so I'd rather wait for a happier occasion when you can give *La Mer* complete.[2]

Perhaps I'm wrong, but 'Jeux de vagues' played by itself doesn't seem to me to have the same significance ... and when you have three children, you can't take just one of them to the Concert Colonne! – Put yourself in their place!

The devil take your programme.

With my regrets
Yours ever
C.D.

[1] A composer and conductor. Debussy met him in Marmontel's piano class at the Conservatoire and again for a few months in Rome. See letter 4.
[2] Pierné was later to give the first performances of two of Debussy's works: *Ibéria* and *Jeux*. See letters 190 and 262.

156† TO GEORGES JEAN-AUBRY[1]

Cher Monsieur   26 October 1907

Forgive my delay in replying to your kind letter and in thanking you for your efforts on my behalf.

If my name can be of any use to you don't hesitate to use it, and I hope England will be kind to you. Talking of which, it seems to me the sympathies of the English for music are only of the official variety, and so far Handel and Sullivan have met their needs perfectly well.

Among the cities you're going to be visiting I don't see Cardiff.[2] It's an important musical centre where French music would gain a sympathetic hearing.

I've seen M. André Caplet.[3] I have every confidence in his good taste and leave him a free hand to organize the concert you are being kind enough to devote to Claude Debussy.

With my thanks and best wishes
Yours
C.D.

[1]   A writer on music who organized lecture–recitals of contemporary works. Debussy had got to know him the previous year through Ricardo Viñes.
[2]   The interest in French music at this time in Wales, and in Manchester, is documented in Martha Stonequist, *The Musical Entente Cordiale 1905–16*, Ann Arbor, 1974.
[3]   See letter 180.

157† TO VICTOR SEGALEN

Cher ami   Wednesday 15 January 1908

Forgive me . . . I've been in constant turmoil lately, as always happens when my music frequents the artistic world.

As you know perhaps, Colonne ought to have played *La Mer* last Sunday.[1] After appalling rehearsals he decided not to play it after all and they came asking me to conduct the performance next Sunday.

It was not without a furiously beating heart I climbed the rostrum yesterday morning for the first rehearsal. It's the first time in my life I've tried my hand at orchestral conducting and certainly I bring to the task a candid inexperience which ought to disarm those curious beasts called 'orchestral musicians'. At least they're full of goodwill.

Further impressions: you really feel yourself to be the heart of your own music . . . When it 'sounds' properly, you seem yourself to have become an instrument embracing all possible sonorities, unleashed merely by waving a tiny stick.

If it entertains you, some day I'll develop these impressions.

To come back to Orpheus,[2] I like the second draft very much . . . without wanting to stifle the opportunity for a third one which will, perhaps, go more easily on the 'fine phrases' . . . they're excellent as they stand, but I'm sure in the final stage they'll be more integrated and shaped to receive music.

For today I won't say anything about our 'constructive' ideas over Orpheus. At first sight they seem to me to be pregnant with possibilities – but perhaps these have already been blocked? Don't you find that you're never the master of a system until you've stood back and surveyed all its consequences?

And don't you value the discoveries, or rediscoveries rather, which come from who knows what kinds of reflection? You think at the time they're sterile, but when eventually the flowers bloom they're all the more beautiful for the suffering they've undergone.

I've no news about the London concert. I'm waiting for some daily.

Don't worry, I'll send you a telegram if there's anything you need to know. In any case, we'll be at the Grosvenor Hotel.

With all best wishes to Madame Segalen
Yours ever
C.D.

[1] In place of *La Mer* on 12 January, Colonne conducted the *Prélude à l'après-midi d'un faune* and a suite by Alfred Bruneau. Debussy conducted *La Mer* on two successive Sundays, 19 and 26 January. His London performance was, as we have seen, fixed for 1 February.
[2] Debussy is referring to the operatic project *Orphée-roi*, for which Segalen was writing the libretto.

158 TO PAUL-JEAN TOULET

Cher ami   Wednesday 22 January 1908

You're one of the few people whose news I welcome. Understandably, you're not particularly keen on writing – except in a *Grande Revue*, to which you've contributed some absolutely ravishing 'Ombres chinoises'.[1]

You may say it's a delightful way of receiving your news, but forgive me if I prefer something more personal.

Since I last saw you I've made my debut as an orchestral conductor . . . It's interesting while you're using the little stick to obtain the colour you want, but after that it's more like an exhibition; and the reception of your success isn't very different, I feel, from that of a conjuror or an acrobat bringing off a successful leap.

I'm going to perform again in England and then in Italy . . . life is full of surprises.

Not wanting to be too emphatic on the subject, I'm disturbed by what you say about your health . . . But even if Saint-Loubès keeps you away from your friends for too long, perhaps we should be grateful to it even so for allowing you to recover.

I look forward to seeing you in March. Everyone will be delighted, including Mademoiselle Claude, who's telling stories in an Anglo-French patois that leaves both her grandmothers somewhat aghast.

With all our best wishes
Yours sincerely
C.D.

[187]

¹ The issue of the *Grande Revue* for 10 December 1907 contained a series of 'Ombres chinoises' by Toulet – short stories illustrated with woodcuts by Léone Georges. They were republished in *Comme une fantaisie* (1918).

159 TO JACQUES DURAND

Mon cher Jacques   [March 1908]

There's a letter for you at the Hôtel Gonnet which contains the news in detail . . . Insist on seeing it, because I'm afraid I can't remember it word for word and I think it might amuse you.

Don't blame the sea for getting on your nerves. It doesn't mean to, you know; and if its caresses are rough, they are at least sincere.

As for the 'whirlwind that is Paris', permit me to keep my distance!

I find the age we live in singularly uninviting in the fuss it makes over nothing. We're wrong to mock the 'bluff' of the Americans; we operate a kind of artistic 'bluff' and one of these days it's going to come crashing down around our ears – all very uncomfortable for French vanity.

The *Images* won't be quite complete by the time you get back, but I hope to play you a large part of them . . . I'm trying to write 'something else' – *realities*, in a manner of speaking – what imbeciles call 'impressionism', a term employed with the utmost inaccuracy, especially by art critics who use it as a label to stick on Turner, the finest creator of mystery in the whole of art!

Don't take the tone of this letter to mean I've become a pessimist. I've no time for that sort of attitude, only from time to time humanity disgusts me and I have to give vent to my feelings to someone who isn't going to interpret it as an illness.

My wife and I send all our best wishes for a pleasant stay, and journey home.

Yours ever
C.D.

160 TO JACQUES DURAND

Mon cher Jacques   Tuesday 24 March 1908

It was wonderful weather last Sunday, just right for enjoying oneself doing nothing . . . And that was the very day that M. Ph. Flon,¹ in his

[188]

profound wisdom, chose to get me to play right through *Pelléas* – with countless repeats. God, who concerns himself with hosts of good-for-nothings, is not kind to composers!

Ph. Flon alternated between appearing to understand and appearing to be at sea . . . in the end he went off very happy with his day, leaving me with a bruised right thumb. Perhaps it was all the ninths in the score – they've been the subject of various complaints in the past.

I'm glad Cannes is restoring your health and strength: it's what the place is best known for, but with these southern cities you never know if they're really to be taken seriously. My memories of the place go back to the time I was six.[2] I remember the railway in front of the house and the sea on the distant horizon, which sometimes gave the impression that the railway came out of the sea, or else went into it (as you pleased).

And then there was the road to Antibes with so many roses that I've never in my life seen so many at the same time – the perfume along that road certainly qualified as 'intoxicating'. I hope they've left the railway – convenient for your return journey – and the roses, which are still the best method of decorating the highway. If I also mention a Norwegian carpenter who sang from morning to night – Grieg songs, perhaps? – then that's the end of my 'Souvenirs'. Fear not, I won't turn them into an orchestral work ('The Carpenter's Apprentice').

I hope you've read Lalo's article?[3] It makes a very edifying read: we learn that *Ariane et Barbe-bleue* is decent people's music and *Pelléas* music for 'degenerates'. Because 'there are unsuspected defects' which are the only explanation for the strange assembly of characters that make up the admirers of this abominable music! The worst thing about it is the lowness of the means employed – namely that the 'good Jew' is defended by the 'bad Jesuit' . . . I wouldn't disagree for a second that the music of *Ariane et Barbe-bleue* is much more likely to satisfy these gentlemen's tastes than that of *Pelléas*. But why prevent the noble 'degenerates' from preferring their 'defects' and eternal damnation?

Richard Strauss, 'the symphonic domestic', was conducting at the Concerts Colonne last Sunday. Thanks to Ph. Flon I couldn't get to it.

Astruc has written to me about a Debussy Festival, to take place at the Opéra-comique, with the assistance of important artists: Planté,[4] Mme de X, etc. I'm going to suggest the Act IV duet from *Pelléas* with Mily-Meyer and Dranem.[5]

That's all for the moment . . .

Don't go on enjoying the delights of Cannes for ever. My wife joins me in sending best wishes to Madame Jacques Durand.

    Yours
    C.D.

[1] Philippe Flon, the director of the Lyon Opera, was putting on *Pelléas* a few weeks later.
[2] It was in 1870 or 1871 that Debussy stayed in Cannes: so he would have been eight or nine.
[3] In his article of the same date in *Le Temps*, Lalo in fact attacked the 'invertebrate descendants of "debussysme" . . . In the battle of *Pelléas* we had some strange allies: some days, we were so upset at finding ourselves alongside them we even began to think that, to attract such supporters, *Pelléas* must contain unsuspected defects. This won't happen with *Ariane* . . . Everyone will rally to his own standard. And the *Ariane* party will consist only of those who know how to value the essential qualities of the French spirit and of French art.'
[4] Francis Planté, 1839–1934, was a famous French pianist. (R.N.)
[5] Emilie Mily-Meyer was an operetta singer who made her debut in *Le petit duc* in 1878; Armand Menard, 1869–1935, known as Dranem, was a singer of popular songs.

161† TO GEORGES JEAN-AUBRY

    Cher ami   [1 April 1908]

I've asked *Musica* for the article on Gounod, but so far no reply . . . What a slack administration! I'll set my bookseller on to them – perhaps he'll get better results than I have.

Yesterday, for the first time, I heard two songs by André Caplet on poems by G. Jean-Aubry.

I like the music very much and have every expectation of liking the poems too when Madame Mellot-Joubert is good enough to articulate her pretty voice more clearly.

Caplet is an artist. He has the gift of conjuring up an atmosphere and, not only is he sensitive, he has a sense of proportion; which is much rarer than you might think, at a time when music is thrown together anyhow, with all the introverted intellectuality you find in a tavern!

I hope you're not still feeling the damage to your hand? At any rate the beauty of your poetry doesn't seem to have been affected.

I look forward to seeing you soon. My best wishes to your wife.

    Yours
    C.D.

162 TO JANE BATHORI[1]

Madame   [April 1908]

Please forgive my delay in answering you kind letter . . . But I must
insist straight away that you exaggerate my possible influence with M.
Carré over the casting of Mélisande! Anyway I never go to the Opéra-
comique, so I know absolutely nothing of the backstairs intrigues.

I've recently heard a young American,[2] Miss M. Teyte. She has a
charming voice and a true feeling for the character of Mélisande. As you
might expect, she also has the accent which the public of the Opéra-
comique has got so used to, thanks to Mademoiselle Garden. I am
convinced, as always, that your fine talent and excellent musicianship
give you the right to suppose that your Mélisande would indeed be an
original conception . . . Once again, I have no influence at the Opéra-
comique.

  With regret, I remain
  Yours sincerely
  C.D.

Please give M. Engel my best wishes. I am entirely at your disposal for
the concert you mention.

[1] Jane Bathori, 1877–1970, born Jeanne-Marie Berthier, was a soprano later to be
important in promoting the works of Les Six. In 1908 she married her singing teacher, the
tenor Emile Engel, who was thirty years her senior. She gave the first performance of Le
Promenoir des deux amants in January 1911 and towards the end of her life, in 1953,
published a book, Sur l'interprétation des mélodies de C. Debussy.
[2] Maggie Teyte was in fact English, born near Wolverhampton in 1888. (R.N.)

163 TO JACQUES DURAND

Cher ami   Thursday 18 June 1908

I came to see you in your office the very day you decided to leave for
your summer holidays . . . Without pretending I'm the only person
these things happen to, I will add that it was pouring with rain and my
nice grey hat is probably done for!

Have you seen in the papers that Miss Maggie Teyte[1] didn't have that
much to suffer from a comparison with her illustrious predecessor? I'm
sure the latter will, at the least, accuse me of ingratitude, as it's not part
of any singer's equipment to imagine she's dispensable. One rather

amusing detail is that everyone says Périer is getting better and better ... The reason, I'm sure, is that he's entirely given up singing what I wrote.

The final news about *Pelléas* is that the final performance of the season will be a matinée on Sunday. Périer is off to Cologne.

I've seen Caplet who's quite willing to lend a hand refurbishing *L'Enfant prodigue*:[2] so we'll soon get through it and be rid of this distinguished *revenant*.

These last few days I've been working solidly on *La Chute de la maison Usher* ... it's an excellent means of strengthening the nerves against all kinds of terror. All the same, there are moments when I lose awareness of my surroundings: and if Roderick Usher's sister walked through my front door I wouldn't exactly be surprised.

> I'll see you next Tuesday for certain.
> Yours till then
> C.D.

[1] Maggie Teyte had just taken over the role of Mélisande on 12 June. (She was to give 19 performances in the two seasons 1907–9, following the 60 performances by Mary Garden. R.N.)
[2] The orchestral score and the vocal score were both published by Durand in 1908.

164 TO PIERRE LALO

Cher Monsieur   Tuesday 23 June 1908

To have shed some light in the debate on *Boris Godunov* and *Pelléas et Mélisande* is an elegant gesture on your part, especially as a number of imbeciles had intervened and the whole thing looked almost like turning into a diplomatic incident.[1]

No point in seeking enlightenment from the Russians, I'm sure you'll agree – not even over Mussorgsky; when I was in Russia some twenty years ago, I found his name was never mentioned.

It was only in France I was able to get to know his music as is the case with many of the Russian composers. On this point the French are not much different. It's remarkable how reluctant we are to admit that one of our compatriots has discovered anything at all ... And how ingenious we are at spotting resemblances at the slightest opportunity.

Are we always going to reserve national pride for our fashionable hats?

[192]

26 Maggie Teyte, the second Mélisande.

But I'm becoming a bore, when all I wanted to do was thank you.

Yours sincerely
C.D.

[1] The relevant passage of Pierre Lalo's review, in *le Temps* of the same day, ran: '*Pelléas* and *Boris* have some successions of chords in common and some orchestral sonorities, that's all . . . Debussy's music is organized with harmonious refinement while *Boris* is full of disorder and chaos . . .' We may note that after the worsening of the personal relationship between Lalo and Debussy, 'cher ami' has become 'cher Monsieur'.

165† TO GIULIO GATTI-CASAZZA[1]

Monsieur le Directeur   Sunday 5 July 1908

Following our conversation earlier today, I confirm my undertaking to give first refusal on the two works herein mentioned:

La Chute de la maison Usher
Le Diable dans le beffroi

to the Metropolitan Opera and to its affiliated theatres in the United States of America, including the Boston Opera Company.

This agreement is made in return for a payment of 10,000 francs for the two operas, of which sum I have already received 2,000 francs, the balance to be paid on delivery by my editor of the complete music.

Further I demand that the two works in question should always be given on the same evening, whether in New York or in the affiliated theatres and that no work of any other composer should appear on the same programme.

I also confirm that I give the Metropolitan Opera the first option on my future works, and in particular on the 'Légende de Tristan'.

I remain
Yours sincerely
C.D.

[1] Gatti-Casazza had just taken up his post as director of the Metropolitan Opera House.

Cher ami   6 August 1908

Here's the signature in my blackest ink . . . for *Children's Corner*, the red on the cover must be an orange-red — try and surround the 'Golliwogg's' head with a golden halo – for the cover, a light grey paper scattered with snow.

For the title of the 'Trois Chansons' – we must have: *Trois Chansons de Charles d'Orléans* and not Poésie de Charles d'Orléans – anyway why 'poésie' in the singular, which is meaningless? Could the layout follow that of the *Trois Chansons de France*?

C.D.

167 TO VICTOR SEGALEN

Cher ami   Thursday 27 August 1908

Forgive the long delay . . . at the moment I'm toiling away like a miner, spending all day furiously digging music out of a brain which doesn't always summon up enthusiasm for this over-production.

The two acts you sent seem to me to be pretty well in their final state.[1] No more needs to be done except to take out some excess wordage: occasionally, too, the rhythm is more suited to reading than singing. By way of explanation I could quote – if I had the patience – pages of Chateaubriand, Victor Hugo and Flaubert which are always said to be lyrical in the extreme, but which – to my way of thinking – contain no music whatever. It's something writers will never admit, because it's a mystery and impossible to explain. I'm sure a couple of hours together will sort out any problems.

I hope you agree we must expand the role of the crowd . . . it mustn't just stay at the back of the stage, grumbling inexplicably. I would point out that this will only add to the stature of Orpheus, as well as getting over more clearly the innate animosity of the crowd towards genius.

I'm delighted to know you're going to be in Paris for a long spell. I hope I can free myself during this period from all my current tasks; then we can work, or do nothing, depending on how we feel.

With best wishes to your wife
Yours
C.D.

[1] This refers to the *Orpheus* project, suggested in letter 153 and discussed in letter 157. In the meantime the Segalens had met Debussy in London when he was conducting at the Queen's Hall in February.

168 TO FRANCISCO DE LACERDA[1]

Cher ami   Saturday 5 September 1908

I was very happy to hear of your appointment and to know that M. Emery[2] wasn't as rough on you as his name might suggest.[3] So now you've got a foot on the ladder and some security; and perhaps you prefer the air of Montreux to the 'Schola's' ecclesiastical vapours?

Talking of which, your friend E. Satie has just finished a fugue in which boredom disguises itself behind wicked harmonies and in which you will recognize the influence of the aforementioned establishment.[4]

In case you're interested, I may say I'm still living an ant-like existence. I'm devouring nearly twenty pages of manuscript paper a day; as you can imagine, from the hygienic point of view it's frightful! I'm not convinced it's terribly good from the artistic point of view, either.

But then we have to justify our right to exist. Even so, an oak tree's life is finer and, above all, more profitable. For example, an oak tree can turn into one of those Henry II dining-rooms girls dream about! Or into a piano on which those same girls can linger innocently over the latest thought from Francis Thomé.[5]

I must stop before I get sentimental.

Yours ever
C.D.

[1] Portuguese composer and conductor who had been in Paris since 1895. He studied and then taught at the Schola Cantorum, and had just been appointed to a conducting post in Montreux where Ernest Ansermet was one of his pupils.

[2] The administrator of the Kursaal in Montreux, to whom Debussy had sent a letter of recommendation on Lacerda's behalf.

[3] '. . . aussi bouché que son nom l'indique'. 'Bouché à l'émeri' means 'totally stupid'. (R.N.)

[4] Erik Satie entered the Schola Cantorum at the age of nearly forty and studied there between 1905 and 1908.

[5] A well-known composer of salon pieces for piano, the most famous being *Simple aveu*. He died in 1909.

Cher ami   Tuesday 22 September 1908

I couldn't get to see you last Saturday, as I promised, because I had an appointment with Mademoiselle E. F. Bauer[1] – an American journalist – who came to ask my advice on how to educate young American geniuses . . . For as I'm sure you're aware, any future artistic discoveries will be reaching us from America.

To make up for lost time, a child's genius will be spotted around the age of 8 or 10. It's so ridiculous, it's rather charming. Anyway I assured Mlle Bauer that her compatriots would come up with a machine into which you could put any old child and it would turn him into a genius in five minutes.

When are you coming back to Paris? With regard to *Printemps*, is there any problem about my including a part for piano duet?[2]

Yours
C.D.

[1] Emily Frances Bauer published the result of the interview in *Harper's Weekly* (29 August 1908). The date at the head of the text is 6 August; all in all, it looks as if Debussy was using her as an excuse not to see Durand. The interview is published in R. Langham Smith, *Debussy on Music* (London, 1977), pp. 232–5.
[2] Debussy did not in fact re-orchestrate his Rome 'envoi' of 1887. This was done in 1912 by Henry Busser, under the composer's supervision; the revised score does include a part for piano duet.

                                            Hotel Cecil London
Mon cher ami   27 February 1909

Forgive me for not sending you any news. I've been ill continuously since arriving here on Thursday evening and so had to cancel my trips to Edinburgh and Manchester! . . .

The concert today went splendidly: 'Fêtes' was encored and, if I'd wanted, the same would have happened to the *Prélude à l'après-midi d'un faune* . . . Only I couldn't stay standing any longer . . . the worst sort of position for conducting anything.

This evening I've got to go to a reception organized by the Society of English Composers . . . What sort of figure shall I cut?

Something on the lines of a man condemned to death; it seems I can't get out of it because of the *Entente Cordiale* and other sentimental notions, invented to hasten the death of one's neighbour, probably.[1]

We're staying here tomorrow, Sunday, so as to be feeling more rested on Monday.

So I'll come and see you in your office on Tuesday. With all best wishes from my wife and myself.

Yours
C.D.

[1] For Henry Wood's memories of the concert, and Arnold Bax's of the reception, see Lockspeiser, *Debussy, his Life and Mind* Vol. II, Cambridge University Press, 1978, pp. 122–4. To these may be added a memory of the reception from the English pianist, the late Mary Antonietti. Although no more than a girl at the time, she was one of the few present who spoke French. She was sitting on the sofa next to the composer, who opened the following brief conversation: 'Aimez-vous Londres?' 'Non.' 'Moi non plus.'

171 TO GABRIEL MOUREY[1]

Mon cher Mourey   29 March 1909

Your letter arrived too late for me to be able to send you tickets: anyway Séchiari[2] isn't doing too well, so he's being fairly mean with them!

'Huon de Bordeaux' is all very well but it's taking us back into a world of helmets and ready-made legend ... I prefer your idea for 'Le Marchand de rêves' ... that doesn't necessitate anything, so we can do everything; and that's just what we want. This is more of a fairy-tale era than Monsieur Clemenceau imagines! It's just a question of finding it.[3]

I mentioned 'Le Chat botté' because it's a solid, well-known basis and the public will then realize more easily the transformations it's undergone.

Keep thinking about it, and come and discuss it when you want to. Only warn me first, as I've a fairly busy week ahead.

Yours ever
C.D.

[1] An art critic and a translator of the poetry of Swinburne and Poe. See also letter 152.
[2] The violinist Pierre Séchiari, 1877–1932, had founded a string quartet and since 1906 had managed the Association des concerts Séchiari. Debussy conducted *L'Après-midi d'un faune* at a concert on 25 March.
[3] An allusion to Clemenceau's attitude, as Minister of the Interior, to the postal workers' strike.

London

Mon cher Jacques   18 May 1909

The première of *Pelléas*, which ought to have taken place today, has been postponed till Friday.[1] Behind that announcement lies a number of strange and ridiculous events! . . .

There's a producer here called Alomanz; he comes from Marseilles, sees platforms where there's nothing but empty space and imagines wonderful flowering bushes on struts as naked as a blind man's stick. You may imagine what can be achieved by a man as forceful as that! I've rarely had such a strong desire to kill anybody.

I have to act as electrician, machine operator . . . God knows how it'll all end up!

Fortunately, the orchestra is doing well. Campanini[2] understands the work fairly well — a little too extrovert — but at least it's warm and alive.

I think Warnery[3] will be very good, though I haven't seen him in costume yet.

Marcoux and Bourbon are good too. As for Mlle Féart she's indescribably ugly and lacking in poetry, and I find myself regretting the absence of the good Miss Teyte.[4] Naturally she sings the notes, but there's nothing behind them. In confidence, it's a disappointment.

The fact is, it could have been an excellent performance but for the usual thing, trying to do a month's work in eight days. I've done everything I can and my artistic conscience will be clear.

It has to be said that Higgins and Percy Pitt[5] are charming and full of goodwill: the real blame lies, as you know, with composers who are happy to have things near enough right, just so long as they're played!

Now the only thing I want is to go back home . . . the theatre atmosphere makes me ill; however anxious people are to please, there's always something run-of-the-mill that comes along and sends you head over heels.

With all our best wishes to your wife and yourself,

Yours
C.D.

---

[1] 21 May. (R.N.)
[2] Cleofonte Campanini specialized in the Italian repertory. (He had conducted the first American performance of *Pelléas* at the Metropolitan Opera on 19 February 1908. R.N.).

[199]

³ Warnery, Marcoux and Bourbon sang the roles of Pelléas, Arkel and Golaud respectively. (R.N.)

⁴ However, on 6 December 1908 Debussy wrote of Rose Féart, 'her voice and musicality please me enormously'; and, in June 1908, of Maggie Teyte, that she showed 'barely as much emotion as a prison door'.

⁵ The manager and musical director of Covent Garden.

173 TO VANNI MARCOUX[1]

Royal Palace Hotel Kensington

Mon cher Monsieur Marcoux   London 22 May 1909

May I express my gratitude for all the real and profound beauty that your wonderful talent has brought out in the character of Arkel.

Since you are an artist and a man of complete understanding, I should like to ask you to emphasize a little more Arkel's great kindness! And that might be done perhaps more by the carriage of the head than in the tone of voice.

Forgive me for mentioning this detail which is not any kind of criticism but advice, prompted by affection and your own high standards.

Thank you once again
C.D.

¹ The baritone and bass Vanni Marcoux, 1879–1962, sang in the provinces and abroad before making his debut at the Opéra in 1909. After singing Arkel in London, he took on the role of Golaud in Boston in 1912 and in Paris in 1914.

174 TO HIS PARENTS

Cher Papa, chère Maman   23 May 1909

Here are some extra details about the première of *Pelléas* in London, relayed to me as I didn't attend this ceremony: signs that it would be a success were visible in the first Act and they became clearer and clearer right through to the end. The singers were recalled a dozen times and for a quarter of an hour there were calls for the composer, who was settled peacefully in his hotel 'far from the vain sounds of applause' . . . Then Campanini came on twice to take a bow and at last the mob consented to go home to bed.

Received opinion states that such a reaction is extremely rare in England, where the temperature of the public tends to remain below zero ... So long live France! Long live French music! And music for ever! [...] I had to concern myself with the scenery and the lighting effects, not to mention the music ...

Your devoted son
C.D.

175† TO JACQUES DURAND

Mon cher Jacques   23 May 1909

Here are some extra details about the première of *Pelléas*, relayed to me because, as you may imagine, I didn't attend this little celebration!

In the first Act signs were visible that it would be a success and they became ever clearer right through to the end. There were calls for the composer for a quarter of an hour. He was resting quietly in his hotel, unconcerned for any kind of glory.

Then Cleofonte Campanini came on twice to take a bow and telephoned me to say the *opera* had had an enormous 'success' such as had rarely been seen in England. He also came to see me the next morning and confirmed the victory, to the accompaniment of Punch-like grimaces, and then embraced me as though I was a medal blessed by the Pope.

Mlle Féart was, it seems, transformed and almost pretty! Warnery didn't think it incumbent on him to come and thank me: so much for man's ingratitude in general and tenors' in particular.

It's likely that in a theatre like Covent Garden, where the final effect is all that matters, everyone saves their utmost for the première. I can tell you, the last dress rehearsal was terrible.

We're leaving tomorrow morning at 11. My wife has been unwell for some days, so that I view the end of the journey with both fear and longing.

I hope to see you on Tuesday and to find you less uneasy about your father's health.

With best wishes from us both
Yours
C.D.

[201]

Mon cher ami   12 June 1909

I was hoping to see you this morning with M. Gatti-Casazza and thank you for last night's performance . . .[1] Chaliapin is absolutely amazing, although the role of Yvan doesn't suit him as well as that of Boris.

As for the ballet, I've probably forgotten what to look for in this kind of spectacle, because I was bored by it. Even so, what a curious way of dressing people up! I fancy we do better than that at the Folies Bergères! Or did I come at a bad moment?

With thanks from us both
C.D.

[1] The programme on 11 June consisted of Rimsky-Korsakov's *Ivan the Terrible (The Maid of Pskov)* and *Le Festin*, a ballet with a scenario by Diaghilev and music by various Russian composers. The costumes Debussy complains about below were mostly the work of Bakst and Benois.

Mon cher ami   26 June 1909

You must blame the lack of news on the appalling weather we're being treated to at the moment . . .

The days pass in a grey, humid, heavy atmosphere, enough to make an oak tree depressed.

In *Pelléas*, it's expressed as follows:[1]

You'll agree, no one can live with those harmonies in his ears every day!

I hope Switzerland[2] is providing better weather for you. Taking the cure in pouring rain seems superfluous . . .

Nothing out of the ordinary's happening here apart from the usual strikes, without which Paris would certainly be a duller place. Caplet has just gone off to do some hard composing at Criquebeuf-en-Caux. I've had the honour of being invited to sit on the jury for the singing examination (ladies).[3] If anybody wants my place I'd be happy to give it to them, perhaps even with a little money attached.

[202]

I've been working on *La Chute de la maison Usher* recently and have almost finished a long monologue for Roderick. It's sad enough to make the stones weep for what neurasthenics have to go through. It smells charmingly of mildew, obtained by mixing the sounds of a low oboe with violin harmonics (B.S.G.D.G.)[4]. I'm very proud of it, so don't tell anyone.

Don't drink more water than you have to and, whatever you do, come back to Paris . . . I look forward very much to seeing you again.

    C.D.

Chouchou's well, her mother's better.

[1]   The chords are an abbreviated version of 3 bars at the beginning of Act III scene 3. Golaud and Pelléas have come up out of the vaults and the chords accompany Pelléas's words: 'Il y a là un air humide et lourd comme une rosée de plomb, et des ténèbres épaisses comme une pâte empoisonnée' (The air down there is damp and heavy like a leaden mist, and the dense shadows are like a poisoned broth.) (R.N.)
[2]   Durand was in fact at Evian.
[3]   At the Conservatoire.
[4]   'Breveté Sans Garantie Du Gouvernement' (Patent not guaranteed by the government).

The Russian Ballet
Images for orchestra

Debussy was the first composer Diaghilev thought of in 1909 to write a work for his company. The first idea came to nothing: Debussy preferred to concentrate on finishing the *Images* for orchestra, which he had been working on for a long time, as well as the first book of *Préludes* for piano, the *Trois Ballades de François Villon* and the first version of the libretto for *La Chute de la maison Usher*.

He suffered loneliness in his house on the avenue du Bois de Boulogne, and his deep depression was only somewhat lightened by Chouchou's gaiety and spontaneous sense of fun. It was at this time that the first symptoms appeared of the disease that was to kill him. The one real compensation for his unhappiness was his new-found friendship with André Caplet, who became an indispensable collaborator.

178† TO JACQUES DURAND

       Cher ami   13 July 1909
I came to your office to bring some proofs and found you'd gone back
to the country. I trust you're well – we certainly need to be to survive
the hydrotherapy we're undergoing at the moment.

       Choisnel tells me you'd like to have the next portion of the *Images*
. . . I confess I've rather put them on one side lately in favour of Edgar
Allan Poe. It's an absorbing task, so I hope you'll forgive me?

       Don't worry, anyway; I will come back to the *Images* and finish them
to your satisfaction.

       I've just been sitting on the jury for the woodwind competitions at the
Conservatoire and I can give you good news of the high standard of the
flutes, oboes and clarinets; as for the bassoons, they're admirable . . .
the sound of the instrument is tending towards pathos and, mark my
words, that's going to alter certain orchestral 'values'.

       Chouchou has just had an operation for enlarged tonsils. She's come
through it well and has almost totally recovered.

       Hoping to see you soon and with all our best wishes to your wife,

       Yours
       C.D.

179 TO JACQUES DURAND

       Cher ami   18 July 1909
I've seen M. S. de Diaghilev,[1] accompanied by Laloy. As the latter speaks
French too well for the former, the conversation ran into a few difficulties.

Naturally, I can't suggest a ballet subject at the drop of a hat; and there they are talking to me about 18th-century Italy! . . .[2] Which, for Russian dancers, strikes me as a bit contradictory.

But they don't need the piano score till 10 January and the orchestral material till the first fortnight in May.

Given these dates, perhaps I could try it? . . . As for contracts, down payments, etc., I confess to total ignorance and would be grateful if you could discuss terms with M. S. de D. As he told me he intended to stage the ballet in Rome, Moscow, etc. . . . he would like to keep certain rights in the work; I imagine we wouldn't let him have them without firm guarantees on his part?

Could we perhaps ask for a down payment on delivery of the piano score?

I hope to come and see you next Tuesday.

> Yours
> C.D.

[1]Diaghilev's successful 1909 season with the Ballets russes was the first to be given over exclusively to ballet. Paris had seen Nijinsky in *Le Festin*, *Le Pavillon d'Armide*, *Les Sylphides* and *Cléopâtre*, as well as scenery and costumes by Bakst and Benois.
[2]The ballet was called *Masques et bergamasques*. Debussy got no further than writing the libretto, which Durand published in 1910. The composer's decision to write it on his own led to a strain in his relationship with Laloy. (see letters 181 and 182 below).

180 TO ANDRÉ CAPLET[1]

Cher André Caplet   20 July 1909

Chouchou Debussy is grateful to you for worrying about her health. It was a matter of enlarged tonsils and the problem was solved in a moment. No need to tell you that the celebrated 'Dagobert'[2] played his most important role in this operation . . . She's quite better now and can go back to singing that renowned repertory of hers, in which opera and operetta live peacefully side by side.

A gap of two days at this point, while I've been writing a ballet scenario for Claude Debussy and the next season of the Ballets russes . . .[3]

I've also had some bad moments since you left, what with feeling low and the rain, which drowns my firm intentions of being a genius every

[206]

27 André Caplet and Debussy.

morning as soon as I get out of bed . . . The only good day I've spent was at the woodwind competition. What clarinets! And oboes, and velvety flutes. As for the bassoons, they're quite admirable . . . as pathetic as Tchaikovsky and as ironic as Jules Renard. And all in a fantasy by Henri Busser, written as if he'd been born in a bassoon . . . – which is not to say he was born to make music.

We've decided to stay in Paris, I think, as without travelling to another world we'd probably only find the same rain we have here with the added disadvantages of not being at home, having to work on tables usually no more than 75 cm. wide and meeting people who aren't always willing to remain anonymous.

As you can gather, I'm in the sort of mood where I'd rather be a sponge at the bottom of the sea or a vase on the mantelpiece, anything rather than a man of intellect; such a fragile kind of machine, which goes only when it wants to and against which the will of man is powerless . . . You give orders to someone who won't obey you and that someone is yourself! It's difficult to treat yourself like an idiot, your thoughts go blankly round and round; like sad horses on a merry-go-round, with no music and no riders.

Perhaps it's the punishment for those who are too fond of ideas, but wear themselves out pursuing just one . . . whence the *idée fixe* . . . the prologue to madness.

We shouldn't chastise ourselves, though, not even with an idea. And don't go shedding tears at this gloomy monologue. I like to think you're in a better state than me, at all events, even if you've no energy. You have the sea to console you and the right to be bad-tempered when you want to be . . . and that's something.

> With all best wishes from the family
> Yours ever
> C.D.

1 Debussy had known this young composer and conductor since 1907. They quickly became close friends and Caplet helped him bring several of his works to a condition where they could be performed.
2 One of Chouchou's toys. (R.N.)
3 *Masques et bergamasques.*

181 TO LOUIS LALOY

Cher ami   27 July 1909

Why are you at Rahon par Chaussin[1] instead of 80 avenue du Bois de Boulogne? . . . where it would be much easier for me to tell you of my decision, come what may, to write the scenario for the Russo-Venetian ballet.[2]

May all the gods whose job it is to guard friendships prevent you from thinking I've forgotten . . . the other arrangement – which you remind me of so tactfully.

I hope you'll be willing to extend your forgetfulness of past wrongs to continuing your moral support in the dealings I shall have to have one day with these people? As you so rightly say, 'they speak and think Russian' and you are the only one who can help me.

I humbly admit that the impulse to take this decision so abruptly came from what I know to be the bad side of my character . . . launching out enthusiastically, only to lose heart later. But I do treasure, in a secret corner of my heart, the idea of working with you on Aeschylus' *Oresteia* . . . in that we shall be completely our own masters, with all the time we need and not bothered either by Russia or the Place de la Madeleine.[3]

I won't offer any further explanations, as you've got me used to your habit of understanding the things I don't say. It may not look like it, but it's much more cunning than Oedipus' game with the Sphinx.

There's no need to alter anything in the advice you've given for playing my music. It remains simply to read and understand.

The dates Géjéon[4] has fixed are somewhat dangerously optimistic – I'll try and change them to something more reasonable.

Despite the first part of this letter, which was very hard to write,

    I remain
    Yours ever
    C.D.

[1] Laloy's country home between Dôle and Poligny in the Jura.
[2] *Masques et bergamasques.*
[3] His publisher Durand.
[4] The nickname of G. Jean-Aubry.

Mon cher ami   30 July 1909

I can't have read your telegram or your letter carefully enough, because
I can't really understand either of them . . . And now you're talking
about going off to Venice to see a dancer? . . . A great honour for him
and what's more, I should think, extremely complicated.

Let's set out the facts in legal fashion, if that's what you want.

1. You come and see me with Diaghilev. The meeting is spent
talking about various ideas but with no clearcut result.

2. I meet Diaghilev at Durand's and he mentions a possible
collaboration with P. J. Toulet . . . (another complication). At
the same time he says that, as he's leaving for Venice in three
days' time to go and see the *maître de ballet*, he'd like to take a
scenario to show him.

3. As it's now a question merely of a divertissement intended to
last fifty minutes at the most, I don't see the point of turning the
universe and yourself upside-down and I write the aforementioned scenario, with the minimum of plot to link the dances.
Diaghilev thinks it's charming. It's agreed instantly that
Nijinsky and Karsavina will take the leading roles. You see how
simple it all is!

I must add that I don't see why my having written the scenario
precludes the possibility of your collaboration. Whether it's to be
'official', as you put it, or 'friendly' is just a matter of words . . . though
I'd be happier with the latter.

Everything will turn out for the best, you'll see, and when the time
comes your help will be both valuable and necessary . . . But so far my
needs are so simple, I don't require any assistance for the moment. Not,
at least, from this 'official' angle you insist on which, coming from you,
I find incomprehensible. The legal document continues: we're dealing
with a Russian who understands French perfectly well and I give you
my word he'll understand everything I ask of him. I have no intention of
asking Nijinsky to describe symbols with his legs or Karsavina to
explain Kant's philosophy with her smile.

I intend to enjoy myself writing this ballet – an excellent state of mind for
a divertissement – and I hope you'll enjoy it too, in spite of everything.

Yours
C.D.

[210]

183 TO M. D. CALVOCORESSI[1]

Cher Monsieur   3 August 1909

My sincere thanks for sending me *Le Coq d'Or*. It's the music of an old conjuror[2] who was very good once and remembers the fact.

My compliments on the translation which, despite the rather breathless comic tone of the libretto, can't have given you much pleasure.

Yours sincerely
C.D.

[1] A critic who in 1907 had published an edition of Rimsky-Korsakov's *Le Coq d'Or* with French words. In a letter to Laloy of 22 February 1907, Debussy calls Calvocoressi a 'valet de chambre' because of his support of Ravel.
[2] Debussy had used the same word to describe Ravel in letter 147 to Laloy of March 1907.

184 TO EDGARD VARÈSE[1]

Cher Monsieur   10 August 1909

As I'm away from Paris I didn't receive your letter till this morning . . . So please forgive this late reply.

The *Fantaisie* you mention is not even published, but I've been intending for a long time to rework it almost entirely. Since 1889, when it was written, I've changed my views about how to combine piano and orchestra. The scoring would have to be altered too, to avoid a slightly ridiculous contest between the two characters![2]

Your story about R. Strauss is charming. But, without wanting to play down the value of what he said, I feel he has nothing to fear from competition these days and can afford to play the generous patron.[3]

I hope your future plans turn out as well as you deserve,

Yours most sincerely
C.D.

[1] Born of a Piedmontese father and a French mother, Varèse had been a pupil of d'Indy and Roussel at the Schola Cantorum and of Widor at the Conservatoire. He introduced himself to Debussy in October 1908 and tried unsuccessfully to introduce Busoni to him in February 1909.
[2] This work was engraved by Choudens but not published. It narrowly missed being performed in 1890 at the Société nationale de musique (see letter 17) and again in 1896 at the Concerts Colonne. It was published and played only after the composer's death.

(Alfred Cortot gave the first performance at a Royal Philharmonic Society concert in London on 20 November 1919. R.N.).

[3] Probably alluding to Strauss's recommendation that *Pelléas* should be staged in Vienna. (The Viennese première took place at the Hofoper on 23 May 1911. R.N.).

185   TO ANDRÉ CAPLET

25 August 1909

No, it's not neurasthenia and it's not hypocrisy either, but the delightful pain of choosing one idea out of many. And then I've been spending my days lately in *La Maison Usher*, which isn't exactly a house to calm the nerves, quite the opposite . . . You get into the strange habit of listening to the dialogue of the stones and expecting houses to fall down as though that were a natural, even necessary phenomenon. What's more, if you press me to, I'd admit to a greater sympathy with that house's inhabitants than with . . . many others, who shall remain anonymous. The man of unbending moral rectitude never inspires me with any confidence whatever . . . There was a great moralist called Carlyle, a Scotsman and something of a Calvinist, who brandished his morality under the noses of his contemporaries. He made his wife very unhappy and travelled eight kilometres every day to play the lovelorn schoolboy at the feet of a young lady who refused his advances, in the name of another, probably superior, morality.[1] I mention it because reading his works forms part of my regular morning exercise . . .

I haven't read Pierre Lalo's article,[2] and you can be sure I won't . . . The father of this excellent critic wasn't a very good composer, but he showed talent from time to time. The son has continued in his father's tradition of being an unsympathetic personality, but without the smiling elegance for which one forgave the father.[3] In short, he's one of the many who don't hear music for itself but for what, to their ears, it brings with it of traditions laboriously learned; and they can't change these without running the risk of no longer understanding anything . . . It's the sort of blind, idiotic superstition which goes on for centuries and spreads itself over everything that's submitted to human judgement; while the artists themselves have a struggle not simply to create new stereotypes in place of the old.

Have you read a piece of news which, so the newspapers tell us, is of prime importance? . . . Arrigo Boito has finished his handiwork (left or right handiwork, one knows not) in the matter of his opera *Nerone*.

[212]

28 An 'official' photograph by Nadar.

This story's been on the go for a little over twenty years now. And by this same stroke Boito throws away his admirable position as a man who might perhaps have written a masterpiece. Why didn't he wait till he was dead? Because, even if people admit he's produced a masterpiece, many of them will never forgive him for making them wait so long . . .[4] When you miss a train, you're more inclined to blame the driver than yourself. With which piece of sound commonsense, I take my leave.

> With best wishes from us all
> C.D.

[1] An allusion to the, apparently Platonic, relationship between Thomas Carlyle and Harriet Baring. Debussy refers to this writer twice in his articles describing him as a 'charming dyspeptic' in 1903, and *Sartor Resartus* as 'that cruel breviary of humour' in 1914.
[2] The article in question appeared in *le Temps* on 18 August. In it Lalo discussed the *Chansons de Charles d'Orléans* and Debussy's imitators.
[3] Nothing we know of this composer confirms Debussy's opinion.
[4] *Nerone* was first published in 1901 as a 'tragedy'. Boito took his time setting it to music and at his death, in 1918, the orchestration was still unfinished; it was completed by Smareglia and Tommasini. The opera was not performed until 1924, and then without much success; d'Annunzio said of it: 'Is it possible to keep a single work "inside oneself" and go on modifying it for fifty years?'

186† TO GEORGES JEAN-AUBRY

> Mon cher ami   9 September 1909

I read your libretto[1] as soon as it arrived . . . It's a charming tale and the plot is, naturally, ingenious and poetic to the utmost degree: I say 'naturally' because poets these days are so often strangely perverse in the way they extract a passionate lyricism from desperately mundane subjects.

I've spent the summer in the shadow of the suburban railway which runs near the house, and I've been absorbed with the idea that one doesn't need to hear the song of the nightingale – the song of the trains is much more in tune with modern artistic preoccupations!

Caplet is good enough to send me some news from time to time; he seems very well both physically and mentally.

I find it very wrong of you to be leaving Paris and your friends are right to complain.

> Yours ever
> C.D.

[1] The subject of this is unknown.

187 TO ADOLPHE ADERER[1]

Cher Monsieur   8 October 1909

Your friend is absolutely right. If, when a musical theatre was being built, more attention were paid to the orchestra pit and less to the cloakroom, then one could seat the instruments as one wanted.

It's one of the many results of – force of habit, which is often the opposite of good sense and even of good taste.

Someone is surely bound to mention Germany? . . . It's true that music there is housed better and listened to more seriously – even if that's only completely true of the most important centres. Our native ingenuity ought to stand in the way of our simply taking the easy path and going on as before, without over-encouraging our passion for brutally disciplined music which is suitable, at best, for audiences outside France.

Yours sincerely
C.D.

[1] The theatre critic of *le Temps*, who published this letter on 13 October, as well as replies from Saint-Saëns, Massenet and Widor, as part of his inquiry into 'Orchestral seating in musical theatres'.

188 TO ALBERT CARRÉ

Cher Monsieur Carré   30 October 1909

I've just heard Mr Coulomb.[1] He's very good and I think there's hope he'll be a perfect Pelléas, at last!

The voice is attractive and intelligent; the curious thing is, he knows about music and even seems to like it!

Could you allow him some free time so that I can do some detailed work with him as soon as possible? I'd be most grateful.

With many thanks
C.D.

[1] Coulomb had just made his debut in Saint-Saëns's opera *La Princesse jaune*. He was never to sing Pelléas.

25 November 1909

Forgive me, all my time lately has been taken up doing boring and exhausting things. I've been dedicating myself to the betterment of the pianistic race in France . . .[1] Life's habitual irony saw to it that the most artistic of all the candidates was a young Brazilian girl of 13. She's not beautiful, but her eyes are 'drunk with music' and she has that ability to cut herself off from her surroundings which is the rare but characteristic mark of the artist.

The jury included some odd musicians who'd have been more at home, I fancy, judging livestock. And I came to unshakeable conclusions on two points: that Beethoven wrote really rather badly for the piano and that there exists a mysterious correlation between people's ugliness and the music they choose . . . When all's said and done, one doesn't often have the opportunity of hearing a fantasy on *Les Dragons de Villars*,[2] not to mention a Scherzo by Vollenhaupt,[3] a composer dead long since, it turns out: a fact which fails of its effect on those who were unaware he'd ever lived.

The Conservatoire remains the same gloomy, dirty place we remember,[4] where the dust of unhealthy traditions still sticks to the fingers. You speak of 'our envelope' like a true spiritualist, but I hope you'll be kind enough to preserve yours for our sake. I don't see any reason why we should actively seek out the dust of history and maybe – who knows? – give rise to one of those awful monuments, to be branded by our grandchildren as being of national importance.

Did you manage to get any work done, before this wretched illness struck? It's important, as my poor friend Charpentier used to say – the era we live in has a need for beauty and especially for 'music', which people dress up in tinsel and ugly masks as though its real face was unpleasant to look at. You may agree, perhaps, that all that is merely an 'establishment' attitude in reverse?

Let me have your news as soon as possible and I hope it's good.

    With all best wishes from the family
    Yours
    C.D.

If there's anything at all I can do to help you, please don't hesitate to ask.

    [216]

[1]   Debussy was serving this year on the jury for the piano entrance examinations at the Conservatoire. (The young Brazilian girl was Guiomar Novaes, 1896–1979, who entered Isidor Philipp's class in 1910. R.N.).
[2]   Quite a number of fantasies were written on this opéra-comique by Aimé Maillart.
[3]   Heinrich Adolf Wollenhaupt, 1827–1863, was a German pianist and composer whose career was centred on New York.
[4]   The Conservatoire moved the following summer from the site on the rue du Faubourg Poissonnière to its present position on the rue de Madrid. (R.N.)

190 TO ANDRÉ CAPLET

Cher André Caplet   25 February 1910

You'll blame me, quite rightly, for my apparent indifference to your health and your news ... as for your health, Jacques[1] has been kind enough to send me words of reassurance, so I naturally thought I'd have time to write to you (I was wrong). To which add all kinds of distractions ... illness, rehearsals, jangling nerves ... the full, horrible gamut of Parisian life.

   As for *Ibéria*, only the third movement worked as it should; with the two others we'll have to start all over again ... The 'ultra-Spanish' rhythm of the first went all 'left-bank' under our young 'Capell-meister's'[2] intelligent conducting and the 'perfumes of the night' seeped out discreetly from under a bolster, presumably so as not to upset anybody. I wish you'd been there to share my suffering; a desire you will please interpret as containing a dash of egoism and a large dose of friendship.

   Today I rehearsed *Rondes de Printemps* ... it's not for me to tell you anything about the music, but the orchestra sounds like crystal, as light as a woman's hand (not Blanche Selva's).[3]

Saturday morning [26 February]

This morning, rehearsal of *Ibéria* ... it's going better. The aforemen-tioned young Capellmeister and his orchestra have consented to be less earthbound and to take wing somewhat ... You can't imagine how naturally the transition works between 'Parfums de la nuit' and 'Le matin d'un jour de fête'. *It sounds as though it's improvised* ... The way it comes to life, with people and things waking up ... There's a man selling water-melons and urchins whistling, I see them quite clearly ... Mind you, not everyone finds it all so obvious – some people

[217]

thought it was a serenade. But that's of no importance whatever, any more than an article by Lalo in which that great critic gives me orchestration lessons, claiming I *never* use instruments for their natural sound.[4] So far I've done nothing but write about myself ... I hope, when you write, you'll pay me back and tell me about nothing but yourself, and that the letter reaches me soon, please.

Yours
C.D.

[1] Jacques Durand.
[2] Gabriel Pierné, who conducted the first performance of *Ibéria* at the Colonne Concerts on 20 February.
[3] The pianist Blanche Selva, who had studied with d'Indy and now taught piano at the Schola Cantorum (She was, to say the least, generously proportioned. R.N.).
[4] Pierre Lalo wrote of *Ibéria* as follows in *Le Temps* on 26 February: 'What an abuse of percussion and woodwind, with oboes and clarinets endlessly nasalizing! And the brass forever muted, never sounding with their natural voice or doing their proper job, but always giving sneering laughs like Mr Punch! Music from a Tunisian café or the rue du Caire ...'

191 TO GEORGES JEAN-AUBRY

Mon cher ami   25 March 1910

My brother's[1] a very nice chap, but he's a man accustomed to 'Music-Halls', something I can't bring myself to blame him for! You must have upset him a little, introducing him to music which, while allowing itself to smile, doesn't descend to outbursts of laughter ... I hope he'll forgive us?

You ask about Mallarmé's opinion of the music for the *Prélude à l'après-midi d'un faune*. That goes back a long way ...

At the time I was living in a small furnished apartment on the rue de Londres.[2] Rather curiously, the wallpaper was decorated with portraits of M. Carnot[3] surrounded by little birds! You can imagine the effect of contemplating such a scene? A strong desire to stay out of the house, for one thing.

Mallarmé arrived looking like a soothsayer, with a Scotch plaid over his shoulders. He listened, and then there was a long silence before he said: 'I wasn't expecting anything like that! This music prolongs the emotion of my poem and conjures up the scenery more vividly than any colour.'

After the first performance he sent me a copy of *L'Après-midi d'un faune* inscribed with these lines:

> If you would know with what harmonious notes
> Your flute resounds, O sylvan deity,
> Then hearken to the light that shall be breathed
> Thereinto by Debussy's magic art.[4]

A document of prime importance, for anyone who's interested.

In any case, it's my happiest memory of a period when I wasn't yet plagued by 'Debussysme'.

> Yours
> C.D.

[1] Alfred Debussy, 1870–1937, was a buyer for a railway company in Cardiff and was comfortably off. At this time he was living in Le Havre and Jean-Aubry had invited him to a Debussy concert given there on 7 March by Jane Bathori, Emile Engel and Franz Liebich.
[2] Debussy's memory is plainly at fault here. He left the apartment on the rue de Londres in July 1893, but the score of the *Prélude* was not finished until September 1894. He was then living at 10 rue Gustave-Doré.
[3] Sadi Carnot, French President, murdered in June 1894.
[4] 'Sylvain d'haleine première / Si ta flûte a réussi / Ouïs toute la lumière / Qu'y soufflera Debussy'. The composer did not receive this copy until June 1897, as we know from one of Mallarmé's visiting cards (sold by Drouot, 15 December 1969).

192 TO RENÉ DOIRE[1]

Cher Monsieur   6 April 1910

Please excuse my delay in replying. Illness has unfortunately prevented my doing so before now.

Thank you for the copy of your review. In Mr P. de Stoecklin you have a contributor who writes most entertainingly about music and passion![2]

You asked me for some lines on Chopin! To tell you the truth I don't see how they would find a place in a review in which my way of looking at music seems to be so much at odds.[3]

Your readers might feel they didn't understand anything about music any more!

> I remain, Sir
> Yours sincerely
> C.D.

[1] Chief editor of the *Courrier musical*.

[2] In the issue of the *Courrier* for 1 January 1910, devoted to Chopin, Stoecklin's article 'Chopin vu par Schumann' ended with this definition of the former by the latter: 'the poet of melancholy and burning passions'.

[3] In the issue of 1 February 1910, for example, Paul Landormy claimed that 'outside a certain highly cultivated circle ... [Debussy's works] will always remain a dead letter.'

193 TO GABRIEL FAURÉ

Cher maître et ami   14 May 1910

Once again I swear on Ambroise Thomas's[1] ashes that, gently but insistently, I decline to sit on the jury for the singing examinations.
Please don't think ill of me for this refusal.

Yours as ever
C.D.

[1] One-time Director of the Conservatoire, who died in 1896. A symbol of conservatism, he wrote some 25 operas including *Mignon*.

194 TO JACQUES DURAND

Mon cher Jacques   8 July 1910

Since you left to take the waters, I've been going along with this curious existence which is my life and will be from now on. Those around me resolutely refuse to understand that I've never been able to live in a world of real things and real people. That's why I have this imperative need to escape from myself and go off on adventures which seem inexplicable because they figure a man nobody knows; and perhaps he represents the best side of me! After all, an artist is by definition a man accustomed to dreams and living among apparitions ... It's pointless expecting this same man to follow strictly all the observances of daily life, the laws and all the other barriers erected by a cowardly, hypocritical world.[1]

In short, I live surrounded by memories and regrets. Two gloomy companions, but faithful ones – more so than pleasure and happiness!

I'm working as much as I can. These are still the moments when I come closest to satisfying my taste for the inexpressible! If, as I hope, I succeed with this exploration of anguish, which is what *La Chute de la maison Usher* will be, then I feel I'll have made a useful contribution to music . . . and to my friend and publisher Jacques Durand!

You haven't said anything about *The Firebird* . . .[2] It's not perfect, but, in certain respects, it's an excellent piece of work none the less because the music is not the docile slave of the dance . . . And every now and then there are some extremely unusual combinations of rhythms!

When you consider that French dancers would never have agreed to dance to music like that . . . So, Diaghilev is a great man and Nijinsky is his prophet, unless that role has been taken by Calvocoressi.[3]

Have you been following Conrad's novel *The Secret Agent* in *Le Temps*? It's full of the most splendid scoundrels, and the end is magnificent. It's expressed in an absolutely calm and detached style and it's only when you think about the story afterwards that you say: 'But all those people are monsters' . . .

Anyway it's extremely individual.

Something else very individual is the Chinese Exhibition I've just been to see at the Pavilion de Marsan . . . If it's still open when you get back, you must go! . . . It's not a thing I can describe on paper, but rarely if ever have I seen such beauty and refinement.

Think of me with sympathy this Sunday. I shall be listening to eleven performances of the Rhapsody for B♭ Clarinet;[4] I'll tell you all, if I survive.

I'll see you soon. Please give your wife my best wishes.

>   Yours
>   C.D

---

[1]   This refers to a period of serious doubts about the future of Debussy's marriage.
[2]   Stravinsky's ballet had been performed by the Ballets russes on 25 June.
[3]   See letter 183.
[4]   Composed by Debussy for the Conservatoire final competition. He orchestrated it the following year.

195   TO EDGAR VARÈSE

>   Cher Monsieur   12 July 1910

It seems Berlin is making you welcome.[1] I'm glad and I congratulate you sincerely. Even so, it must surely need a lot of courage getting used to a foreign country? So many things, so many habits must be irritating, not to say offensive! We take our mother country with us, more or less, and

I admit that even in France I've felt a foreigner; all of which is to tell you how amazing I think you are!

Send me the *Pelléas* score and, although I have no confidence in metronome markings, I'll do what you ask.

It's a good idea of yours to work at the piano, for your future both as a conductor and as a composer. One is so often betrayed by so-called pianists! I mean it – I can't tell you the extent to which my piano music has been deformed; so much so that often I have a job to recognize it![2] Forgive this personal outburst, but there are good reasons for it . . .

> Yours as ever
> C.D.

[1] Varèse had founded the Symphonisches Chor and, with the help of Busoni and Richard Strauss, had succeeded in getting some pupils.

[2] It is not clear which pianists Debussy is referring to: to the 'scholiste' Blanche Selva, whose playing he seems never to have liked, or to Ricardo Viñes, whom he accused of being 'too dry' in a conversation with Victor Segalen (and, in a letter to Jean-Aubry of 1908, of 'distorting the expression' of the second book of *Images*. R.N.).

196† TO JACQUES DURAND

Mon cher Jacques   15 July 1910

The delightful countryside on the postcard you sent looks strangely like a chimney-breast! . . . When nature decides to be Swiss, she really lets herself go with green – the most unpleasant shade one can imagine – it's a country of cardboard and billiard cloths . . . I don't want to know about a country where one has to be climbing all the time or else watching other people climb. It doesn't even fulfil its expected function of curing people, when you've managed to acquire a stomach ache there . . . !

It seems to me you could do that on the avenue de l'Alma.

The clarinet competition went extremely well and, to judge by the expressions on the faces of my colleagues, the *Rapsodie* was a success! (Talking of which, thank you for your plans over the sight-reading piece).[1]

One of the candidates, Vandercruyssen, played it by heart and very musically. The rest were straightforward and nondescript.

You've no idea of the sort of thing these poor devils are given to play! In particular a *Concertstück* for bassoon, enough to make a negro tremble. And it's not even well written for the instrument . . . That's one of the many areas where changes are needed; let's hope our friend Dukas will put things straight.[2]

Personally, this competition has meant several tiresome days leaving me 'without strength or courage', as the hero of *l'Enfant prodigue* and various other musical dramas sings to such poignant effect!

As you say, I'm spending my time in *La Maison Usher* . . . not exactly a nursing-home and sometimes I emerge with my nerves stretched like the strings of a violin.

At moments like that I'd be capable of giving the Good Lord himself a rude answer, except that this divine personage long ago chose the path of eternal anonymity!

I've seen M. Russell.[3] He's full of enthusiasm for *L'Enfant prodigue* but claims he can't put on *Pelléas* till next season as he wants different scenery and a different production from Hammerstein's[4] – in fact, a whole series of ideas to show that the Boston Theatre is the best in the world, as H. Russell is the most perfect of managers.

I must leave you now to go to Bellevue and see Laloy, a man with whom – in your absence – one can exchange something other than tittle-tattle and catty remarks.

I hope this letter finds you relaxed and enjoying your 'Swiss green' undisturbed.

> With all best wishes to your wife
> Yours
> C.D.

[1] Durand had decided to publish it under the title *Petite pièce*.
[2] Paul Dukas had just been appointed a member of the governing council of the Paris Conservatoire.
[3] Henry Russell was the manager of the Boston Opera House, as well as being one of Debussy's creditors. He appointed André Caplet as permanent conductor and gave *Pelléas* on 1 April 1909. He had previously brought models of the Boston stage and sets over to Paris to show Debussy and Maeterlinck.
[4] Oscar Hammerstein I was the founder of the Manhattan Opera House. His production of *Pelléas et Mélisande* on 19 February 1908 was the opera's American première, with Mary Garden as Mélisande, and three other members of the original cast.

Cher ami   25 August 1910

I've examined the 'brasserie-style' orchestration of *La plus que lente*[1]
and it seems to me to be needlessly decorated with trombones, timpani,
triangle, etc. . . . and therefore designed for a kind of 'brasserie de luxe'
I've never come across! I've no desire to upset monsieur H. Mouton[2]
who is probably a master of the genre, but there are one or two clumsy
passages that could easily be avoided! I have taken the liberty of trying
out another kind of arrangement which strikes me as more practical.[3]
One other point: it's impossible to start a piece in a brasserie the way
you would in a salon; you simply must have a few introductory bars . . .
Anyway, don't let's limit ourselves just to brasseries, we must think of
the innumerable 'Five o'clocks',[4] and the gatherings of beautiful
listeners I had in mind![5]

I'll talk to you about it again tomorrow . . . It may not seem worth
the trouble, but it is.

Yours ever
C.D.

[1] A waltz for piano which Durand had just published.
[2] Henri Mouton, who arranged a number of Debussy's works for small orchestra.
[3] A questionable judgement. Debussy's orchestration is for string orchestra, flute,
clarinet, piano . . . and cimbalom. (R.N.)
[4] The most popular of these concerts were the ones organized by *Le Figaro*.
[5] 'les belles écouteuses': a quotation from Verlaine's poem 'Mandoline', set by Debussy
in 1882. (R.N.)

Cher André Caplet   21 November 1910

I was delighted, as you may suppose, to receive the enthusiastic
telegrams confirming and proclaiming your glory, in the shadow of
which Azaël[1] remains modestly seated. So: 'sempre avanti'; 'quite well';
'toujours à mieux',[2] and may the angels in heaven accompany you on
their lutes – provided you've had a chance to rehearse them first.

Sadly, my father died a short while ago,[3] after a long and painful
illness. Even though we hardly ever agreed about anything, it's a loss I
feel more deeply with every day that passes. He had some admiration at
least for *L'Enfant prodigue* and the success in Chicago would surely

[224]

have increased this beyond measure; it's a matter for regret (I speak without irony) that this simple pleasure was denied him.

I'd be most grateful for your own, written, comments on the performance of *Children's Corner* which, thanks to you, is so gorgeously apparelled.[4] I do wonder if it will behave as it should in this new guise? I should be sorry if it looked pretentious: I have every confidence in you, all the same.

I'm getting ready to leave for Vienna and Budapest in several days' time. I'm playing the orchestra in the first and the piano in the second. To say that my delight is unalloyed would be to tell a lie . . . I don't have the necessary qualities for missions of any kind; what's more, when my music is involved I undergo an almost physical suffering. If you'd been there I'd certainly have asked you to take over, which would have been better for everybody. But let us put this melancholy cup from us, and may I say how happy I am at your success, – which, between ourselves, was never in doubt.

> Yours ever
> C.D.

Madame Debussy and your friend Chouchou join me, as usual, in sending their kind regards.

[1] Azaël is the Prodigal Son in Debussy's cantata of that name. Debussy re-orchestrated it in 1908 with Caplet's assistance, and Caplet had just conducted it in the USA.
[2] These three mottoes are in Italian, English and French in the original. The English one seems to be slightly the odd man out. (R.N.)
[3] 28 October.
[4] Caplet had just orchestrated the piano suite and conducted the first performance in New York on 10 November.

Journeys
Le Martyre de Saint Sébastien

In 1910 Debussy laid his favourite projects aside to work on incidental music for Gabriele d'Annunzio's *Martyre de Saint Sébastien*. Thanks to Caplet, he managed to finish the score on time but its success was muted.

Financial difficulties, caused by his extravagant life-style, go some way to explain this forced labour as well as the journeys he made to conduct in Austria and Hungary. Caplet invited him to go to Boston, where he might have supervised a *Pelléas* entirely in accordance with his tastes, but he did not dare face his wife's opposition.

A Hungarian journalist, who interviewed Debussy in Budapest, has left this portrait of him: 'Debussy is a friendly and highly strung Frenchman. He's still young, barely forty-eight, but his hair and dark beard make him seem younger. With his crinkly hair (which he doesn't wear long as most artists do), his swarthy complexion and broad nose he looks like a negro . . . His face is attractive, he has a velvety look in the eye and his conversation is friendly; his voice is gentle and seems to come from the depths. He carries about him an aura of cheerful satisfaction and extraordinary naïvety. Sometimes he looks like a replete faun, sometimes like an astonished child . . .' (4 December 1910).

199 TO GABRIELE D'ANNUNZIO[1]

Hotel Krantz Vienna
30 November 1910

Mon cher Maître

Your letter has been forwarded to me here where I am staying for some time and for my sins. Forgive me for not writing at once to say how happy I am to have received it. How could I not love your poetry? The very thought of working with you gives me a kind of *advance fever*.

I shall be back in Paris around 20 December. I'm sure I have no need to say how pleased I shall be to see you.

Yours most sincerely
C.D.

[1] Slightly eccentric and bombastic wordsmith, lover of formal art, poet, playwright and novelist. He had just discovered in Ida Rubinstein the Saint Sébastien of his dreams. For the music to accompany this mystery he thought first of Roger-Ducasse. Debussy accepted the task on 10 December. D'Annunzio went off to Arcachon and sent the text bit by bit between 9 January and 2 March 1911.

200† TO EMMA

Vienna
2 December 1910

Chère petite mienne

I owe you a pleasant awakening this morning thanks to your lovely letter ... You know what it's like to have your brain in fragments, to think till it hurts and have just a handful of nothing to show for it. But you're living among familiar things, while I'm in an anonymous room of no particular kind whose past history I'm certainly not going to delve into. The people round me will never be anything except strangers; not that I would have it any other way, but this regime of intense concentration ends up by suffocating you: never saying any of the things you usually say, knowing that nobody will answer for the simple reason that nobody is really listening. When I talk to you, it's often not you I'm addressing but another me, whom I can question and who replies like the voice of my own thoughts. Maybe this is a peculiarly subtle way of missing someone. There are more directly human ways of doing so, which I also feel, please believe me. Although the first way too is not without value, I'm sure you'll agree with me . . .

This morning we had the final rehearsal. I got rather angry, as I don't think a man playing the viola should consider he has the right not to play – what a nonsense! – and gaze at me as though I were a shop-window! The pretentions of the Viennese seem to me to go absolutely beyond what's tolerable, but they're not unique, alas! It didn't go badly and in spite of everything I had the last word, because I exercised my will-power without letting up for an instant. With these 'lads' it's like being the tamer in the cage with the wild beasts: you must never take your eye off them or you're done for . . . So please believe that, at 7.30 this evening, it will only be by thinking of you and Chouchou that I'll be able to hide the traces of endless boredom and even a touch of distaste . . . Because, to be frank, one's trying to win the approval of an audience made up for the most part of idiots – a fairly ridiculous enterprise, with a certain ironical contradiction about it. We must hope I'll have enough nervous energy left to surmount this feeling which makes me my own worst enemy!

As long as Chouchou can rely on 'Teddy' and 'Weagle Top', all will be well. I dare say she loves them because they're constitutionally unable to contradict her.

> With fond kisses
> Your
> Claude

I'm sending Mlle Chouchou some postcards with very nice soldiers on.

201† TO CHOUCHOU[1]

Vienna
2 December 1910

The memoirs of 'outre Croche'[2]

1. Once there was a papa who lived in exile . . . 2. and every day he missed his little Chouchou. 3. The inhabitants of the city saw him walking past and murmured 'Why does that gentleman look so sad in our gay and beautiful city?' [. . .] 5. So Chouchou's papa went into a shop run by an old, very ugly man and his even uglier daughter, he politely removed his hat and using deaf-mute gestures asked for the most beautiful postcards they had, so that he could write to his darling little daughter . . . The ugly old man was very moved by this and as for his daughter, she died on the spot! 6. The said papa went back to his hotel, wrote this story which would make a goldfish weep, and put all his love into the signature below, which is his greatest claim to fame.

LepapadeChouchou

[1] A series of six postcards showing Austrian soldiers in a variety of humorous situations. The fourth card is missing.
[2] A reference to Debussy's *alter ego*, Monsieur Croche, and to *Mémoires d'outre-tombe*, the autobiography of the writer and statesman François-René, Vicomte de Chateaubriand, 1768–1848.

202 TO EMMA

Budapest
Chère petite mienne   3 December 1910

As my telegram has told you, the concert went very well: the audience were moved and listened like good little children. *Ibéria* was stunning. I've never heard it like that before. You'd have been proud of your Claude and it's the first time an orchestra has ever thought to thank me for conducting them. I can't say my fans unhitched the horses from my carriage because I was in a motorized taxi and no mob, however besotted, can turn itself into an engine.

I didn't dare send you a telegram immediately after the concert, in case it frightened you. You're too easily alarmed and are always inventing troubles that make you ill and disturb your dear little liver. Again, I can't understand why you've had only one letter from me. From the day I arrived in Vienna I haven't missed a single opportunity of writing to you.

I wrote to d'Annunzio from Vienna. Had he already left Arcachon? Probably, to judge from Mlle Rubinstein's letter.[1] This business doesn't sound very promising; added to which, I should start looking like a specialist in female dancers. We mustn't forget Miss Maud Allan, *Khamma* . . . (sutra)![2]

It seems the Amsterdam people pay very badly . . . And then I really don't want to be far away again from my darlings. As I see it, that's an end of the matter.

I've already rehearsed the young quartet who are due to play next Monday [5 December]. All four of them are superb. The finale, which other quartets find such a stumbling block, is child's play to them . . . Dear God! . . . It's all very fine, but these rehearsals do go on:[3] I've had enough of all these people ending in 'ois' . . . I want to see my little darling and my Chouchou once again.

This morning on the way from Vienna to Budapest we stopped at a station called Eusellugvar, for those whose larynx is made for such things (if you say 'j'aime le caviar' very fast you get somewhere near it). On the platform was a gypsy band, dressed with a barbarian elegance and hats to go picking mushrooms in, and all the time the train was standing there they played the Ratkowsky[4] march like the very devil! I was so excited I cheered. The simple explanation is that a rich Hungarian in his will left a sum of 600 crowns annually to pay for a performance of the said march every time a train stops there, to maintain patriotic sentiment in the hearts of his fellow citizens. Hartmann[5] used to tell one of his famous tales about gypsies playing all day and all night in the railway stations; it was just a tall story, except in 'j'aime le caviar'.

Forgive me for not writing more: I'm too tired . . . and impatient. With all my love . . . Give Chouchou a big, big kiss for me.

    Your
    Claude

[1]   Ida Rubinstein, a Russian dancer and pupil of Fokine, was engaged by Diaghilev and danced in *Cléopâtre* and *Schéhérazade*. Later she was to have her own troupe.
[2]   An allusion to the Canadian dancer Maud Allan, who had commissioned from Debussy a pantomime ballet, *Khamma*. The contract had been signed on 30 September, inaugurating a stormy relationship between patroness and composer. See letter 228.
[3]   A play on the word 'répétitions'. (R.N.)
[4]   The Rákóczy march, attributed to the Hungarian composer János Bihari. It has become a patriotic song and was popularized by Berlioz's transcription.
[5]   His previous publisher, Georges Hartmann.

Budapest

Mon cher Jacques   4 December 1910

My stay in Vienna was full of such a succession of irritating and ridiculous incidents, I didn't feel I should bother you with an account of them . . .

But the concert went well, especially *Ibéria*. Lack of time prevented us playing either *La Mer* or the *Nocturnes*. Naturally, I was assured that the orchestra knew *La Mer*, having played it three times. My dear Jacques, if only you could have heard it! Come back, Chevillard! And the same with the *Nocturnes*. So I decided to confine myself to the *Petite Suite, L'Après-midi d'un faune* and *Ibéria*. And, I may say, sorting out *Ibéria* in two rehearsals represents quite a considerable effort. I'm not asking that this signal feat be engraved on the marble of eternity but, even so, it's not an everyday undertaking; my nerves are in pieces. Remember, these people could only understand me through an interpreter − a doctor of law by trade − and whether he mangled my instructions in translating them we shall never know!

I left no means of communication unexplored, though: I sang, I made Italian pantomime gestures, etc. It was enough to soften the heart of a buffalo.

Well, in the end they understood and, in spite of everything, I had the last word. I was recalled to the platform like a ballerina and if my besotted fans didn't unhitch the horses from my carriage, that's only because I was in a simple motorized taxi.

If there's any ultimate moral to be drawn from this journey, it is that I'm not cut out to be 'the composer abroad'. It needs the heroism of a commercial traveller and a willingness to compromise which I find decidedly repugnant.

This evening's concert in Budapest is being held in a hall like a Turkish bath . . . I can't wait for 10 to 7 tomorrow morning, the blessed moment when I catch the train straight back to Paris.

So you'll probably see me in your office on Thursday when I'll give you a lively account, with all the details, of this memorable and exasperating journey.

Yours ever
C.D.

[231]

Cher Monsieur Barczy   19 December 1910

I've been caught up again by the hectic, demanding life of Paris which leaves little time for correspondence, however pleasant, so I wasn't able to reply straight away to your kind letter.

Thank you for sending the Hungarian music. But how different it is from my memories of [Radics . . . !][2] It's like a beautiful butterfly in a glass case! The wings are still striking but they don't move any more and their rich colouring has faded. I wonder whether you, as a Hungarian, can appreciate this music at its true value? It's so much a part of your life, so familiar that you don't see its real, profound artistic importance.

But just look at what it turns into in Liszt's hands! For all his genius, he domesticates it . . . It loses its freedom and its characteristic feeling of the infinite.

When you listen to Radics, you lose awareness of your surroundings . . . You breathe the forest air and hear the sound of streams; and it's a melancholy, confidential message from a heart that suffers and laughs almost at the same moment . . .

In my opinion, this music should never be touched. It should indeed be defended, as far as possible, from the clumsiness of the 'professionals'.[3] So . . . have more respect for your gypsies. They're not merely 'entertainers', whom you get along to play for parties or to help the champagne go down! Their music is every bit as beautiful as your old lace and embroidery . . . So why don't you show them the same respect, the same love?

Your young composers could do worse than find their inspiration there, not in copying but in transposing the gypsies' freedom, their gifts of evocation, of colour and rhythm . . . Wagner's ideas have had a bad influence on a lot of music and a lot of countries . . . The popular music of one's homeland must be used only as a basis, never as a procedure. That is particularly true of yours . . . So love this music as passionately as you wish, but don't dress it up in school uniform or put gold spectacles on its nose!

Forgive me for meddling in matters which are perhaps none of my concern . . . it's just that I'm utterly devoted to music – not just French music! – so I'm always sad to see its riches being wasted; or people misinterpreting its true feeling, I could say its *natural feeling*!

[232]

There's too much German influence in France and we're still suffocated by it. Don't you go the same way, don't let yourselves be taken in by false profundity and the detestable German 'modernstyl'.

I've received some music from your friend Guillaume Zágon[4] and you may be sure I shall have a look at it. He's certainly a nice young man and very promising! As for the members of the Waldbauer Quartet,[5] they have my warmest sympathy . . . If there's ever anything I can do for them, I shall be very happy to oblige. They sent a postcard to Mlle Chouchou Debussy, which touched me greatly. Would you send me M. Waldbauer's address so that I can thank him?

Please remember me to Mme Barczy.

> Yours most sincerely
> C.D.

I should also like the addresses of your friend Angyan and of Monsieur de Fodor!!!

I left a walking-stick behind in the Hotel Hungarian – not that it's at all valuable, but I have a superstitious attachment to it. Would you make inquiries about it and ask the hotel management to send it on to me?

[1] The impresario who had arranged Debussy's visit to Hungary.
[2] Gypsy violinist.
[3] This opinion may be compared to the one expressed in letter 102.
[4] Géza Vilmos Zagon, 1889–1918.
[5] Imre Waldbauer had just founded a quartet with Temesváry, Molnár and Kerpely.

205 TO GABRIELE D'ANNUNZIO

29 January 1911

My apologies for being so deeply buried in manuscript paper, I didn't reply immediately to your charming and terrifying letter. It gives off triumphant fanfares as it marches towards glory. So much so that I now feel any music will seem inadequate beside the ever-burgeoning splendour of your imagination.

Which is why I feel a certain terror as I see the moment approaching when I really must write something. Will I be able to? Will I have any ideas? This fear is perhaps healthy; one must not penetrate mystery steeled with an empty pride.

What would you have me do, faced with the torrential beauties of your two, simultaneous offerings; above all, how shall I choose? For the great final chorus, you will allow me to prefer your French translation to the traditional text.

I've seen M. de Rigaud; he has written to Russell,[1] which is much better than any intervention on my part. The word 'business' for me conveys nothing but gloom and misery! It would be kind of you to write and reassure the 'Benefactress'[2] of the safe arrival of the parcel I mentioned in my last telegram. It contains a fountain-pen which looked the very thing for your magician's hands. It would be so annoying if, by some diabolical mischance, it had found its way into the paws of a railway clerk at Arcachon.

Your letter holds out some hope that I may see you soon; I needn't impress on you how happy that would make

> Yours fraternally
> C.D.

My wife sends her kindest regards. A kiss from Chouchou.

[1] Henry Russell. See letter 196 footnote 3.
[2] Debussy's wife. (R.N.)

206 TO ROBERT GODET

6 February 1911

This long-delayed letter was begun, I promise you, immediately after our last meeting; and really it's no fault of mine I've had to take up commercial travelling . . .

First, Vienna; an old city covered in make-up, overstuffed with the music of Brahms and Puccini, the officers with chests like women and the women with chests like officers.

There we had an orchestral concert – which was what I went for! Numerous congratulations in German, which I don't understand, so I can interpret them as I wish.

Then, Budapest: where the Danube refuses to be as blue as a famous waltz would have us believe. The Hungarians insincere and nice. The best thing there was a gypsy whose name is spelt Radics, but pronounced Raditche – don't ask why. He loves music far more than many people who have a reputation for doing so.

[234]

In an unpretentious, run-of-the-mill café, he gives the impression of sitting in the shade of a forest and, from the depths of men's souls, seeks out that peculiar melancholy we so rarely have the chance to make use of. He could extract confidences from a safe.

There we had chamber music (1,500 people listening to *Children's Corner* – a fearsome lack of proportion).

But I've brought back some really beautiful embroidery and some marvellous chocolates sold by a Monsieur Gerbaud (one of your compatriots) who is a genius in his way.

Back in Paris, I got down to a ballet for a Miss Maud Allan, as English as you please. To make up for that, the ballet's Egyptian;[1] the plot would fit into a baby's hand, typically devoid of interest.

Plots of another kind have pushed me into writing it, as well as reasons of domestic economy.

It was precisely at that moment that Gabriele d'Annunzio arrived with *Le Martyre de Saint Sébastien*, for which I've agreed to write incidental music.

It's much more lavish than the poor little Anglo-Egyptian ballet. I need hardly tell you that in it the cult of Adonis mingles with that of Jesus; that it is very fine, beyond a doubt; and that in fact, if I'm allowed enough time, there are some opportunities for good music.

The two Poe stories are postponed till I don't know when! Between ourselves, I may say I don't mind, because there are a lot of 'accents' I'm still not happy with; nor am I with a certain flabbiness of organization, especially in *Le Diable dans le beffroi*. Here I want to find an extremely simple sort of choral writing, but extremely mobile as well . . . That's to say, I don't like the veneer in *Boris* any more than the relentless counterpoint in the second act of *Die Meistersinger*, which ultimately is no more than an unimpassioned chaos . . . There's certainly another way of doing things: masterly illusion, for example. It's damned difficult! Not to mention the stupid habit of positioning the choirs as if they were taking a cold bath: men on one side, women the other. That'll have to go. And someone, you'll see, will invent long, difficult words to describe something very simple.

So, for somebody like me who has a highly developed taste for idleness, there's not much time to lose.

And now it's your turn to write to me. First of all, it's a pleasure I've been deprived of for too long – all my own fault; and then I need your moral support. As you know, any number of people have taken it upon

[235]

them to give me rude proof that friendship can turn into double-dealing.

Some music will reach you at the same time as this letter; that's probably still what I'm best at. And if there's any of it you haven't got, don't hesitate to let me know.

Chouchou has the flu and her mother is in bed with her liver. Even so they both send you their kindest regards.

Yours ever
C.D.

¹ *Khamma*: see also letters 202 and 228.

207 TO GABRIELE D'ANNUNZIO

11–12 February 1911

I too write in great haste. The days fly past without my noticing. It's tomorrow already – the agony is unbearable.

Could you tell me, in the way you find easiest, the exact moment when 'the dance on the red-hot coals' begins? There are words to be spoken during this dance, aren't there? Forgive me; when you're there next to me I hear the music suggested by your words, but all the same I need to have some firm reference points. Your notes for the designer and the composer are like an enchanted forest full of images, and at times I feel like Tom Thumb.

I like the rhythm of the Seraphs' Chorus enormously. I think that for the beginning of Saint Sebastian's assumption we may have to employ a broader structure. There could be a danger that similar rhythms in the poetry might lead to a too insistent repetition of sounds in the music. Also I don't seem to have marked in the 'Notes' the telling moment where the chorus discover the name Sébastien . . . Sébastien.

The man who possessed himself unlawfully of your fountain-pen must have been touched by grace after several nights of remorse.

My wife's a little better. Her mother continues to hover between life and death. Chouchou is more chouchou than ever. They send you their warmest greetings, and I my fraternal devotion.

C.D.

[236]

Ami   [February 1911]

I've been taken up with unavoidable rehearsals for the revival of *Pelléas et Mélisande*[1] – forgive them! – and so didn't thank you at once for the last splendid instalment.

I must tell you that it's so lofty and other-worldly, the music is very difficult to find. In any case it's impossible to agree to Madame Rubinstein's request, that's to say to detach the dances from the rest of the work so that she can work out the choreography! The dances are intimately bound up with what is spoken simultaneously or else with what is going to be spoken after them.

Protect me!
C.D.

[1] The revival of *Pelléas et Mélisande* took place on 18 February. It had not been given in the 1909–10 season and Marguerite Carré now took over the role of Mélisande from Maggie Teyte.

209 TO EDGAR VARÈSE

Cher Monsieur   12 February 1911

Please forgive me for not writing earlier, due to pressure of work which obliges me even now to write to you in great haste.

You're absolutely right not to worry about the hostility of the public. The time will come when you'll be the best of friends. But disabuse yourself quickly of the idea that the critics here are more perceptive than in Germany . . . And don't forget that a critic rarely loves what he has to talk about . . . Indeed he often guards jealously his ignorance on the subject! Criticism could be an art if it were exercised under the necessary conditions of free opinion. But as it is, it's no more than a trade . . . Mind you, there's no denying that so-called artists have made a generous contribution to this state of affairs.

I haven't had time to go to Prague for the same reasons I can't write an article. The review you mention – is it the same *Pan* that appeared some fifteen years ago? That one was excellently illustrated but very expensive.[1] If you could possibly send me a copy, I should be most grateful. I'd consider becoming a subscriber, as I love pictures almost as much as music.

It's true I'm collaborating with d'Annunzio. I'm writing incidental music for the mystery of *Saint Sébastien*: it's two years' work and, of course, I have barely two months!

I hope life continues to turn out well for you.

> With all best wishes
> Yours
> C.D.

[1] *Pan* was published in Berlin between 1895 and 1899. A French supplement, subtitled 'artistic and literary review' ran to at least four issues in 1895.

210 TO ANDRÉ CAPLET

> Cher André Caplet   [March or April 1911]

D'Annunzio has not done me the honour of turning up this afternoon![1] Could you please persuade Léon Bakst[2] that Paradise is a place known to one and all as being 'dazzling'. And, unless he's determined to join forces with Mr . . .[3] in stifling, or rather neutralizing the music, let him come up with something!!!

It is agreed that *Mlle Vallin* will sing and not Mlle Féart![4] I should point out that the result of all this is to hurt the feelings of someone who has given proof of nothing but charming good nature. If she is upset, such was not my intention!

> Yours as ever
> C.D.

[1] For a rehearsal of *Le Martyre*.
[2] One of Diaghilev's principal designers who was responsible for both sets and costumes for *Le Martyre*.
[3] The producer Armand Bour or the choreographer Fokine?
[4] Rose Féart had sung Mélisande at Covent Garden in 1909. Ninon Vallin sang the 'Vox coelestis' and the Virgin Erigone in *Le Martyre* (see also letter 172).

211 TO GABRIEL ASTRUC

> Mon cher ami   [May 1911][1]

As the producer's efforts come to a halt on the threshold of Paradise, stemming from a belief that because there is no more music everyone can take their leave: some to Larue's, others to Zimmer's,[2] or less

[238]

29 Léon Bakst's drawing for the décor of the 'magic chamber'
(*Le Martyre de Saint Sébastien* Act II).

imposing hostelries – then perhaps it would be for the best if Paradise were suppressed?

But there are more important things which must on no account be allowed to continue. For one, the lack of co-ordination between the action and the music. If you require details, I have them ready for you. It is vital to find some other way of arranging the end of Act IV . . . As things stand, the spectators see the actors leave – with all the pomp of some paltry village funeral – and naturally think they have the right to do so too.

I have already asked if, at the assumption of Saint Sebastian's soul, it could kindly be arranged for the seven seraphim to reappear as angel musicians. And during the final chorus, wave the golden palms! I wouldn't claim it was an idea of genius, but it is a way of getting some movement into the background which, at the moment, remains resolutely uniform . . . When all's said and done, it is Paradise![3] It isn't enough just to let down a backcloth with rays painted on it – rays which don't even radiate, what's more.

The departure of Saint Sebastian's body could perhaps be started later; it could then halt at the moment when light fills the scene and resume its funereal progress – with rather more in the way of resources – during the unaccompanied choruses.

This is all important, believe me, and I look forward to your reply.

Yours ever
C.D.

The light on the procession of women of Byblis, Adonis worshippers, etc., must be moonlight. We must have some torchbearers – and the torches should be extinguished at the end of the lamentation 'Quench the torches, Eros! Weep!'

The audience must not be allowed to enter the theatre during the Preludes . . . For a start it's not polite and it's a rule observed in all similar situations elsewhere.

Thank you for the tickets for the box which have just arrived.

[1] The première of *Le Martyre* took place at the Théâtre du Châtelet on 22 May. (R.N.)
[2] Larue was a restaurant on the Place de la Madeleine; Zimmer a brasserie in the rue Blondel.
[3] This Paradise is the one referred to in the story about Bakst who, nettled by Debussy's observations, asked him: 'You've been to Paradise, have you?' To which the composer replied: 'Yes, I have, but I never talk about it in front of strangers.'

[240]

30 Léon Bakst's costume for the seven seraphim in *Le Martyre*.

Cher frère et ami   19 June 1911

What a beautiful book and what a really beautiful work![1]

I've read it through again with a pleasure untarnished by the ponderousness, the contradictions and the discord with which the theatre surrounds anything beautiful. I didn't want to bother you by asking for another meeting, as I imagined you would be much too busy. But I should dearly have liked to see you and given you the score of *Saint Sébastien* myself. And now I'm leaving this evening to go and conduct an orchestral concert in Turin. Will you be here when I get back, on the 22nd of this month? I do hope I shall have this pleasure.

> With all my best wishes
> Yours ever
> C.D.

Would you care to pick up the score I've got for you from my house? I don't want to entrust it to the uncaring hands of the postal service.

[1]   D'Annunzio had sent him a copy of the text, published by Calmann-Lévy. (R.N.)

213 TO JACQUES DURAND

Grand Hôtel et Hôtel d'Europe Turin
Mon cher Jacques   25 June 1911

I really think the Turin concert will be the end of my conducting career. . . ![1] I've been leading a dog's life! Six hours of rehearsal a day are enough to give you a distaste for any sort of music, your own included. And then one can't help feeling that deep down Claude Debussy's music is a matter of indifference to them and that at the first opportunity they'll be back with their Puccini, Verdi and all the others from the language of 'si' (to quote our most recent national poet . . . G. d'Annunzio). In addition to all these problems, my wife has been ill ever since we got here. So this journey instead of being enjoyable, as it was supposed to be, has turned out to be a ghastly nightmare. My malevolent fate has struck again, as usual — and Turin is rectangular and horrid. I've never seen so many tramlines for getting about on. Very convenient, but murder for the eardrums! We can't wait to get back . . .

> Yours ever
> C.D.

[242]

¹ Vittorio Gui provides some explanation in his memoirs (*Battute d'aspetto*, Florence, 1944, p. 222) for the gloomy tone of this letter. Debussy had arrived in Turin with Emma, Chouchou and Dolly Bardac and wanted to rehearse *L'Après-midi d'un faune* and *Ibéria* himself with an orchestra that had never played them before. In the event, realizing that he was unable to get what he wanted from the orchestra, he agreed to hand the stick over to the young Vittorio Gui, who took all the rehearsals and let Debussy conduct only for the concert itself.

214† TO JACQUES DURAND

Cher ami   13 July 1911

I too have been ill: heat, overwork, nervous exhaustion? . . . anyway, I've been ordered to have a total rest for a month, at least.

The truth is that *Le Martyre de Saint Sébastien* tired me out more than I thought and the journey to Turin finished me off. Everything in this world has its price! As the old saying has it, 'Don't force your talent!' Which we might put into modern words as 'Don't let's get carried away!' I'm glad to say my wife's a little better and we'd be getting ready to leave for somewhere with lots of water and less railway, only she's worried about her eldest daughter whose position of young married woman has brought the usual events in its train!

How right you are, my dear Jacques, to love your house in the country . . . Everything in life is so transitory, there must be a unique charm about a house that has seen you playing as a child and dreaming as a young man — it's sad, at my age, not to have anything of the sort. Not a very American or up-to-date sentiment, but very sincere and very 'old France', I feel.

I called in at your office to find both furniture and staff in their summer clothes . . . Another hint to me to leave Paris!

Yours ever
C.D.

Chouchou is like a peony and joins her good wishes to ours.

215 TO JACQUES DURAND

19 July 1911

I was getting a little worried, my dear Jacques, when your kind letter at last arrived to reassure me . . . Things are better but still far from perfect, especially as I don't quite see how we're going to be able to get away.

July bristles with bills, landlords and a whole collection of domestic worries which repeat themselves every year with a distressing regularity. Whatever ingenious plans I invent I always end up 3,000 francs short, and even by selling my soul to the devil I don't know where I shall find them.

We were thinking of going to Houlgate, which is a quiet, family resort! Arcachon is out of the question because of the cost of travelling.

So one's nerves begin to fray and, as one no longer knows who to blame, the result is acid repartee on topics far removed from the matter in hand . . . That's life: not a joke, and full of wanton complications! Can you imagine how exhausting it is to struggle against a void? And how unfortunate it is to have an imagination in those circumstances! Forgive these untimely complaints.

Yours as ever
C.D.

216† TO ANDRÉ CAPLET

Le Grand Hôtel Houlgate [Calvados]
Cher André Caplet   Tuesday 15 August 1911

Life is a queer business and, as lived in this den around me here, more unappetizing still. Jesus Christ, Cecil Rhodes and Americans are all hotel people. They're instantly adaptable, quite content to be merely a number, and manage to stay cheerful while changing their clothes four times a day. It's amazing. Still, the beach at Houlgate is by far the best. The Sea's unreservedly beautiful and there are even trees with real leaves. But all that's utterly spoilt by a civilization so excessive, it comes curiously close to barbarism.

There's also a M. Paul Vizentini who conducts a band of malefactors in a variety of stupid pieces, even though the Sea takes the opportunity to retire in indignation – me too!

. . . 'And the children come down to the beach to bathe' . . . Some of them are actually rather nice. But dear God! Their mothers and fathers are a horrid sight! It's hard to compare the children with their parents without concluding that one of the parties, at least, has not been the soul of virtue. It seems there are more things go towards the making of a child than one dreams of, as Horatio might say to Hamlet . . .

[244]

31 Debussy and Chouchou at Houlgate, 1911.

Are you aware that the sea journey from Le Havre to Dives – just along the coast from Houlgate – is a delightful experience? I won't lay too much stress on how happy the three Debussys would be to see you, and Claude Debussy in particular.

I'm doing precisely nothing, not out of idleness but because it's impossible to think amid this caravanserai. I'm reading some really extraordinary 95 cent novels and I've discovered the Chronicles of Joinville, who was the wonderful biographer of Saint Louis (King Louis IX). It's never too late to become erudite; but there's no cause for alarm, I won't overdo it!

The firm of Durfils, who are not in the business of marketing leisure, have sent me the proofs of the orchestral score of *Le Martyre de Saint Sébastien*. They reminded me of those treasured moments during the early rehearsals – when we were still in control. They remain one of my happiest and most vivid memories, no doubt about that, nor about the fact that I owe them to you. What a real joy it was to be able to listen to music without anxiety; to feel an atmosphere of joy surrounding you and becoming ever stronger, till in the end you weren't sure whether you really existed, and whether you hadn't turned into that menacing timpani roll or that harmonic on the cello . . .

Enough! Enough! Enough!

Yours ever
C.D.

217 TO JACQUES DURAND

Houlgate
Mon cher Jacques   Saturday 26 August 1911

Here life and the sea go on their way . . . The former contradicting our primitive instincts, the latter going tunefully to and fro and soothing the melancholy of those who have chosen the wrong beach!

As you see, even my pen is weeping![1]

And the truth is that at the end of this holiday we have to admit we don't know why we came.

Is it really that we've lost the ability to enjoy things together? I don't know. But apart from the air we're breathing, which human industry hasn't been able to do anything about, everything else is less than mediocre.

[246]

The orchestration of the *Rapsodie*[2] is almost entirely sketched and when I get back to Paris, that is on 1 September, I'll just have to write it out. It's impossible for me to do it here being, as you know, a man of settled habits.

I can only deplore the fact that *Pelléas* is to be given at Nice[3] and at Cannes . . . I realize it's a necessary cog in the glory machine, but I'm also thinking how ridiculous such performances are where everything is brought down to the scale of the participants! (performers and public).

Still, one has to put up with the things one can't change.

I'm particularly happy to be able to pen the words: see you soon.

Yours ever
C.D.

1 An ink blot on the original letter.
2 In its original form as a Conservatoire test piece, see letter 196, the *Clarinet Rhapsody* was written with piano accompaniment.
3 *Pelléas* was to be given at the Nice Casino in February 1912.

218 TO ANDRÉ CAPLET

[October 1911]

Are you angry with me? I must tell you that since we parted in the corridor of the Métro, my life has been stupid and empty and not to be wished on anybody . . .

Naturally we must abandon all hope of travelling to Boston . . .[1] I know perfectly well the shape the obstacles are taking but I don't know what lies behind them. You know what a horror I have of contradiction? Well, everything in this business is contradictory and upsetting. And I imagined the natural thing would have been to support me as lovingly as possible! The thought of describing to you the continual arguments and battles was so painful, I've put off writing to you as long as possible! The worst thing is that I feel lost in it all. I can no longer find my tranquil egoism – an admirable force which I know well how to use.

Frankly, I'm extremely depressed. Give me a little more time in which to recover.

With all my best wishes
Yours as ever
C.D.

It might be possible, if I made a slight effort, for me to *come by myself* . . . But then, I don't dare to!

Let me know soon what you think.[2] *Don't forget that your letter will have to be seen.*

[1] Henry Russell had invited Debussy to come to Boston to conduct *Pelléas*. After much hesitation, Debussy refused to go because of his wife's opposition.
[2] As letter 222 shows, Caplet chose not to reply.

219 TO HENRY RUSSELL

Cher Monsieur Russell   Sunday 22 October 1911

I must resolutely decline to come to Boston . . . I take this decision, I promise you, with regret and for family reasons too serious for me to ignore.

What you have told me about your plans for putting on *Pelléas et Mélisande*, and what I have myself seen of the decor, constitute temptations I find it painful to resist because I am sure your production will be unique. I saw my friend André Caplet at work during the performances of *Saint Sébastien* and it's a rather rare occurrence in the life of an 'executee'[1] to be able to sit in on rehearsals — normally such bad-tempered affairs — without any kind of fear. But you know his innate gifts as a conductor and his marvellous understanding of this complex and delicate art. And he is passionately fond of *Pelléas*.

All of which are fine guarantees, are they not? Finally, I must say that you are not the one who feels my absence the most.

> With my warmest gratitude and best wishes
> Yours sincerely
> C.D.

[1] 'Exécuté' means 'victim of an execution'. (R.N.)

220† TO JACQUES DURAND

Cher ami   Friday 8 December 1911

The consternation into which the *Rapsodie* has plunged the Russians[1] seems to me rather excessive, especially as this piece is one of the easiest on the ear I've ever written . . . ! Are they now regarding the clarinet as an instrument of revolutionary propaganda?

Forgive me for not being able to send you the proofs of *Gigues* today. While I was orchestrating it I found some slight modifications were necessary. It's better to delay a little now rather than come back with revisions later.

Yours ever
C.D.

[1] The *Clarinet Rhapsody* had just received its first performance in Russia.

221 TO ROBERT GODET

18 December 1911

Even though I've been slow to reply, so scandalously so that no possible explanation can be found, don't imagine I've forgotten you . . . I can see you as you were the last time we met – so quick and aggressive – with that beard which does make you a bit different. I can hear you talking to that parrot which, like all family pets, is discretion itself. I can see you longer ago still: in the rue Cassini, so calm you could hear the silence move – sorry!

Yesterday I went to the Salon d'Automne to see an exhibition by Henry de Groux[1] and there I encountered the Past!

It's a wonderful exhibition! . . . A Napoleon leading the retreat from Moscow which makes you shiver more than any amount of snow and in which you can feel all the bitterness of the disappointments yet to come. A large bronze of Tolstoy marching, as it seems, in the face of Destiny, much finer than Rodin's ingenious mutilations! A portrait of Wagner looking like an old, cynical magician, guarding his secret . . . A whole succession of images and shapes which haunt you continuously. I saw de Groux there, hardly changed. Still giving the impression of a talented clown, with all the dreams of the world in his eyes.

As I remember, it was with you I saw for the first time his *Christ aux outrages*,[2] in a sort of barn at the bottom of the rue de Vaugirard. De Groux was with Pierre d'Alheim,[3] a kindly giant in a cap, who was leaving for Moscow that evening and was probably afraid of forgetting about it. His wife, Marie Olénine, was there too – you remember, she used to sing Mussorgsky songs, very simply. They were the ones who founded a 'Maison du Lied' in Moscow, where you can hear songs from the four corners of the world at the drop of a hat . . . They also run

[249]

competitions to find the best harmonies for spoiling popular songs. I wouldn't say it was exactly useful, but it's better than playing around carelessly with explosives.[4]

De Groux has been so thorough about disappearing from view, people thought he was dead. He's a fine example of moral courage – among others I know . . . His advice is to avoid the nasty fumes from the censers of the elect, though it's not a bad idea to spit into them when you need to.

Today I've sent you the score of *Saint Sébastien*, the sort of writing you may perhaps prefer to this letter! And you'd be right!

Did you know that quite near you, in Clarens, there's a young Russian composer: Igor Stravinsky, who has an instinctive genius for colour and rhythm? I'm sure you'd like both him and his music . . . And 'he's not all tricks'. He writes directly for orchestra, without any intermediate steps,[5] and the outline of his music follows only the promptings of his emotion. There are no precautions or pretentions. It's childish and savage. Even so, the organization is extremely delicate. If you have the opportunity of meeting him, don't hesitate.

Talking of organization, I haven't managed so far to find what I want for my two Poe stories . . .[6] They smell of the lamp and you can see the 'seams'! The longer I go on, the more I detest the sort of intentional disorder whose aim is merely to deceive the ear. The same goes for bizarre, intriguing harmonies which are no more than parlour-games . . . How much has first to be discovered, then suppressed, before one can reach the naked flesh of emotion . . . pure instinct ought to warn us, anyway, that textures and colours are no more than illusory disguises!

Your letter arrived this morning to cheer me up . . .

All this scribbling will only make your eyes worse . . . Tell me! Is it from too much writing? Or too many cigars? Forgive me for sounding like a schoolmaster, which I've no right to do, only it's important that you of all people should be free of problems like that!

You've kept your ability to see further than music which, as you know, is an increasingly rare gift! It's one your good friend Claude Debussy values, though he generally hears rather different bell sounds.

Why aren't you here with me more often!

Sometimes I'm so miserable and lonely . . . though there's no way round it and it's not the first time. Chouchou's smile helps me through some of the darker moments, but I can't bother her with stories she would only see as irritating variations on the Ogre's wicked deeds! So I remain alone with my discomfort!

[250]

I'm rather nervous about *Pelléas* in Geneva. It isn't the sort of thing that'll go down well there . . . The emotion in it, lacking stereotypes or leitmotifs, will be regarded as indecent! Perhaps I'm wrong, but even so I have the feeling Geneva is a hive of professors, and that ideas are only admitted wearing white ties.[7]

No, what I'd much rather do is climb a mountain with you and listen to the wind . . !ies8 You may be sure it would sing only that music made of all the harmonies it gathers as it passes over the treetops (a sentence all the more beautiful for being entirely meaningless!).

If Destiny, then, sends you to Paris, that'll be the best thing it's done for a long time. I hope you'll stay on a little and won't have too many 'jobs' to do. 'We have so much to say to one another,' as someone once said![9]

I must stop in case you start thinking this correspondence is going to end up as 'memoirs', which are only excusable when someone dies . . . if then!

> Yours as ever
> C.D.

[1] Belgian painter, sculptor and lithographer, 1867–1930. He first met Debussy in 1902 and in 1909 made a portrait and a bust of him. He was an unconventional character, closely involved in the symbolist movement. His 1911 exhibition caused all the more of a sensation because, as Debussy says later in the letter, he was thought to be dead.

[2] This sculpture was exhibited in 1890 at the Salon des Beaux Arts in Brussels but turned down by the jury of the Salon du Champ de Mars in Paris in 1892.

[3] Pierre, Baron d'Alheim, wrote a book on Mussorgsky and made French versions of his songs; his wife, Marie Olénine, introduced Mussorgsky's work to the Paris public in 1896.

[4] While being wholly in accord with Debussy's opinions as expressed elsewhere (in letter 204, for example), these sentiments derive added piquancy from the fact that the winner in four of the seven categories for folksong harmonization in the 1910 competition was Ravel. Mme Olénine d'Alheim performed all seven winning songs in Paris in December of that year. (R.N.)

[5] Stravinsky himself claimed he always worked at the piano. (R.N.)

[6] See letter 206, also to Godet. (R.N.)

[7] *Pelléas* was given in Geneva on 8 March 1912.

[8] Godet was a mountaineer, among other things. 'At the age of seventy, accompanied by his two daughters but without a guide, he climbed to the summit of Mont Blanc' (Lockspeiser, *Debussy, his Life and Mind*, Vol. I, p. 104). (R.N.)

[9] 'Nous avons tant de choses à nous dire': Pelléas in Act IV scene 4.

Mon bon Caplet   22 December 1911

Not to have replied to my last, disoriented letter,[1] written under the double influence of spleen and bad temper, is entirely understandable. But not to reply to poor Saint Sebastian, that's not kind! Even if he has got used to arrows, he didn't expect any from you . . .

But don't let's exaggerate. I know your life of 'hard labour'[2] is designed to blunt the sharpest sensibility. I have not, of course, told anybody what it cost me to give up my journey to America . . . First, because of my feelings for you, built up by thousands of those tiny crystallizations which happen almost without our knowing it. And secondly, because a performance of *Pelléas* prepared by you promised to be a beautiful and moving affair. I'm rather like a child who's been shown a cake, which is then eaten by other people – character-forming maybe, but at my age it's a little late for that sort of experience! The short answer is that I suffered. Let's say no more about it.

Music is not helping much, either . . . I can't finish the two Poe stories, everything is as dull as a hole in the ground. For every bar that has some freedom about it, there are twenty that are stifled by the weight of one particular tradition; try as I may, I'm forced to recognize its hypocritical and destructive influence. The fact that this tradition belongs to me by right is hardly relevant . . . it's just as depressing, because whatever masks you wear, underneath you find yourself. In fact, we ought to destroy what devours the best of our thoughts and reach a position where we love nothing but ourselves, with a fierce attention to detail. But what happens is the opposite: first of all there's the family, which clutters up the path, either with too much kindness or with a blind serenity. Then come the Mistresses or the Mistress, with whom we don't really reckon because we're so happy to lose ourselves in passion. I keep clear of these, and of stronger temptations . . . Truth to tell, there's nothing we can do. We have a soul bequeathed to us by a bunch of totally unknown people who, through the family tree, act upon us very often without our being able to do much about it.

I read about your magnificent conducting of *Samson et Dalila*! You are capable of anything, even resuscitating stuffed crocodiles. For my sins I heard *La Mer* conducted by G.P.;[3] it was awful and frustrating. The same *La Mer* conducted by C. Ch.[4] much better. After these two performances Jacques Durand and I decided not to present *Gigues* this year. We'll wait

[252]

for next spring when Durand is going to organize some new orchestral concerts. May we hope that André Caplet will be kind enough to lend his support? And will the aforementioned *Gigues* be conducted by him? And, with your permission, may we call that 'good news?'[5]

Chouchou is still a good little girl who doesn't forget her friend Caplet. She talks about him to people who have never heard of that illustrious capellmeister – which brands them in her eyes as some kind of savage Iroquois.

Satie hasn't yet had the ten spare minutes he needs to go off to America, but he speaks of you and claims that a true Norman will never get used to the Americans[6] and that this joke of thinking you have to spend six months over there won't last long. I agree with him entirely. You don't think you might have a moment to see the New Year in with us? This Boston of yours is much too far away! When you think that to you, my best friend, I have to convey my good wishes in writing, to be cooled perforce by the long journey and the humidity of the Atlantic. But our day will come and then we'll make up for lost time!

That last paragraph doesn't make any claim for immortality or being engraved on marble. It's just a confused expression of what I sincerely feel and of the affection of

> Your true friend
> C.D.

My wife and Chouchou send you, as always, their kindest regards.

[1] Letter 218.
[2] Debussy uses the English expression.
[3] Gabriel Pierné conducted *La Mer* at the Colonne Concerts on 5 November 1911.
[4] Camille Chevillard conducted *La Mer* at the Lamoureux Concerts on 17 December.
[5] *Gigues* was first performed on 26 January 1913, conducted by the composer.
[6] Satie and Caplet were both born in Normandy, on opposite sides of the mouth of the Seine: Satie in Honfleur, Caplet in Le Havre. (R.N.)

223 TO JACQUES DURAND

> Cher ami   22 December 1911

As you may suppose I've heard nothing from M. d'Annunzio. I get the impression this archangel is not taking us altogether seriously?

> Yours ever
> C.D.

Jeux
The ballet world
More travels

The ballet *Jeux* was Debussy's only specially written contribution to Diaghilev's repertoire, but the performance laboured under an indecisive choreography. Debussy was no happier with the ballet production of *L'Après-midi d'un faune* and carefully did not involve himself in the moral scandal it provoked. His ties with Stravinsky became closer and *Le Sacre du printemps* made an enormous impression on him. Three more journeys – to Moscow (1913), to Rome and The Hague (February 1914) and to Brussels (April 1914) – added to his feeling of exhaustion. He returned to writing newspaper articles, this time for the revue *S.I.M.*

Mon cher Jacques   [January 1912]

I can't let the day go by without thanking you for your kind telegram.

Between ourselves, it seems quite clear to me that M. Russell and his people in Boston have discovered the true and only way of putting on *Pelléas*!

Even so I'm still doubtful. I feel the Americans are only a foreign version of the Marseillais. After all, they invented the idea of 'bluff' which is very close to the spirit of the Midi.

Your colleague Choisnel told me that you preferred Biarritz to Pau – believe me, these towns of the Midi will never be popular except with the English, who are so easy to please because of their native fog.

Here it's raining – your sympathy accepted – but we have a new government,[1] which is bound to bring back the sun and put an end to the taxi strike.

Myself, I'm desperately trying to find ideas which won't come and to finish anything at all, whatever the cost! A curious disease which afflicted Leonardo da Vinci. Only he had genius to go with it. It helps in all sorts of ways. I must content myself with everlasting patience which, someone once said, can sometimes be a substitute for genius.

Have you considered the influence a ballet scenario might have on a ballerina's intelligence? In *Khamma* – which I hope to play for you soon – one feels a curious vegetation invading the brain, so the dancers are forgiven.

Yours ever
C.D.

[1] Under Raymond Poincaré.

Mon cher ami   Sunday 25 February 1912

I haven't forgotten you, believe me. I should be delighted if you would conduct *Children's Corner* in Rome, as my opinion of you hasn't changed; I'm still prepared to swear before God, and even before men, that you are a conductor of the very first rank.

Really, I don't see the necessity of putting one's grey cells into orbit in order to become a *debussyste*. I feel it's just a question of having a modicum of taste! You may say that's not a quality to be found internationally, still less nationally . . . the public is the same everywhere and always follows anyone who can show them the latest in miracles. It suffers too from the hereditary, traditional habit of preferring lies to sincerity – an observation just as valid on the moral front as on the spiritual one . . . I long ago gave up trying to do anything to change this deplorable state of mind. I content myself with serving music as lovingly, as loyally as possible, and that's all!

You're right, *Ariane et Barbe-bleue* is a masterpiece, but it's not a masterpiece of French music . . . And the longer I live, the more I find we're wrong to forget our past and listen to foreign voices which don't perhaps sing as well in tune as our own! You say you'll be in Paris in the spring, so I hope to see you soon.

With my kindest regards to your wife

Yours
C.D.

Please give M. Depanis[1] my best wishes, if you have the chance.

[1] Giuseppe Depanis, a Turin lawyer, who organized concerts and exhibitions there and with whom Debussy had stayed the previous summer. See letter 213.

226 TO IGOR STRAVINSKY

Cher ami   Saturday 13 April 1912

Thanks to you I've spent a lovely Easter holiday in the company of Petrushka, the terrible Moor and the delightful ballerina. I imagine you too must have spent some incomparable moments with these three puppets . . . and I know few things as good as the passage you call 'le tour de passe-passe' . . .[1] There's a sort of sonorous magic about it,

32 Debussy and Stravinsky photographed by Satie.

mysteriously transforming these mechanical souls into human beings: it's a spell which, so far, I think you are alone in possessing. And then there are orchestral *certainties* such as I have encountered only in *Parsifal* – I'm sure you'll understand what I mean! You'll progress beyond *Petrushka*, of course, but you can still be proud of what the work stands for.

Please forgive me for not thanking you earlier for so kindly sending me the score, though the dedication on it is much too flattering about what I have done for the art of music, which we both serve with a similar disinterested zeal ... Unfortunately, these last few days I've been surrounded by invalids! Especially my wife, who has been ill for some time ... I've even had to become a 'man about the house' and I must tell you straight off it's not a role I have any aptitude for.

I hope to have the pleasure of seeing you back in Paris soon as there's talk of playing some more of your music, I'm glad to say.

Don't forget where we live or how delighted we shall all be to see you again.

> Yours ever
> C.D.

[1] The passage Debussy refers to runs from figs. 58 to 64 in scene 1 of the score: the showman plays his flute and brings the three puppets to life.

227 TO JACQUES DURAND

Mon cher Jacques   2 July 1912

It seems to me we differ in our interpretations of what the English 'girl'[1] means by one passage in her letter ... What she has in mind is not merely an arrangement of my music but a complete rewriting of it by one of those musicians of genius that only England can produce. How does she reconcile not being able to cope with my music and at the same time insisting there must be more of it? It's a nasty business altogether and she deserves to have her nose politely rubbed in it! She's been rather swift in replacing her genius for understanding things with her genius for being a pest.

What right has she got to decide that nothing can be done with *Khamma* when she doesn't know the resources it uses and hasn't tried to stage it? Forgive me for bothering you with this business which makes a complete nonsense of the *Entente Cordiale* ...

[258]

So far I've had nothing from the smooth Diaghilev except a telegram promising the scenario for *Jeux* by the end of last week. I'm concentrating on *Gigues* as well as the *Préludes*[2] and some other things . . .

My wife has been poisoned by some mushrooms . . . Given the sensitivity of her 'vaso-motor' system, it's had a devastating effect.

> With all best wishes to you both
> Yours ever
> C.D.

[1] The Canadian Maud Allan ('girl' is Debussy's own term for her. R.N.).
[2] He was working on the second book of *Préludes*, published the following year. (R.N.)

228 TO MAUD ALLAN

Mademoiselle   16 July 1912

In reply to your letter of 26 June:
1. I see that you agree with me over the terms of paragraph 3 of our contract which lays down no publication date for *Khamma*. That is a step forward.
2. I can only reiterate what I said in my previous letter about the music of *Khamma*. It is impossible that you be permitted to arrange this music to suit your own taste.
                     Thus I composed it
                     Thus it shall remain.

> I am
> Yours sincerely
> C.D.

229 TO RENÉ LENORMAND[1]

Cher Monsieur Lenormand   Thursday 25 July 1912

Forgive me for not writing sooner to thank you for the parcel and for the trouble you have been to. Until today I have been so overwhelmed with work that I had no time to accede to your request. It's all extremely accurate and almost implacably logical. You have obviously gained the impression, rather ironically, that all these colours were finally plunging us into a kind of uneasiness from which we shall

[259]

emerge with a question mark driven into our heads like a nail. Whether it was intentional or not, your study is perhaps the most powerful critique of 'modern harmony'.

You are sometimes ruthless in divorcing your quotations from their context, because then they lose almost all their 'curiosity value'. You should consider the untrained hands that are going to fumble their way carelessly through your book, using it only to finish off all those beautiful butterflies that are already a little bruised by analysis.

But enough! Too bad about the dead, and the wounded who will be put out of their misery. That's how it always is with wars. And may I congratulate you exceedingly on a task which demanded manifold abilities.

> Yours sincerely
> C.D.

[1]   A composer who was keen on contributing to the development of the *Lied* in France and founded a society to that end. He had asked various composers of the time for their opinions, to be included in his *Etude sur l'harmonie moderne* which was published in 1913.

230 TO JACQUES DURAND

Mon cher Jacques   9 August 1912

My wife's already told you we had a good journey back . . .[1] What a beautiful house it is! And how well you and your wife have preserved its ancient feel without spoiling it. That sounds rather rude but most people, as you know, use the Past only to make you feel 'you don't belong' . . . 'you never will' and you should stick rigidly to playing the role of guest.

Having Bel-Ebat in my mind's eye always makes me a little sad when I come back home . . . This avenue du Bois de Boulogne smelling of Brazilians and Americans, not much ancient feel here! I also come back to my landlord, the English alcoholic, who'll have no compunction in throwing me out if ever he finds a millionaire adventurer! But an end of grumbling – back to the matter in hand.

I had a visit from Nijinsky and his 'niania'[2] (S. de D.), who came through Paris on their way to Deauville. We sorted out one or two details that were still rather vague. They're in a great hurry to have the music of *Jeux* because Nijinsky wants to work on it during his stay in

[260]

Venice! Apparently the peaceful air of the lagoons will inspire his choreographic reveries. I refused to play them what I'd done, not wanting Barbarians sticking their noses into my experiments in personal chemistry! But *at the end of the month* I must get down to execution in the most disagreeable sense of the word.[3] May God, the Tsar and my country stand by me in my hour of need.

I swear to you I'm not wasting a minute and, in the variable, enervating weather we're having this summer, that's not always much fun. Talking of which, Chouchou has composed a little song in English, a rather ungracious one, saying 'the sea is annoyed not to have had a visit from M. and Mme Debussy or their charming daughter' ... I expended much eloquence trying to persuade her that this year the sea had gone out so far, people were despairing of ever finding it again; which didn't go down very well. There are times when being a father is a very delicate business!

Thanks to *Jeux* I've had to interrupt the orchestration of Gigues.[4] Don't be too cross with me, I'll get back to it soon and it won't take long to finish.

> Yours ever
> C.D.

[1] Debussy and his wife had been staying with the Durands at their house in the country. (R.N.)
[2] 'Nurse' in Russian. 'S de D' is Diaghilev.
[3] A pun on 's'éxécuter', which means to comply or oblige. See letter 219 footnote 1. (R.N.)
[4] The orchestral draft of *Jeux* is dated 23 August 1912, with additions made on 1–2 September, but the full score was completed only on 24 April 1913.

231 TO ANDRÉ CAPLET

Cher André Caplet   25 August 1912

Switzerland is a 'charming country' only in fusty opéras-comiques. Am I right in thinking the one in question is about China? With music by Bazin, who wrote a treatise teaching you how not to understand harmony.[1]

Since you left I've been eking out my existence as usual – in which your kind wishes have been some support – and I've finished the piece called *Jeux* I spoke to you about. How I was able to forget the troubles of this world and write music which is almost cheerful, and alive with quaint gestures . . . I'll have to invent for it an orchestra 'without feet'. Not that I'm thinking of a band composed exclusively of legless cripples! No! I'm thinking of that orchestral colour which seems to be lit from behind, which there are such wonderful examples of in *Parsifal*![2]

If I didn't know the welcome America keeps for you, I'd confess that I miss you extremely. Of course, egoism plays a large part in this, so you can take it to heart just as much as you feel like doing. You're one of the rare people with whom I like swapping ideas because you never sound a wrong note in reply . . . It's extremely rare! ('extremely' and 'rare' are repeated deliberately). You're on your way to a life in which, apparently, there's no time to look back at the past. And as it would be unbecoming for me to send you a photograph to go on your desk, I can only put myself in the hands of the gods who control the memories of men!

I'm thinking about the piece on Rameau[3] you want.

> As ever
> Yours
> C.D.

P.S. If it's still possible – without making a fuss about it – don't forget 11 September.

[1]   François Bazin, 1816–1878, wrote several opéras-comiques of which *Le voyage en Chine* (1865) was the most successful. He was also the author of a *Cours d'harmonie théorique et pratique*.
[2]   Compare his remark about *Petrushka* to Stravinsky in letter 226.
[3]   An article on Rameau which he eventually sent to Caplet on 19 November.

232† TO JACQUES DURAND

Mon cher Jacques   5 September 1912

The title of 'great French innovator' is a little more than I deserve. Even so, I'm grateful to have this encouragement for the future.

The few extra bars D.[1] asked for meant that I've had to change the end of *Jeux* – to its advantage . . . it's a better shape and passion now flows through every bar (Russians are like Syrian cats).

Jacques Charlot[2] has intimated to me your impatience . . . on this point, I think D. doesn't trust the French and is bending the truth

[262]

considerably! Anyway, I'm doing all I can and I don't think we'll be behind schedule. (The new copyist is very efficient.)

Yours ever
C.D.

[1] Diaghilev.
[2] A cousin of Durand's who worked in the publishing house. He transcribed several of Ravel's works and, after he was killed in the First World War, Ravel dedicated to him the 'Prélude' from his *Tombeau de Couperin*.

233 TO JACQUES DURAND

Mon cher Jacques   12 September 1912

Choisnel has sent me the reply you've decided to give to the wretched Maud Allan. It's perfectly in order; but I must say a few words about this young woman's appalling behaviour. It's intolerable that she should start issuing opinions with no backing whatever and expressing them in language hardly suitable for a bootmaker who's got his instructions wrong.[1] I'm probably not philosophical enough, because this whole argument depresses me profoundly. I ask you! She supplies a scenario so boring a negro could have done better. Somehow, by the aid of what providence I know not, I manage to write the music. And then this young woman gives me lessons in aesthetics, talking about her taste and that of the English – it's beyond everything. It's enough to make you weep, or better still give her a smart blow! But even if one doesn't go to that extreme, it might still be possible to give her a lesson in good manners.

You'll find considerable changes at the end of *Jeux*. I've been working on it up to the last moment.[2] It's hard to get it right because the music has to convey a rather *risqué* situation! Even though in a ballet immorality passes through the ballerina's legs and ends in a pirouette.

Tired as I am, I've gone back to my *old projects*.[3] My love for them should give me new strength; that's the hope, anyway.

Our best wishes to your wife and yourself.

Yours ever
C.D.

[1] Maud Allan found *Khamma* 'far too short' and not 'altogether in accordance with the full text thought which was submitted'.

² Debussy is here referring to the piano score which was published in 1912. The full score was completed only on 24 April 1913 and published the following year.
³ Probably the two tales of Edgar Allan Poe. (R.N.)

234 TO ANDRÉ CAPLET

Cher André Caplet   11 October 1912

Despite my natural inclination to oblige you, I've had to think the matter over carefully and so wasn't able to reply straight away ...

I should say first that I've always refused to orchestrate my songs, and have done so politely, obstinately and fiercely.¹ Several great singers – large ones anyway – have asked me to do so and my view remains the same. But in your case, the position's different . . . If you think it's a good idea and would like to do it, then choose any of the *Ariettes* you think worthy of your ingenuity. But I hope you'll agree with me, there can be no question of Mlle Garden making her own choice . . . That sort of thing is absolutely incompatible with the freedom an artist must have in dealing with his own work. I've never acknowledged autocracy except in the form of a government; in one's daily life, it strikes me as dangerous.

If you don't mind, the question of anonymity won't arise . . . If you orchestrate the songs, then your name will appear on the title page. I myself have a number of reasons for approving of that, chief among them my affection for you.²

You may know that M. Russell was kind enough to do everything he could on my behalf? In spite of the material nature of his help, I trust he appreciates how sincerely grateful I am.³ If I didn't write to you as soon as possible, it was because of other problems – I only have to bend down to pick them up – and because there are days when I no longer have the strength to complain and bother my friends with tales that are all too closely bound up with my domestic economy.

I've started the article on Rameau. It's trickier to write than you'd think, simply because in forty lines you have to outline the life, the work, the influence on music of a man who suddenly disappeared from the history books – one wonders why, or maybe one knows all too well.

I hope to see you soon . . . and wish you every success in your enterprises; I imagine it's a country where help takes the form of adroitly cutting off your hands.

Yours as ever
C.D.

[264]

¹ Caplet orchestrated two of the *Ariettes oubliées*: no. 1, 'C'est l'extase', and no. 5, 'Green'.

² In 1898 Debussy wrote to Pierre de Bréville that he thought it was 'pointless' for his *Proses lyriques* to be 'inflated with a nondescript orchestral hubbub'. But in 1901 he orchestrated two of them himself, for a performance at the Société nationale which never took place.

³ Two years earlier the English impresario had lent Debussy the sum of 5,000 francs which the composer had been unable to repay.

235 TO IGOR STRAVINSKY

[5 November 1912]

Don't fall over, cher ami, it's only me!!! If we both really applied ourselves, in your case to understanding why I haven't written and in my case to explaining it, then I promise you neither of us would have a hair left on his head!

But the good news is that here your name is mentioned once a day – at least – and your friend Chouchou has composed a fantasy on *Petrushka* which is enough to make a tiger roar ... For all the punishments I threaten her with, she still goes on claiming 'you'd find it excellent'. So how can you imagine we're not thinking of you?

I still think of the performance of your *Sacre du printemps* at Laloy's house . . .¹ It haunts me like a beautiful nightmare and I try in vain to recall the terrifying impression it made. That's why I wait for the performance like a greedy child who's been promised some jam.

As soon as I have a reasonable proof of *Jeux* I'll send it to you . . . I'd like to have your opinion on this 'trifle' . . . for three people! You're surprised at my calling it *Jeux* and prefer 'Le Parc'! Please believe me, *Jeux* is better. For one thing it's shorter; and for another it's a convenient way of expressing the 'horrors' that take place between the three participants. When are you coming to Paris? It would be good to have some real music at last.

With kindest regards from the three of us to your wife and yourself.

Yours ever
C.D.

¹ In his memoirs, *La musique retrouvée* (1928), Laloy has left a description of this performance of the piano duet version of the score, which took place in his country house at Bellevue on 9 June 1912, with Debussy playing the bass and Stravinsky the treble: 'We were dumbfounded, flattened as though by a hurricane from the roots of time.'

Mon cher Jacques   Saturday 7 December 1912

As you gave me to expect, I've had a letter from Chevillard.

The outcome is that he's offering to conduct *Gigues* but doesn't say anything about the other two *Images*. I imagine that on this point you agree with me and would prefer to have all three together.

Don't you think Pierné might be given the opportunity?[1]

He's always been willing to do the three and said so again yesterday evening on the telephone. Chevillard could still have *Saint Sébastien*; and perhaps *Printemps*, which we mustn't lose sight of.

I'll wait to reply to Chevillard until I've agreed something with you; we shall, of course, continue to walk hand in hand — over the head of exterior conflict! . . .

Between ourselves, I have a soft spot for the Colonne orchestra[2] and I wouldn't like to be disobliging to them without a very pressing reason.

It's for you to decide.

Yours ever
C.D.

[1] 'Gigues' was conducted in the end by Debussy himself at the Colonne concerts on 26 January 1913.
[2] Debussy had written a few words in homage to Edouard Colonne in *Excelsior* in 1910, to mark the association's 1,000th concert. Also, it was with them that he made his debut as a conductor, in *La Mer* on 19 January 1908.

Mon cher Jacques   Tuesday 7 January 1913

You'd already have had the two missing Préludes if I hadn't got hung up on 'Tomai des Eléphants'. I've been soldiering away at it but as a prelude it doesn't work! I've already decided on a replacement and you'll have a complete set by the end of the week.

As for the *Petite suite* you're absolutely right: I've had occasion too often to appreciate the danger of arrangements like these to let myself in for similar treatment.[1] Let Mr Rumbold exercise his choreographic genius on more suitable subjects.

[266]

Since I saw you, things haven't gone too well on the arterio-sanguinary front and my nerves are definitely the worse for it.

I enclose Trouhanova's[2] letter.

> Yours ever
> C.D.

[1]   The *Petite suite*, written in 1888–9, had already been transcribed for various media, even for organ and for wind band.

[2]   A Russian dancer who gave some 'Concerts de danse' at the Châtelet in April 1912, including the first performance of Dukas's *La Péri*.

238 TO EMILE VUILLERMOZ[1]

Mon cher Vuillermoz   Friday 17 January 1913

Your article is beautifully put together, and I admire the subtle artifice with which you pass from *Idomeneo* to *Fervaal* . . .[2]

If the composer of this mystery from the Cevennes has any conscience left, he'll thank you for pointing out to him the attitude he ought to adopt. Unfortunately, he won't do any such thing, mark my words – he'll go on 'doing his duty' ('duty' to be understood in the strictly scholastic[3] sense). And so will the rest of them . . . Quite a few days lie ahead consecrated to Boredom.

Don't worry, my own condition has nothing tetralogical about it. It's the story of a little cyst that wanted to go on growing. A pair of sharp scissors have cut it off in its prime; and that's all.

> Yours
> C.D.

[1]   A critic who wrote for numerous journals and was a passionate champion of contemporary music. He had been one of the founders of the Société Musicale Indépendante and was editor-in-chief of the review *S.I.M.*

[2]   The title of the article, in the issue of *S.I.M.* for 15 January, was 'Idomenée. La Sorcière. Fervaal', passing from Mozart to d'Indy, of whom he goes on to speak in the second paragraph.

[3]   A putative adjective from 'Schola (Cantorum)'. (R.N.)

Paris
Saturday 18 January 1913

No, mon cher Toulet, I haven't forgotten you and I value your friendship too highly ever to question it.

You must believe me when I assert, calling as witness the holly which provides a solemn border to my window, that I haven't yet got used to the idea of your departure, which gave the impression of being an escape from everything and more besides! I never explained that, as I saw it, it was a cover for wounded feelings and stifled sensibilities – there are times like those when neither advice nor consolation is of much use; they can even seem indiscreet or hypocritical!

If one is to have the right to tell anyone he's on the wrong track, one has to be able to offer him, straight away, a means of getting off it, and have the conviction that one is oneself in the right . . . It's a difficult business!

Particularly in your case, with the complications of your health and the strain you've put on it with all your conflicting life-styles.

It's a disconcerting dualism which leads you, on the one hand, to enjoy company and, on the other, to have a secret and more refined taste for solitude . . . It could result in perplexity, at the least! I'm worried in case your voluntary exile to Saint-Loubès[1] satisfies only one side of you?

Forgive me if, in my extremely timid attempts to understand you, I'm sounding out of tune. I'll say no more . . .

Let's pass quickly over my delay in writing to you and please accept my fondest and best wishes for your health and peace of mind, while this month of January 1913 is still with us. These wishes come also from my wife and your not-so-little friend Chouchou whose imagination has recently been stimulated by a piano teacher, a lady in black who looks like a drawing by Odilon Redon or a nihilist caught up in a bomb blast.[2]

Yours as ever
C.D.

What do you think of the story 'Duel à mort' in *Le Temps*?[3]

[1] Toulet had decided to leave Paris and had just settled at Saint-Loubès (Gironde), in S.W. France.
[2] See letter 308.
[3] An adventure story by Guy Thorne (pseudonym of Cyril A. E. Ranger Gull) of which the first instalment appeared in *Le Temps* on 26 December 1912.

[268]

Cher Godet   Saturday 18 January 1913

Passing quickly over my delay in writing and all my other sins, may I offer you my fondest and best wishes while this month of January is still running its course!

The Opéra-comique has had the delightful notion of reviving *Pelléas* in conditions that could not be more aggravating . . . Madame Carré[1] brings a furious zeal to the task of portraying Mélisande as a kind of melancholy washerwoman; a Monsieur Boulogne(?)[2] regularly allows you a choice of two notes with every one he sings; and my poor Périer[3] has nothing left except good intentions; from which you can see I haven't had much joy out of my New Year presents.

You're aware maybe that I've gone back to being a music critic, in the *S.I.M.* You'll say, quite rightly, it's not an event to change anything in the established order! Or, to be more accurate, organized disorder. Still, one must go on religiously trying to put things back where they belong: in an attempt to recover the values falsified by arbitrary judgements and capricious interpretations, so that people can no longer distinguish between a Bach fugue and the *Marche Lorraine*! One of the characteristics of the age is to follow leaders who have barely learned to walk! Wherein have I much grief received, and much discouragement. Living the life of an artist in Paris becomes daily less compatible with the spirit that reigns here! We're becoming stupid fantasists like the Viennese . . . And you can't imagine the technical standards of our so-called 'spectacles d'art'.

If family commitments didn't keep my wife so firmly in Paris, I can assure you I'd be asking you to find me a little spot in Savoy, which you certainly seem to find agreeable. I could then soak myself in real sunlight and shake off this atmosphere of false grandeur which comes sliding under the front door, no matter what we do to try and avoid it.

In short, I'm haunted by the Mediocre and it terrifies me . . . (God knows, I'm not just pretending!)

But enough of this gloom. Instead news of Chouchou – who is unacquainted with the flowers of melancholy. She was delighted with your present and intends to thank you herself. (It may be some time in arriving. You will excuse this shortcoming which she gets from her father's side.)

She's just started learning the piano with a lady utterly in black – to

[269]

the tips of her fingernails, if I may so express it. She gives the impression of having escaped from some terrible catastrophe and her patience is inexhaustible, as Chouchou very quickly discovered.

In a fortnight or so I'll send you a new book of piano *Préludes*. Please treat them as an informal visiting card.

Remember, I always prefer reading your letters to writing mine.

> Yours ever
> C.D.

My wife asks me to send you her best wishes.

[1] Marguerite Carré was the wife of the director of the Opéra-comique. She took over the role of Mélisande from Maggie Teyte in 1910 and was still singing it in the 1920s.
[2] M. Boulogne did not reappear after this season.
[3] See letter 163.

241† TO ANDRÉ CAPLET

> Cher André Caplet   29 May 1913

The whimsical destiny that governs my life has just played me another shrill flute solo . . . I'm not going to England after all.[1] So that's five thousand francs at the bottom of the Channel for good! I suppose it's better than being made President of the Republic, but it's very annoying. I'm writing by the same post to Lady Speyer, on your behalf; she's an excellent woman and influential, if I'm not mistaken! My wife will write to Lady Grey. She's ill again (my wife) and again it's 'very annoying'!

Le sacre du printemps is extraordinarily wild . . . As you might say, it's primitive music with all modern conveniences!

Naturally I'm very upset and have lost all hope of hearing *Pelléas* as I wrote it!

> Yours ever
> C.D.

[1] Debussy had been hoping to see Caplet conduct *Pelléas* at Covent Garden.

33 Karsavina, Nijinsky and Schollar in *Jeux*, May 1913.

Cher Robert   9 June 1913

Rather than think of you having to go into a music shop, I'd prefer to bring you the parcel myself – you'll probably get it at the same time as this letter.

I curse your 'business commitments', even if they still leave you with time for me and, I'm sure, for others as well. But I find it hard to forgive them for depriving me of you this summer! Heavens! It's not as though you come that often . . . and whatever Arkel-Leblanc-Maeterlinck says: meaningless events certainly do happen.[1] Among them I might include the production of *Jeux* in which Nijinsky's perverse genius applied itself to a special branch of mathematics! The man adds up demisemiquavers with his feet, checks the result with his arms and then, suddenly struck with paralysis all down one side, glares at the music as it goes past. I gather it's called the 'stylization of gesture' . . . It's awful! Dalcrozian, even – I consider Monsieur Dalcroze one of music's worst enemies! And you can imagine the havoc his method is capable of causing in the breast of a young savage like Nijinsky![2]

The music of course doesn't defend itself! But is content to place its light arabesques in the way of all those ill-omened feet – which don't even apologize!

I saw Bloch at the Théâtre des Champs-Elysées.[3] He's still determined to use that cavernous voice of his to introduce people who, one is surprised to learn, are 'friends of Godet' . . . He must be exaggerating!!!

On reflection I think I'd rather leave Paris than see you here. At the moment it's what they call 'La Grande Saison'.[4] You can't have any idea to what extent that increases the number of idiots one comes across. Not content with mangling the French language, they bring along with them artistic ideas they believe to be modern but which are already giving off a smell of putrefaction: a bad taste even more blatant than our own. And we're so overwhelmed, we haven't the strength to resist. All in all, the exhibitions at the zoo in the Bois de Boulogne are greatly to be preferred.

It's kind of you to worry about my worries . . . My wife still isn't very well. Mademoiselle Chouchou is the only one representing health in the household.

If you can find a way for us to meet, I shall be grateful beyond the end of time, because 'autumn' is the opposite end of the year and in December I'm going to Russia!

[272]

Yours ever
C.D.

[1] A misquotation of 'Il n'arrive peut-être pas d'évènements inutiles' from Arkel's monologue in Act I scene 2 of *Pelléas*. (R.N.)

[2] E. Jacques-Dalcroze, 1865–1950, a Swiss composer and author of theories on the physical and musical manifestations of rhythm. At this time he had a large number of followers, notably Diaghilev and Nijinsky; the choreography of *L'Après-midi d'un faune* was based on his ideas.

[3] Ernest Bloch, 1880–1959, a Swiss composer who was now teaching composition in Geneva.

[4] The 8th season of the Ballets russes saw the first productions of *Jeux* (15 May) and of *Sacre du printemps* (29 May), as well as Karsavina in Florent Schmitt's *La tragédie de Salomé* (12 June) which Trouhanova had danced in 1911.

243 TO GABRIELE D'ANNUNZIO

12 June 1913

What an evening, cher d'Annunzio![1] So beautiful, but in a different way from *Le Martyre*, for which I none the less retain a special affection.

If I may say so, your style is too fine: for the mouths of the actors and for the ears of the public, battered as they are by the motley uproar of the staging. In my opinion it's exactly the wrong style to use.

Why give the eyes so much work when the ears have so much to take in? For years we've been a prey to influences from the North and from Byzantium which together are stifling our Latin genius, with its grace and clarity.

You know it as well as anyone. I don't know whether, after such a long oppression, the time to react has arrived. I'm sure we'll have the opportunity to talk about it at greater length in the future.

But all this concerns only one, very detailed point. All I wanted to do today was to say how much I enjoyed it, a sentiment my wife shares to the full.

With our warmest admiration
Yours ever
C.D.

[1] D'Annunzio's *La Pisanelle ou la mort parfumée* had been given the previous evening at the Châtelet with Ida Rubinstein. The incidental music, conducted by Inghelbrecht, was by Ildebrando da Parma, a pupil of Puccini.

Cher André Caplet   23 June 1913

I continue without more ado:[1] you would have been delighted with
Mlle Vallin singing the *Proses lyriques* and especially *Le Promenoir des
deux amants*. It was enough to make one weep – as your friend Pelléas
says, more or less – I don't know where she finds that voice. It
understands the curves which the music describes through the words
. . . but it's utterly beautiful and very simple . . . They also played, at the
same 'Gala Debussy',[2] your two-piano arrangement of *Ibéria*. I wish
you'd been there, I missed you every moment – I know the careful
balance of each sound so well and every time I felt as though I'd sat on a
gas lamp! . . . And those tremolos sounding like the rumble of so many
dead pebbles.[3] There's no doubt about it, for many of the people who
call themselves 'musicians' the art of music is closed on Sundays and
weekdays too. No need to go on . . . How happy I'd be to forget all
these galas and take myself off to a little farm in your beloved
Normandy, with no music except hens singing 'a cappella' and sceptical
ducks performing an ironic scherzo.

You've said practically nothing about Maguenat, the one-time
painter? Was he good, or just 'serviceable'? I'm thinking of Périer who's
leaving the Opéra-comique, apparently. If it's worth considering, I'll
speak to Carré about him; otherwise Heaven knows what monstrosity
he'll wish on me. Maybe he'll even take it as an opportunity not to put
on *Pelléas* ever again . . .[4]

Aren't you coming to spend some time in Paris? The 'Grande Saison'
comes to an end very soon with *Pénélope*,[5] so we'd be able to enjoy
some blessed repose. And considering I've hardly seen you, you're not
going to play a dirty trick on me and go back to that damned America,
pausing only to stock up with new ties? I have a playthrough of *Sacre
du printemps* lined up for you, something you can't ignore.

I wouldn't want to influence you, but you can see what has to be
done: take the train, then the boat . . . to take you to the train. And
finally to 80 avenue du Bois de Boulogne where a very warm welcome
awaits you.

Yours as ever
C.D.

---

[1] Debussy had written only three days before. (R.N.)

34 Portrait of Debussy by Ivan Thièle, 1913.
Tretiakov Museum, Moscow.

² The Debussy gala took place on 19 June at the Comédie des Champs-Elysées. Apart from Vuillermoz, who introduced it, the performers were Ninon Vallin, the violinist Gaston Poulet, the pianist Ricardo Viñes and L'Association chorale de Paris.
³ 'Remuer de sourds cailloux': a reference to 'le roulis sourd des cailloux', a line from the first of Verlaine's *Ariettes oubliées*, set by Debussy as 'C'est l'extase' in 1887. (R.N.)
⁴ Maguenat made his debut in 1908 in *La Traviata*. He was singing Pelléas in London (and did indeed replace Périer at the Opéra-comique the following season. R.N.).
⁵ Fauré's opera was performed for the first time in Paris on 10 May.

245 TO JACQUES DURAND

Mon cher Jacques   15 July 1913

As the postal service celebrated 14 July by refusing to deliver the smallest letter, today's the first chance I've had to thank you for your kind help. You might think writing this letter was a chore, unless you'd known for years what a miserable life I'm leading.

For instance, this year Dr Crespel strongly advised my wife to go and take the waters at Vichy. He even insisted it was imperative! You can imagine, with a sensitive nature like hers, what sort of atmosphere ensued, pregnant with thoughts which are never spoken. It's unbearable and offensive.

Struggling on one's own is nothing! But struggling 'en famille' is terrible! Not to mention the domestic demands of a material comfort one has enjoyed for a long time and which one cannot believe has now become impossible to afford.

In my case the struggle is to uphold a point of honour: a crazy one, perhaps, but explicable in the sense that I don't want one day to be reproached for accepting the present situation in order to turn it to my own advantage (there's a fine irony!).

Perhaps I'm to blame, because my only energy is intellectual; in everyday life I stumble over the smallest pebble, which another man would send flying with a lighthearted kick! And then I have an innate horror of any kind of discussion . . .

Forgive these painful details and accept my gratitude and affection – the latter free of all histrionics.

C.D.

[276]

Mon cher Jacques   Friday 8 August 1913

I don't find the story of the Mallarmé–Ravel family amusing. What's more, is it not strange that Ravel should have chosen the same poems as me? As a phenomenon of auto-suggestion ought it to be communicated to the Academy of Medicine?[1]

I'd written to Dr Bonniot before getting your letter – which doesn't matter in the least and can't alter my relationship with Mallarmé himself!

Chouchou didn't have whooping-cough; I think it was probably an attempt at bronchitis; she's clever enough to be getting better slowly, because of the special treatment illness brings with it.

My apologies for wasting your time – which you have better things to do with, my lord? – with this latest news.

    With best wishes from us all
    Yours ever
    C.D.

Perhaps the Mallarmé family is afraid Nijinsky will invent some new choreography for the three songs?

[1] Without knowing it, Debussy and Ravel worked simultaneously on *Trois poèmes de S. Mallarmé*. Their choices of two songs were identical: 'Soupir' and 'Placet futile'. Debussy's songs appeared first but without permission from the poet's heirs and it was Ravel who obtained it for him from Mallarmé's son-in-law, Dr Bonniot. Ravel's own songs did not appear until 1914, also from Durand.

Mon cher Jacques   30 August 1913

I think we can accept Chevillard's proposals . . . But don't you think it would be sensible to find out what Astruc and Diaghilev have in mind? This is just a hesitant opinion, not a token of opposition . . . Perhaps it's not relevant anyway? Forgive me, I'm paralysed with worry. You can't possibly envisage the hours of torment I'm going through at present! I promise you, if my little Chouchou weren't here I'd blow my brains out, stupid and ridiculous as that might be.

I'll see you on Tuesday. I really need your support.

    Yours as ever
    C.D.

Mon cher Jacques   3 September 1913

I'm most grateful for the observations you made yesterday which are very much to the point . . . But I came to ask you whether you would be kind enough to lend me one or two thousand francs . . .

I feel rather ashamed, given how little you had to say to me . . . I'm afraid that between us it hasn't been a question of 'advances' for some time! But I don't know what to do any more . . .

My mother's ill and needs things I can't give her. As you know, I have to keep working and I'm at the end of my tether.

You will appreciate what it costs me to write to you like a pauper.

> I am, none the less
> Yours ever
> C.D.

As soon as I get back the orchestral score of *Jeux*, I'll make a two-piano arrangement of it.[1] May we enter that among my credits?

[1] This arrangement seems never to have been made. (R.N.)

Mon cher Jacques   27 September 1913

I was delighted to get your letter. For one thing, I was afraid I'd been somewhat forgotten; and for another I didn't dare write to you as I didn't have any good news to deliver. Luckily the second tableau of *La Boîte à joujoux* has replaced my prose − from your point of view a distinct improvement.

The third tableau is going slowly. The soul of a doll is more mysterious than even Maeterlinck imagines; it doesn't easily tolerate the kind of humbug so many human souls put up with.

There's to be a money-box, but I shan't be interpreting that: lack of practice, probably?

But I hope to finish it off even so. I don't know why they don't make M. Deutsch (of la Meurthe) director of the Opéra. He certainly likes music because he's not afraid to put it on; even though he can't have got much pleasure out of it so far! I don't always understand Astruc's artistic aims but there's no doubt he can be made to do good work, and he's infinitely more disinterested than certain directors of our acquaintance.

> Yours as ever
> C.D.

250† TO GABRIEL ASTRUC

> Mon cher ami   Sunday 19 October 1913

After serious reflection, I think you are wrong to abandon *our* theatre.[1] People are certain to come down on you for this desertion. It would be preferable, in my humble opinion, to continue the struggle and if you have to die, better to die a beautiful death.

You haven't taken sufficiently into consideration that transferring our company to the Opéra is absolutely impossible. The Opéra is not a place for revolutions – believe me. You've inspired so much devotion in the past; it must be possible for you to go on doing so!

> Anyway I remain
> Yours as ever
> C.D.

[1] Financial problems had forced Astruc to close the doors of the Théâtre des Champs-Elysées, which had opened with such high hopes on 31 March.

251† TO GABRIEL MOUREY

> Mon cher Mourey   30 October 1913

Would it be possible for Mme Mors to put back the dates you've given me to December?[1] The reason being that the music cannot possibly be ready in time; don't forget we have to leave room for rehearsals. What's more (when I think about it) if we don't have the complete music for the second Act, the groans from the choir will sound ridiculous for the simple reason they won't relate to anything!

Don't you think it would be better to stick to your first idea of *La Flûte de Pan*? On 14 November I have to be in Lausanne to rehearse and conduct a concert which takes place on Monday 17th . . . You can see how little time I have.

May I say that when it comes to the theatre one must fight shy of

hasty productions . . . Disaster generally looms over the first performance. By that time there's nothing more one can do, except weep!
Consider what I've said! You're too fond of having things done properly
not to share my point of view.

> Yours
> C.D.

[1] Mourey's play *Psyché* was first given privately, in the Mors household, on 1 December
1913. The only surviving music for it by Debussy is a flute solo, played at the moment of
Pan's death. It was published in 1927 under the title *Syrinx*.

252 TO ANDRÉ GIDE[1]

Mon cher Gide   24 November 1913

In the face of the kindness of the *Nouvelle Revue Française* and its
secretary Jacques Rivière, and of your own kind insistence, I am left
without excuses . . . As you know, I'm writing as a music critic in the
review *S.I.M.* So far these articles have taken up all the time I can spare
for the curious and pointless task of expressing my opinion.

Would I not have to find something rather novel to say to justify a
double dose of this chatter?

I'm leaving for Russia in a few days and we can discuss it again when I
return around 20 December. For the moment it gives me the opportunity
of sending you my best wishes.

> C.D.

[1] Debussy had met Gide and Paul Valéry in Pierre Louÿs's circle around 1894.

253† TO EMMA

[Moscow]
Saturday 6 December 1913

What's going to become of us? Your letters are more and more miserable!
Like you, I feel nothing will calm you and that makes me very uneasy . . .
Once again, I beg you, grant us *both* a little patience and goodwill.
Unhappy as we are at present, it's unthinkable we shouldn't be rewarded
for our suffering; otherwise one couldn't rely on the simple justice which
is meted out to the humblest among us – they don't put themselves out to
get it either, because it's merely rightful compensation.

35 Emma and Claude Debussy around 1913.

I've no rehearsal this afternoon because Koussevitzky[1] needs the orchestra for this evening's concert. Someone called Busoni is playing a piano concerto which lasts an hour and ten minutes . . . As you might suppose, he wrote it! From the score the music looks rather swampy, with Richard Strauss's worst faults made worse still by someone with none of his virtues.

I didn't know Diaghilev was in Moscow, but he telephoned and is coming to dinner this evening [. . .]

---

[1] Serge Koussevitsky was the instigator of Debussy's Russian visit. He began as a double-bass player and then in 1909 founded an orchestra in Moscow which bore his name. The repertoire it played was predominantly modern.

254 TO EMMA

Moscow

Chère petite mienne   Monday 8 December 1913 7 p.m.

The rehearsal is just over and in great haste I want to tell you that I love you, that you are my one and only *petite mienne* and that even so I'm still miserable.

Do you realize that you wrote: 'I don't know how I'll manage not to be jealous of your music'? Don't you think that's enough to upset one's equilibrium somewhat? First of all if there were to be any jealousy between you and music, it would be on music's side; if I go on creating it and loving it it's because this music, which you're so unfair to, was responsible for my meeting you,[1] loving you and so on. The chances are that if I were never to compose again, you would be the one to stop loving me, because I could hardly rely on the somewhat restrained charms of my conversation or on my physical advantages to keep you by me. And you know how diplomatically music intervenes in those moments of ill-humour which I still tend to be so bad at handling.

We now go straight to the banquet given by the painters, sculptors, musicians, men of letters, etc., to annoy Claude Debussy. And on leaving this fraternal love-feast we take the train for St Petersburg, at exactly half past midnight.

As soon as we arrive we have a rehearsal at half past midday and another that afternoon; the next day, Wednesday, a final rehearsal in the morning and the concert in the evening. There's nothing like hard work. If I'm not ill with it all it's because I'm still tough, despite my great age . . .

[282]

Keep loving me! Although I'm such a long way away, pay no attention to the treacherous consolations you're bound to be offered. Tell yourself that Claude is spending a sort of season in purgatory and keep him a place in Paradise, which for him consists only of you.

With all my love
Claude

[1] Debussy had been introduced to Emma by her son Raoul, who was a member of Fauré's composition class at the Conservatoire. (R.N.)

255 TO CHOUCHOU[1]

St Petersburg Grand Hotel d'Europe
Ma chère petite Chouchou   11 December 1913

Your poor papa is very late replying to your nice little letter. But you mustn't be cross with him . . . He's very sad not to have seen your pretty face for so long or heard you singing or shouting with laughter, in short all the noise which sometimes makes you an unbearable little girl, but more often a charming one.

How is that genius M. Czerny getting on? Do you know:

the 'air de ballet' for fleas?

And old Xantho?[2] Is he still being good? Is he still digging up the garden? You have my permission to give him a thorough scolding!

At the Koussevitsky's house in Moscow there are two lovely bulldogs with eyes like the frog in the salon (we're great friends, I think you'd like them) and a bird which sings almost as well as Miss Teyte.

It's all very nice but don't imagine I can forget you even for a second. Far from it, the only thing I think about is when I'm going to see you again. Until then, love and lots of kisses from your old papa.

C.D.

Be very nice to your poor mama; do all you can to see she doesn't get too worried!

[1] Chouchou had had her 8th birthday on 30 October.
[2] The Debussys' dog.

[283]

Cher Vuillermoz   23 December 1913

I knew you were a tyrant, but now the blackness of your soul is revealed utterly. Here am I, barely home from a horribly exhausting journey, following days when I had to conduct two three-hour rehearsals . . . and it seems I'm not allowed to be tired or ask for respite! No, I have to write an article on my memories of the tour . . . Why not, in addition, a study of the comparative merits of the various railway companies, which have thrown me about so rudely! Vuillermoz, you are, in my opinion, a one-man Inquisition; despite general belief that it's a thing of the past! And what harm have I ever done to you?

Ah! Who can tell what feelings pass through the soul of an editor-in-chief?

Affectionately
C.D.

257 TO CHARLES GRUET, MAYOR OF BORDEAUX[1]

Monsieur   6 January 1914

Allow me to commend most especially to your notice a young musician called Edgard Varèse, who has applied for the post of Director of Music at the Bordeaux Opera House.

He has all the necessary qualities for the task and I should personally be grateful to you if you would use your influence thus to ensure that he will be able to make his career in France.

I remain, Sir, your humble servant
C.D.

[1] The Bordeaux opera house had been closed for renovation since May 1913 and was to reopen in October 1914. The directors finally chosen were Louis Perron and René Chauvet. Varèse left (from Bordeaux) for the United States in December 1915.

Mon cher Jacques   16 January 1914

I hope you're now free of the flu, in spite of the very cold weather we're
enjoying, if that's the word?

I'm sure you're aware of M. Gheuzi's[1] generous, if curious, ideas for
La Boîte à joujoux? They're characteristic of our times, in which it's the
thing to make much ado about nothing at all!

Can you imagine those poor marionnettes in a setting normally
reserved for the demands of Ariane or the fury of Golaud (though as
infrequently as possible, it's true!). There's been talk of a revival of
Pelléas. That's much more interesting for the Opéra-comique. As for *La
Boîte*, we must allow it to retain its unaggressive aspect and present it in
some fairly novel manner.

I fancy you agree without my needing to press the point?

Let me have your news.

Yours as ever
C.D.

P.S. M. Edgard Varèse, a young musician, will be asking if you'd be
kind enough to see him. He's just conducted an orchestral concert in
Prague including *Le Martyre de Saint Sébastien*.[2] Apparently it was
'magnificent'. He's obviously energetic and able to get things done (even
though I can't say I know a lot about him!).

[1] P. B. Gheusi, the Director of the Opéra-comique.
[2] Varèse had conducted the Czech Philharmonic Orchestra on 4 January in works by
Gabriel Dupont, Dukas and Roussel, and a symphonic suite from *Le Martyre* put together
by André Caplet. (The critic of the *Prager Tageblatt* wrote of Varèse: 'After only three
rehearsals with an orchestra that he had never met before he succeeded in revealing to us
the very soul of the compositions which had been entrusted to him.' R.N.)

259 TO D. E. INGHELBRECHT[1]

Cher Inghel   Sunday 18 January 1914

Despite long and patient research I haven't been able to find the full face
portrait of Debussy your father-in-law[2] was asking about! And the
same goes for the one by M. Jacques-Emile Blanche in which I look like
a custard that's been up all night . . .[3]

Thinking about it, I can't help feeling the highly illustrious poets in

[285]

your programme may take offence at seeing themselves represented by Debussy and no one else! May we all shelter under the patronage of Charles d'Orléans, sweet prince, beloved of the muses and so excellently French!

Yours ever
C.D.

[1] Inghelbrecht conducted the choruses for *Le Martyre*. In 1913 Gabriel Astruc appointed him musical director of the Théâtre des Champs-Elysées.
[2] The artist T. A. Steinlen.
[3] The portrait in question is Blanche's second, smaller one of Debussy. The painter says in his memoirs that it was done at Auteuil in the open air. Today it is in the municipal museum at Saint-Germain-en-Laye.

260 TO GUSTAVE DORET[1]

Mon cher Doret   30 January 1914

Forgive me! I've got so much work on hand I forget my obligations – writing to you, that's to say.

Three piano preludes:

    I. Dancers of Delphi

    II. The Girl with the Flaxen Hair

    III. La Puerta del vino (The Gate of Wine)

In fact that's all my limited capabilities allow me to play! If necessary, I could always improvise on the Dutch national anthem?

I don't have the orchestral parts for the *Nocturnes*, but I'm sending you the score with corrections ... It's a long, delicate business, especially in 'Sirènes'. Would you be able to find a stylish copyist for this finicky task? Apart from mistakes, there are a number of changes.[2] Please note I need this score for Rome!

As you're rehearsing in Amsterdam on the 23rd, may I ask your advice on where to put the 24 singers? You know the hall and I have every confidence in your experience of these kinds of detail.[3]

No one will be happier to see you in Rome than I shall.

Yours
C.D.

[1] The Swiss musician Gustave Doret, 1866–1943, had conducted the first performance of *Prélude à l'après midi d'un faune* in 1894. (R.N.)
[2] On his own score of the *Nocturnes*, published by Fromont in 1900, Debussy made numerous corrections which were printed only in 1930 in a new edition by Jobert.

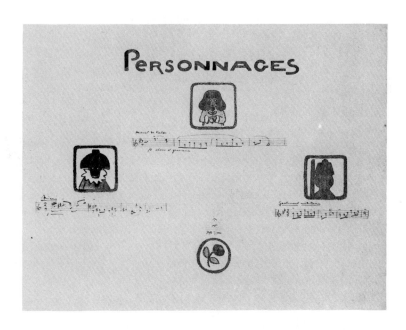

36 André Hellé's design for the Durand edition of Debussy's *Boîte à joujoux*. The manuscript quotations are in the composer's hand.

³ Debussy conducted the Concertgebouw Orchestra on 1 March. As well as the *Nocturnes*, the programme included the three Préludes, *L'Après-midi d'un faune* and the *Marche écossaise*.

261 TO X . . .

Mon cher confrère   5 March 1914

Do you not think that recitative, as the old masters understood it, has by now almost entirely disappeared? Or at least it has changed its character to such an extent that one can no longer call it that. It has become part of the melodic web, woven over the harmonic framework and linking the various episodes of the musical drama; it is therefore a delicate matter to decide what is or is not recitative! Personally I should find it very difficult to send you the 'typical' example you ask for, although I have pleasure in acknowledging the courteous manner of your request.

I remain
Yours most sincerely
C.D.

262 TO GABRIEL PIERNÉ

Cher vieux   5 March 1914

I couldn't find a suitable way of thanking you this morning . . .; nervous strain and my anxiety to express all I had to say quickly and clearly, it all left me feeling paralysed and in turmoil!

You know me well enough to be aware of my affection and gratitude for the way you committed yourself so thoroughly to the performance of *Jeux*.[1] I had the impression the orchestra liked it much less than you did; was I wrong, perhaps? As far as the *piccolos* are concerned I think, even so, 'personalities' come into it . . . ! Don't let's go into that too deeply. I also felt the various episodes lacked homogeneity! The link between them may be subtle but it exists, surely? You know that as well as I do. And the last thing, by and large it's too loud . . . And . . . forgive me. . . ?

Yours ever
C.D.

[288]

I call your attention to the entry of the cellos and basses at fig. 53 which marks a new state of things!

At fig. 51 not too fast.

Would you be kind enough to send me tickets for a box on Saturday! My thanks again.

[1] Pierné conducted the Colonne Orchestra in *Jeux* at the Châtelet on 29 February and was to give a second performance on 6 March.

263 TO JACQUES DURAND

Mon cher Jacques   [April 1914]

It was in fact agreed that G.[1] would put on *La Boîte à joujoux*. Even so I don't understand his behaviour, given that there's no one at the Opéra-comique any more and, what's more, nothing *in writing* between you and G.?

As for the orchestral score, I've made a start on a very detailed sketch which can be filled out when the time comes.[2]

The important thing in all this is to find out exactly what G.'s intentions are. It's not easy, I can tell you, with his friendly vacillation!

Hellé's[3] gone off to his island; however we're fully in agreement on the following points: he'll take care of the scenery and costumes and the characters will be played by children. As for the production, we don't need a ballet master as, for the most part, they're *movements* and not traditional *ballet steps*. All we want is an ingenious producer – and there is just one such at the Op-c.

I'll write to G.

Yours as ever
C.D.

[1] Gheusi, see letter 258.
[2] The orchestration of *La Boîte à joujoux* was only 'in process of completion' even in 1917. It was finished by André Caplet and the ballet was not performed until after Debussy's death, in 1919.
[3] The painter André Hellé was the originator of the ballet's scenario and had contributed colour engravings to the piano score, published by Durand in December 1913.

1914–1918

The War
The Final Years

The outbreak of war affected Debussy profoundly. Under the pressure of events his artistic nationalism became more pronounced. He spent the summer of 1915 at Pourville and here he recovered his ability to 'think in music' and he composed 'like a madman': *En blanc et noir*, the *Douze Etudes* for piano, the sonata for cello and piano and the one for flute, viola and harp. But his cancer continued to grow and in December 1915 he had an operation which left him exhausted. 'I'm suffering the tortures of the damned,' he wrote to Robert Godet.

He spent the summer of 1916 at Le Moulleau and the following one at Saint-Jean-de-Luz. The third sonata, for violin and piano, caused him considerable difficulty; it was his last work. He managed to complete a new version of the libretto of *La Chute de la maison Usher* and continued to make plans with Paul-Jean Toulet for an adaptation of Shakespeare's *As You Like It*. But his strength was failing. At the end of 1917 he took to his bed and died on 25 March the following year.

Mon cher Jacques   Saturday 8 August 1914

I was reassured by your letter and am truly delighted to have news of you.

As you know, I'm quite devoid of sang-froid and even more so of the military mentality, never having had occasion to handle a gun. Then there are my memories of 1870[1] which prevent me reaching a pitch of enthusiasm, as well as the anxiety of my wife who has a son and a son-in-law both in the army!

As a result my life is one of intensity and disquiet. I'm nothing more than a wretched atom hurled around by this terrible cataclysm, and what I'm doing seems to me so miserably petty! It makes me envious of Satie and his real job of defending Paris as a corporal.

So if you have any work you can put my way, please think of me. My apologies for counting on your friendship but, to be honest, you are all I have!

Yours ever
C.D.

---

[1]   None of Debussy's friends knew at this time that his father had been a supporter of the Commune, captured and condemned by a tribunal in 1871 to four years' imprisonment (after a year he was released under a further four-year suspension of his civil rights. R.N.).

Mon cher Jacques   18 August 1914

Now that they've removed all the workers from Paris, either by shooting them or expelling them, it's immediately become a charming spot. I met Erlanger[1] in a grocer's shop yesterday and he told me proudly that he'd put himself at the disposal of the Minister of War! He'll be inspecting the inkwells, perhaps? I also saw Paul Dukas, who isn't at any minister's disposal but declares he's as ready to get his head blown off as the next man.

At my age and with my military aptitude, the best I could do would be to man a barricade! If there's an imperative need for one more 'body' to ensure victory, I'll offer mine without hesitation.

M. Dalimier[2] is looking after the wives and children of the orchestral musicians who've gone off to the war. They've formed a committee – a good old French custom – and I'm one of the members. It's one way of spending the time which, at the moment, hangs more heavily than ever!

Anyway it's impossible to work! To tell you the truth, I don't dare to. The side-effects of the war are more distressing than they seem.

Let me have your news.

Yours ever
C.D.

[1]   Camille Erlanger, 1863–1919, was a pupil of Delibes at the Conservatoire and won the Prix de Rome in 1888. Dukas won the second prize the same year.
[2]   The Under-Secretary of State at the Arts Ministry.

266 TO NICOLAS CORONIO

                                                            [Angers]
Mon cher Coronio   [September 1914]

[. . .] This dreadful journey convinced my wife there was no point in leaving Paris . . . I agreed . . . I won't get on to the subject of German barbarity. It's exceeded all expectations. They've even found it convenient not to distinguish between brutishness and intellectualism – a charming combination! With such terrible things going on I haven't yet got round to thinking about personal tragedies . . . I think we're going to pay dearly for the right to dislike the music of Richard Strauss and Schoenberg.[1] As for Beethoven, someone's just made the fortunate discovery he was a Fleming![2] When it comes to Wagner, they're bound to exaggerate! His glory will always be to have summed up centuries of music in a formula. It's certainly something and only a German could attempt it. Our mistake was to keep trying for too long to follow in his footsteps . . . our generation won't ever be able to change its tastes any more than its forms! What could be interesting and surprising is what those who have fought in this war – who have been 'on the march' in all senses – will do and think? French art needs to take revenge quite as seriously as the French army does! And its cathedral of Rheims goes back further in time . . .[3]

I'm doing a little piano-playing again, notably on a Bechstein; my only excuse is that it's not paid for! It can go under the heading of 'War Contributions' . . .

Jacques Durand is at Noirmoutiers, cutting down on expenses!!! After all, who's bothering to buy music? Everyone's much more interested in the potato crop. . . ! [. . .]

C.D.

¹ For another reference to Schoenberg, see letter 277.
² Beethoven's grandfather was born at Malines and moved to Bonn around 1731–2. See E. Closson, *L'élément flamand dans Beethoven*, Brussels, 1928.
³ The sense of this reference to Joan of Arc is that whereas the French army lost to Germany only in 1870, French music (Rameau) was overwhelmed by German music (Gluck) a century earlier. (R.N.)

267 TO JACQUES DURAND

Mon cher Jacques   9 October 1914

I was particularly pleased to get your letter as your silence was beginning to worry me – I know the post at the moment comes to take on an exaggerated importance, perhaps.

Anyway you're well, that's the main thing.

My wife and I have been to see her son.¹ There was obviously no question of his fighting but at least he has been making himself useful: as interpreter, cyclist and secretary at the mixed hospital in Melun . . .

The continual encouragement we're receiving to be patient seems to me to be to the point! Obviously you can't move an army corps as easily as a chair! . . . A basic truth clearly understood by those townspeople playing with little flags . . . even so, it's very hard on the nerves!

I've had a letter from M. André Charlot:[2] he speaks of *No-ya-li* (*Palais du silence* that was) as if he intended to stage it this year! That strikes me as premature.[3] Anyway, I don't want this music played until the destiny of France is decided: she can't laugh or cry while so many of our men are dying heroes' deaths!

If I dared to and if, above all, I wasn't afraid of the 'routine' element which haunts this kind of composition, I'd be happy to write a Heroic March . . . But, as I've said, to play the hero while sitting peacefully a long way from the action seems to me ridiculous . . .

Not that there'll be any shortage of this kind of thing. I can predict that when you get back to Paris you'll have enough offers to fill every cupboard Messrs Durand possess.

You suggest I may see you in Paris soon. Needless to say, I look forward to it.

As I write, little soldiers are at their exercises, some with bugles, some with drums . . . Fanfares and rhythms which remind me irresistibly of the two 'Richards'' best themes.[4] If you have a taste for drawing morals, you can make something of that.

I look forward to seeing you shortly.

> With all best wishes to your wife and yourself
> Yours ever
> C.D.

My further congratulations to Jacques Charlot![5] I'm sure he has a firm sense of duty and, if fortune continues to favour him, will come back a general! More simply, we must just hope he comes back . . . in one piece!

[1]   Raoul Bardac.
[2]   The director of the Alhambra Theatre, London.
[3]   According to a contract of 21 November 1913, *Le Palais du silence* or *No-ya-li* (on a scenario by Georges de Feure) was to be given at the Alhambra. Only a few sketches survive.
[4]   Richard Wagner and Richard Strauss.
[5]   See letter 232 footnote 2.

268†   TO ROBERT GODET

Cher Godet   1 January 1915

You're probably the only person who would understand that . . . silence does not mean forgetfulness! But in these troubled times delicacy is a rare flower and its perfume unusually sweet.

[294]

The worst horrors are forgotten – it's a necessity for the future. What will take a long time to remove is these false, heavy, foreign tastes that have insinuated themselves – God knows how blindly and hypo-critically – into our ways of thinking, listening, even of feeling. For forty-four years we've been playing at self-effacement; even in France, the French were determined to cultivate thickheadedness and claimed to be lending some weight to our ideas!

As for music, I confess that for months I no longer knew what it was; the familiar sound of the piano had become something hateful. Pythagoras (?)[1] working on his mathematical problems right up until a soldier killed him, Goethe writing *The Elective Affinities* during the French occupation of Weimar, these are admirable intellectual achieve-ments. I can only deduce that I'm inferior, and do some mathematics, possibly?

At the request of the *Daily Telegraph* I've had to write something for *King Albert's Book*.[2] It was very hard, especially as the 'Brabançonne' stirs no heroic thoughts in the breasts of those who weren't brought up with it.[3]

The result of these divagations is called *Berceuse héroïque* . . . it's the best I could do, feeling the continued proximity of hostilities as a physical restraint. Added to which there's my military inferiority – I wouldn't know how to use a gun . . .

I haven't been to see your daughters yet, because I'm very definitely not surrounded by a halo of light as you are kind enough to imagine. When people are quietly doing their duty, that's not the moment to approach them with forced smiles. I'll wait for a more suitable occasion and hope they'll forgive me?

A rather empty letter – I'd far rather be able to greet you face to face.

Wishing you were here
Yours as ever
C.D.

[1]   In fact, Archimedes.
[2]   *King Albert's Book* was organized by Hall Caine in order to offer 'a tribute of admiration to Belgium, on the heroic and ever-memorable share she has taken in the war . . .'. Apart from Debussy, the other musical contributors were Johan Backer-Lunde (Norway), Sir Frederick Cowen, Sir Edward Elgar, Edward German, Peter Lange-Müller (Denmark), Liza Lehmann, Sir Alexander Mackenzie, Pietro Mascagni, André Messager, Camille Saint-Saëns, Ethel Smyth and Sir Charles Stanford.
[3]   The 'Brabançonne' is the Belgian national anthem.

Mon cher Jacques   24 February 1915

I find the Chopin 'manuscripts' truly terrifying . . . ! How can you expect three manuscripts, certainly not all in Chopin's hand, to agree with each other? Of course, only one can be right . . . and that's where the story begins. Chopin, impressionable and sensitive as he was, must have *corrected* his proofs – when he had the time, poor man! That's why I have considerable confidence in the 'Friedman' edition. It takes into account *all* the previous editions and testifies to a lively understanding of Chopin's style.

As for Scholtz (Peters), he's an imbecile.[1]

I've just finished revising the *Etudes* and they're ready for you to take away. In the *Trois Etudes*, for M.'s[2] method, I think we should remove the slurs in the third one (in fact, the second). In the other two sets the pedal indications should go in their normal place and not between the staves, where they take up space unnecessarily and block the view, so to speak.[3]

I'm still not allowed out and I'm coughing loudly enough to blow a hole in an oak-tree.

Yours as ever
C.D.

The edition of the *Six Epigraphes* is utterly 'desirable'.[4]
Have you got an original edition of the *Barcarolle*?

---

[1] Debussy is referring to German editors of Chopin: Ignaz Friedman (Breitkopf) and Hermann Scholtz (Peters).

[2] Moscheles.

[3] As German editions were not available in France during the war, Durand commissioned various new ones. Debussy revised Chopin's complete works and they were published between 1915 and 1917.

[4] A reworking of the incidental music he had written in 1901 for a staged version of some of Louÿs's *Chansons de Bilitis*. Durand published it for both piano solo and piano duet in 1915.

Pourville[1]

Cher ami   14 July 1915

Don't be jealous, but there's some rain left over for Pourville . . . A light, continuous drizzle has been falling all morning and looks like lasting till the end of the world.

Apart from that, I've been working as removal man and carpet-fitter, all the jobs a move entails, given man's instinctive need to take a little of his familiar surroundings with him. Arkel (the toad)[2] is back exactly where he belongs; he's as solemn as ever, but seems to like it here . . . As I said, the best part is the garden . . . It's rather untidy, with none of the proud orderliness of the gardens laid out by Le Nôtre, but it's a gentle sort of jungle, well suited to those who aren't keen on playing Robinson Crusoe. Once you get to the top, you come upon a fine expanse of sea, enough to make you think there's more beyond – that is, the sea of infinity! At midday you can hear bells – as in *Pelléas*; if 'the children don't come down to the beach to bathe' (P. et M.), it's probably because they're not in the mood!

Today the sea looks like zinc, bored . . . and boring! Which makes me think of the personal contributions one might be making to this state of mind; it's true, surely, that one can experience calm even with a house of worries on one's back, like a poor snail buried in debt!

But no grumbling, lest we disturb the Fates . . .

The Angelus is ringing timidly, as though convinced it's not bringing any peace to men's hearts.

Even if my work-table can't compare with the one at home in Paris, it is large enough to take the manuscript paper called 'Soleil' (what a hope!).

I must confess I've made a slight change in the colour of the second of the *Caprices*[3] (Ballade de Villon contre les ennemis de la France); it was too profoundly black and almost as tragic as a 'Caprice' by Goya!

It won't delay my sending them unduly.

Today I've been correcting proofs of 'Chopin' . . . Some minor errors which, even so, wouldn't escape the 'Doktors'' hostile spectacles.

It's getting dark, so I must light the lamps and say goodbye.

With best wishes to your wife
Yours as ever
C.D.

[297]

Please note: on page 5 of the Mazurkas, a rather imaginative *rubato*, and the same on page 18.

1   Debussy and his wife stayed at Pourville till the middle of October in 'Mon Coin', the house of the playwright Ferdinand Hérold.
2   A small wooden figurine which Debussy called his 'fetish object' and which he always had on his desk while composing. A note has survived, written to Emma just before a move: 'Don't put Arkel in the trunk! He doesn't like it.'
3   The pieces for two pianos published in December 1915 as *En blanc et noir*.

271†   TO JACQUES DURAND

      Mon cher Jacques   Thursday 5 August 1915

It's because of mankind's unfortunate inability to regulate its 'thinking machine' as the mood takes it that you've found no peace at Bel-Ebat, for all its charms . . . I must admit that I too, despite the sea, the garden and 'Mon Coin' itself, am feeling the desperate anxieties of this war. It's got to the point where I daren't open the newspaper, which has no real news and speculates according to its fancy so as to keep its readership; otherwise I'd slip back into the mood I was in in Paris, and I want to work – not so much for myself, as to provide a proof, however small, that 30 million Boches can't destroy French thought, even when they've tried undermining it first before obliterating it.

I think of the youth of France, wantonly mown down by those Kultur merchants, and of its contribution to our heritage, now for ever lost to us.

The music I'm writing will be a secret homage to them; what's the use of a dedication? However you look at it, it's the result of egoism in a state of uncertainty and that won't bring anyone back to life.

As for the Russians, people forget, it seems, that they were once our most treacherous enemies and that now, quite simply, it's the Germans' turn to face them – and the Germans haven't burned Moscow yet . . . !

They're talking now about Japan entering the war.

Why not the Martians, while we're about it?

All of which can only make the Boches prouder still and, Heaven knows, there's no need for that. And there'll be a terrible cost to be counted when it's all over! Why have so many people been invited to eat a cake which isn't even cooked yet? Monsieur de la Fontaine wrote a nice fable on the subject, but that was in an era when France had enough common sense for the whole of Europe.

    [298]

The sonata for cello and piano will reach you, perhaps, before this letter. It's not for me to judge its excellence but I like its proportions and its almost classical form, in the good sense of the word. I'm also sending some new music for part of the second *Caprice*; it goes from:

(piano I, left hand)

up to the return of the motif:

(augmentation of the theme)

(a procedure used by the old masters long before the 'school' fugue, as you know).

It's my concern for proportions which has made this change necessary; also, it makes things clearer and cleans the atmosphere of the poisonous vapours momentarily emitted by the Luther chorale – or rather by what it represents, because it's still a fine tune.

I'll get back to the proofs of the Chopin *Polonaises*. My apologies over these but the Muse who, as you kindly put it, is 'visiting' me at the moment has taught me not to rely on her constancy and I'd rather hold on to her than have to run after her.

So much for what goes on in my 'thoughtery' (not to mention the *Etudes*[1] I'm working on).

I hope that even if you don't find reassurance at Bel-Ebat, you may find hope.

> With all our best wishes
> Yours ever
> C.D.

Please greet Choisnel for me.

[1] Debussy's own *Douze Etudes* for piano.

272† TO JACQUES DURAND

Pourville

Mon cher Jacques   28 August 1915

Forgive me! For some days I've been in the same condition as Russia! That's to say, no supplies; no more of the manuscript paper 'Quarto Papale' which I've recently become so attached to. In order to finish the six *Etudes*, which will reach you at the same time as this letter, I've had to employ a devilish cunning worthy of the Boches. Talking of which, you mentioned in one of your letters how hard it was to be patient . . . ! I tell you, one needs the most implacable patience to copy out the study 'pour les octaves' or the one called 'pour les degrés chromatiques'! I realize there's no agony involved and that this is a very personal view.

For a long time the continuous use of sixths reminded me of pretentious young ladies sitting in a salon, sulkily doing their tapestry work and envying the scandalous laughter of the naughty ninths . . . So I wrote this study in which my concern for sixths goes to the lengths of using no other intervals to build up the harmonies; not bad! (Mea culpa . . .)

The six *Etudes* I've written so far are almost all 'on the go'; don't worry, there'll be some calmer ones! I started with these because they're the hardest to write and to get some variety into . . . the easiest combinations of the original *datum* are soon used up. The other *Etudes* deal with the search for special sonorities, including 'Pour les quartes' in which you'll find unheard-of things, even though your ears are well accustomed to 'curiosities'.

You haven't given me an answer about the dedication: Couperin or Chopin?[1]

Not enough has been made, perhaps, of the fact that the Grand Duke Nicholas is too tall. He doesn't look often enough at his feet, round which his armies are crumbling . . . He sees Petrograd, Moscow, maybe even the capital of Tibet – I've forgotten its name, is it Lhassa? – But don't let's cause trouble.

As for the secret meeting of Parliament the deputies are after, it sounds like the idea of some concierge with power mania. Monsieur Viviani[2] is a good speaker but eloquence is no more than dilettantism or armchair heroics. These reflections are totally unimportant, especially coming from me. Still, it's dispiriting to see how little politicians change and how fast the number of imbeciles grows . . .

To return to music and decency . . . I've invested a lot of passion and faith in the future of the *Etudes*. I hope you'll like them, both for the music they contain and for what they denote.

I'm sure you'll agree with me that there's no need to make technical exercises over-sombre just to appear more serious; a little charm never spoilt anything. Chopin proved it and makes this desire of mine seem somewhat overweening, I know. Neither am I so dead to the world as not to be aware of the comparisons that my contemporaries, colleagues and others . . . will studiously make to my disadvantage.

> Yours ever
> C.D.

I've received the manuscript paper from Bellamy and also the parcel from Gaston . . . with which to write a 'Sixthology' . . . Please thank Gaston, I'll write to him. Rest assured I won't be troubling my friend and publisher with any sort of 'ology'!

[1] The *Etudes* are dedicated 'à la mémoire de Frédéric Chopin'.
[2] René Viviani was the French Prime Minister. His administration fell in October 1915.

273† TO JACQUES DURAND

Pourville

Mon cher Jacques   1 September 1915

Pourville is drenched with rain and your letter brings the only ray of light I can expect to see today . . . It's true 'we must carry our light within us', as the ancient Greeks believed when they imprisoned poor Socrates because his ideas about light were different from theirs! If I had lots of money I'd buy 'Mon Coin' immediately, out of gratitude at being able to think and work again. When I think back to the void of last year, I get shivers up my spine and I'm afraid to go back to Paris and the factory of nothingness[1] my study had become . . . ! But at least I'll see you again and be able to play you these *Etudes* which are giving your fingers such a fright . . . I may say there are certain passages which sometimes bring mine to a halt too. Then I have to get my breath back as though I'd been climbing a flight of stairs . . . In truth, this music wheels above the peaks of performance! It'll be fertile ground for establishing records.

Despite my respect for Saint-Saëns's great age,[2] what he says about Chopin's pedalling isn't entirely true. I have very clear memories of what Mme Mauté de Fleurville[3] told me. He (Chopin) recommended practising without pedal and, in performance, not holding it on except in very rare instances. It was the same way of turning the pedal into a kind of *breathing* which I observed in Liszt when I had the chance to hear him in Rome. I feel Saint-Saëns forgets that pianists are poor musicians, for the most part, and cut music up into unequal lumps, like a chicken.

[301]

The plain truth perhaps is that abusing the pedal is only a means of covering up a lack of technique, and that making a lot of noise is a way to drown the music you're slaughtering! In theory we should be able to find a graphic means of representing this 'breathing' pedal . . . it wouldn't be impossible. Come to think of it, isn't there a work on the subject by Mme Marie Jaëll,[4] who was severe in the matter of piano technique?

The sun's come out at last . . . what can it have been doing over the other side, to get here so late?

With that I leave you.

Yours ever
C.D.

[1] 'les usines du néant', a phrase taken from the writings of Jules Laforgue.
[2] Jacques Durand had passed on to Debussy some of Saint-Saëns's ideas about Chopin pedalling. Saint-Saëns was 80 in 1915.
[3] See introduction to Chapter I (p. 1). Whether she ever was a pupil of Chopin must remain doubtful.
[4] The Alsatian pianist Marie Jaëll, 1846–1925, had acted for a time as Liszt's secretary. Her main theoretical work was *Le mécanisme du toucher*, 1897.

274 TO D. E. INGHELBRECHT

Pourville
Mon cher Inghel   30 September 1915

I beg to acknowledge receipt of your letter of the 25th instant – as my wine-merchant would say. I enjoyed reading it enormously because of your exact, ironic description of the Luxembourg gardens . . . I love them, all the same. They represent a fine period of French history and if those who walk around in them are rather a special breed, they're preferable, by and large, to the smart 'cocktail' habitués of the avenue du Bois de Boulogne. After all, the poor Luxembourg isn't responsible for the terrible statues with which our artistic leaders have thought fit to decorate it. But what a delightful walk it is along the 'allée des Reines'!

The reason I haven't written before is that I'm re-learning about music . . .[1] It's good, even so. It's even better not to be thinking in terms of the various societies: Nationale, Internationale and other places of ill-repute . . . The emotional satisfaction one gets from putting the right chord in the right place can't be equalled in any of the other arts. Forgive me. I sound as if I've just discovered music. But, in all humility, that's rather what I feel like.

[302]

We return with regret, and via the Gare Saint-Lazare, round 12 October. Then my head will be full of strings of pianists. Farewell silence! Farewell the incomparable noise of the sea, with its stern advice not to waste one's time!

But we mustn't complain. One can't always be the darling of the gods. Let's think of the poor devils who are being killed in the trenches. No modern conveniences there.

> Yours ever
> C.D.

With fondest best wishes.

¹ The summer of 1915 had been very productive: the Cello Sonata and the *Douze Etudes* were finished and the sonata for flute, viola and harp begun.

275 TO BERNARDO MOLINARI¹

Pourville

Mon cher ami   6 October 1915

Your kind letter has reached me in a little spot by the sea where I've come to try and forget the war. For the last three months I've been able to work again.

When I tell you that I spent nearly a year unable to write music . . . after that I've almost had to *re-learn* it. It was like a rediscovery and it's seemed to me more beautiful than ever!

Is it because I was deprived of it for so long? I don't know. What beauties there are in music 'by itself', with no axe to grind or new inventions to amaze the so-called 'dilettanti' . . . The emotional satisfaction one gets from it can't be equalled, can it, in any of the other arts? This power of 'the right chord in the right place' that strikes you . . . We're still in the age of 'harmonic progressions' and people who are happy just with beauty of sound are hard to find.

I take the liberty of talking about this to you, because you're more sensitive than the 'musicians' are to that emotion which lives beyond a frontier they will never cross . . .

I haven't written much orchestral music, but I have finished: *Douze Etudes* for piano, a Cello Sonata, and another sonata for flute, viola and harp, in the ancient, flexible mould with none of the grandiloquence of modern sonatas. There are going to be six of them for different groups of instruments and the last one will combine all those used in the previous five.[2] For many people that won't be as important as an *opera* . . . But I thought it was of greater service to music!

I assure you I haven't forgotten my promise to orchestrate 'L'Isle joyeuse' . . .[3] only the troubled times we're going through have taken me away from the project . . . Forgive me . . . ! I'll try and find something else for you.

As for your kind invitation to come back to Rome, I'm delighted, of course, but unfortunately I don't think it's possible at the moment. It's not a question of 'Bank notes',[4] but we really don't know what difficulties still lie ahead. And then, if I did have the pleasure of coming to Rome again, I'd want to bring my wife. She adores Italy, but while she was there she never went to Rome . . . what a mistake!

Talking of my wife, am I dreaming or did I receive a notice of the wedding of Bernardino Molinari? And did I not send the aforesaid B.M. my congratulations? Without wishing to pry, I should love to have some news of this event. How could you leave your dear old father, your lovely sister − I often think about them − and your elderly maid who has such a nice way of being difficult? As I write I remember the wonderful taste of macaroni, the marvellous little cakes and your habit of leaping up innumerable flights of stairs . . . and, most of all, the kind welcome you gave all three of us.

What's become of the Count San Martino[5] and his wife? Is he fighting on a front somewhere? Is she making bandages for the wounded? And what of our friend who looks like a blond faun?

So many questions . . . Writing to you brings back memories of a stay which may have been short but will never be forgotten . . . Please write. I'm going back to Paris, with regret I may say, so the usual address will do for your letter, or letters even.

> With all best wishes to your family
> Yours ever
> C.D.

[1]   A conductor who took a keen interest in contemporary music. Since 1912 he had been artistic director of the Augusteo in Rome.
[2]   Only the first three were written. The fourth was to be for oboe, horn and harpsichord and the fifth for trumpet, clarinet, bassoon and piano. (The last sonata was also to feature 'the gracious assistance of a double-bass'. R.N.).
[3]   A piano piece Debussy had written in 1904. It was orchestrated by Molinari after his death, following 'the composer's indications'.
[4]   In English in the original. (R.N.)
[5]   Count Enrico di San Martino was president of the Accademia di Santa Cecilia. He had been organizing concerts of contemporary music since 1911.

Pourville

Mon cher Jacques   Saturday 9 October 1915

You know what I think about metronome marks: they're right for a single bar, like 'roses, with a morning's life'. Only there are 'those' who don't hear music and who take these marks as authority to hear it still less!

But do what you please.

The fatal hour of departure draws near!

None the less I shall keep writing till the last moment, like André Chénier writing verses on his way to the scaffold! A comparison which, macabre as it may be, is not entirely beside the point.

The brain is a delicate instrument which seizes up at the slightest shock: 'ambience' is more than a cliché.

I'll ring you as soon as I get home and will probably see you tomorrow.

Yours ever
C.D.

277 TO ROBERT GODET

Cher Godet   14 October 1915

You, or rather life, are being hard on me! I would so much like to have seen you and told you things I don't feel able to write. Fate is certainly stupid rather than kind − let's say no more about it.

I've just been staying by the sea in a place which regrets its lack of cosmopolitan brilliance: it's called Pourville-sur-mer. There I redis-covered my ability to think in music, which I'd lost for a year . . . Not that my writing music is indispensable but it's the only thing I know how to do, more or less well, and I confess its disappearance made me miserable . . . Anyway, I've been writing like a madman, or like a man condemned to die the next morning.

Certainly I haven't forgotten the war during these three months . . . indeed I've come to see the horrible necessity of it. I realized there was no point adding myself to the number of wounded and, all in all, it was cowardly just to think about the atrocities that had been committed without doing anything in return; by re-fashioning, as far as my strength allowed me, a little of the beauty these 'men' are destroying, with a meticulous brutality that is unmistakably 'Made in Germany'.[1]

[305]

What a disgusting business, even so . . . and what a sad lesson for us! I don't just mean the concrete emplacements and the two-way espionage – that's awful, I agree. I'm talking about the heavy hand laid on our thoughts and our structures, and accepted with a careless smile. That's the serious damage, impossible to forgive and difficult to repair because it's inside us like tainted blood. To take one example among many, the theatre directors have lost their footing (some footing!) and no longer know where to turn because they can't consult the Wagner directory.[2] There's talk of Rameau . . . 'he's boring', but no one cares to admit his performing style has been forgotten. It certainly won't be M. d'Indy, the Schola contractor, who's going to revive it.

One asks oneself at the moment whose arms music might be falling into. The young Russian school is extending hers but, as I see it, they've become as un-Russian as could be. Stravinsky himself is leaning dangerously towards Schoenberg,[3] though he remains the most wonderful orchestral technician of his age.

So, what about French music? Where are our old harpsichordists who produced real music in abundance? They held the secret of that graceful profundity, that emotion without epilepsy which we shy away from like ungrateful children . . .

Forgive me, it's turning into an article . . . This letter isn't about that but about you. I say it again, sadly: I'd have loved to see you! You're really the only one I could have talked to . . . the rest of them are a species of businessman upset by the war, grumbling, complaining, asserting, etc. . . . I find it all so dull. I'd have found some comfort in your gently ironic outlook on life, which doesn't shut itself off from emotion. How are you, that's the real question? It's not banal curiosity or vulgar prying, as you know. Thinking about you has become the most natural thing in the world for me, even though you haven't realized it . . . rather like a landscape where one has been happy and whose colours remain in the mind's eye.

Writing is necessarily a poor substitute – it's organized. It doesn't satisfy the whim of 'saying' things the moment you think of them. How many times have I said to myself, 'I'll tell Godet that . . .' And in fact I really think I have. I've missed you! To be honest, we didn't deserve to be separated. I take the liberty of writing 'we'.

Yours ever
C.D.

[306]

¹ In English in the original. (R.N.)

² Performances of Wagner's music were banned in France during the war. (R.N.)

³ Probably an allusion to Stravinsky's *Three Japanese Lyrics*, written in 1913 under the influence of *Pierrot lunaire*.

278 TO GUSTAVE DORET

Cher ami   Friday 15 October 1915

On my return to Paris I found waiting for me your excellent book, and I must thank you for the particularities it offers. I'm sure it's the first time such a large book on music hasn't been a bore!

You know what a rare compliment that is! Although I don't entirely share your opinions on Debussy's music, I'm deeply touched by your response to it.¹

Yours sincerely
C.D.

¹ The book was Doret's *Musique et musiciens*, Lausanne, 1915. He praised *Pelléas* and the subtlety and sobriety of Debussysme, while expressing his satisfaction that several composers were escaping from 'the slavery of a system which is contrary to their temperament'.

279 TO FRANCIS POULENC¹

Cher Monsieur   Saturday 23 October 1915

This is a time when we should be trying to regain a hold on our ancient traditions: we may have let their beauty slip from us, but it has not ceased to exist.

None the less the respect due to César Franck compels us to admit that he is one of the greatest of Flemish composers.

I remain
Yours most sincerely
C.D.

¹ 'I pretended I was a young Belgian critic passing through Paris and asked him . . . his opinion of Franck – needless to say, this was in order to get his autograph.' (Poulenc in the catalogue of the Debussy exhibition at the Opéra-comique in 1942, p. XIII).

24 October 1915

First of all, très cher ami, I'm delighted to have some news from you . . . Your friends told me something about you but, for some reason, made a mystery out of your health and the place you were staying in?

We're all reasonably well here: that's to say, we're as well as the majority of Frenchmen. We've had our disappointments and our spiritual and domestic difficulties, as is only natural, now that Europe and the rest of the world have taken it upon them to participate in this tragic 'concert'. Why don't the inhabitants of the planet Mars join in as well? As you say, 'they won't drive us crazy'.[1] All the same, it's something over and above brute force; 'closing the windows' on beauty is a complete nonsense and destroys the true meaning of life at the same time. But eyes and ears will have to be opened when the insistent noise of the cannon gives way to other sounds . . . ! We shall have to wipe this evil crop from off the face of the earth. We shall have to kill this microbe of false grandeur, of organized ugliness, which we haven't always recognized as being no more than weakness.

You are, I know, one of those who can fight and win against this kind of 'gas', just as deadly as the other and against which we've had no 'masks' to protect us.

My dear Stravinsky, you are a great artist! It's a fine thing to belong to one's country, to be attached to the earth like the humblest of peasants! And when the foreigner sets foot on it, all the talk of the internationalists has a bitter taste!

During these last few years, when I've felt the Austro-German miasma spreading over art, I've wished I had more authority to give vent to my fears and issue warnings about the danger we're heedlessly running into. How could we not have foreseen that these men were plotting the destruction of our art, just as they had planned the destruction of our country? Worst of all is this racial hatred which will end only with the last of the Germans! Will there ever be a last German? I'm convinced their soldiers reproduce among themselves!

Concerning the *Nocturnes*, the Swiss composer Doret is right, I've made a great many changes. Unfortunately they're published by a publisher (Fromont, in the rue du Colisée) whom I no longer deal with. Another problem is that there are no copyists at the moment capable of doing this delicate work! I'll keep trying and hope I can find a way of satisfying M. Ansermet.[2]

[308]

Music is in a sad condition, one has to admit . . . It's of no use except for charitable purposes, although we certainly shouldn't complain about that. Personally, I've spent over a year unable to write anything. It's only in the last three months, staying in the house of friends by the sea, that I've been able to think in music once again. Unless one's directly involved in a war, it makes thought very difficult. Only that olympian egoist Goethe could work through one – even, apparently, on the day the French marched into Weimar . . . Then there was Pythagoras[3], killed by a soldier just when he was about to solve some problem or other. I've actually written nothing except 'pure' music: twelve *Etudes* for piano; two sonatas for various instruments, in the old French style which was kind enough not to ask for tetralogical efforts from its listeners.

And you, what have you been doing? You may, of course, tell me to mind my own business, although the question is prompted not by vulgar curiosity, but simply by the affection I feel for you.

And your wife and children? Have you been worried about them?

My wife has had a serious eye illness with unbearable neuralgia. Chouchou has . . . a cold in the head, which she has turned into something very important by taking herself so seriously.

It's hard not to know when we shall see each other again and to have to rely on the feeble resource of 'words'. . . !

> Yours as ever
> C.D.

All our fondest wishes to your family.

P.S. I've again seen a friend of mine in the Society of Authors who tells me that you've chosen me as sponsor for your entry into the said Society; my thanks.[4]

---

[1]   In his letter to Debussy written from Morges on 11 October, Stravinsky had said: 'It's enough to drive you mad, which is exactly what the Boches are after. But they can rest assured I shan't give them that satisfaction and nor will you . . .'

[2]   Ernest Ansermet was a young Swiss conductor mentioned by Stravinsky in his letter to Debussy: 'I've spoken to you before about my friend Ansermet. He's now conducting orchestral concerts in Geneva and would like to give the *Trois Nocturnes* there this winter. He was the one who gave them their first complete performance in Switzerland, at Montreux . . .'

[3]   See letter 268 footnote 1.

[4]   Stravinsky was finally admitted into the Société des Auteurs, Compositeurs et Editeurs de Musique on 10 February 1921, with Gabriel Pierné as his sponsor.

281 TO EMMA

24, Square du Bois-de-Boulogne
6 December 1915 11 p.m.[1]

As one never knows the outcome of even the simplest event, I want to tell you one last time how much I love you and how sad I should be if any sort of accident were to prevent me ensuring our happiness, either now or in the future.

And you, my darling, love me in the person of our little Chouchou . . . you are the only two for whose sake I do not want to leave this earth altogether.

Your husband
C.D.

[1] Debussy was to be operated on next day.

282 TO ROBERT GODET

Très cher   4 January 1916

There are unpleasant reasons for my silence . . . I'd been ill for some time: not enough exercise, with the usual consequences, but I could live with those without coming to a halt. Suddenly it all got worse, so they operated; nasty moments and painful after-effects, etc. . . .

Recovery will be slow and by natural means. Nature alone has all the time in the world; mine is beginning to run out. So it's not very jolly and I'm complaining – not that there's any point, because Mother Nature is usually deaf to her children's suffering.

Ironically, this incident caught me working at full tilt; as someone said, 'That doesn't happen every day.'[1] One has to take advantage of the good times to make up for the bad. I was on the point – more or less – of finishing *La Chute de la maison Usher*, but the illness has quashed my hopes. Obviously it's not a matter of importance on Aldebaran or Sirius whether I write music or not, but I don't like being crossed and I find it hard to lie down under this blow of fate! And I'm suffering like a condemned man!

I'd rather talk about your letters which are a great comfort to me. Maybe there's a simple explanation, but you give answers to questions I've formulated only in my head.

I was deeply touched by the story of your wounded man . . . Some

[310]

37 Debussy at Le Moulleau in 1916.

consolation, surely, for admirers of *Pelléas*, including Gustave Doret whose wooden features and gilded soul are rather familiar to me? Those thoughts confided in you are to be treasured all the more because one can tell from them that this man loves music for what it is and not for what people have told him about it. It was right that you should find him: those are things written in a secret book which, luckily, only a few people know how to read.

My thanks to Madame Rollan-Mauger[2] for being all you tell me. You're certainly collecting 'golden moments' – I'm talking about the lady's voice.

Talking of which, you know how deep mine used to be? Since I've been ill it's completely disappeared: there are worse things to lose!

I've seen Stravinsky recently . . . He says: my *Firebird*, my *Sacre*, like a child saying: my top, my hoop. And that's exactly what he is – a spoilt child who, from time to time, cocks a snook at music. He's also a young savage who wears noisy ties and kisses the ladies' hands while treading on their toes. When he's old, he'll be intolerable. That's to say, he won't be able to tolerate any music; but, for the moment, he's amazing. He claims to be a friend of mine because I've helped him climb a ladder from which he can hurl grenades – not all of which explode. But, as I say, he's astonishing. You've had a close look at him and, what's more, you've analysed what makes him tick so implacably.

And so, all my best wishes for a very happy New Year. Madame Debussy and Mademoiselle Chouchou send theirs too.

> Yours ever, even if feebly
> C.D.

---

[1]   Possibly a reference to Golaud's words in Act II scene 2 of *Pelléas*: 'Et puis, la joie, on n'en a pas tous les jours.' (R.N.)
[2]   Mme Rollan-Mauger was to give the first performance of the 'Noël des enfants' on 9 March 1916 at the Casino Saint Pierre in Geneva.

283† TO JACQUES DURAND

Cher ami   13 January 1916

I'm very sorry not to have seen you today – the Laloys came to dinner. You're so busy, I don't often get a chance to talk to you.

Paul Dukas came yesterday and seemed in very good form – a rather depressing thing for me to have to say when my existence is circumscribed by a rubber ring! Tomorrow I start taking the medicine which has very surprising effects — mysterious even.

As I'm extremely sensitive — thank you! — they're having to reduce the dosage, so the treatment will go on for longer . . . Nature has no pity on her creatures.

My best wishes to your wife
Yours ever
C.D.

284 TO EMILE VUILLERMOZ

Mon cher Vuillermoz   Tuesday 25 January 1916

You're right, and all the more so because the dimensions of the *Berceuse*,[1] which you're being kind enough to concern yourself with, are precisely those of an *Estampe* . . .[2] Now an 'estampe' is not a fresco, which I certainly didn't have in mind. Anyway, do we need another 375 pages in order to get our feelings down on paper?

This lullaby is: melancholy and discreet and the 'Brabançonne' doesn't make a racket. If you don't hear enough of the ravaging of Belgium in it, let's say no more on the subject.

It's no more than a visiting-card, with no pretentions other than to offer a homage to so much patient suffering.

I was asked to write it for a book dedicated to the king of the Belgians and you know me well enough to be aware that I don't like being intrusive.

There's no doubt it was not understood. It's a shame the splendid performance it had didn't help the audience.

Finally (as I've already written more words than the *Berceuse* has bars) there's no way of writing war music in wartime. To be honest, there's no such thing as war music, as you know!

You do me a great honour by calling me a pupil of Claude Monet.

Yours as ever
C.D.

[1] See letter 268. Debussy's orchestrated version was performed under Chevillard on 26 October 1915.
[2] Debussy refers both to the set of three piano pieces he wrote in 1903 and to the general meaning of the word: 'prints' or 'engravings'. (R.N.)

[313]

Très cher   Friday 4 February 1916

Bring your brain to bear on *En blanc et noir* . . . These pieces draw their colour, their emotion, simply from the piano, like the 'greys' of Velázquez, if I may so suggest? Anyway all the orchestral musicians are at the front and those who are left behind – by whatever piece of administrative providence – are hard to put up with because they can't console themselves by comfortably hamming it through 'The Ride of Valkyries' as usual!

I've just started a new treatment. It's all shrouded in mystery and I'm asked to be patient . . . Good God! Where am I to find patience? after sixty days of various tortures.

I'm wallowing in 'factories of nothingness', as our friend Jules puts it:[1] I watch the hours go past, each the same as the other and still worth living when they're not too painful. Never have the fortifications looked so ugly . . . People go past, some of them waving ridiculous walking-sticks, others clad in Marshal Joffre blue, the foulest blue ever invented. The war continues – as you know – but it's impossible to see why . . . I realize it's not easy to find a solution but there's something irritating in the way they go about the war so nonchalantly! Death exacts none the less its blind tribute . . . When will hate be exhausted? Or is it hate that's the issue in all this? When will the practice cease of entrusting the destiny of nations to people who see humanity as a way of furthering their careers?

It's time for my treatment, so I must leave you . . .

Yours ever
C.D.

[1] See letter 273 footnote 1.

286 TO VICTOR SEGALEN

Cher ami   5 June 1916

Re-reading *Orpheus* has left me not unmoved . . . I remembered us sitting there, armed with two pencils; our long discussions, and my longer silences.[1]

What a lot has happened since then! Only our friendship has remained, a vigilant guardian defending its house and its gods. Which is perhaps the best treatment one could hope for from that old tease called Time? As for the music to go with the story, I hear it less and less. For one thing, we can't have Orpheus singing, because he is song itself – the whole conception is wrong; but parts of what we wrote are still very beautiful.

I've come to the conclusion (though this is a different point) that heroes ought to be left in their legends. Otherwise they become ridiculous and inflated.

I'm still cultivating my rectal flora. Without realizing it, I've spent a full six months now contemplating my misery; it's too long for someone who hasn't the time to lose any more. Will I ever again know what it is to be well? I don't dare to think so and I'd much rather have a sudden end than this pursuit of health in which, so far, the disease is always one step ahead of me.

I must stop before I go on too long.

> Yours ever
> C.D.

[1] The project dated from 1907 (see letter 153). Segalen spent the years between 1909 and 1913 in China, from where he sent copies of his works to Debussy.

287 TO ANDRÉ CAPLET

Cher André Caplet   10 June 1916

You're an amazing fellow . . . As bold as a lion, you manage to find a piano, a cellist and a sonata[1] and to get them all together just a few metres away from the Boches . . . such elegant bravura is and always will be the very 'essence of France'. As for the bowing, do what you like! The fact is, every cellist will find a bowing he thinks is best . . . Except when they're playing together in an orchestra, I don't think it's anything to worry about, do you?

As for printing mistakes, contact Jacques Durand.

I was overjoyed to see you again. Even if I didn't think you were lost for good, I was beginning to have my doubts (invalids are easily worried!). And now without so much as thinking about it you've put my fragile machine back together again. For me, poor human wreck that I am, it was a comfort to see a man who had passed through the guns without leaving anything important behind. For a moment it made my own miseries seem trivial.[2]

[315]

If I could force my body to concentrate on avoiding accidents, perhaps the rest would follow? But I'm too old . . . I know nothing of the skills of using the terrain and I'd get myself killed like a rabbit in a field.

I hope to see you soon . . . There's a lot of music waiting for you; like a sister, if I may put it like that.

Yours ever
C.D.

1   The Cello Sonata which Debussy had finished in 1915.
2   Caplet was later gassed and died from the effects in 1925. (R.N.)

288 TO JACQUES DURAND

Mon cher Jacques   21 July 1916

Begging Maeterlinck's pardon, but meaningless events do happen . . .[1] Things are still menacing! To tell you the truth, I don't know how I'm going to get through. I've been spared nothing: illness; Chouchou ill; as the last straw, Mme Texier also ill! It's enough to drive one to suicide at the least. If I didn't have the desire as well as the duty to finish the two Poe operas, I'd have done it already.

Whichever way I turn, I'm met with disasters . . . just as I enjoy a struggle on manuscript paper, so I hate struggling with people because it can suddenly turn so nasty – when it's a matter of day-to-day living.

When life starts to treat you with such hostility, isn't it a sign and a suggestion not to resist any longer?

I don't know any more.

Yours ever
C.D.

1   See letter 242 footnote 1.

289† TO MAUD ALLAN

Chère Miss Maud Allan   30 July 1916

I have been sitting for hours in front of the score of *Khamma* which is precisely tailored to a complement of 90 players. I am utterly at a loss as to how it could be reduced to suit an orchestra half the size. What

[316]

would you do if you were asked to dance with just one arm and one leg? There is some analogy between such an insult and the amputation you are asking for. I can only leave you to act as you see fit, but I decline all responsibility in the matter. Why send the score back to Durand, when it is Ernest Bloch who has to take charge of this hazardous operation?

> With renewed regrets, I remain
> Yours sincerely
> C.D.

290 TO ROBERT GODET

Paris
Cher Godet 4 September 1916

The monotony of my life and all it contains is such that I couldn't bring myself to write to you . . . I have to choose, though: if I don't write to you, it's goodbye to your letters which I like and goodbye to your friendship which is as vital for me as bread. So, again, forgive the monotony of my life and all it contains.

I watch the days go past, minute by minute, as cows watch trains go past: I go to bed, fairly certain I shan't sleep, hoping tomorrow will be better, and it starts all over again! The cause of my suffering hasn't undergone any particular change. The disease – that old servant of death[1] – has chosen me as a testing-ground. God knows why. I work, and the only result is to convince me I shouldn't have bothered. When will it all end?

It would be better if we could leave this house . . . Did I tell you that first Chouchou and then her mother had the whooping-cough? It's a stupid illness and they've still not recovered. The doctor prescribes a change of air. You know how little real understanding they have of domestic life; they turn apartments upside down and suggest you move, when often you're within an ace of dying of hunger.

This house has some curious points of resemblance with the House of Usher . . . Even if I haven't got Roderick Usher's cerebral disorders or his passion for (?) Weber's last waltz, we share a certain hypersensitivity . . . I could give you details which would make your beard fall out . . . it's extremely unpleasant, not for your beard (which has nothing to fear), but for me, as I don't like to draw attention to myself.

My poor Godet, living like that is the most awful nightmare! I'm

[317]

getting letters from one of my friends – André Caplet – who's a liaison officer in the area round Verdun. He toys with death from morning till night and manages to keep in high spirits. He's got a collapsible piano in the trenches with him! The other day he was interrupted by a burst of gunfire which almost made him as collapsible as the piano . . . He went on playing several metres under ground. He's a hero, no doubt about it! If it were possible, I'd willingly go and replace him . . . But with my usual luck I'd have been killed several times already.

The authorized spokesman for the Bloch[2] tribe came to see me last month, before leaving for America as kapellmeister to an English dancer – Miss Maud Allan – who commissioned a ballet from me some time ago (I don't think I told you about it). His voice still sounds like that of a eunuch bursting into a harem. He even exaggerates it. He's destined for higher things, like selling guaranteed rings on the streets – so much for this brilliant cosmopolitan whose presence here makes us the envy of Europe. Naturally, he complained bitterly about his quarrel with you. While he was talking, I was thinking, 'How could Godet have put up with this cross between a commercial traveller and a dangerous lunatic?'

In a few days you'll receive the sonata for flute, viola and harp.[3] It dates from a time when I was still in touch with music. It's a memory too of a Claude Debussy of long ago, of the *Nocturnes* perhaps?

I have no compunction about saying I hope you'll write back without delay!

> Yours ever
> C.D.

[1] A reference to Arkel's phrase in Act IV scene 2 of *Pelléas*: '. . . la maladie, la vieille servante de la mort . . .' (R.N.)
[2] Ernest Bloch, see letter 242. He had been engaged by Maud Allan to give the first performance of *Khamma* in New York, but this never came off.
[3] It was played privately at Durand's on 10 December.

291† TO JACQUES DURAND

> Mon cher Jacques   12 October 1916

Le Moulleau definitely doesn't agree with me and I won't be bringing back any masterpieces . . . perhaps one or two useful pointers to the future? Hotel life has never seemed so difficult . . . the very walls are hostile, not to mention life in a numbered box.

[318]

Yesterday I had a visit from Mr L. Roos . . .[1] For a moment he made me feel sorry I'd composed a sonata and I began to wonder whether my writing was at fault! There's no escaping the fact, bad musicians are everywhere! This episode has worried me considerably; the ramifications are many and I'm not surprised any more that my poor music is so often not understood. Without dramatizing things unduly, it was terrifying. Why wasn't I taught to polish spectacles, like Spinoza? Then I'd never have had to rely on music to provide my daily bread . . .

It's a miscalculation, indeed I'd go so far as to call it dishonest! If only it weren't too late, unfortunately, to make something out of this bitter truth.

I hope we'll be returning soon – perhaps the 20th. I can't wait to get back to my old house with all its faults, its annoyances and its bugles. It knows me better than this outpost, which has been a wretched disappointment . . .

D'Annunzio has left a lasting reputation behind him in these parts. People are still talking about his dogs, his suits and various other things in which the comic Muse has the best role.

> Yours ever
> C.D.

[1] In fact Rosoor – see the following letter.

292 TO JACQUES DURAND

[Le Moulleau]

Mon cher Jacques   17 October 1916

M. Louis Rosoor the cellist comes not from Bordeaux but from Lille and won a first prize at the Paris Conservatoire. That doesn't stop him having his own individual understanding of my music.[1] We must be particularly tolerant with those who've been invaded by the Germans! If the world's now coming to 4 place de la Madeleine to buy my music and treating it any old how, that doesn't worry me, but when self-styled 'virtuosi' spread error and desolation in so-called 'concert' halls, I continue to find that irritating. But if you don't see anything wrong, we'll say no more about it.

Going for a walk recently at Cap Ferrat, I found the 'cellular' idea for the finale of the Violin Sonata . . . Unfortunately the first two movements don't want to have anything to do with it . . . Knowing myself as I do, I'm certainly not going to force them to put up with an awkward neighbour.

For reasons of domestic hygiene we can't go back home until the 24th, which means a slight delay to my hopes of seeing my three trees again: but I've weathered delays before.

My skin is blacker than King Dagobert's wife's!

With that sensational information, I leave you.

Yours ever
C.D.

[1] Louis Rosoor used to hand out descriptive commentaries to Debussy's Cello Sonata ('Pierrot wakes up with a jolt . . .'), claiming he had been given them by the composer.

293† TO ROBERT GODET

Cher Robert   11 December 1916

What does the paper matter as long as one gets the letters! The substance of yours is so rich, they've no need of the finest vellum. Replacing beauty of style with glamorous paper is a trick we can leave to amateurs.

For someone who can't sleep any more your mind is remarkably open to the sort of 'correspondences' which leave the 'vulgar mob' gaping like chickens. I congratulate you and . . . benefit from it.

Sakousky and Hummel are curiously blind.[1]

Naturally, I don't take this poor tattered body for walks any more, in case I frighten little children and tram conductors. But if they could see inside my head! Still it's not important, there are ruins that are better hidden. And even if I'm old, I can't yet expect people to get a historical thrill out of looking at mine.

Despite the weather yesterday, which was the sort for staying at home in, I went to Jacques Durand's house to hear a performance of the sonata for flute, viola and harp. The harp part was taken by a young lady who looked like one of those priestess musicians you see on Egyptian tombs – nothing but profile! She's just come back from Munich, which she had a job to get away from; she spent a little time in prison and eventually left without her harp . . . worse than losing a leg. Even though it was chromatic (not her leg, the harp she played on yesterday), which distorts the sonority rather, it didn't sound bad, all things considered. It's not for me to say anything about the music . . . Although I could do so without blushing, because it's by a Debussy I no longer know! . . . It's terribly sad and I don't know whether one ought to laugh at it or cry? Perhaps both?

[320]

A Danish newspaper has written to ask: 'Has the current World War diminished or increased your hope in the prospect of eternal peace in the future?' What's your reaction to this 'neutral'? Does he think I'm a prophet? And why ask questions which can never be answered while mankind still exists?

Of course there are highly intelligent people capable of treating this boring theme to variations more numerous than the sands of the sea! Frankly, I've never liked 'variations'. They're just a slick procedure for making *a lot* out of *very little*: sometimes it's an act of vengeance; occasionally the poor theme gets cross and rejects its ingenious finery in disgust.

Do you know a book by G. K. Chesterton called *The Napoleon of Notting Hill*? It has some delightful imaginative touches. For a start, it's nothing to do with Napoleon, but with a king who solves a variety of serious problems by dancing! As you can read English, I'm sure you'd enjoy it. It's the companion of my sleepless nights at the moment and I can't blame it for prolonging them. I've also tried reading the Civil Code, but I've had to give up. It's extremely disturbing! After three pages the 'articles' start doing a savage dance, some of them telling you that you're right and others that you're wrong. Certainly reading them gives you a jaundiced view of the law.

Talking of which, I don't suppose the head of the Bloch tribe's[2] stay among the Americans is going to advance his cause or develop his soul? If only they could make his voice break, then it might stop sounding like a bad-tempered parrot's, giving his every little remark an edge of unpleasantness! Is there no news of him or of his gentle companion Miss Maud Allan? Together the two of them are quite capable of stupefying the Americas. She with her arms, he, of course, with a symphony – which he carries respectfully round with him. I was not in the least anxious to get to know him, but he put me through a torture like King Lear's. He is not forgotten.

So that's how things are! . . .

I'm terrified of planning any sort of work whatsoever – that in itself is enough to condemn it to the waste-paper basket, the cemetery of bad dreams.

What an existence! I'm exhausted by chasing phantoms but not tired enough to sleep. So I wait for the morrow, for better or for worse; and it starts all over again.

In a cowardly way my thoughts go back to the morphine I used to take. It made me feel ill, but like a shell at the bottom of the sea.

I expect I've bored you enough?

A parcel of music should reach you in a few days. I hope it'll make you forgive me.

> Yours in disarray
> C.D.

1 Debussy's nicknames for two of his friends.
2 See letter 290 footnote 2.

294 TO EMMA[1]

24 December 1916

In this year of 1916 Father Christmas is at the front and communications are so difficult, he hasn't been able to respond to my requests. I've no flowers or music . . . Nothing but my poor anxious heart and an urgent desire to see the end of this marking time which is like a premature burial.

This waiting for better days is enough to drive one crazy and if your courage wasn't here with me I would long ago have gone off to read the communiqués on another planet.

Never has your love been more precious or more necessary to me. I worry when you go away! Noël! Noël! The bells are cracked. Noël! Noël! They have wept too long!

Be patient, I beg you, and let me recover . . . until the times return when we can count our kisses. I don't care about anything except that — believe me.

If I didn't know your spirit was so strong, I'd be afraid for you, living this life with an invalid. But you will be the source of my ease from all the cares that oppress me.

Forgive me for loving you . . . Wait for me.

> Your Claude

1 One of the notes Debussy used to send up to her in her bedroom, on the storey above his study.

295† TO JACQUES DURAND

Mon cher Jacques   23 February 1917

You were right to be sorry I abandoned the 'Neapolitan' finale;[1] after having great hopes of its replacement I've come back to it – with some changes. It's one of a thousand little personal tragedies which occur without so much noise as the fall of a rose-petal and without disturbing the universe. So in a few days you'll see Naples again . . . and you won't die!

But do try and like this definitive finale!

Yours ever
C.D.

[1] To the Violin Sonata.

296† TO JACQUES DURAND

Mon cher Jacques   15 April 1917

Never correct J. S. Bach's accompanied violin sonatas on a rainy Sunday . . . ! I've just finished revising the above[1] and I can feel the rain inside me . . .

When the old Saxon Cantor hasn't any ideas he starts out from any old thing and is truly pitiless. In fact he's only bearable when he's admirable. Which, you'll say, is still something!

All the same, if he'd had a friend – a publisher perhaps – who could have told him to take a day off every week, perhaps, then we'd have been spared several hundreds of pages in which you have to walk between rows of mercilessly regulated and joyless bars, each one with its rascally little 'subject' and 'countersubject'.

Sometimes – often indeed – his prodigious technical skill (which is, after all, only his individual form of gymnastics) is not enough to fill the terrible void created by his insistence on developing a mediocre idea no matter what the cost!

I can't find Choisnel's realizations, which you mention. I thought he took them back the last time he came to see me. But I can't be certain, with my memory in its present feeble state.

Over *Jeux*, we mustn't forget that the Nijinsky version didn't leave very happy memories behind it; we shouldn't start renegotiating until

[323]

we get some 'assurances'. Don't forget the Sonata . . . Poulet gives me gooseflesh![2]

Yours ever
C.D.

[1] His versions of these and of the three cello (viola da gamba) sonatas were not published by Durand until 1923.
[2] Gaston Poulet and Debussy gave the first public performance of the Violin Sonata in the Salle Gaveau on 5 May 1917.

297 TO GABRIEL FAURÉ

29 April 1917

My slowness in replying to your kind letter, cher maître et ami, is due to the simple reason that I can no longer play the piano well enough to risk a performance of the *Etudes* . . . In public a peculiar phobia takes hold of me: there are too many keys; I haven't enough fingers any more; and suddenly I forget where the pedals are! It's unfortunate and extremely alarming.

I assure you I'm not just being difficult; I should have been particularly happy to do you a favour.

With my apologies
Yours ever
C.D.

298 TO ROBERT GODET

Cher Godet   7 May 1917

I was just going to write to you . . . As usual, you'll say! But it's the sad truth at a time when events can't be overcome and the best resolutions die before they can resolve anything.

So life goes on like a tired old machine. It's clear it's had enough . . . and so have we!

I've at last finished the sonata for violin and piano . . . By one of those very human contradictions it's full of happiness and uproar. In future don't be taken in by works that seem to fly through the air; they've often been wallowing in the shadows of a gloomy brain. Such is the finale of this same sonata. It goes through the most curious contortions before ending up with a simple idea which turns back on itself like a snake biting its own tail – an amusement whose attraction I take leave to doubt!

It was played last Saturday at a concert for the benefit of blind soldiers. The public had come with charitable purposes and applauded it. But not as loudly as the 'Noël', after which they went mad, demanded an encore, etc. . . . My low tolerance of noise prevented me from fully appreciating these manifestations.

As for my health, it could be good if my spirits were better . . . This life in which you have to fight for a lump of sugar or for manuscript paper, not to mention your daily bread, needs stronger nerves than mine.

You describe in your letter, not without humour, a catalogue of disasters. I hope you weren't the victim? Please reassure me on this point!

Is it really true you're coming to Paris in June? This writing paper is too small to contain the violence of my feelings – I hardly dare hope!

I'm very fond of the father of your little American girl. If he ever had his riddles published I'd buy a copy at once. Let's hope the gods still exist! We're sorely in need of them, and I even more of your friendly lucidity.

> Yours as ever
> C.D.

299 TO ROGER-DUCASSE[1]

Cher ami   9 May 1917

As you already know, your two studies had a success which can be unhesitatingly described as 'considerable', especially the study for repeated notes which was encored.[2]

For my humble part, I've rarely heard such a dynamic use of sonorities – I won't use the facile metaphor of 'fireworks', but even so . . .

Madame Long's[3] fingers seemed to have multiplied and you owe her an enthusiastic encore.

> Yours happily
> C.D.

¹ A pupil of Fauré, he won second prize in the Prix de Rome in 1902. He was a friend of Debussy's and had given the first performance of *En blanc et noir* with him the year before.
² Ducasse did not attend the concert of the Société Musicale Indépendante at which his two studies were played. The one on repeated notes was published by Durand in 1915.
³ The pianist Marguerite Long had met Debussy in July 1914 and was to do so again at Saint Jean-de-Luz in the summer of 1917. In her book *Au piano avec Debussy* (1960; Eng. trans. 1972) she fills out her memories a little.

300 TO PAUL-JEAN TOULET

Cher ami   20 May 1917

I admit I was deeply moved by your delicate fly-prints . . . they brought back to me the stuffy 'Bar de la Paix', the crowded 'Weber' and all the other places on which your presence is inscribed in letters of fire (oh yes). But nothing's left of those good old times. People have become nastier still, and one can even feel some nostalgia for the 'undesirables' of yore . . .

And you are no longer here, no room for discussion on that point. As far as I can see, no one's taken your place. I expect you know about the obscure punishment visited on me for nearly two and a half years now? Fear not, I shan't darken your fine horizon with stories that are a meticulous blend of the grotesque and the horrible. The war may not have touched me physically but spiritually it's destroyed me: I'm lost and I don't have the money to offer a realistic reward for my recovery.

Perhaps we'll meet in some more peaceful time? Seeing you again is one of the things I'd like most . . . writing to you simply isn't enough. I tell you straight!

Yours ever
C.D.

301 TO SERGE DE DIAGHILEV

26 May 1917

You have had the notion, mon cher Diaghilev, of clothing the distinctly French charm of Fauré's *Pavane*¹ in a Spanish gravity; and it's a *tour de force* on which I congratulate you: you and the wonderful Massine . . .

[326]

Petrushka is definitely a masterpiece. They haven't anything of the sort in Germany and never will have.

> With my thanks
> Yours ever
> C.D.

[1] Fauré's music was used for Massine's ballet *Las Meninas*, after the painting by Velázquez. It was danced at the Châtelet on 25 May.

302 TO ROBERT GODET

> Cher Godet   Thursday 7 June 1917

Your enthusiasm over the Violin Sonata will, I'm afraid, be abruptly dampened when you actually have it in your hands . . . much as the gods may approve your attitude, if you want to stick to it you would perhaps do better not to look through the score!

I must admit I wrote this sonata only to get rid of it, and because I was spurred on by my dear publisher.

You know how to read between the staves, so you'll see traces of that Imp of the Perverse who urges us on to choose the very idea we ought to have left alone . . . This sonata will be interesting from a documentary point of view and as an example of what an invalid can write in time of war. But enough about the sonata!

As my brain is only moving slowly, I couldn't work out from your letter when you're coming to Paris? We leave, disasters permitting, around the end of the month.

No need to labour the point, but I'm looking forward to seeing you.

Le poison noir is a whimsical tale which has no connection with my music, apart from the poster.[1] So rest easy and don't worry.

I take the liberty of begging you to come to Paris as soon as you can; I'm terrified of missing you.

> Yours ever
> C.D.

[1] *Le poison noir* was a play in one act by Jean Bernac and Albert Jean, given at the Grand Guignol on 11 May.

7 June 1917

If your distaste for Paris is such that you find everything about it odious, then the following proposition may not be to your liking . . . It's about *As You Like It*.[1]

I went to see Gémier,[2] Shakespeare's guardian, before one of his performances as Shylock and talked to him about my ancient passion for *As You Like It*. I told him that if he had any plans to put it on, I should like the honour or writing the incidental music . . . Gémier's face assumed the mask of Comedy and said 'Agreed'. At this point a brief interlude: the energetic G.M.[3] . . . to whom Gémier tells this story in confidence (!). M. at once slips him the idea of letting him do the translation; and turns up on my doorstep one morning with the 'thing' all ready for the oven! So, gently I recount to M. the past history of *As You Like It*. Which can be summed up by saying, '*As You Like It* and Toulet have gone together in my mind for a long time. I couldn't do one without the other.' The M. leaves, neither ashamed nor confused, but appearing to understand.

You've already guessed my ideal dénouement? All it needs is for you to agree to put your grey cells to work. When the weather gets hot, grey cells go indoors — and could you tell me (being impatient, I won't say how soon) whether the idea interests you?

Apart from which there's the war, as you know. I'm sorry my health has reduced me to the role of spectator, like all those people in theatre audiences who say bluntly, 'I wouldn't have played the part like that' . . .

> May the gods guide you.
> Yours ever
> C.D.

[1] See letters 103, 104 and 110.
[2] Firmin Gémier was an actor in Antoine's troupe. He then took over as manager of the Théâtre de la Renaissance in 1901 and of the Théâtre Antoine in 1906.
[3] Gabriel Mourey.

Paris
Cher ami   20 June 1917

Like poor Mélisande 'I cannot do what I want' and that's the worst thing of all!

You invest Gémier with too much Shakespearian rigour – if you knew the translation of *The Merchant of Venice* you'd be less worried!

He (Gémier) is chiefly after an opportunity to display his gifts as a producer, as a manipulator of crowds . . . *As You Like It* won't be very suitable from this point of view, but I'm sure he'll find a way. If he has to, he'll manoeuvre the usherettes; or else the audience in the stalls will go up to the third gallery and vice versa. Seriously, though, you could do *As You Like It*, couldn't you?

I didn't keep a copy of the work you did on it and I have too much respect for your work to have mislaid it. It can't have got lost?[1]

The vocal element could play a large part in *As You Like It* . . . I don't intend to leave out any of the 'songs' that decorate the text. In passing, I commend them to your goodwill; and what's more, to your lyricism?

Unless we change our minds we'll probably be coming down to your part of the world. I tremble as I say it because it's enough for me to express a wish for it to evaporate immediately.[2]

Yours ever
C.D.

[1] The text of Toulet's adaptation of *As You Like It*, with Debussy's annotations, is now in a private collection in Paris.
[2] Toulet was at Guéthary, down the coast from Biarritz. The Debussys went a little further south, to Saint Jean-de-Luz. (R.N.)

305 TO WALTER RUMMEL[1]

Cher ami   28 June 1917

I'm sure you forgave me after your last recital for not coming round to express my admiration?

It's hard to say that kind of thing in public . . . or rather, you either say too much or too little! . . . Meanwhile the object of this attention looks at you anxiously, as if to say, 'How's he going to get out of that one? Why tell me things I know better than he does?'; and that's the truth of it.

[329]

One doesn't congratulate a sunset, does one, or the sea on being more beautiful than any cathedral?[2] You are a force of nature . . . like her you go from the great to the little with no visible effort. You therefore understand both the great Sebastian Bach and the little Claude Debussy, so that for a moment they stand together in the public's mind . . . My thanks for that and for everything.

> Yours most sincerely
> C.D.

[1] Rummel gave the first performance of the *Etudes* in December 1916. He had just played a recital consisting of pieces by Bach and Debussy. See letter 309 for Debussy's opinion on this 'prince of virtuosos'.
[2] A reference to Verlaine's poem 'La mer est plus belle que les cathédrales' which Debussy had set in 1891 as the first of his *Trois mélodies*. (R.N.)

306† TO D. E. INGHELBRECHT

Cher ami

[Saint Jean-de-Luz]
[July 1917]

Our departure was in the nature of an escape, as usual! Anyway here we are in the delightful Basque country. There's everything one could need to make one happy, if only this old carcass didn't have to be dragged along as well; its only change is to become harder to cope with. There are a lot of famous pianists in the area including R. Viñes, J. Nin,[1] Mme M. Long, etc. . . . but I have the advantage of staying in an outlying part of the town, so I don't hear them. True, I don't see the sea either and that's something I'm very sorry about. The piano here is a curious instrument which takes holidays for a week at a time. There are keys, sometimes in the bass and sometimes in the treble, which go for days without functioning. But as they do it at different times one can always manage. Or one can desist altogether. You have a decided taste for proselytism . . . Nobody could mind less than I do. Count on me and remind me of the names of your two protégés – I haven't got them with me – when the holiday is over. Chouchou has it in for a little prelude by J. S. Bach in E major. And every morning she gives it a bad time, I must say; I can't bring myself to hold it against her. Keep me abreast of your news – but don't be offended if I don't answer straight away. How is your father-in-law?

> With best wishes to Mme D. E. C. Inghelbrecht
> Yours ever
> C.D.

[330]

[1] Joaquín Nin, 1879–1949, Spanish pianist and composer.

307 TO JACQUES DURAND

Châlet Habas Saint Jean-de-Luz

Mon cher Jacques   27 September 1917

Not wanting to start every letter with everlasting variations on 'I'm no better' and 'I'm very tired', may I be allowed to tell you about Francis Planté?[1] He's been at Saint Jean-de-Luz these last few days and gave two concerts at the Ch.B. Society.[2] He's prodigious. He played – very well – the 'Toccata' (from *Pour le piano* by C. Debussy) and was marvellous too in Liszt's *Feux follets*. Much less good in Ravel's *Jeux d'eau*. This piece's butterfly wings can't support a virtuoso's weight (or his pedalling, whichever you will).[3] At the second concert he's going to play 'Reflets dans l'eau' and 'Mouvement' and he's asked my advice. Otherwise we've talked a lot about you because your friend P. Fournier was one of the party . . . You can easily imagine the conversation! Your ears ought to have been glowing furiously. (Especially the left one.)

Your last letter didn't entirely quell my worries about your wife's health . . . I'm extremely sorry to hear about it and needn't emphasize how much I would have you free of this all too human source of anxiety. There'll always be enough of these left, that's for certain!

If you understand anything of what's happening in Russia, it would be very kind of you to let me know. These people have a curious sense of responsibility! I notice people always talk about 'Russia the mysterious' . . . If by 'mystery' they mean 'imbecility', then we're in agreement. The truth is, the country's absurdly large! (It ought to have two 'presidents' at least.)

The telephone brings ears closer, but not necessarily hearts . . .

And you'll never put a stop to the continual disagreements between 'Petrogradians' and 'Muscovites'.

With those stirring words I must go to bed and try and get some sleep . . . Sleep! 'Tis a little like death![4]

Yours ever
C.D.

[1] The pianist Francis Planté was then 78 years old. He gave a series of concerts for war charities in the department of Landes and in the Basque country between June and November 1917.

² Charles Bordes.
³ Debussy makes a play on words between 'poids' and 'pied'. (R.N.)
⁴ A reference to the French saying, 'Partir, c'est mourir un peu'. (R.N.)

308 TO CHOUCHOU'S PIANO TEACHER

Mademoiselle   24 October 1917

For two years now Chouchou has made no noticeable progress. This is not anyone's fault and I am not going to reproach you for it. Only it is vital she should be in the hands of someone stricter.

There is also the matter of times – you often change them, but it is not for me to enter into a discussion on the subject. So we have decided, her mother and I, to orientate her musical studies in a different direction. Please believe me when I say that your personality is not at issue in all this. In any case your future does not lie wholly within the confines of the teaching profession, at least for your sake I hope not.

With our thanks for the help you have given Chouchou until now,

I remain
Yours sincerely
C.D.

309 TO ROBERT GODET

Très cher   [31] October 1917

At last we're back in this little nook. To be frank yet again, we should never have left it.

Travelling at the moment is a strange and dangerous enterprise . . . For example, we had to stay on Bordeaux Saint Jean station, in the rain, surrounded by draughts, for longer than it takes to die a hero's death.

We arrived on a cold, clear morning.

The old avenue du Bois de Boulogne was charming. (Even so there are more neutrals in Biarritz!) Our garden had an abandoned look under its dead leaves . . . The two trees, which you know, were in their autumnal garb; the usual magic somewhat soured by the excessive reds of the bugle calls.

Being a tree-lover, you'll understand how I felt.

[332]

It was a relief to be away from the international vexations of Saint Jean-de-Luz . . .

I was beginning to think I might be in for a peaceful time when I saw trees that hadn't been wasting time looking for new outfits, and then my luck turned and I found myself gazing at those dreary sheets of manuscript paper – empty of music and yellow with boredom. I mean it, I've come back with nothing, not even any unpublished Basque songs. Probably Bordes has got them all[1] and the Basques have transferred their affection to bad music – the sort that brings tears to the eyes of negroes and nervous little children.

It's kind of you to be enthusiastic about this journey to Switzerland, but so far it remains an enigma . . . If it's just someone stringing us along, I don't find that entertaining. Anyway we can't forget my deplorable state of health – it puts a stop to my finest bursts of good intentions.

Have you seen the portrait Edmond Dulac's just done of the prince of virtuosos, Walter Rummel? (Dulac was born in Marseille but has recently taken English nationality.) It's astonishing: his forehead makes him look like a café waiter with genius – to quote Carjat on Baudelaire[2] – and it lights up the frame. But I still prefer Liszt's – forehead that is; it's wider, more generous. Rummel's temples are narrow, and it's obvious he'll never go mad . . . He (Rummel) told me he might possibly be appointed 'professor of virtuosity' at the Geneva Conservatory! Isn't he rather young? Will the young pianists of Geneva take him seriously? (Couldn't he at least wear glasses?) But I sincerely hope he succeeds. I'm afraid he won't get very far here in Paris! You know how people hold on to their opinions! And in Geneva all the things I now see as being difficult for him could well turn out to be advantages!

Don't be upset that I haven't mentioned my plans for some time . . . Music's completely abandoned me. Even if it's not a cause for tears, it's a trifle ridiculous, at least. But there's nothing I can do about it, and I've never forced anyone to like me. If music thinks I'm treating her badly, then she can go elsewhere: if necessary I could give her some useful addresses, even if not particularly sympathetic ones! The hard part in all this is to have to go on writing about it: that's certainly the worst thing! Why haven't I the energy to become a writer on military matters? That's a good life at the moment. Look at Bidou in the *Débats* and Laloy in *Excelsior* – you'd think they were born wearing zouave's trousers. Seriously, I think Bidou is marvellously clear at explaining the most complex military situations —perhaps his skill as a drama critic is more help to him than one might imagine?[3]

> Yours ever, but a little exhaustedly,
> C.D.

[1]   Charles Bordes had died in 1909. Before founding the Chanteurs de Saint-Gervais he had done fieldwork collecting 'Archives of Basque traditions' and had published several musical works based on popular tunes of the region.
[2]   No printed source has been discovered for this phrase of Etienne Carjat, who was a caricaturist, photographer, writer and painter of numerous exaggerated portraits.
[3]   Henry Bidou was a literary and dramatic critic who became a military chronicler and went on to write a history of the First World War.

310 TO JACQUES DURAND

> Mon cher Jacques   1 November 1917

There's no way I can go out any more without risking an 'incident' . . . So we must write!

Do what you like about La Boîte à joujoux, only don't let's add to the 'restrictions'. I may say, in passing, that the orchestral score is nearing completion.[1] At the first real opportunity, let's not hesitate any more. This work is, after all, conceived in a truly French spirit and if we wait too long we run the risk of not being able to turn this to our advantage.

Laloy and I have been working on the operatic version of Le Martyre de Saint Sébastien. It's an improvement; isn't it strange that in some 3,995 lines there should be so little substance? Just words, words . . . I think we'll manage it all the same.

I've also got plans to write incidental music for Shakespeare's As You Like It (Gémier wholly approves).

But to all these fine ideas I bring only ill-health which reacts to the slightest shock, I could even say to the slightest change in the weather!

> Yours ever
> C.D.

Tell Gaston I'm thinking of him . . .[2]

[1]   Debussy had begun it in the spring of 1914; it was completed after his death by André Caplet and first performed in Paris on 10 December 1919.
[2]   Gaston Choisnel.

Mon cher Raoul   8 April 1918

Did you receive the last telegram? You must have done. I was the one who thought to send you the first one. I wrote it and then I realized that being only a little girl I didn't have the necessary documents to show at the post office, so I asked Dolly[1] to send it. She was here because I sent for her when I saw Mama's face so utterly distraught. When she'd gone, Mama was called to Papa's bedside because the nurse thought he was 'very bad'! We sent at once for two doctors and they both said he should have an injection to stop the pain. I understood then – Roger-Ducasse was there and said to me, 'Chouchou, come and kiss your Papa.' At once I thought it was all over. When I went back into the bedroom, Papa was asleep, breathing regularly but very shallowly. He went on sleeping like that until 10 o'clock in the evening and then, gently, like an angel, he went to sleep for ever.[2] I can't describe what happened afterwards. A flood of tears was building up behind my eyes but I forced them back because of Mama. All that night, alone in her great bed, I couldn't sleep for a minute. I had a fever and with dry eyes I gazed at the walls and couldn't bring myself to believe the truth!

The next day far too many people came to see Mama and by the end of it she couldn't hold out any longer – it was a release for her and for me. Thursday arrived, the Thursday when he was to be taken from us for ever! I saw him one last time in that horrible box – lying on the ground. He looked happy, so happy and then I couldn't control my tears. I almost collapsed but I couldn't embrace him. At the cemetery Mama, naturally, couldn't have behaved better and as for me, all I could think of was, 'I mustn't cry because of Mama'. I summoned up all my courage. Where did it come from? I don't know. I didn't shed a single tear. Tears restrained are worth as much as tears shed, and now it is night for ever. Papa is dead. Those three words, I don't understand them or rather I understand them too well. And to be the only one here struggling with Mama's indescribable grief is truly terrible – for several days it's made me forget my own, but now I feel it more bitterly than ever. You're so far away, Raoul! Think occasionally of your poor little sister who would like to embrace you so much and tell you she loves you. Can you understand all I feel but can't put into words?

[335]

A thousand kisses and all my love
Your little sister
Chouchou

It's unbelievable. I don't know how I stay alive, and I can't believe the awful truth.[3]

[1] Dolly Bardac, Raoul's sister, who became Mme de Tinan.
[2] Debussy in fact died a little before midnight on Monday, 25 March.
[3] Chouchou was twelve and a half years old when she wrote this letter. She died after receiving the wrong treatment for diphtheria, sixteen months after her father, on 16 July 1919.

Chief published collections
of Debussy's letters

Caplet — *Lettres inédites à André Caplet, 1908–1914, recueillies et présentées par E. Lockspeiser* Monaco, éd. du Rocher, 1957.

Chausson — *Revue musicale*, 1 December 1925 and 1 May 1926; Charles Oulmont, in *Mercure de France*, December 1934, reprinted in *Musique de l'amour*, Paris, 1935.

D'Annunzio — *Debussy et d'Annunzio, Correspondance inédite présentée par Guy Tosi*, Neuchâtel, éd. du Griffon; Paris, Denoël, 1948.

Durand — *Lettres de C. Debussy à son éditeur*, Paris, Durand, 1927.

Emma (Debussy) — *Lettres de C. Debussy à sa femme Emma, présentées par Pasteur Vallery-Radot*, Paris, Flammarion, 1957.

Godet et Jean-Aubry — *Lettres à deux amis*, Paris, Corti, 1942.

Laloy — *Revue de musicologie*, 1962.

Louÿs — *Correspondance de C. Debussy et P. Louÿs, recueillie et annotée par H. Borgeaud*, Paris, Corti, 1945.

Messager — *La jeunesse de* Pelléas. *Lettres de C. Debussy à A. Messager*, Paris, Dorbon, 1938.

Segalen — *Segalen et Debussy. Textes recueillis et présentés par Annie Joly-Segalen et André Schaeffner*, Monaco, éd. du Rocher, 1962.

Toulet — *Correspondance de C. Debussy et P. J. Toulet*, Paris, Le Divan, 1929.

Index of works

Page numbers in *italic* refer to the illustrations

Ariettes oubliées, 146n., 264, 265n., 276n.

Berceuse héroïque, 295, 313 and n.
La Boîte à joujoux, 278, 285, 287, 289 and n., 334 and n.

Cendrelune, 78 and n., 89, 94
'Chanson de la Mère', 96n.
Chansons de Bilitis, 94, 97n., 98, 101–2 and n., 114n.
Chansons de Charles d'Orléans, 74n., 195, 214n.
Children's Corner, 195, 225, 235, 256
La Chute de la maison Usher, xxi, 139n., 170, 171, 192, 194, 203, 204, 212, 220–1, 223, 235, 250, 252, 290, 310, 316
Cinq Poèmes de Baudelaire, 23, 28n., 31n., 43n., 45–6, 48n., 60
Clarinet Rhapsody, 222, 247 and n., 248, 249n.
La Damoiselle élue, 23, 24, 26n., 39n., 43, 44n., 52, *53*, 59, 60, 66n., 114, 116
Danses for harp and orchestra, 176n.
Le Diable dans le beffroi, xxi, 138–9 and n., 141–2 and n., 170, 171, 194, 235, 250, 252, 316

Diane au bois, 8, 10n., 12–13, 14–15, 16
Douze Etudes, 290, 299 and n., 300, 301 and n., 303 and n., 309, 324, 330n.

En blanc et noir, 290, 298n., 314, 326n.
L'Enfant prodigue, 2, 169n., 179, 182 and n., 192, 223, 224–5 and n.
Estampes, 136, 137–8 and n., 144n., 313 and n.

'Fanfare', 150n.
Fantaisie for piano and orchestra, 23, 26, 28n., 30 and n., 32, 33–4n., 38, 81, 82n., 211–12 and n.
Fêtes galantes, 148
Les Frères en Art (F.E.A.), 96, 97n., 103n.

Gigues, 249, 252–3 and n., 259, 261, 266 and n.

Ibéria, xxi, 171, 172n., 185n., 217–18 and n., 229, 231, 243n., 274
Images for orchestra, xxi, 172n., 180 and n., 181, 184, 188, 204, 205, 266
Images for piano, 154, 155, 158, 168, 169n.
L'Isle joyeuse, 304 and n.

Jeux, 185n., 254, 259–65 and n., 271, 272, 273n., 278 and n., 288–9 and n., 323–4

Khamma, 230 and n., 236n., 255, 258, 259, 263n., 316–17, 318n.

Marche des anciens comtes de Ross, 88n.
Marche écossaise, 88 and n., 288
Le Martyre de Saint Sébastien, 226, 227n., 235, 236–7, 238–42 and n., 239, 241, 243, 246, 248, 250, 252, 266, 273, 285 and n., 286n., 334
Masques, 148
Masques et bergamasques, 206–10 and n.
La Mer, 137, 141, 145, 154, 155 and n., 158, 163 and n., 168, 179, 185, 186, 187n., 231, 252, 253n., 266n.

No-ya-li, 294 and n.; see also *Le Palais du silence*
Nocturnes, 103, 105, 108, 231, 318; composition, xxi, 42, 73, 75, 82, 86, 87, 93, 94, 98, 100; original title, 38, 39n.; dedication, 92n., 93; performances, 109, 112, 116–17 and n., 118n., 122, 155, 167n., 168, 288n., 309n.; publication, 111; corrections, 286 and n., 308
Les Nuits blanches, 105

Orpheus, 183, 196n.

Le Palais du silence, 294n.; see also *No-ya-li*
Pelléas et Mélisande, 59, 74n., 98, 105, 111, 141–2, 160, 164, 189, 190n., 191–2, 203n., 222, 273n., 285, 297, 312 and n., 318n.; composition, xvi, 50, 52, 54–6, 60–1, 63–4 and n., 70, 73 and n., 75, 76, 80, 86; orchestral draft, 81n.; première, xvii, 77n., 119, 120, 123n., 124 and n., 126, 130, 173; Debussy refuses to allow extracts to be performed, 87; dedication, 92n.; Fauré's version, 99–100; further French performances, 132, 174–5, 237 and

n., 247 and n.; publication, 135 and n.; Belgian première, 170, 172, 174–5; English performances, 184, 199, 200–2, 270 and n.; Italian première, 184n.; American performances, xviii, 199n., 223 and n., 226, 248, 252, 255; Viennese première, 212n.; Swiss première, 251 and n.; proposed revival at Opéra-comique, 269
Petite Suite, 231, 266, 267n.
La Plus que lente, 224 and n.
Pour le piano, 132n., 144n., 331
Prélude à l'après-midi d'un faune, 51, 82, 84–5, 98, 231; first performance, 50, 75n., 83n., 286n.; further performances, 108, 167n., 179, 187n., 197, 198n., 243n., 288n.; Mallarmé's opinion of, 218–19 and n.; ballet production, 254, 273n.
Préludes, 204, 259 and n., 266, 270, 286, 288n.
Printemps, 20–1 and n., 24, 26n., 197 and n., 266
Proses lyriques, 42, 43n., 47 and n., 52, 54n., 66n., 68, 69n., 88, 90n., 105, 144, 265n., 274

Rapsodie for saxophone and orchestra, 136, 137n., 158
Rodrigue et Chimène, 23, 34n.

Salammbô, 12–13
La Saulaie, 87, 88 and n., 105, 108, 109
Scènes au Crépuscule see *Nocturnes*
Siddhartha, 170, 181 and n., 182–3
Six Epigraphes, 296 and n.
'Le sommeil de Lear', 150 and n., 158
Sonata for cello and piano, 290, 299, 303 and n., 309, 315, 316n., 320n.
Sonata for flute, viola and harp, 290, 303 and n., 309, 318, 320
Sonata for violin and piano, 290, 319, 323, 324–5 and n., 327
String Quartet, xvi, 23, 42, 43n., 47, 60n., 65, 66n., 68, 75n., 122 and n., 230
Syrinx, 280n.

Tristan, 170, 180, 182 and n., 194
Trois Ballades de François Villon, 204
Trois Chansons de France, 146n., 195
Trois mélodies, 34n., 330n.

Trois poèmes de S. Mallarmé, 277 and
  n.

Zuleima, 8, 10n., 12–13

General Index

Page numbers in *italic* refer to the illustrations

Académie des Beaux-arts, 26n.
Accademia Santa Cecilia, 304n.
Adalbert, J., *Paysages de femmes*, 21
Aderer, Adolphe, 215n.; letter from Debussy, 215
Aeschylus, *Oresteia*, 209
Algeria, 72n., 73, 90n.
Alhambra Theatre, London, 294n.
Alheim, Baron Pierre d', 249, 251n.
Alioth, 123
Allan, Maud, 230 and n., 235, 259n., 263 and n., 318 and n., 321; letters from Debussy, 259, 316–17
Alomanz, 199
America, 38n., 197, 226, 247–8 and n., 252, 253, 255, 262, 321
Amsterdam, 230, 286
André, General, 139
Angyan, 233
Annamite theatre, 23
Ansermet, Ernest, 196n., 308, 309n.
Antibes, 189
Antoine, André, 150n.; letter from Debussy, 150
Antonietti, Mary, 198n.
Arcachon, 59 and n., 60n., 227n., 234, 244
Archimedes, 295n.
L'Art et la vie, 77

L'art moderne, 140n.
Asnières, 88, 90n.
L'Association chorale de Paris, 276n.
Astruc, Gabriel, 179n., 189, 277, 278–9, 286n.; letters from Debussy, 179, 202, 238–40, 279
Au Ménestrel, 92n.
Auberge du Clou, xvi, 141n.
Augusteo, Rome, 304n.
Austria, 226, 227–30, 231, 308
Auteuil, 286n.
Avellan, Admiral, 59

Babaïan, S., 174n.
Bach, J. S., 58, 70, 184, 269, 323, 330 and n.
Bachelet, Alfred, 45–6 and n.
Backer-Lunde, Johan, 295n.
Bailly, Edmond, 37, 57 and n., 61n., 65; bookshop, xvi, 23, 44n., 50; publishes *Proses lyriques*, 42; biographical note, 43n.; publishes *La Damoiselle élue*, 54n., 59
Bakst, Léon, 202n., 206n., 238, 239, 240n., *241*
Ballets Russes, xx, 206 and n., 221n., 273n.
Balzac, Honoré de, *La Grande Bretèche*, 82 and n.
Bambara tribe, 133
Banville, Théodore de, xv, 2; *Diane au bois*, 8, 10n.

[343]

Barczy, 233n.; letter from Debussy, 232–3

Bardac, Emma, *see* Debussy, Emma

Bardac, Hélène (Dolly), 146n., 243n., 335, 336n.

Bardac, Raoul, xv, 146n., 167n., 283n., 293, 294n., 335–6; letters from Debussy, 120–2, 164–7; *Hérodiade*, 122

Bardac, Sigismund, 146n., 167n.

Baring, Harriet, 214n.

Baron, Emile, 16n., 20n.; letters from Debussy, 18–21

Basques, 333

Bathori, Jane, 191n., 219n.; letter from Debussy, 191

Baudelaire, Charles, xv, xvii, 13n., 54n., 101, 333

Baudry, 15 and n.

Bauer, Emily Frances, 197 and n.

Bauer, Henry, 124n.; letter from Debussy, 124

Bax, Arnold, 198n.

Bayreuth, 23, 48n., 66n., 70, 72n.

Bazin, François, 261, 262n.

Becque, Henry, 18, 20n.; *Michel Pauper*, 20

Bédier, *Roman de Tristan*, 180

Beethoven, Ludwig van, 60, 77, 78n., 89, 168, 216, 292, 293n.

Bel-Ebat, 158, 260, 298, 299

Belgium, 295n., 313

Bellamy, 301

Bellevue, 265n.

Ben Brahim, Zorah, *91*

Benois, Alexandre, 202n., 206n.

Benoit, Camille, 24n.

Berlin, 221, 238n.

Berlioz, Hector, xix, 41, 140, 230n.

Bernac, Jean, *Le poison noir*, 327 and n.

Biarritz, 255, 332

Bichain, 120, 122n., 135, 136

Bidou, Henry, 333–4 and n.

Bihari, Janos, 230n.

Biskra, 70, 72n., 136

Bizet, Georges, xix, 72

Blanche, Jacques Emile, *19*, 44n., 285, 286n.

Bloch, Ernest, 272, 273n., 317, 318 and n., 321

Bloy, *Sueur de sang*, 57 and n.

Boieldieu, François Adrien, *La Dame Blanche*, 130 and n.

Bois, Jules, xv; letter from Debussy, 35; *Les Noces de Satan*, 35n.

Bois de Boulogne, 117, 272

Boito, Arrigo, *Nerone*, 212–14 and n.

Bonaparte, Princess Charlotte, 3n.

Bonaparte, Princess Mathilde, 4n., 18n.

Bonheur, Raymond, 27, 48, 74n., 81–2; friendship with Debussy, xii, xvi, xvii, 23, 54n.; letters from Debussy, 30, 80; biographical note, 31n.

Bonnières, Robert de, 52, 54n.

Bonniot, Dr, 277

Bordeaux, 332

Bordeaux Opera House, 284 and n.

Bordes, Charles, 43n., 74n., 332n., 333, 334n.

Boston, xviii, 226, 247–8 and n., 253, 255

Boston Opera House, 194, 223 and n.

Boston Orchestral Club, 137n.

Bouchardy, Joseph, 56, 57n.

Bouchor, Maurice, xv, 28n.; *Tobie*, 28 and n.

Boulez, Pierre, 50

Boulogne, M., 269, 270n.

Bour, Armand, 238n.

Bourbon, Jean, xix, 199, 200n.

Bourgeat, General, 112, 130n.

Bourgeois, *Le Bossu*, 56, 57n.

Bourget, Paul, xv, 2, 11 and n., 12, 16, 21 and n., 40, 88

Boyer, Georges, 10n.

Brahms, Johannes, 234

Brayer, Jules de, 28, 30n., 33

Bréval, Lucienne, xiii

Bréville, Pierre de, 24n., 265n.; letter from Debussy, 66

Bruneau, Alfred, xiii, xx, 82n., 110, 187; letter from Debussy, 82; *Messidor*, 90, 92n.

Brussels, 60, 65, 68, 170, 172, 174–5, 254

Brussels Conservatoire, 140n.

Bucci (operatic tenor), 56

Budapest, 225, 226, 230–1, 234–5

Burger, M., 35

Busoni, Ferruccio, 211n., 222n., 282
Busser, Henry, 126, 128n., 197n., 208

Café Pousset, xv
Café Vachette, 28, 30n.
Café Weber, xv, xvi, 133n.
Caine, Hall, 295n.
Callot sisters, 108
Calvocoressi, M. D., xix, 221; letter from Debussy, 211
Campanini, Cleofonte, 199 and n., 200, 201
Campbell, Mrs Patrick, 100n.
Cannes, 1, 189, 190n., 247
Cap Ferrat, 319
Caplet, André, xvii, 185, 207, 214, 223n., 285n.; friendship with Debussy, xiv, xix, 204, 208n.; compositions, 190, 202; musical collaboration with Debussy, 192, 208n., 225n., 226, 289n., 334n.; letters from Debussy, 206–7, 212–14, 216–18, 224–5, 238, 244–6, 247–8, 252–3, 261–2, 264–5, 270, 274, 315–16; in First World War, 318; death, 316n.
Cardiff, 185
Carjat, Etienne, 333, 334n.
Carlyle, Thomas, xv, 212, 214n.
Carnot, Sadi, 218, 219n.
Caron, Rose, 182n.
Carré, Albert, 98, 99n., 105, 119, 120, 121, 123, 191, 274; letters from Debussy, 123–4, 215–16
Carré, Marguerite, 237n., 269, 270n.
Carrière, 59n.
Carvalho, 78n., 94n.
Casino Saint Pierre, Geneva, 312n.
Chabrier, Alexis Emmanuel, Briséis, 142–3 and n.
Chaliapin, Fedor, 179n., 202
Chamberlain, Houston Stewart, 83 and n.
Charlot, André, 294
Charlot, Jacques, 262, 263n., 294
Charpentier, Gustave, xix, xx, 89, 97, 140, 216; Louise, 105 and n., 110–11 and n., 117; La Vie du Poète, 41, 43n.
Chassaigne, Anna-Marie (Liane de Pougy), 117, 118n., 137 and n.

Le Chat Noir, xv, 92n., 102n., 141n.
Chateaubriand, François-René, Vicomte de, 195, 229n.
Chausson, Ernest, 24n., 27, 44n., 57n., 74n., 78n.; friendship with Debussy, xii-xiii, xvi, 23; letters from Debussy, 24, 44–9, 51–62, 64–70; Le roi Arthus, 45n., 54n., 58; Ballade, 46n.; quarrels with Debussy, xvii, 50, 60n.; death, xvii
Chausson, Mme, 45, 47n., 49, 54n., 56, 68, 69
Chauvet, René, 284n.
Chénier, André, 305
Chesterton, G. K., The Napoleon of Notting Hill, 321
Chevillard, Camille, 157, 158, 231, 277; Debussy critical of, xix, 117, 155, 162–3, 164, 180; conducts Debussy's works, 116, 155n., 252, 253n., 266, 313n.; biographical note, 117n.
Chicago, 224–5
China, 261
Chinese Exhibition (1910), 221
Choisnel, Gaston, 158 and n., 205, 255, 263, 299, 323, 334n.
Chopin, Frédéric, 1, 51, 158, 219, 220n., 296 and n., 297–8, 299, 300–2 and n.
Choudens, 211n.
Christen, Jules, 109–10
Civil Code, 321
Clarens, 250
Clemenceau, Georges, 198 and n.
Colette, 85n.
Colonne, Edouard, 108, 112, 158, 166, 168, 172, 180, 186, 187n., 266 and n.
Colonne Concerts, 81, 83n., 112, 167n., 185, 189, 211n., 218n., 253n., 266n.
Colonne Orchestra, 289n.
Comédie des Champs-Elysées, 276n.
Commune, xii, 1, 291n.
Compagnie Fives-Lille, 18n.
Concertgebouw Orchestra, 288n.
Concerts Lamoureux, 30n., 111n., 117n., 122, 144n., 155n., 167n., 253n.

Conrad, Joseph, xv; *The Secret Agent*, 221
Conseil supérieur du Conservatoire, 170
Conservatoire, xiv, xv, xvi, xix, 1, 64n., 153 and n., 179, 185n., 203n., 205, 211n., 216, 217n., 221n., 223n., 247n., 283n., 292n., 319
Coppier, André-Charles, 67
Coronio, Nicolas, 162n.; letters from Debussy, 162, 292–3
Cortot, Alfred, 212n.
Costallat, 142n.
Côte-d'Or, 1
Coulomb, 215 and n.
Couperin, François, 300
Courrier musical, 220n.
Covent Garden, 128n., 200n., 201, 238n., 270n.
Cowen, Sir Frederick, 295n.
Cozanet, Albert, 162n.
Crespel, Dr, 276
Crickboom Quartet, 78n.
Cros, Charles, xv, 28n., 31n.
Curnonsky (Maurice Sailland), 85n., 133n., 136, 139
Czech Philharmonic Orchestra, 285n.
Czerny, Karl, 283

Daily Telegraph, 295
Dalimier, M., 292 and n.
Damrosch, Walter, 38n.
d'Annunzio, Gabriele, xx, 214n., 230, 253, 319; letters from Debussy, 227, 233–4, 236–7, 242, 273; *Le Martyre de Saint Sébastien*, 226, 227n., 235, 236–7, 238, 242; *La Pisanelle ou la mort parfumée*, 273n.
Danube, River, 234
Dardel, Otto de, 28 and n.
De Bussy, Abbé, 43n.
Debussy, Alfred, 218, 219n.
Debussy, Claude: character, xi–xii; relations with women, xiii; friends, xiii–xiv, xvii; relations with his parents, xiv; early life, 1–2; at the Villa Medici, 2, 5–22, 9; and Gaby Dupont, 23, 50, 70n., 86, 88–9, 103; engagement to Thérèse Roger, 50, 60n., 66 and n.; marriage to

Lilly Texier, xvi–xvii, 86, 108–9 and n., 145, 149n.; ill-health, 98–9, 112, 204; leaves Lilly for Emma Bardac, xvii, 145, 146, 149n.; divorce, 145, 150, 155n., 156, 162n.; biographies of, 170; conducting career, 170, 179–80, 186, 187 and n., 266n.; depression, 204, 206–8, 250; marriage to Emma Bardac, xvii, 221n., 281–3; financial problems, 226; in Vienna, 227–30, 231; in Budapest, 230–1; in Turin, 242–3; visit to Russia, 272, 280–4; portraits, 285, 286n.; in the First World War, 290–334; cancer, 290, 310 and n., 313, 314, 315, 317; death, 290, 335–6
Debussy, Claude-Emma (Chouchou, Debussy's daughter), xviii, *165*, 187, 203, 204, 208n., 228, 233, 243 and n., *245*, 250, 253, 261, 272, 283n., 310; birth, xvii, 145, 167 and n.; letters from Debussy, 229, 283–4; ill-health, 205, 206, 236, 277, 309, 316, 317; fantasy on *Petrushka*, 265; piano lessons, 268, 269–70, 330, 332; letter to Raoul Bardac, 335–6; death, 336n.
Debussy, Emma (formerly Emma Bardac, Debussy's 2nd wife), xix, *151*, 167n., *281*, 304; Debussy leaves Lilly for, xvii, 145, 146, 149n.; letters from Debussy, 146, 227–8, 229–30, 280–3, 310, 322; biographical note, 146n.; ill-health, xviii, 166, 236, 242–3, 259, 272, 276, 309, 317; refuses to let Debussy go to America, xviii, 248n.; in the First World War, 291, 292, 293; and Debussy's death, 335
Debussy, Rosalie (Lilly Texier, Debussy's 1st wife), *107*, 113, 126–8; marriage to Debussy, xvi, 86, 106n., 108–9; letters from Debussy, 105–6, 131, 147–8; ill-health, 114 and n.; Debussy leaves, xvi–xvii, 145, 149n., 150, 152n., 156
Debussy, Manuel-Achille (Debussy's father), xii, xiv, 1, 17, 224–5, 291n.; letter from Debussy, 200–1

Debussy-Manoury, Victorine
(Debussy's mother), xiv, 1, 40, 278;
letters from Debussy, 200–1
Degas, Edgar, 38n., 59n.
Delibes, Léo, 292n.
Delmet, Paul, xv, 90, 101
Demest, Désiré, 88 and n.
Denis, Maurice, 53, 54n., 61n., 66n.
d'Ennery, Adolphe, 56, 57n.
Depanis, Giuseppe, 256 and n.
Desjardins, Dr Abel, 108n.; letters
from Debussy, 108
Desrousseaux, Mme, 54
Deutsch, M., 278
Diaghilev, Serge de, xix, 204, 221,
230n., 238n., 260, 273n., 277, 282;
concerts at the Opéra, 179n.; Le
Festin, 202n.; asks Debussy to write
ballet music, 205–6, 210; first Paris
season, 206n.; Jeux, 254, 259, 260,
262–3; letters from Debussy,
326–7
Dickens, Charles, xv
d'Indy, Vincent, xv, xix, 24n., 52,
54n., 74n., 142n., 211n., 218n.,
306; Fervaal, 267 and n.; Un jour
d'été à la montagne, 164, 167n.;
letter from Debussy, 30
Dives, 246
Doire, René, 219n.; letter from
Debussy, 219
Doret, Gustave, xvii, 78n., 286n.,
307n., 308, 312; letters from
Debussy, 286, 307
Dranem (Armand Menard), 189,
190n.
Dubois, 114
Dubus, Edouard, 35; Quand les
violons sont partis, 36n.
Ducasse, Roger, 137n., 227n., 326n.,
335; letter from Debussy, 325
Dufranne, Hector, 173n.; letter from
Debussy, 173
Dujardin, Edouard, 46 and n., 47,
83n.
Dukas, Paul, xv, 125, 223 and n.,
285n., 292 and n., 312–13; Ariane
et Barbe-bleue, xiv, 178 and n.,
189, 190n., 256; friendship with
Debussy, xvii, xx, 64n.; letters from
Debussy, 64, 117–18, 178; Sym-

phony in C, 89, 90n.; on Debussy's
Nocturnes, 118n.; La Péri,
267n.
Dulac, Edmond, 333
Dumas, Alexandre, xv; La Dame de
Monsoreau, 56, 57n.; Francillon,
21n.
Duparc, Henri, 74n.
Dupin, Etienne, 47, 48n., 56, 81–2
Dupont, Gabriel, 285n.
Dupont, Gaby, xvi, 23, 34n., 50, 55,
70n., 86, 88–9, 92, 103
Dupuis, Sylvain, xix, 176n.; letter
from Debussy, 175–6
Durand, Jacques, xii, xiii, xviii, xxi,
142n., 159, 173n., 177, 209n., 217,
252–3, 315, 320, 326n; letters
from Debussy, 137–8, 148, 150–2,
153–5, 158, 162–3, 168–9, 171,
174–5, 177, 179–80, 181–2, 184,
188–90, 191–2, 195, 197–8, 199,
201, 202–3, 205–6, 220–1,
222–4, 231, 242–4, 246–7,
248–9, 253, 255, 258–9, 260–1,
262–4, 266–7, 276–9, 285, 289,
291–2, 293–4, 296–302, 305,
312–13, 316, 318–20, 323–4, 331,
334; publishes Debussy's music,
xix, 43n., 60n., 77, 78n., 137n.,
145, 149n., 155n., 192n., 206n.
Durand Ruel, 169
Duval, Paul (Jean Lorrain), 76, 77n.

Eastbourne, 153, 156
Echo de Paris, 77n., 85n., 94n.
Echo de Paris illustré, 142n.
Edinburgh, 197
Elgar, Sir Edward, 295n.
Eliot, George, 16 and n.
Emery, M., 196
Engel, Emile, 191 and n., 219n.
England, 185, 186–7, 199–201, 270
English Channel, 181
Enoch, Messrs and Company, letters
from Debussy, 142–4
Enoch, Wilhelm, 142n.
Entretiens politiques et littéraires,
90n.
Erb, 78n.
Erlanger, Camille, 292 and n.; Le Juif
polonais, 105 and n.

Ernst, Alfred, 46n., 85n.
Eusellugvar, 230
Excelsior, 266n.

Falla, Manuel de, xiv, 176n.; letter
from Debussy, 176
Fashoda affair, 102n.
Fauré, Gabriel, xix, 54n., 66n., 78n.,
99–100 and n., 135n., 153n., 283n.,
326n.; *La Bonne Chanson*, 146n.;
letters from Debussy, 153, 220, 324;
Pavane, 326, 327n.; *Pénélope*, 274,
276n.
Féart, Rose, xix, 199, 200n., 201, 238
and n.
Ferrier, Paul, *Chilpéric*, 77, 78n.
Le Festin, 202n.
Feure, Georges de, 294n.
Féval, *Le Bossu*, 56, 57n.
Le Figaro, 82n., 92n., 94, 123n.,
124n., 152n., 224n.
First World War, 290–334
Fiumicino, 10–11, 17n.
Fiumiselino, 16, 17n.
'Five, The', 179n.
Flaubert, Gustave, 13n., 18, 54n., 195
Fleurville, Antoinette Mauté de, 1, 301
Flon, Philippe, 189, 190n.
Fodor, M. de, 233
Fokine, Michel, 230n., 238n.
Folies Bergères, 202
Fontaine, G., 64
Fontaine, Lucien, 74 and n., 82n.,
109n.
Fontaine family, 66n., 108
Fontenailles, Count Hercule de, 122
Forain, Jean-Louis, 89, 90n.
Fournier, P., 331
Fragerolle, Georges, 101, 102n.
Franck, César, 56, 66n., 307 and n.
French Institute, 20n.
Friedman, Ignaz, 296 and n.
Fromont, Eugène, 43n., 113, 135n.,
141, 142n., 286n., 308
Fuchs, Henriette, letter from Debussy,
4

Ganne, Louis, 140, 141n.
Garden, Mary, xiii, 100n., 126, 128n.,
130–1 and n., 175n., 191, 192n.,
223n., 264

Gatti-Casazza, Giulio, 194n., 202;
letter to Debussy, 194
Gauguin, Paul, 66n.
Gauthier-Villars, Henri (Willy), 85n.,
109, 110n., 164, 167n.; letter from
Debussy, 84–5
Gautier, Judith, 45n.
Gautier, Théophile, 2
Gémier, Firmin, 328 and n., 329, 334
Geneva, 251 and n., 309n., 312n.
Geneva Conservatory, 333
Georges, Léone, 188n.
Gérard, General, 132n.
Gerband, M., 235
German, Edward, 295n.
Germany, 215, 233, 237, 292–3, 298,
305, 308, 319, 327
Ghent, 60
Gheusi, P. B., 285 and n., 289 and n.
Gide, André, xv, 72n., 73, 74n., 75n.,
90n., 280n.; letters from Debussy,
280; *Le Voyage d'Urien*, 61n.
Gigout, Eugène, 162n.
Gil Blas, xix, 119, 135n.
Giordano, Umberto, 155 and n.
Gluck, Christoph Willibald, 135n.,
172, 183, 293n.
Godet, Robert, xii, xiv, xv, xvii, 23,
28n., 29, 34n., 251n.; letters from
Debussy, 26–8, 31–4, 109–10,
128–30, 234–6, 249–51, 269–70,
272–3, 294–5, 305–6, 310–12,
314, 317–18, 320–2, 324–5, 327,
332–4
Goethe, Johann Wolfgang von, 309;
The Bride of Corinth, 142n.; *The
Elective Affinities*, 295
Gounod, Charles François, 14, 41,
43n., 190
Goya y Lucientes, Francisco José de,
297
Granada, 136
Grand Guignol, 327n.
Grande Revue, 187 and n.
Gravollet, Paul, 123n.
Greece, 301
Greffulhe, Countess, 167, 168n.
Grey, Lady, 270
Grieg, Edvard, 57n., 189
Groux, Henry de, 36n., 57n., 249–50,
251n.; *Christ aux outrages*, 249

Gruet, Charles, letter from Debussy, 284
Gui, Vittorio, 243n.; letter from Debussy, 256
Guide musical, 68
Guiraud, Ernest, 16, 17n., 64n., 78n., 102n., 128n.
Gulon, 141

The Hague, 254
Hahn, Reynaldo, 101
Hall, Elise, 137n., 158
Hamelle, xix
Hammerstein, Oscar I, 223 and n.
Handel, George Frideric, 185
Harper's Weekly, 197n.
Hartmann, Georges, 78 and n., 79, 80, 81, 86, 92n., 112, 113, 230 and n.; letters from Debussy, 92–3, 97–101, 103, 104–5, 108–9, 111–12
Hauptmann, Gerhart, xv; *Les Tisserands*, 96, 97n.
Le Havre, 246
Hayot, 144 and n.
Hébert, Ernest, 10, 11n., 16, 17
Heine, Heinrich, *Almanzor*, 10n.
Hellé, André, 287, 289 and n.
Helmann, 52, 54n.
Hérédia, José-Maria de, 89, 90n.
Hérédia, Louise, *see* Louÿs, Louise
Hérold, A. Ferdinand, 75n., 77 and n., 298n.
Hérold, Louis, 77n.
Hervé, 78n.
Heugel, Henri-Georges, xix, 92 and n.
Higgins, 199
Hochon, M., 16
Hocquet, Vital, 54n.
Hofmann, Josef, 179n.
Holland, 26
Hôtel Gonnet, 188
Hotel Hungarian, 233
Houlgate, 244–6, *245*
Hüe, 78n.
Hugo, Victor, 61, 122n., 195
Hungary, 226, 230–1, 234–5
Huret, Jules, 94n.; letter from Debussy, 93–4

Ibsen, Henrik, 124n.

Inghelbrecht, D. E., 273n., 286n.; letters from Debussy, 285–6, 302–3, 330
L'Initiation, 35
Italy, 1, 2, 5–22, 187, 206, 242–3, 304

Jacques-Dalcroze, E., 272, 273n.
Jaëll, Marie, 302 and n.
Jammes, Francis, 31n.
Japan, 158n., 298
Javanese music, 23, 76, 77n.
Jean, Albert, *Le poison noir*, 327 and n.
Jean-Aubry, Georges, xix, 186n., 209n.; letters from Debussy, 185, 190, 214, 218–19
Jehin, 59, 60n., 63
Jersey, 148
Jesus Christ, 244
Joan of Arc, 293n.
Jobert, 286n.
Joffre, Marshal, 314
Joinville, 246
Le Journal, 77n., 113n., 116
Jusseaume, 123, 124n.

Kant, Immanuel, 210
Karsavina, Tamara, 210, *271*, 273n.
Keats, John, 28 and n.
Kerpely, 233n.
King Albert's Book, 295 and n.
Koussevitsky, Serge, 282 and n., 283
Kufferath, Maurice, 68, 69n.
Kunc, 78n.
Kursaal, Montreux, 196n.

La Fontaine, Jean de, 298
La Jeunesse, Ernest, 89, 90n.
La Scala, Milan, 184n.
Labergement Sainte-Marie, 82n.
Lacerda, Francisco de, xiv, 172–3 and n., 196n.; letter from Debussy, 196
Laforgue, Jules, xv, 43, 48n., 123n., 149n., 302.; *Complaintes*, 47 and n.; *Moralités légendaires*, 47 and n.; *Notre-Dame de la Lune*, 47
Lalo, Edouard, 212; *Namouna*, 116 and n.
Lalo, Pierre, xix, xx, 116n., 164n.,

189, 190n., 194n., 212, 214n., 218 and n.; letters from Debussy, 116, 163–4, 192–4

Laloy, Louis, xix, *143*, 144n., 145, 162n., 170, 173n., 174n., 178n., 180, 205–6 and n., 223, 265 and n., 312, 333, 334; letters from Debussy, 144, 152–3, 156, 160–2, 167–8, 172–4, 176–8, 209–10

Lamoureux, Charles, xix, 26, 28, 30n., 32–3 and n., 117n.; *see also* Concerts Lamoureux

Landormy, Paul, 144 and n., 220n.

Lange-Müller, Peter, 295n.

Laparra, Raoul, *Alyssa*, 135n.

Larousse, 59n.

Larue (restaurant), 238, 240n.

Lassus, Orlando de, 14

Lausanne, 279

Le Bargy, 105 and n.

Le Nôtre, André, 297

Leblanc, Georgette, 123n.

Lehmann, Liza, 295n.

Lenormand, René, 260n.; letter from Debussy, 259–60

Leonardo da Vinci, 255

Leoncavallo, Ruggiero, 135

Lerolle, Henri, xii, xvi, xvii, xxi, *52*, *59* and n., 64, 70n., 74n.; letters from Debussy, 72–4, 80–2

Lerolle, Mme, 81

Levadé, Charles, xxi, 141n.; letter from Debussy, 140–1

Liapunov, 179n.

Librairie de l'art indépendant, xv

Libre esthétique, 66n., 155n.

Liebich, Franz, 219n.

Liszt, Franz, 232, 301, 302n., 333; *Faust Symphony*, 117; *Feux follets*, 331

Lockspeiser, Edward, 97n., 100n., 251n.

London, 160, 170, 179, 186–7 and n., 196n., 199–201

Long, Marguerite, 325, 326n., 330

Lorrain, Jean (Paul Duval), 76, 77n.

Louis, Dr Rudolf, 128–30

Louis, Saint, King of France, 246

Louÿs, Louise (née Hérédia), 90n., 104

Louÿs, Pierre, xiii, xiv, xvii, 43n., 62, 75n., 105n., 109n., 110n., 280n.;

friendship with Debussy, xii, xv, xvi, 23, 50, 60, 61n., 70n., 147n.; photography, *55*, *71*, *115*; letters from Debussy, 61, 70–2, 76–8, 83–4, 88–92, 94–5, 101–2, 103–4, 110–11, 112–13, 114–15, 116–17, 120, 134, 136–7, 146–7; biographical note, 61n.; visits Algeria, 70, 72n., 74, 90n.; *Chansons de Bilitis*, 76, 77n., 94, 101–2 and n., 296n.; *Cendrelune*, 78 and n., 89, 94; *Aphrodite*, 83, 84 and n.; marriage, 86, 90n., 104–5; translates *La Saulaie*, 88; at the première of *Louise*, 111n.; *Les aventures du Roi Pausole*, 112, 113 and n.

Lucian of Samothrace, *Scenes from Courtesans' Life*, 105 and n.

Ludwig II, King of Bavaria, 36, 38n.

Lugné-Poë, 100n.

Luxembourg gardens, 302

Lyon Opera, 190n.

M. Croche antidilettante, 174n.

Mackenzie, Sir Alexander, 295n.

Maeterlinck, Maurice, *125*, 180, 278, 316; *Pelléas et Mélisande*, 50, 54n., 60–1 and n., 99, 100n., 119, 123 and n., 130, 223n.

Maguenat, 274, 276n.

Maillart, Aimé, *Les Dragons de Villars*, 216, 217n.

La Maison de l'Oeuvre, 100n.

Mallarmé, Stéphane, 36n., 38n., 48n., 50, 75n., 164, 218–19 and n.; salon, xv, xvi, 23, 61n., 75n., 77n.; sonnets, 58; letter from Debussy, 75; banquet for the publication of *Divagations*, 89, 90n.

Mallarmé family, 277

Manchester, 186n., 197

Maquet, *La Dame de Monsoreau*, 56, 57n.

Marcoux, Vanni, 199, 200n.; letter from Debussy, 200

Marlborough, Duke of, 13

Marmontel, 185n.

Marnold, Jean, 162n., 174n., 183n.

Marot, Blanche, 102n., 142; letter from Debussy, 114

Marty, Georges, 5, 6n.
Mascagni, Pietro, 295n.
Massenet, Jules, 56, 90, 92n., 215n.;
 Manon, 149n.; *Werther*, 41
Massine, Léonide, *Las Meninas*, 326,
 327n.
Mauclair, Camille, xv, 75n., 99,
 100n., 142n.
Maupassant, Guy de, 4n., 72
Maus, Octave, 66n., 140n.; letter
 from Debussy, 139
Meck, Mme von, xiv, 1, 60n.
Mellot-Joubert, Mme, 190
Melun, 293
Menard, Armand (Dranem), 189,
 190n.
Mendès, Catulle, xv, 23, 34n., 44,
 45n., 46 and n., 110, 142 and n.
Mercier, Henry, 28 and n.
Mercin, 81, 82n.
Mercure de France, 83, 84n., 183n.
Mercure musical, 156 and n., 160,
 162n., 173, 174, 181n., 183n.
Merolle, Mme, 74
Messager, André, xiv, xvii, 56, 57n.,
 98, 119, 124, 127, 128n., 295n.;
 letters from Debussy, 126–7,
 130–1, 135, 141–2, 149
Messager, Madeleine, 128, 149
Metropolitan Opera, New York, 194
 and n., 199n.
Meyerbeer, Giacomo, xv, 13, 18; *Les
 Huguenots*, 110, 111n.
Midi, 255
Mikhaël, Ephraim, 142n.
Milan, 179
Millet, Jean François, *L'Angélus*,
 122n.; *Les Glaneuses*, 122n.
Mily-Meyer, Emilie, 189, 190n.
Missa, Edmond, 150n.
Molinari, Bernardo, 304n.; letter from
 Debussy, 303–4
Molnár, 233 and n.
Monet, Claude, 313
Montépin, Xavier de, 88, 90n.
Montreux, 196 and n., 309n.
Moréas, Jean, 28, 30n.
Moreau-Santi, Mme, 4n.
Morice, Charles, xiv, 75n.
Mors, Mme, 279, 280n.
Moscheles, 296n.

Moscow, 249, 254, 280–3, 298, 300
Le Moulleau, 290, 318
Mourey, Gabriel, xiv, xviii-xix, 170,
 180, 181n., 182, 198n., 328n.;
 letters from Debussy, 198, 279–80;
 Psyché, 280n.
Mouton, Henri, 224 and n.
Mozart, Wolfgang Amadeus,
 Idomeneo, 267 and n.
Musica, 153, 190
La musique en Suisse, 130n.
Mussorgsky, Modest, 249, 251n.;
 Boris Godunov, 30n., 179 and n.,
 192, 194n., 235

Nadar, *213*
Napoleon I, Emperor, 249
Neuilly, 61n.
New York, 318n.
Nice, 247 and n.
Nicholas, Grand Duke, 300
Nietzsche, Friedrich Wilhelm, xv, 111
Nijinsky, 206n., 210, 221, 260–1,
 271, 272, 273n., 277, 323
Nin, Joaquín, 330, 331n.
Noirmoutiers, 293
Normandy, 253n., 274
Nouvelle revue, 21 and n.
Nouvelle Revue Française, 280
Novaes, Guiomar, 217n.

Offenbach, Jacques, *La Grande-
 duchesse de Gerolstéin*, 137n.
Ohnet, Georges, 18, 20n.
Olénine, Marie, 249, 251n.
Ollendorf, 138
Olonne, Max d', 78n.
Opéra, Paris, xv, 42, 44, 92n., 116,
 179n., 278, 279
Opéra-comique, Paris, 43n., 78n., 93,
 94n., 105n., 124n., 128., 173n.,
 178n., 182n., 189, 289; *Pelléas et
 Mélisande* at, 86, 99n., 126, 191,
 269, 270n., 274, 285; and *Le
 Diable dans le beffroi*, 142n.
Orléans, Charles d', 286

Palestrina, Giovanni Pierluigi da, 14,
 42, 45
Pan, 237, 238n.

Paris Universal Exhibition (1889), 23, 77n., 114n.
Parma, Ildebrando da, 273n.
Pau, 255
Péladan, Joseph, 36n.
Périer, Casimir, 72, 74n.
Périer, Jean, 126, 128n., 192, 269, 274, 276n.
Perron, Louis, 284n.
Peter, Alice, 97n.; letter from Debussy, 96–7
Peter, René, xiii, xx, 95 and n., 97, 123n., 150n.; letters from Debussy, 95–6, 102–3, 106, 123; *Le Roman de Rosette*, 103; *Tragédie de la mort*, 95n., 96n.
Petrograd, 300
Philipp, Isidor, 217n.
Pierné, Gabriel, xvi, 5, 6n., 185n., 218n., 252, 253n., 266, 289n., 309n.; *La fille de Tabarin*, 105 and n.; letters from Debussy, 185, 288–9
Pissarro, Camille, 66n.
Pitt, Percy, 199
Planchet, 78n.
Planté, Francis, 189, 190n., 331 and n.
Plato, 137
Poe, Edgar Allan, xv, xviii, 33n., 51, 109n., 205, 235, 250, 252, 264n., 316; *The Devil in the Belfry*, 138–9 and n., 142n., 170; *The Fall of the House of Usher*, 54n., 139n., 170; *The Narrative of Arthur Gordon Pym of Nantucket*, 9n.
Poictevin, Francis, 57, 59n.
Poincaré, Raymond, 255n.
Polignac, Armande, de, 160, 162n.
Polignac, Prince Edmond de, 77, 78n.
Poniatowski, Prince André, xiv, 38n., 43n.; letters from Debussy, 36–43
Popelin-Ducarre, Claudius, 18n.; letter from Debussy, 17
Popelin-Ducarre, Gustave, 17, 18n.
Porte Saint-Martin, 57, 95n.
Pothier, 141
Pougy, Liane de, 117, 118n., 137 and n.
Poulenc, Francis, xiv, 307 and n.; letter from Debussy, 307

Poulet, Gaston, 276n., 324n.
Pourville, *151*, 290, 297, 298n., 301, 305
Prager Tageblatt, 285
Prague, 237, 285
Primoli, Giuseppe, 3n., 11, 16, 17n.; letter from Debussy, 3
Prince of Wales theatre, London, 100
Prix de Rome, 2, 3, 5, *9*, 135 and n., 141n., 292n.
Proust, Marcel, xiii, 78n., 95n., 168n.
Puccini, Giacomo, 140, 234, 242, 273n.; *Manon Lescaut*, 56, 57n.
Pugno, Raoul, 45n., 81
Pujo, Maurice, 78n.
Puvis de Chavannes, Pierre, 59n., 76
Pyrenees, 114
Pythagoras, 295, 309

Queen's Hall, London, 196n.
Quillard, P., 75n.
Quittard, Henri, 35n.

Radics, 232, 234–5
Rahon par Chaussin, 209
Rachmaninov, Sergei, 179n.
Rameau, Jean Philippe, 172, 173n., 262 and n., 264, 293n., 306; *La Guirlande*, 135 and n.
Ranger Gull, Cyril A. E. (Guy Thorne), 268n.
Ravel, Maurice, xix, xx, 66n., 135n., 168, 177–8, 211n., 251n., 263n.; *Histoires naturelles*, 177 and n.; *Jeux d'eau*, 331; *Trois poèmes de S. Mallarmé*, 277 and n.
Redon, Odilon, 44n., 66n., 268; letter from Debussy, 43
Régnier, Henri de, xv, 39n., 43n., 48n., 51–2
Renan, Ernest, *L'abbesse de Jouarre*, 20n.
Renard, Jules, xv, 177n., 208
Renoir, Auguste, 66n.
Reszke, Jean de, 126, 128n.
Revue blanche, xix, 85n., 119
Revue bleue, 144
Revue hebdomadaire, 118n.
Revue indépendante, 20, 21
Revue wagnérienne, 46 and n.
Reynold's Bar, xv

Rheims, 293
Rhodes, Cecil, 244
Richepin, Jean, *Braves Gens*, 18–20
Riemann, Hugo, 183 and n.
Rigaud, M. de, 234
Rimbaud, Arthur, 28n.
Rimsky-Korsakov, Nikolai, 78n.; *Le Coq d'Or*, 211 and n.; *Ivan the Terrible*, 202n.; *Schéhérazade*, 164, 167n.
Rist, Edouard, 110 and n.
Rivière, Jacques, 280
Robert, Paul, 70, 72n.
Rodin, Auguste, 59n., 249
Roger, Thérèse, xvi, xvii, 50, 60n., 66 and n., 67, 68, 69n.
Rollan-Mauger, Mme, 312 and n.
Rome, 2, 5–22, 179, 254, 256, 286, 301, 304
Romilly, Mme Gérard de, 109n., 132n.; letter from Debussy, 131–2
Ronsin, Eugène, 123, 124n.
Rosoor, Louis, 319 and n., 320n.
Rossetti, Dante Gabriel, xv, 26n., 33; *La Saulaie*, 87, 88n., 109
Rostand, Edmond, *Cyrano de Bergerac*, 94, 95n.
Rouquairol, Mme, 59, 65
Roussel, Albert, 211n., 285n.
Royal Philharmonic Society, 212n.
Royan, 59, 63
Rubinstein, Anton, 37
Rubinstein, Ida, 227n., 230 and n., 237
Rumbold, 266
Rummel, Walter, xiv, 330n., 333; letter from Debussy, 329–30
Russell, Henry, 223, and n., 234 and n., 248n., 255, 264, 265n.; letter from Debussy, 248
Russia, 1, 158n., 192, 248, 249–50 and n., 272, 280–4, 298, 299, 300, 331

Sailland, Maurice (Curnonsky), 85n., 133n., 136, 139
Saint-Germain-en-Laye, 1, 286n.
Saint-Gervais, 42, 43n., 57
Le Saint Graal, 35n.
St Jean-de-Luz, 290, 326n., 329n., 330–1, 333

Saint-Loubès, 187, 268 and n.
Saint-Marceaux, Mme de, 64, 66n.
St Petersburg, 282, 283
Saint-Saëns, Camille, xv, 215n., 295n., 301, 302n.; *La Princesse jaune*, 216n.; *Samson et Dalila*, 252
Salle d'Harcourt, 78n.
Salle Gaveau, 169n., 324n.
Salle Pleyel, 24, 75n.
Salon d'Automne, 249
'Salon de la Rose-Croix', 36n.
Salon des Beaux Arts, Brussels, 251n.
Salon du Champ de Mars, Paris, 251n.
Salvayre, Gaston, 18; *Egmont*, 20n.
Samain, Albert, 31n.
San Martino, Count Enrico di, 304 and n.
Santa Maria dell'Anima, Rome, 14, 15n.
Satie, Erik, xvii, 35n., 36n., 109n., 141n., 196 and n., 253 and n., 257, 291
Satory, 1
Savoy, 269
Schmitt, Florent, *La tragédie de Salomé*, 273n.
Schoenberg, Arnold, xx, 292, 293n., 306; *Pierrot lunaire*, 307n.
Schola Cantorum, 156n., 196 and n., 211n., 218n., 267n.
Schollar, 271
Scholtz, Hermann, 296 and n.
Schopenhauer, Artur, xv, 28
Schott, 78 and n.
Schumann, Robert, 158, 220n.
Scriabin, Alexander, 179n.
Séchiari, Pierre, 198 and n.
Segalen, Victor, xii, xiv, xix, 170, 181n., 196n., 315.; *Dans un monde sonore*, 183 and n., 186; letters from Debussy, 180–1, 182–3, 186–7, 195, 314–15
Segard, Achille, 101, 102n.
Seidl, Anton, 38n.
Selva, Blanche, 156n., 217, 218n., 222n.
Sens, 136, 139
Séverac, Déodat de, xiv, 156 and n.
Seville, 76, 77n.
Shakespeare, William, *As You Like It*, 132–4 and n., 138, 139, 290, 328,

329, 334; *King Lear*, 150; *The Merchant of Venice*, 329
Signac, Paul, 66n.
S.I.M., 178n., 254, 267n, 269, 280
Simon, Jules, 172, 173n.
Sisley, Alfred, 66n.
Sivry, Charles de, 1
Les Six, 191n.
Smareglia, 214n.
Société des Auteurs, Compositeurs et Editeurs de Musique, 309 and n.
Société des grandes Auditions musicales de France, 168n.
Société internationale de musique, 178n., 302
Société Musicale Indépendante, 267n., 326n.
Société nationale de musique, xvi, 24 and n., 30n., 46n., 58, 65, 66n., 75n., 164–6, 169n., 211n., 265n., 302
Society of English Composers, 197–8
Socrates, 301
Soissons, 82n.
Sonzogno, Edoardo, 184 and n.
Spain, 76, 77
Speyer, Lady, 270
Spinoza, Baruch, 319
Stanford, Sir Charles, 295n.
Steinlen, T. A., 286n.
Stoecklin, P. de, 219, 220n.
Strauss, Richard, xix, 189, 211, 212n., 222n., 282, 292, 294 and n.; *Ein Heldenleben*, xx, 111 and n.; *Salome*, 176, 179 and n.
Stravinsky, Igor, xix, xx, 250, 251n., 257, 265n., 306, 309n., 312; *The Firebird*, 221 and n.; letters from Debussy, 256–8, 265, 308–9; *Petrushka*, 256–8 and n., 262n., 265, 327; *Le Sacre du printemps*, 254, 265, 270, 273n., 276; *Three Japanese Lyrics*, 307n.
Street, George, 54 and n.
Suarès, André, 54n.
Sullivan, Sir Arthur, 185
Sulzbach, Mme, 45–6 and n.
Svendsen, Johan, 56, 57n.
Swinburne, Algernon Charles, xv
Switzerland, 202, 222, 251, 261, 309n., 333

Symbolists, xv, xx, 50, 251n.
Symphonisches Chor, 222n.

Tailhade, Laurent, 36n., 48n.; letter from Debussy, 35–6
Taskin, 182n.
Tchaikovsky, Peter Ilich, 1, 37, 208
Teatro de la Comedia, 176n.
Temesváry, 233n.
Le Temps, 34 and n., 116n., 182, 190n., 194n., 214n., 215n., 218n., 221, 268 and n.
Texier, Rosalie (Lilly) *see* Debussy, Rosalie
Teyte, Maggie, xiii, xix, 191 and n., 192n., *193*, 199, 200n., 237n., 270n., 283
Théâtre Antoine, 97n.
Théâtre d'art, 35n.
Théâtre des Bouffes-Parisiens, 100n.
Théâtre des Champs-Elysées, 179n., 272, 279 and n., 286n.
Théâtre du Châtelet, 240n., 267n., 289n., 327n.
Théâtre libre, 150n.
Théâtre Royale de la Monnaie, Brussels, 176–7
Thièle, Ivan, *275*
Thomas, Ambroise, 220 and n.; *Hamlet*, 41
Thomé, Francis, 196 and n.
Thorne, Guy (Cyril A. E. Ranger Gull), 268n.
Tibet, 300
Tiersot, Julien, 59, 60n.
Tinan, Jean de, 44n., 85n.
Tolstoy, Count Leo, 18, 249
Tommasini, 214n.
Toulet, Paul-Jean, xii, xvii, xix, 85n., 123n., 145, 169n., 188n., 210, 290, 329n.; letters from Debussy, 122–3, 124, 132–4, 138–9, 169, 187, 268, 326, 328–9
Toulouse-Lautrec, Henri de, 111n.
Trocadéro, 114n.
Trouhanova, 267 and n., 273n.
Turin, 242–3, 256n.
Turner, J. M. W., 33, 188

Udine, Jean d' (Albert Cozanet), 162 and n.

Valéry, Paul, xii, xv, 61n., 74n., 75n., 90n., 280n.
Vallin, Ninon, 238 and n., 274, 276n.
Van Dyck, Ernest, 182n.
Vandercruyssen, 222
Vanier, Léon, 21, 47, 48n.
Varèse, Edgard, xiv, xx, 222n., 284 and n., 285 and n.; letters from Debussy, 211, 221–2, 237–8
Variétés, 78n.
Vasnier, Eugène, xii, xv; letters from Debussy, 2, 4–16, 21–2
Vasnier, Marguerite, 5, 6
Vasnier, Marie-Blanche, xv, 1–2, 4n., 11n., 23, 15, 19
Vasnier, Maurice, 5, 6
Velázquez, Diego de Silva y, 40, 314, 327n.
Venice, 210, 261
Verdi, Giuseppe, 13, 242
Verdun, 318
Verlaine, Paul, 28n., 34n., 101, 146, 224n., 330n.; Ariettes oubliées, 276n.
Vichy, 276
Vidal, Paul, xiv, xvi, 4n., 5, 6n., 28
Viélé-Griffin, Francis, 48n., 89, 90n.
Vienna, 172, 212n., 225, 227–30, 231, 234, 269
Vieuille, Félix, 173
Villa Medici, xv, 2, 4n., 5–22, 9
Villiers de l'Isle Adam, Comte de, 45n.
Villon, François, 136
Viñes, Ricardo, 144 and n., 156n., 169n., 186n., 222n., 276n., 330
Vittoria, 42, 57
Viviani, René, 300, 301n.
Vizentini, Paul, 244
Vuillermoz, Emile, 267n., 276n.; letters from Debussy, 267, 284, 313

Wagner, Eva, 83n.
Wagner, Richard, xv, xvii, xx, 11n., 13, 18, 23, 45n., 54, 58, 61n., 64–5, 73, 87, 110, 140, 172, 232, 249, 292–3, 294 and n., 306, 307n.; The Mastersingers of Nuremberg, 235; Parsifal, 258, 262; Das Rheingold, 44–5 and n., 46; Der Ring des Nibelungen, 45n.; Tristan und Isolde, 32, 180; Die Walküre, 45n., 46
Waldbauer, Imre, 233n.
Waldbauer Quartet, 233 and n.
Waldeck-Rousseau, 139n.
Wales, 186n.
Warnery, Edmond, 199, 200n., 201
Watteau, Jean Antoine, 4n.
Weber, Carl Maria von, 317
Weber, Louise (La Goulue), 111 and n.
Weimar, 295, 309
Whistler, James, 75n.
Widor, Charles Marie, 211n., 215n.
Wilder, Victor, 46 and n.
Wollenhaupt, Heinrich Adolf, 216, 217n.
Wood, Henry, 179, 180n., 198n.

X, letter from Debussy, 288
Xantho (dog), 283 and n.

Yonne, 137n.
Ysaÿe, Eugène, xvii, 60, 68, 75n.; letters from Debussy, 74–5, 87–8
Ysaÿe Quartet, 60n., 75n.

Zágon, Géza Vilmos, 233 and n.
Zamoiska, Countess, 64
Zimmer (brasserie), 238, 240n.
Zola, Emile, 111; Messidor, 90, 92n.

89